BUTCHER

BUTCHER
MY AUTOBIOGRAPHY

TERRY BUTCHER WITH BOB HARRIS

highdown

Published in 2005 by Highdown
an imprint of Raceform Ltd
Compton, Newbury, Berkshire, RG20 6NL

Raceform Ltd is a wholly-owned subsidiary of Trinity-Mirror plc

A catalogue record for this book is available from the British Library.

ISBN 1-905156-00-6

Cover designed by Tracey Scarlett

Interiors designed by Fiona Pike

Printed in Great Britain by William Clowes Ltd, Beccles, Suffolk

DEDICATION

I would like to dedicate this book to my wife Rita,
for her understanding, her help and
her encouragement in this project,
as in all we do together. Also to my three sons
Alistair, Christopher and Edward.

ACKNOWLEDGEMENTS

Terry Butcher and his co-author Bob Harris would like to thank publisher Jonathan Taylor for his enthusiasm and professionalism with this project; editor Daniel Balado Lopez; the staff at Highdown; John Russell of the Association of Football Statisticians; Pam Wilby and Julian Groom of the Meridien Hotel group for their help and advice; agent Jonathan Harris and, of course, Mr Hyde for the added spice.

BOB HARRIS

Bob Harris is Terry Butcher's co-author and long time friend. Indeed, the friend who tapped him up for Glasgow Rangers! A well known and much travelled sports writer, Harris is the author of several best-selling sports books involving such legends as Sir Garfield Sobers, Sir Viv Richards, Dennis Lillee, Sir Bobby Robson, Graeme Souness, Kevin Keegan, Graham Kelly, Stuart Pearce, John Charles, Denis Law, Steve Coppell and Bruce Grobbelaar. He witnessed first hand each and every one of Butcher's international matches and most of his club highlights.

CONTENTS

INTRODUCTION ... AND MR HYDE   9

1   FROM SINGAPORE TO PORTMAN ROAD   15

2   WELCOME TO IPSWICH   34

3   THE LONGEST AWAY TRIP   61

4   THE BEST SEASON OF MY LIFE   75

5   NEAR TO DEATH   85

6   OUT BUT UNDEFEATED   95

7   THE CHANGEOVER   103

8   BREAKING UP IS HARD TO DO   112

9   SURVIVAL   121

10   THROUGH THE TRAP DOOR   131

11   NEARLY IMMORTAL   135

12   DOUBLE TOP   152

13   GOLDILOCKS AND THE THREE BEARS   173

14   BACK TO ACTION   184

15   BLOODY HERO   197

16   NEARLY IMMORTAL AGAIN   206

17   SENT TO COVENTRY   223

18   THE MANAGER MUST GO   236

19   MORE WHINE, SIR?   245

20   THE DOTCOM REVOLUTION   258

21   JUMPERS FOR GOALS   269

22   SCOTTISH FOOTBALL IS BANKRUPT   389

23   ENGLAND, MY ENGLAND   395

24   FIVE ALIVE!   307

POSTSCRIPT   321

TERRY BUTCHER'S CAREER RECORD   327

INDEX   339

INTRODUCTION

... AND MR HYDE

Everyone has a positive and negative side to his or her character. I was brought up to be polite, proper, to speak to people the right way, but inside me there is a certain element that wants to rebel, a streak which from time to time rears its ugly head. Occasionally the cause is alcohol, but usually it's simply a red mist which appears when something, usually football-related, has upset me.

It's hard to understand or explain, mainly because I am staunchly conservative and it goes against everything I hold true. I believe in the state, the police, and law and order. My father, a prison officer, wanted me to be a lawyer; indeed, there is nothing I like better than watching *Judge John Deed* or *Rumpole of the Bailey*, and I love reading Quintin Jardine who writes about the Edinburgh policeman Bob Skinner, who happens to be a Motherwell supporter. I was mortified when he appeared to die in the last book I read.

Law and order attracts me because in my life there is discipline. My desk at the office is nice and neat, and I always like things to be done at home and work in the right way. The blinds have to be drawn exactly level, the bed covers have to be correct, my reading book is by the side of the bed and the glass of water placed exactly in the middle of the coaster on the bedside table. If I set a table for dinner, the placemats and cutlery have to be exactly aligned. I am fanatical about symmetry and neatness.

So that is, if you like, the Dr Jekyll aspect of my personality, but there is another side. A certain Mr Hyde, who is lurking in the shadows waiting to come out and shame me, to go against everything I stand for. He is my alter ego. There are times when I need to explode and let the passion flow, and that's when the monster appears.

My rants after Motherwell games are becoming legendary for all the wrong reasons. At Livingston we lost 1–0 to a goal that came three minutes from the end when a point would have been a great help in our relegation battle. Alan MacDonald, the kit man, the best I have ever known – he arrives at the ground three or four hours before everyone else – loves Motherwell and the job, and he has a rack where he hangs the washed spare shirts and others not being used. I went apoplectic about the manner in which we gave the goal away and as I came into the dressing room I picked up the rack and hurled it into a corner. Poor Alan was mortified at seeing his pristine kit fly around the dressing room among the mud and rubbish. It needed another wash when he got it back to Fir Park.

It's been the same at nearly all the other grounds. At Dundee recently I booted the fire extinguisher off its holder on the wall, painful for me as well as the man who had to put it back up. I then ripped off my top like the Incredible Hulk, and a flask of hot tea was bounced around the room. I hadn't lost it but I was livid because we hadn't won a match we should have won. I felt cheated and wronged. At Hibs last season their dieticians produced bacon butties, potato wedges and pizza for our post-match meal. I couldn't let my players eat such rubbish, so I took the trays outside and let them drop from a height of five feet to the floor. There were one or two players, namely those who had not played, who regretted my actions, not from any moral standpoint but because they fancied a snack!

The door I kicked in at the same ground on another occasion, when we lost 3–1 and had three players sent off, was a prime example of one of my rants. There are two fire doors at Hibs; one was open and one was shut, so I kicked at the closed one with the sole of my boot. It flew open, but because it was locked at the top it swivelled and the lock flew past the right ear of my coach Maurice Malpas, coming to rest embedded in the opposite wall. The door began swinging slowly back for me to boot again, and this time the hinges sprang as it hit the wall. Not surprisingly it wouldn't shut properly, so I rammed it closed because I wanted to have a rant at my players in private about their poor performance. Carlsberg sponsored Hibs, and there was a case of 24 cans of lager waiting for us. This became another target. I booted one can, which exploded, showering beer everywhere. The can stuck to my foot, and it must have looked ridiculous, but I ignored the looks around me and picked up the case, ready to throw it against the wall. But as I lifted it the cans fell out, bouncing off my feet. I still had the first can stuck to my boot, so I thought I had better leave to calm down a little. I pulled on the door and it promptly collapsed, just missing my number three Chris McCart. He had to jump to one side because this big, heavy door would surely have broken his legs had it caught him. It was so heavy that afterwards Chris had a job lifting it off the floor. When we went back to Hibs after the incident I noticed that the broken door had been put on to a cupboard right next to the dressing room, the damage in full view.

There was another door, at Aberdeen, which also received my full attention. One of my team-mates had suffered a serious injury during the game and I was so irate I put my foot through the referee's door and all but landed in prison. I was charged by the police for vandalism and breach of the peace; but for the intervention of former Aberdeen manager Alex Smith I might well have gone down in view of my previous record.

Doors have usually been the object of my anger, although, like my shooting, I sometimes miss the target. Once, at West Ham when I was playing for Ipswich, I speared my leg through a wall right up to my thigh trying to kick a door down. Quite rightly I was made to apologise to the Hammers' manager John Lyall, who was as charming as only John could be and forgave me. Even so, it could have been much worse. At the time I was trying to get at the referee who had given a very dubious penalty against us. To this day I do not know what I would have done had I grabbed hold of him. Had I done so I doubt very much whether I would ever have been allowed to play organised football again.

And that is the thing about Mr Hyde: I can't be sure what his limits are. I just don't know how far he will go, though I have never yet made my way right to the edge. Fortunately, as I've just described, my anger is usually expelled on inanimate objects, invariably dressing-room doors – at Motherwell they have only recently replaced the toughened glass in the boot-room door following another violent assault – walls or plates of sandwiches. Rubbish bins are also a regular target because they are always handy in a dressing room and are a perfect size to kick. Bottles of water, too, are easily to hand in a dressing room. But certainly the referee at Upton Park came close to being my first genuine assault.

The one time I was hauled before the courts, when some action in an Old Firm derby led to me, two colleagues and an opponent being charged with of a breach of the peace, it was Terry Butcher and not Mr Hyde. The Celtic player concerned can count himself lucky: had it been Mr Hyde who went after him, who knows what would have happened. There was also the room wrecking in Zeist, Holland, on a drunken evening with Ipswich when alcohol took hold and led to some very childish nonsense. I was, quite rightly, severely reprimanded by the club.

But booze doesn't make me want to become aggressive and pick fights; it is when I feel cheated, that justice has not been done, that I will snap. Sometimes it's down to not getting our just rewards, probably through our own ineptitude or bad luck. I honestly thought I was beginning to mature as I got older, but those events at places like Dundee and Hibs show I am not. After one home defeat to Aberdeen, I punched the cupboard in the coaches' room, not once but twice, breaking my knuckles on the solid, old-fashioned door. My tail was between my legs when I went in to see the physio and told him I thought I had broken my hand. He confirmed it.

After such incidents I always feel terrible. It is just so against everything I stand for in my normal life. I tell my wife Rita about it and she slaughters me, as does my secretary at Motherwell, Betty. My assistant Maurice also has a go, and I vow not to do it again, but then something upsets me and I will boot our metal skips at Fir Park, putting my feet in the same danger as my hands. It's sheer stupidity. I've even had cause to attack the furniture at home. I once jumped down the stairs in our split-level bungalow, only to scrape the top of my head on the ceiling halfway from the top of the steps. I grabbed the painful area with both hands and promptly smashed both of my elbows through the door at the bottom of the stairs, leaving two sizeable holes in the woodwork.

When I first became manager at Coventry City I was determined to set an example to the players, to be quiet and restrained rather than attacking players and their attitudes. I was probably the same in my second job at Sunderland. How I have changed! A lot of it comes from confidence. If you are in a situation where you are comfortable and sure of yourself then you can go on and do something off the wall to express yourself and make a point. In other words, when you go into a rage you have to know you are 100 per cent right. In my first two posts I wasn't at all sure of myself and didn't go off at all.

But I also have the ability to channel the aggression in me, as I have displayed in front of many a surprised international footballer in the tunnel before a game by hammering on the walls and screaming at the top of my voice to try to put my opponents off. And Mr Hyde also stays locked away where the family are concerned. I have three grown boys, and I admit to throwing several wobblies, but never have I gone into a full-scale rant in front of them, limiting myself to wagging a finger in their faces or banging them on the top of the head with my big bony finger. They shout, 'Not the finger! Not the finger!' But even that's rare, and more often than not I keep my cool.

To go from thinking about my family to understanding that I could easily have ended up in prison for kicking a door in at Pittodrie sends a shiver down my spine. I could also have been done at Dundee and Hibs for malicious damage without a shadow of doubt. Clubs could conduct tours around Scottish Premier League dressing rooms showing the doors I have kicked. Fortunately, most football clubs understand the emotion and tension involved and I guess some of them just shake their heads and say, 'There goes Terry again! Give the carpenter a call.'

The players generally know when the blue touchpaper is about to be lit, and when it is going to be pretty meaty. I have never seen Maurice as angry as me but I have seen him go off on one. The strange thing is, when it happens I suddenly turn into Dr Jekyll and become the peacemaker because my mind tells me there is no use both of us blowing a gasket together.

So, given that I don't go mad at every match because generally the reaction is not warranted, and given the fact I feel so guilty after I've done it I could slap myself, why do I do it? Because I believe my team should play at a decent standard every week and always try to be better. Of course there are times when we are better than we should be – it evens out, more or less, over the course of a season. Still, football is an emotional game, and I cannot stand people who sit on the sidelines and do and say nothing. I have tried it and failed miserably. The fourth officials get hell from me every week, and I guess the only reason why I haven't been dispatched to the stands is because they think I am a complete loony and they don't want to get involved. Either that or they don't understand my English. Whatever the reason, I am grateful to them and to other officials who catch a whiff of what I think of them from time to time.

I am big, I am aggressive, and I am deeply passionate. When I played the game I know I was intimidating because I have seen pictures of myself venting my anger at some unfortunate who, more than likely, has just kicked one of my team-mates rather than me. My only defence is I love the game, love to be involved with it, whether it is as a summariser for BBC's Radio Five Live or as the manager of Motherwell FC in the SPL. Perhaps when you have read the rest of my autobiography you will have an even better understanding of both Terry Butcher and Mr Hyde.

CHAPTER ONE

FROM SINGAPORE
TO PORTMAN ROAD

Yes, I am a passionate Englishman, but I was born in Singapore, though I have to confess I don't remember a thing about it. A few years ago I decided it was time I discovered a little more about my birthplace, so I recruited Wee Tiong, a friend from Hong Kong who was also born and raised in Singapore, and we travelled out, together with former Scottish international footballer Dave McPherson and our wives, on a trip arranged by the Singapore government: we were to coach underprivileged children in the game of football for three days. We stayed at the Fullerton Hotel, right on the quayside. Singapore's sports minister was also involved, and he came out to join us as we trained for a day in the National Stadium and then in a ground close by.

Naturally I was keen to see where I had spent the first days of my life and went armed with addresses I'd got from my parents to view the two houses where we'd lived. One of them was in Ripley Crescent, a very English name that reflects Singapore's history, and I took pictures and some video to show Mum and Dad on my return. But I have to confess it meant nothing to me at all. I left at the age of about fifteen months – it was always going to be a temporary home as Dad was in the Royal Navy and worked on the base – so it's hardly surprising. At least my parents confirmed I had visited the right place.

In a bid to strike a chord or two we went round the shops where they used to take me. Apparently my dad had a Lambretta scooter, so we must have been a sight, Mum carrying me on the back seat and between Dad's legs was our mongrel dog Menace. I was told we used to drive round the shops as a little family unit with no crash helmets, nothing. We would pick up the supplies and then return to base. We even visited the hospital where I was born. It was easy to find as it was close to the thoroughly modern airport, but despite the fact it was still part of the military base it was in a state of disrepair. It was exhilarating to return to the place where I was born, but also weird. I had no memories of it at all.

My dad, Leonard Charles, began his naval career on *HMS Ganges*, the training school near Harwich in Suffolk. He went there as a fifteen-year-old, fell in love with the Navy, became a signalman and travelled the world serving on the famous *Ark Royal.* My mum, Valerie May, married him while he was based in England but stayed at home until she joined him in Singapore. I like to tell people I was conceived in England, but I doubt the truth of the statement as Mum was out there well before.

Dad decided to quit the Navy in about 1960. We returned to Petersfield in Hampshire for his debriefing and then moved to Lowestoft, birthplace and home to both of them. Dad must have liked uniforms because he then trained to become a prison officer, at Blundeston Prison just north of Lowestoft, where he served for a number of years before his retirement. One of his most famous 'guests' was John Stonehouse, the former MP. Dad was in charge of the laundry, which was a perk in prisoner terms because it was a warm, comfortable room and the inmates tended to receive special treatment because it was such a soft touch. He had a good unit and he looked after the prisoners. They, in turn, looked after him and gave him no trouble. But as the years progressed he felt standards of morality in the prison were slipping. There was a growing drug culture and stabbings were commonplace. When he started the job, people went to prison and got on with serving their time; he was completely disillusioned by the time he left because the culture had changed so much. He felt he had to get out of it because he feared he would end up with a knife in his back.

Dad was around six foot tall and my mother was five foot seven, taller than my wife Rita who is only five feet four inches. Strangely, my height is attributable to my mother's side where they were all on the tall side. I was a reasonably tall child, but I didn't spring up until about the age of fourteen. By then I was wearing size eleven shoes plus extra-length jackets and trousers. It wasn't good because footwear – football boots and ordinary shoes – only went up to size nine in the local shops. Luckily, mail-order catalogues came to the rescue.

I wasn't an only child. I have a sister Vanda who, later on in life, came to work for me in my hotel in Scotland. And who says blood is thicker than water? I ended up sacking her as manager of my hotel and we didn't speak for many years because of the fall-out. She was born in 1961 so she's two years younger than me, and we were close in those early days. We went to the same primary school, Fen Park, just half a mile from where we lived, though we attended different senior schools. My wife Rita also went to Fen Park.

I was a good pupil in those early days and I passed my eleven-plus at the age of ten and was accepted into Lowestoft Grammar School. It was probably a case of being too clever too soon; maybe I just had too much carrot juice. Dad was and is an intelligent, articulate person who wanted me to go to university and become a lawyer. He encouraged me in my schooling and used to give me spelling tests at night. I had to spell the words correctly before I could get down from the table. It wasn't the Bruce Rioch school of discipline – the former Luton and Aston Villa player had a Sergeant Major for a father – it was more like encouragement to progress in life. As a result I had a good grasp of the English language at an early age. Dad was a perfectionist and wanted everyone to get things right. I picked up the same trait. It has done me no harm at all and has carried me through life so far.

Fen Park was excellent because it was local and blessed with small classes, and I really enjoyed my time there. Football seemed to be around right from the start. One of the best presents I ever received was a leather football. I used to dribble it along the pavement on my way to school, playing one-twos off the wall as I went. Other boys rode their bikes or their scooters, but for me it was a football. I doubt I was more than five or six, but I just loved having the comfort of that football and to be able to do with it what I wanted. I suppose it is why I was always comfortable on the ball when I began playing, even as a defender.

The urge didn't come from anywhere in particular. Dad watched matches but didn't play much, and there was no football on television at the time other than the FA Cup Final. You had to be rich to have a colour television in those days, so we would all crowd round to Uncle Ivan's house on Cup Final day to suck in the atmosphere. They were special days. Everyone, it seemed, played football in those days.

There was a real sense of community in Lowestoft. We didn't live in the prison in their staff quarters; instead we lived by my great aunt

Sophie, where my mum was raised. We lived there for a while before moving into a new house in Carlton Road, and in those days it was something special. Dad didn't earn a lot but Mum worked at a local cannery called Morton's and it brought in some extra money. Strangely, my wife Rita also worked there during the summers when she left school, to get herself through college. Mum would bike home from work as Dad had the car to travel the four miles to the prison. Living in would have been cheaper, but he didn't want to live in the prison for all our sakes.

School was a little further away when we moved to the new house, but it didn't matter. I still ran with the ball, and it probably upped my fitness levels. There was also a park close by and we were able to play football until dusk, when the park keeper rang his bell. That was the signal to get the last shot in on goal, or in my case the last tackle. Not that I thought of myself as a defender then. I would play anywhere for a game. I played outfield at my primary school – I recall losing one game 7–1 playing left-back in the old 2–3–5 system – and I became a goalkeeper when I went to grammar school. In fact, the only position I didn't play was striker because I liked to step on to things rather than play with my back to goal.

Life can be shaped by some strange events, and my future as a footballer was given a helping hand when I was a very young lad. At home the dining-room table was quite high for me, and one day I reached up for the teapot cover, which looked something like a bobble hat and as a kid I liked to wear it. As I pulled it off the table, I dragged the teapot off with it. As luck would have it it had just been filled with scalding hot water and it spilled over my right foot. I screamed, of course, Mum came running, and my foot was immediately jammed into a bowl of cold water. The skin peeled away and the burn was bad, but I was quite resilient. I don't even remember being taken to the doctor's, never mind the hospital. I still have the scar, but the most significant consequence was I became left-footed.

I used to go to the local beach a lot in those days and I had to put a plastic bag over the plaster to stop the wound becoming infected. Because I couldn't kick with my right foot, I did what any kid of that age would do and used my other foot. I don't advise it as a method to help a youngster become two-footed. In fact, I became so one-footed I used my right leg only to stand on. It is, however, a salutary lesson, for it shows the ability is there in all of us. I believe it is a matter of the mind, so why can't all players become two-footed? It's just a question of adapting and practising, giving yourself the confidence to do it.

So my unlucky injury became lucky for me. I am right-sided in every other respect, right-handed and right-footed in terms of cricket, tennis, etc., but I'm a left-footed footballer. There is no doubt left-footed players have more chance of breaking into teams because they provide balance. Just look at the England team over the past few years under Sven Goran Eriksson, struggling to find a top-quality left-sided midfield player. It certainly helped me: I became left-back for the school team at a very young age.

At the same time I was considered quite a smarty pants. Whenever there was a test the teacher would send me out of the room and give the class half an hour to do it. When I came back in he would ask me the questions and the rest of the class would mark their papers from my answers. (Needless to say, things went rapidly downhill after that!) I was the boffin, the check sheet for the others. Because it was so easy for me they put me up a year, and I could still cope with it. There was no doubt as a schoolboy I peaked too soon. I was too bright too early, and then preferred football to schoolwork.

Our local football club was Lowestoft Town (my dad is still a season-ticket holder and watches them most weeks). Dad used to take me to football when he could, but often he would be working his prison shifts on a Saturday. It was his brother David who took me more often. It was great sport to watch as there were often crazy scores like 7–4 and 8–3 – just the ticket for a youngster like me. I loved it so much I can still remember Tooley and Cassidy the strikers, and some other fantastic players like 'Rocky' Stephenson. I watched some incredible end-to-end games against teams like Histon Town, Stowmarket, Ely and Chatteris. When I pass through those towns in my car on my visits home my mind goes back to those games. It was an immense experience for a youngster. I would watch a bit of the game, then join in the kickabout with other youngsters behind the goal before watching a bit more. I used to be the proud owner of a big wooden rattle, and the bigger the rattle the more kudos you had. After the game we would be back on Fen Park until the attendant rang his bell to send us in for our tea.

I didn't really have too many professional football heroes in those days, but as I grew older I would go with my friends on the train to watch Norwich City. But I have to say the Canaries never grabbed my attention.

There was just something about them I didn't like. Even now when I meet up with Jimmy Bone, who used to play for them and is now assistant manager at Partick Thistle, I cannot raise any enthusiasm. I watched him play with a huge striker named John Manning, but my interest in professional football was always more in the direction of Portman Road.

When Dad had time off on a Saturday he would take me to Ipswich – a real day out I used to look forward to. We would drive into Ipswich, have lunch in the car, and then Mum would go off shopping with Vanda while Dad and I went to the ground. We watched Ipswich gain promotion to the First Division in 1968 under the management of Bill McGarry. My favourites were the big centre-half Billy Baxter; 'Chopper' Jefferson, the number six who used to cut opponents in half, John O'Rourke and Charlie Woods, who was to become my youth-team coach. It was a young but good side in those days and I always looked forward to that 80-mile round trip on roads that weren't as good as they are now. The journey would take an hour and 40 minutes – an adventure on its own.

Lowestoft Town used to frequently reach the first round proper of the FA Cup, and I remember them playing Watford on a bone-hard, freezing pitch. My parents also went to watch them play a cup-tie at Leyton Orient. They didn't take me, but they brought me a little gift back with them. Lowestoft also regularly won the Eastern Counties League and often won through to the final stages of the East Anglian Cup, the final of which was played at Portman Road. The professional clubs didn't enter the competition in those days, but it was always a day out we enjoyed. My parents loved their football and I will always be indebted to them for the way they encouraged and helped me. They never overdid it or insisted I was going to be a footballer. They came to watch me at school games, particularly when I was older and played for Lowestoft and Suffolk Schoolboys, and they would take me to games and talk about them afterwards.

Lowestoft Grammar School became Denes High School, a comprehensive, while I was still attending. It was tragic, as the standards plummeted. You could see from the intake what was coming. The kids would arrive at school on mopeds with their crash helmets on, and clad in leather jackets. There were fights, vandalism, and trouble with the teachers. But when I first went there as a ten-year-old we wore uniforms, and Mum and Dad were given a massive checklist of equipment they had to buy. They had wanted me to go to a private school called St Joseph's in Woodbridge, a rugby-playing school, but the fees were too high. They had been told I would be able to handle it, and it would have been a great step up in my education, but in those days there was no suggestion of an assisted passage. It was as much as they could do to afford the uniform, school bag, shoes, PE gear, reversible sports tops, slide rules and all sorts of other gear for the Grammar School.

I remember being very impressed with the school when I first went there, with the teachers in their flowing gowns and the strict rules which made everyone walk on the left. There was detention, and bells to signal the start and end of lessons, and the sport was varied: rugby was played in the autumn term, football in the spring term, then cricket and athletics in the summer term. I loved it, and I did everything. I represented the school in rugby, football and cricket, and went on to become captain in all three.

Sports were my thing. On sports day I would win four or five events, once netting the Victor Ludorum (but only after it had been erroneously awarded to Inspector Ball's son Christopher). The shot putt was my best event because I was so tall I could just lean forward and pop it out. I also found the high hurdles easy because I could just step over them with my long stride. The other events where my height helped me were the triple jump and long jump. I loved the triple jump, a highly technical event that stretched you mentally and physically. I have the utmost respect for Jonathan Edwards and what he achieved. I was keen on cross-country running too. I certainly wasn't the best, but I would regularly finish in the top ten. I also ran for the school and in county trials, but didn't make it into the team. Another sport we played was volleyball, where I also represented my school. I enjoyed it because it's a hard, clever event with a lot of finesse about it. We would travel around the county playing mainly against men's teams. Basketball wasn't a big sport back then but I played that for the school too. In all I represented my school in half a dozen sports.

When I played rugby for the school against other schools like Langley, Holy Joe's or Felixstowe, we usually played on Saturday mornings or, if we were really lucky, on a school afternoon. After the games we had meals of sausage, beans and chips. We thought we were in heaven, sitting in these ornate dining halls in our school uniforms. I used to think, 'This is sport – this is how it should be played!' When we played football, it was a quick shower and away. Even in East Anglia rugby was a gentlemen's game. But I also enjoyed the confrontation . I was big for my age and I wanted to play in the forwards, but I was a long kicker with my left foot and I was told I was to play stand-off. I was very comfortable with any kind of ball, whether it was a basketball, a football or a rugby ball, but I didn't enjoy the role. I would often get caught with the ball in a ruck and finish with a punch-up – the first appearance, I suppose, of Mr Hyde!

Yet for all that I was a well-behaved boy. I received only one detention in my entire school life, and that, if I remember rightly, was because a group of us were behaving boisterously and I karate-kicked a window accidentally, showering the woodwork teacher's car with shards of glass. They still used the cane in those days and I would have died had I ever received it, not because of fear of it hurting but because of what my father would have said afterwards. I couldn't let my parents down because of the support I had received, especially after passing for Grammar School. Neither was I ever sent off in rugger or football. I was a complete gentleman in those days. Mr Hyde was only really forced out of me when I became a professional sportsman.

The worst onfield incident I can remember as a kid was when my mother and father were watching and I was trying to wind my team up. I shouted at the top of my voice, 'Come on you fuckers, let's get stuck into this lot!' It all went very quiet. The referee came over, told me it was not the sort of language he expected from me, and awarded a free-kick to the opposition. No one swore in our house, and my mum was mortified. She didn't know what to do with herself. As for Dad, he just laughed. He'd heard a hundred times worse every day of his working life in Blundeston Prison. But he didn't swear himself.

I played football for the prison staff team sometimes, and I also played against the prisoners for Fen Park on a Sunday morning. They were in the league, but of course couldn't play away games. They were hard too and would kick you as soon as look at you. If I knocked anyone down in those days I would pick them up, but I wasn't soft. If there was a tackle I was in there – I loved a tackle even then; I was a bit of a John Charles character – but I would never deliberately kick anyone. As for the verbal exchanges, I leave those to your imagination. Some of those prisoners weren't bad footballers and could play as well as they could swear.

But there was a touch of controversy in the Butcher household over Sunday-league football. Dad, who was a tremendous influence on me not only in terms of how the game should be played but also the way life should be lived, didn't go to church because he would often be working on Sundays. Mum, however, was a real Church of England lady who went every week, while my Aunt Sophie went to the Methodist church. When Aunt Sophie's legs got too bad for her to walk, I would wheel her to church. I can honestly say I enjoyed it; it was a modern church and it was warm. Afterwards I would wheel her back to our house for Sunday lunch. The farming programme would be on television after lunch, and then the football came on with *Anglia Sport*'s Gerry Harrison, followed by *Songs of Praise*. Afterwards I would wheel Aunty back to her own home where I would make her a cup of tea. When I started playing Sunday football it somewhat shocked Mum because she thought I should still be taking Aunty to church. But Sunday was bleak apart from the football as far as I was concerned. Nobody did anything on Sunday. To play football was a bit radical for some families, but Mum knew how much I wanted to play. Still, I didn't play every week.

After the game on a Sunday morning everyone went down to the pub where I would have half a pint. That was enough for me. I much preferred to get back for my Sunday lunch at 1.30, the big roast meal of the week with Yorkshire puddings – now there was something I really looked forward to. My mum made two trays of them, two dozen in all, and my personal record at one sitting was thirteen: seven or eight with the meal and then the rest for dessert with jam in the middle. It's still a family record. But I remained as thin as a rake and I knew I had to eat to keep up my strength because I was playing so much sport. I remember my dad used to have bread and dripping with salt on it, and I still like lots of salt on my tomatoes. No wonder people had heart attacks in those days, dipping spring onions and radishes into big piles of salt on the side of the plate.

The prison staff team were a great bunch of guys. One of them was so disgusted when we gave away a goal near the end of one match to make it 4–4 he took the ball from the restart, charged down the pitch and blasted it into the net from all of 40 yards to leave everyone, especially the prisoners, completely stunned. Oddly, I did much the same in 1990 playing for Rangers against Raith Rovers in a League Cup tie. I scored an own goal against Chris Woods to pull them back to 3–2, and then from the kick-off I took possession, ran forward as the prison officer had done, and smashed it in from 35 yards.

We also played some matches at Lothingland Hospital, a mental institution. The patients would often wander on to the pitch and we would have to stop the game until they were escorted off. Streatham Borstal were also opponents of ours. Dad used to run the line during these prison games, despite his lack of knowledge of the laws. He wore a pork pie hat – how bizarre is that? – and ran the line for our back four, waving for offside. One day this big, burly prison officer ran through and was flagged offside by my dad. I thought the two were going to have a fight until Dad called the referee over and demanded the player be sent off.

There were some lovely people involved in the football, though some of the men would roll up with a hangover from the night before. Still, I learnt a lot playing with older men, people who were streetwise and knew when to kick you and when to wind you up. Certainly football had a great effect on the prison officers, creating a good spirit. There was such solidarity, a real winning mentality, and when they lost they were absolutely mortified. But they took it the right way. I was brought up to take defeat the same way, only for it to change when I turned professional.

I developed a really good sense of right and wrong through my father, and he also bestowed upon me the value of hard work and respect. Seeing prisoners also made you more determined never to be in a situation where you could be put away yourself (how those experiences came back to me when I found myself up in court in Glasgow – but more of that later). It was a good way to be brought up, though maybe a little boring compared with some of the other lads of the same age. It all stemmed from the discipline stamped on him in the Navy and then the prison service. His life was all about order and regimen. A classic example was when he wrote he did so with a ruler under the script to keep the lines straight and orderly. When I'm writing the team list or something else, I use a ruler in the same way. I am so like my father, and my third son is so much like me, it's eerie. We do and say the same things. Crosswords, for example, I do just like my father before me, and my son after me.

It wasn't long before I became involved with a club outside school, the Ashlea Boys' Club, sadly now disbanded. We played in the Anglian Combination, about two leagues lower than the Eastern Counties

League. I had a season with them and played goalkeeper, left-back, centre-half, wherever. In those days just having a game was the important factor. When I played in goal I wore a roll-neck sweater; only if you were wealthy did you wear the Peter Bonetti shirt and gloves. Neighbour and friend David Baldry had a set and I used to borrow them to play on a Saturday morning for the school if I had been asked to keep goal. Goalkeepers didn't really wear gloves in those days as the balls were raw leather rather than plastic-coated. Then the prickly gloves came in, and soon after the padded jerseys. It was all right being in goal, but I was already shouting and throwing orders around and I wanted to play out and be more a part of the game. The teachers would get so cheesed off with me shouting and screaming at my players they soon moved me forward, but even then I wanted to play everywhere. I wanted to take the free-kicks and corners, I wanted to cross the ball, I wanted to tackle everyone. I was full of natural enthusiasm.

I spent so much time on sport that for the first time I began to struggle in class. No longer was I considered the child genius. It was sport, sport, sport for me; even during break we had a tennis ball or a football out, and at lunchtime we indulged in mini leagues in the playground. Sadly, schools don't seem to allow this these days. We would come back into class with scraped knees, scuffed shoes, dirty hands and holes in our sweaters. No wonder we didn't feel like lessons in the afternoon. They were fantastic sessions, really competitive and very enjoyable.

Lowestoft Grammar School was about three or four miles from our house – not far enough for a free bus pass – and after the final bell I would be on my bike and heading for a game in the park. It was all uphill to school in the morning, so riding the bike helped to keep me fit. Sometimes, if I forgot my PE kit or a book, I had to bike it back home, as I couldn't ring up Mum or Dad and ask them to bring it in by car because they were away at work. Needless to say, I often did an extra round trip, which meant fifteen or so miles a day in the saddle, as well as all the sport. No wonder my fitness levels were so high.

All that activity made me eat like a horse. As I rode along on the bike I would have a big family-size chocolate Swiss roll in one pocket and a pint of milk in the other. It was my pre-match meal, and if I was hungry after playing I would do the same on the way back. I would eat for fun in those days. Mum was a great cook, and so was Aunt Sophie. Mum always used to feed me before we went out because I could never get enough food. I would go to the relatives, eat another meal, and I would still come back hungry. We had lots of roast dinners. Mum also used to make suet puddings and beef pâté in pastry, but I passed on those, preferring solid slices of meat. The turkey at Christmas was absolutely obscene, the mother of all turkeys, weighing in at around 24lb. One year Mum, Dad and Vanda were so ill they couldn't eat it and I finished most of it on my own. I never became bored with roast turkey, and Boxing Day for me is still as good a meal as Christmas Day, with cold turkey and pickles plus bubble and squeak with brown sauce. But my favourite dish was toad in the hole. Rita took the menu on board when we married, and for a while it was almost all I asked for.

When I was about fifteen I found myself an after-school job with Dewhurst as a butcher's boy. My boss was a guy named Richard with whom I got on rather well. One of my duties was to clean out the large fridges at the back of the shop. In those days you walked out of the shop into the walk-in fridges, huge things with trays at the bottom to gather the blood. If it had been there the whole day the blood would be congealed, and it used to make me gag. After cleaning it out I would put sawdust down on the floor. All that has changed now because environmental health laws state that you cannot take meat from one building to another. I also cleaned out the yards and the huge butcher blocks where they cut up the meat. I would have to scrub them with a metal scrubber and sawdust to get rid of the blood and guts. I would finish off by cleaning the windows. Then in December I'd help to dress the turkeys, getting them ready for delivery or collection – a busy time, but fun.

I did this for a couple of years, and my reward, apart from my 'wages', was meat for the family. Those big loins of pork were a good source of protein for me. Some of the customers didn't want the skin, which was sliced off and hung up for sale. If it didn't go I would ask for the crackling at the end of the day to take home with me. They were about six inches wide, and I used to put them under the grill. Giant pork scratchings! Richard was great. There was a chippie across the road from the shop – coincidentally where Rita was working. I would buy chips when the customers had gone and we would have them with slices of corned beef and fresh tomatoes.

I left the shop when it closed down, but because of my experience I quickly found a job in another butcher's named Wharton's, a more traditional butcher, as Dewhurst were part of a chain. They had their own slaughterhouse and would make their own sausages. We used to make them in the back, putting the meat in the skin. They were fantastic to eat. I used to arrive at around seven a.m. on Saturday, pick up the butcher's bike complete with basket on the front and metal nameplate in the middle, pack all the deliveries carefully in order, with the last deliveries at the bottom and the first at the top, and set off on my round. When I returned I would have one of those sausages in crusty bread and a cup of tea. That was a real treat. Saturday afternoons were quiet, so we would start clearing up at around eleven. I was able to do all this because the school didn't have matches every week. When I was playing, Mum used to deliver the meat for me, but I would still take my wages! It wasn't great money but it was enough at that age to allow me to do things I otherwise would not have been able to do. It was even better in the school holidays: not only did it give me something to do, it also gave me a nice little income. Sadly Wharton's has been taken over now, but I shall always remember the sausages and the little chipolatas.

As for those Saturday matches, my PE teacher, Dan Maddocks, would only let me play football for Ashlea and Fen Park (on Sundays) if I played rugby for the school. They were quite entitled to do that in those days, though I'm not sure they would get away with anything like it now. And when it came to the spring term I would have to play football for the school on Saturday morning in order to continue with my other teams. I was exhausted come Sunday evening.

I played a lot of football during those years. At the age of thirteen I was picked to play for Lowestoft Schoolboys U-15, at left-back. One of the teams I played against was Newham, in one of the later rounds of the English Schools Trophy. We travelled down to east London on the bus for the game, and in the Newham team was a certain Alan Curbishley, now manager of Charlton, and Ade Coker, a good striker who went on to be successful in the professional game, playing for West Ham. We played at the Terence MacMillan Stadium, and although we lost 4–0 it was another great day out, with a meal in a restaurant afterwards and our team dressed up in school uniform. 'Curbs' was a good player, and he went on to represent England at schoolboy level.

I also played for Suffolk Schoolboys for a couple of years. I can't remember whether there were any others who went on to make it in the professional game, but I guess there were some as we played against teams like Essex which was always a hard game, and our best result against them was a goalless draw. A little easier were the games against Bedfordshire, Hertfordshire, Norfolk (our local rivals) and Cambridgeshire. But Essex were always the most difficult and would often put five or more past us. I progressed on to the U-19s, and we were involved every year in the Skegness Festival. Teams would gather in the seaside resort and play a tournament. I had a long spell in schoolboy football without ever being approached by a single professional club, not even Ipswich or Norwich, who were right on my doorstep. It only happened when I was seventeen.

By that time I had managed to achieve seven 'O' levels: two English (Literature and Language), Geography, Latin, Maths, French and Additional Maths. Notice no sciences, which I disliked. As for my 'A' levels, I only passed Maths, which I loved, failing English and French due to football dominating my revision periods. It's funny, but now I enjoy French as a language whereas at school it was just another subject. We had a number of French players at Motherwell, my boss Eric Black spoke it fluently, and when I was out in France for the 1998 World Cup with the BBC I had plenty of opportunities to practise. I understand more than I can speak, and can read the French papers and restaurant menus. I regret now I didn't do more than just enough to pass my exams. In truth, sport just took over. I was far happier kicking a ball in the back garden or in the park than studying. It's a pity I didn't mix both equally, though.

As for girls, I was never bothered in my teens. Rita and I were the same age – there's about six months between us – but remember, I had been moved up a year so I saw little of her. People who know her now would not believe in those days she was a bit of a tearaway. Perhaps that is what attracted me eventually, but though we were often in close proximity to each other, especially when she worked at the fish shop where I bought my chips, and later at the Post Office where I had to take the mail, there was little or no contact. She didn't take any notice of me either, especially with my then long hair, to cover my big ears, with its fringe at the front and no parting. The hairstyle didn't change until 1977 when I went to Hawaii, Canada and the USA for three weeks with Ipswich and it was decided I should go to a hairdresser in Vancouver, where I had it brushed back. I looked a different person. When I returned home it was considered fashionable rather than a complete mullet, and things changed from then on. But Rita can remember me with a mullet. Fortunately she was trained as a hairdresser and kept me in shape after that.

Before then I was a gangling youth, more paint by numbers than an oil painting. Besides, girls didn't play football in those days, so I wasn't really concerned with them. I did go out with the butcher's daughter and a couple of girls from school, but all it meant was walking them home or having a coffee together. It was all very proper at the time. The most I did with the butcher's daughter was go to her home and listen to music – but definitely not in her bedroom the way kids do now. I used to enjoy listening to groups like Mott the Hoople and Queen, but I wasn't really into the Beatles or the hippy music which was all a bit before my time. My era was more Deep Purple, Bad Company, The Who and similar groups. I enjoyed my heavy-metal music too, Alice Cooper and some of the other wild guys. I hated discos because I was over six feet tall, had a scarecrow haircut and stood out a mile – and I was still a virgin.

Not that there wasn't a naughty side to the young Terry Butcher. When I was still at school we would go down to the pub for three or four pints, a game of darts and a packet of pork scratchings while someone else signed us in. I remember my first visit to a pub, when I was fifteen. I went with David Baldry, and we asked for two pints. The barman asked, 'Two pints of what?' We immediately began to panic and looked hard at the bottles and cans on the shelf. The first beer to catch my eye was Carlsberg Special Brew, so we asked for two pints of that. The barman raised an eyebrow as the beer did not come in either pint or half-pint cans. I thought he was going to ask how old we were, but he didn't; he just served us with this rocket fuel someone had called beer. We drank it fairly quickly because we were still worried he had sussed out our ages. We put away a can and a half each – to make up the pint – and scooted out of the pub as quickly as we could. We had barely made the sea front when we were both violently sick. I went home and straight to bed. I was so ill, but it didn't teach me any lessons.

But I was never a rebel. Apart from drinking a pint or two, I was very much a good family boy and enjoyed things like Christmas and summer holidays. The Christmas/New Year season was a time for the family, and we took turns to throw the parties. The kids would play games, cards and a racing game called Newmarket; we even played football in the hallway sometimes. Perhaps as a result, I didn't have many friends from school, because home was comparatively far away. It was mainly the fellow sports players I mixed with, but generally I was a bit of a loner who enjoyed my own little life. I had a lot of mature acquaintances through football, but they were not people I knocked around with away from the sports fields.

Summer was spent mainly on the beach with my pal David. We would take a football down there and it was a great escape for us. The best ball we had was at the start of every summer, a really heavy plastic ball with a fake hexagonal pattern to make it look as though it was a real leather ball. It had the names of teams on it, whether it was the English First Division, as it was then, the World Cup or European Championship nations, or whatever had captured the public imagination at the time. Those balls were good because they wouldn't wobble or fly about in the sea breezes like the more traditional beach-type ball. A leather football was no good because if it went into the sea, as it usually did, it would be so sodden and heavy it was impossible to kick. One of us would be in goal and the other out, and as we played we would commentate: 'Law to Best … Best to Charlton …' and so on. The sand was soft and lovely to dive on, then it was into the sea for a 'shower'. When it became dark the lights would come on over Claremont Pier, and by those lights plus the lights from the bar we would resume our now 'floodlit' match. We even had dressing rooms, because Mum and Dad had a beach hut where they kept the deckchairs and a primus stove. We could adjourn, make ourselves a cup of tea and some beans on toast, and we were ready for the off again.

We didn't feel the need to go abroad for our holidays as we had everything we required on our doorstep. We were in the sea come May. It was freezing cold, but we didn't feel it. Once you were in it was fine. We would swim out and hunt for crabs on the groynes. In the summer the sea would go out a long way, four or five hundred yards, and it would leave a big stretch of flat sand for cricket. We used the groyne as the stumps and even the dads would join in. Football, when played with the group, was somewhat fiercer but it was a lovely flat surface, cleaned up by the tide every night. There was also a stretch called the Denes where the sand met the land, and we would run along the beach, past the Denes Oval (where they still play cricket), up the hill, up the cliff and along the promenade. It was a hard run but enjoyable.

But as my schooling days came to a close, I had to knuckle down and make a decision. No one had yet approached me about a career in football, so I had to look around. My dad was still a prison officer, and at this time Mum was working in the Lowestoft Careers Office, but sometimes in those circumstances it's difficult to discuss jobs. I knew a bit about the butcher's trade, of course, but I didn't see it as a long-term future; as for football, I didn't have the confidence to believe I could go on and earn a living at it. I had had a couple of trials with England Schoolboys and been turned down, so fear of further rejection was a part of the problem.

I remember a boy named Paul Clark, a centre-half who played for Essex boys, who received the call-up for England. I went to watch with the other boys on the coach thinking it could have been me rather than should have been me. I felt no envy at all, even though I knew in myself I was as good as him. Later on in life I actually played against him when he was playing for Southend. But in those days very few of the England U-15s used to make it long term in the professional game, whereas these days it's almost seamless from school level right through to full international. Terry Venables was one of the few who went right through the system before then.

Lack of confidence is linked with fear, and I still have this fear of doing something wrong, to go along with the neatness and order thing. It started young, and it leads into superstition. If I played a game in the afternoon I would have to prepare in a certain way. A voice in my head would tell me if I walked on a line on the way to school we would lose the match. I was paranoid about doing everything in the right order, and then if the game was lost I would accuse myself of having done something wrong in the preparation. Putting my gear on in a certain order was something else I did. I even do it as a manager. It's a real worry, an intense fear of doing something wrong. It comes from my dad – it's a question of doing things in the right and proper way. It even extends to my broadcasting for Radio Five. If I'm on air and say or do something wrong it will gnaw away at me all night and will still bother me the next day.

When I lose a game as a manager I am so self-doubting and critical. I go through everything I did that week – the training, the warm-up, meals, team selection, tactics, everything. I was the same as a player. If I did something wrong on the field or in an interview I would be mortified. I guess it's called paranoia. The more famous I became, the more I wanted to be in the background and not to be noticed. I can understand the problems so-called stars suffer. It is driven, for me, by a total fear of failure. It's intense, and it doesn't just affect me in football but in general matters too. Rita laughs whenever she asks me to do something like put up a mirror because I will ask her three or four times how best to do it and why. I always need the green light. Again, driving the family in a strange country and having to stop for lunch is a black hole for me. Somehow I feel wherever we pick is going to be wrong, or there will be a better place just down the road. The ideal for me is to be somewhere familiar so I know it's right. The alternative is to do a reconnoitre so I know what food they serve, what time they open and where you can park your car. I will never, according to Rita, park in the right place. Fortunately that side of it has waned a little as I have become older, but I'm still paranoid. It is, I repeat, a fear of failure, a fear of being rejected and being made to look stupid. If anyone embarrasses me I can still flip. Mr Hyde again.

And there is, as I have said, this other side to me where I do, of my own free will, really stupid things and make the situation worse. In the eighties I loved the group Madness, and they were promoting a T-shirt with the legend 'Fuck Art – Let's Dance'. I wore it on the team bus on a Friday going to Birmingham to play Villa the next day, and Bobby Robson went apoplectic. He screamed at me, 'Butcher [he always called me Butcher], you can't wear that! You are a footballer, you are representing Ipswich! You can't wear that!' Sir Bobby probably knows me better than anyone else, and he once said to me, 'Butcher, you have a problem. You have a safety valve. Your safety valve is alcohol, and that is where you seek your relief, your escape from stress.' It's true. I drink to celebrate and I drink to forget. You look at society now and you see that attitude reflected in all walks of life. I am a real Jekyll and Hyde.

Still, my confidence might not have been high when I left school, but I was a winner and I was up and at 'em. I decided I was going to go to Trent Polytechnic in Nottingham (in the days before it became a university) to study to become a quantity surveyor. I knew a couple and it seemed to be a job that took you out and about and was Monday to Friday, which left weekends free to carry on with my amateur sports. I thought it would suit me down to the ground. It was a three-year diploma course reputed to have seven women to every man. Again, it sounded good to me.

And then my life changed completely. By now I was playing centre-half regularly, and I had been playing for the county U-19s. Ron Gray, the Ipswich scout and a lovely man, was at most of the games. At the time I had never met him or been introduced to him, and it was a fluke I came to his attention at all. I had a friend, Reg Regis, who I played tennis with and who owned a sports shop almost next to Dewhurst where I had spent so many hours working. Reg's son Mike wrote to Ipswich's youth-team coach Charlie Woods and told him he should have a look at me. Subsequently I was invited to train on Thursday nights at their School of Excellence. I loved it there, just to be in the club with those big kicking blocks to kick your boots against, the distinctive smell of a dressing room with the liniment, sweat and everything else. Upstairs was a big gymnasium where we trained. I went along for a few nights at the end of the 1975/76 season, and I must have done something right as they asked me back.

Sure enough, Bob Bagshaw, a local scout for Norwich, also got in touch with me and asked me to go along to meet John Sainty, their youth-team coach. It was just like London buses: you wait for ever for one to come along, then two come together. I had to wear the Norwich strip of yellow shirts and green shorts, and I was almost physically sick because I was such an Ipswich man by then. I was pants in the match I played in; all I wanted to do was get the kit off. Sainty asked me to come back but I told him I was going on a school-organised canoeing trip down the Ardèche, which I was. By then I had been offered a three-week trial at Ipswich anyway. He told me to go ahead but not to do anything in terms of signing without speaking to him first.

I went down to Portman Road and had a wonderful time. It was hard work, but I loved every minute of it, and after those three weeks they offered me terms. To the credit of Trent Polytechnic they kept my place open for a year in case I didn't make it as a professional footballer, but I never had to take them up on the offer.

CHAPTER TWO

WELCOME TO IPSWICH

I was playing in a practice match marking David Geddis, who was later to become coach at Newcastle United with Bobby Robson towards the end of his days at St James's Park. David was a big, rough, tough centre-forward with windmill arms. He was quick and strong, and we had a right battle, elbowing and kicking each other. It was a good fierce contest, which I really enjoyed. Two days later Bobby Robson called me into his office and offered me a contract. The money was £50 a week, and I have to say I was delighted as it was good money for a seventeen-year-old, plus bonuses of £2 for a win in the youth team and £1 for a draw. If he had offered me a tenner I would still have snapped his hand off.

Dad was ecstatic, but Mum was worried because so many young, hopeful footballers fail to make the grade. What made the difference was my open place at Trent Poly. It was good of them, and I appreciated it, but when you consider it there's little difference between that and having a gap year to travel around the world, as so many students do now. As it was, I fell in love with the professional game straight away. Then Charlie Woods reminded me just because I had signed professional forms it didn't mean I was anywhere near making it as a footballer. 'You cannot pass the ball,' he continued, 'you cannot control the ball. You think you are a big star but all you have done is sign a bit of paper.' I thought he was winding me up, but then he told me to take a football every day after training to a concrete area under the stand and practise against the wall, heading, passing, shortening the distance then elongating the distance, and to do it for twenty minutes every day. It was the best bit of advice I've ever had as it developed my touch, my confidence on the ball and my control. Others did it too, and they all benefited. It's something I pass on to my own youngsters at Motherwell, even to our first-team players – just twenty minutes before training. I was proud of my touch, control and passing. There were few left-sided centre-backs as comfortable on the ball as I was, especially at six feet four inches tall. In the English Premier League now players know they have to be able to pass the ball, but nearly three decades ago at Ipswich every single player could pass and control the ball.

I had seen Bobby Robson a couple of times in pre-season training when he mixed everyone together, senior professionals, apprentices and triallists. It was a wonderful experience mingling with my heroes, in particular Kevin Beattie, who was my favourite player. We still keep in touch. When Mr Robson offered me the contract he had me bring in Mum and Dad to talk it over. His room was quite dark but it was full of pennants from all over the world and his big windows overlooked the ground. It was very impressive to a youngster, and I was in awe of him. I thought he was a wonderful guy then and I still do to this day. He had been manager of the team I supported since 1969. I used to stand on a wooden box to watch his team play. I'd even watched them away: I was at Leicester's Filbert Street ground when they drew with Leeds in the FA Cup quarter-final replay in 1975, though I missed the next game when they beat Leeds 3–2, only to lose to West Ham in the semi-finals due to a poor refereeing performance from the notorious Clive Thomas. I was still watching as a fan from the Churchman Stand when Ipswich beat Barcelona 3–0 in the UEFA Cup in November 1977. Now here I was signing a contract to play for the manager I admired most. I had seen them play lots of times and was comfortable at the ground, but the one thing I still feared above all else was rejection. It was the same feeling I'd had at the England Schoolboys trial, but this was different. This was my future.

In many ways as a manager it is easier to tell a professional you are not renewing his contract than to tell a kid that he is not good enough to fulfil his dreams. I know the situation so well. I was able to go to the Ipswich trials because I knew I had back-up with the place at Trent Poly. Would I have risked it otherwise? Who knows?

I was fortunate I had Charlie Woods as my coach. He was a man I had watched and liked as a player, a tough Cumbrian who put on good training sessions. He was a good coach, working on the technical side as well as on tactics and team play. And we were fortunate in other ways.

Our training pitch was right next to the main pitch, and even if the seniors were using it we would still only have a short walk to the park over the road. We also enjoyed a very good gymnasium upstairs which we could use to develop upper-body strength. We had good practice matches too, and it was all very professional. I relished every minute of it.

We usually played our matches on a Saturday morning in the South East Counties League where the furthest trip was to Portsmouth, and even then we would always make the journey on the day of the game. We would travel, play, and then return to Portman Road to watch either the reserves or the first team, as in those days the reserves played on Saturday as well, which they no longer do. It was perfect, playing in the morning and then back to watch the team I supported. On our return we would stand in the little enclosure next to the tunnel. If we had won it would be announced to the always receptive crowd. We were given one season ticket each and a couple of complimentary tickets per home game. Mum used the season ticket while Dad used to stand with one of his pals near us. Mum and Dad would take me home in the car afterwards, but they would have to wait until we completed our jobs after the game. There was a rota, and duties included tidying the dressing rooms, putting the kit away, cleaning the baths and brushing the boots, and sometimes we would also go out on the pitch to replace divots. One thing we were never asked to do, unlike some other clubs, was to clean the terraces. We would probably get away just after six.

It was nothing to do with cheap labour; it was all part of the discipline of the club. Initially when I was with the youth team I travelled in every day with reserve goalkeeper Laurie Sivell, but it meant I missed the jobs at the ground in the morning, so I took digs closer to the ground with the delightful Mrs Seggars along with Johnny Stirk, the reserve-team skipper. Now, I make sure we have jobs for the youngsters at Motherwell. I'm not so sure they do it at Rangers and Celtic, but as far as I am aware the rest of the clubs do. I understand in England clubs that have academies don't allow the boys to do it. But I believe in it intensely. If you are going to cheat or be slack in your jobs then you are liable to do it as a footballer on the pitch. It reflects the character.

My specific job at Portman Road was in the laundry, looking after the kit and sorting out the hampers. I only did a year and missed out on doing the boots. One thing I could never understand was why the club had only one washer and one dryer. The kit was hung up to dry on Monday in the drying room with its three boilers whether it was dirty, wet, sweaty or whatever. The room used to stink. There were two lots of kit, one for the morning and the other for the afternoon. But when you picked it up out of the dryer it was stiff like a piece of cardboard. There would be fresh kit only after two days. Nowadays the kit is done every day.

For lunch we used a restaurant called the Centre Spot at the ground, but before then we used to go to a pub called the Sporting Farmer where we would have chips with gravy. It may sound awful but it was lovely, and we used to eat while listening to Bryan Ferry on the jukebox. When we moved to the Centre Spot we would have soup and sandwiches or whatever we wanted. There was surprisingly no check on our diets. In the late seventies we used to go into a pub in town that had good bar food and order big portions of scampi and chips or fish and chips – everything with chips. We would eat a monster portion for lunch then go back to our digs and have a whopping meal in the evening. Pre-match meals weren't much better. The seasoned professionals used to have steak and eggs, but I was more into scrambled eggs and boiled chicken. I was learning, but slowly, because it just wasn't considered important.

In the days of chips and gravy we had only ten minutes before we had to rush back to our jobs, and Friday was the big clean-up day when we had to buff all the floors ready for the weekend. You had to get all the water down, suck it up, and then buff it. Now they have office cleaners. The jobs used to be inspected, and if they weren't done properly they had to be done again. We knew this and made sure all was spick and span. If anyone mucked it up the person would be given some serious bother from the rest of us. Little Cyril Lea, the coach who is now at Rushden and Diamonds, was the man who used to check the jobs, and he would always find something by grubbing about behind the boilers and prying into all the nooks and crannies. It was all part of our education, and the spirit of Cyril lives on at Motherwell where I do the same sort of thing, finding Scotch mist and making the youngsters do laps if I find anything wrong. We used to panic as kids during inspections. They still do today.

I really do think that young players at big clubs who don't do this any more miss out on essential discipline – and it shows. I came through the ranks with solid fellow internationals Alan Brazil and Russell Osman, but there was also a big striker named Alan Bond who had problems with his weight, though he was quick and could score goals. He wasn't the most technically gifted but he could bulldoze his way through defences and, more importantly, he could put the ball in the net, the most prized commodity of them all. But he had a problem – he would always cheat on his job. He was a Cockney and thought he was clever; he would go missing, away buying Mars Bars, when he should have been working.

Generally speaking, though, our youth team was a good, disciplined unit. Another of the young players was Stevie Gardner, a good footballer and technically gifted in midfield. Nigel Crouch was another – my best man, as it happens, who now has his own building company in Manningtree in Essex. They were all part of it and all good lads. We could have a laugh and a joke. It was a successful youth team, too: we won our league by a big margin with Brazil scoring 40 goals in the season. My first youth-team game was away against Arsenal at London Colney in August 1976, and we beat them 2–1. I played with Russell, and we have been joined at the hip ever since. We had trials for England Youth together (he won a place, I didn't) and eventually progressed to the full England side. We are still only a telephone call away. The experience was an excellent education for me. My fitness levels went up, as did my awareness under the eagle-eyed coaching of Charlie Woods.

I received my first injury the week before Christmas when I fractured my cheekbone in a game against Chelsea at Mitcham. A corner came in and I headed it out. I remember watching it arc away and thinking to myself 'That's a good header!' when suddenly there was an almighty bang as I was hit with a late challenge from John Sitton. I never felt it was deliberate and just assumed he was committed and went through with his challenge, as I would have done. I suffered a depressed fracture. The physiotherapist came on and asked me if I could clench my teeth together. I tried, there was an immediate shooting pain, and he diagnosed it immediately as a break and called an ambulance, which took me to Kingston-on-Thames hospital. The club called my parents and operated on me the same afternoon. Suddenly I found myself at home for Christmas. It wasn't a good one as far as I was concerned. As it happened, it was a portent of things to come. I seemed to suffer more injuries to my head than to anywhere else on my body.

I eventually came back to the team and we continued to do well through the 1976/77 season. We did all that was asked of us, and to have three players come through from one youth team to represent their countries is about as good as it gets at most clubs. It was a great learning process, and much I picked up in those early seasons has served me well through my playing days and into my managerial career. It also taught me not just to play for the love of the game, although that has always been important to me: it taught me to be a professional and to play to win, whatever it took. For instance, at Portman Road we opted to play with a red and white football called the Surridge Cobbler. Our opponents hated it – it was, I admit, an odd football: the red panels made it look as though it had a strange shape as it flew through the air – so we loved it even more.

That summer we flew to Toronto, from there to Hawaii for nine days of training – or was that drinking? – and then on to Portland where we landed and went straight from the hotel to eat dinner. We didn't have anything organised, we just went out and bought our own dinner. Ten of us went into the bar and ordered ten beers from a waiter whose T-shirt read 'Are there fairies at the bottom of your garden?' When we spotted it we had a look round and there was not a woman to be seen. We cancelled our order and made a hasty exit from my first ever gay bar – not so freely thought of then as they are these days. As eighteen-year-olds we were well under the drinking age of 21 in the States anyway, but we weren't stopped.

It was a great trip, even though I played just twenty minutes of football. In Toronto against the Blizzards, Alan Brazil scored the winning goal in a 2–1 victory. He, like me, was a youngster, and his place on the trip had been touch and go until Trevor Whymark pulled out because his wife was about to have a baby. Brazil had all his gear and stood waiting by the bus. Bobby Robson gave Whymark until two o'clock to make the bus, but then, typically, gave him another fifteen minutes' grace before he gave in to Brazil's pleading to make the journey. It was a great lift for the three of us from the youth team – Alan, Russell Osman and me – to be replacing the players who were on home international duty.

Ipswich, like other clubs, went on these trips because they received good money for the club and we were given decent expenses. Three weeks was a long trip, though, and it wouldn't happen now because the game has changed so much. The club directors came with us, among them John and Patrick Cobbold. The Cobbolds were great fun, and when we arrived in Hawaii in this Silver Jubilee year they instructed us to meet in the hotel bar the next day at noon to drink a toast to Her Majesty. I arrived with Laurie Sivell and Roger Osborne, and immediately Mr Patrick and Mr John said they had already sampled the local cocktail, a Mai Tai, and recommended them to us. We tried them and loved the drink so much that we drank them until four p.m., at which point Mr John said it was time to toast the Queen once more. I went to rise but couldn't get to my feet. I had to toast Her Majesty sitting down and was then helped to bed to sleep it off, leaving Mr John and Mr Patrick to carry on drinking. They were fantastic people – worth a chapter of their own. They were a great foil for Bobby Robson and I doubt whether their kind exist in football these days. When Robson was under pressure with results and became the target of irate supporters, they backed him by giving him a ten-year contract! It was brilliant because it settled the entire club, allowing him to put scouting, youth team, coaches and everything else in place. It's no use having good kids coming through if you haven't the coaches to handle them once they are there. If you have poor coaches, the kids have no chance. Some of the young players who didn't look as though they would make it did so because the right coaches were there to bring the best out of them. It was a hard environment, but it worked.

We trained in Hawaii, but it was a joke because the players were drinking a lot and were more concerned about where they were going at night. But Robson was well aware of what was going on and training was hard, very hard. That was the case for most of the footballers I knew in my era. If you drank hard you had to train hard to sweat out all the rubbish. The only problem was that all that sweaty work left plenty of space for more alcohol at night.

It was while I was in Hawaii I learnt a little more about women. I met a young lady from San Diego who was some eight years older than me, but we had been told on the plane all we needed to do to enchant the ladies was to speak because they would love our English accents. We didn't exactly have the girls flooding around us, but it certainly helped; what's more, if the lads needed to communicate between themselves all we had to do was talk very quickly and they couldn't follow what we were saying. I was with Roger Osborne, who wasn't interested in the girls because he was happily married, but he sportingly told me that if I wanted to take anyone back to the room I could just take the keys from reception and he would find alternative accommodation. But as I vaguely recall, the keys were not very often at reception.

After Hawaii we flew into Portland where we won again, and then it was on to Vancouver to play the Whitecaps, where Bobby Robson had spent some time before taking over at Ipswich. Unfortunately I roomed with Northern Ireland international Pat Sharkey, a lovely guy under normal circumstances, but the night before the game he was plastered and he was down to play on the artificial surface. He not only flooded the bathroom but also came after me a couple of times – whether the advances were amorous or aggressive I didn't hang about to find out. I took my camera, my wallet and my room key and went into Russell Osman's room, which was a sanctuary in comparison. I left Sharkey to it and only went back for a shower the following morning. He played, but he didn't touch the ball for the first 45 minutes as he ran around with a scarlet face. Robson realised what was up at half-time and brought him off, and later on he gave me my twenty minutes, which I really enjoyed, despite the odd warm-up the night before.

I returned to Ipswich with a tan and a new hairstyle, feeling great about the new season. That was when I got together with Rita. The meeting that would change my life for ever happened in a pub called the Wherry Hotel in Oulton Broad. I was there with a player called David Dunthorne, who was at Norwich and had been at Lowestoft Schoolboys with me. I came back from a game and, as often happened, we went out. He introduced Rita to me as one of his friends. I had my trendy gear on: a pair of flared jeans, a polo shirt and a *Starsky and Hutch* jumper. I thought I looked very smart, but Rita and her friends took the rip out of it. We chatted, and finished up at a disco at the end of South Pier. I still hated discos but I was pleased to be with Rita and her pal Lesley. Rita lived about a mile from the pier so it was local for her and she knew most of the people. She would dance with her friend, come back and have a drink, then go off and dance some more, so it could hardly be said we were together or on a date. Whenever she came back for a drink she stood on some steps; I was at the bottom so she was on a level with me. I spoke to her about it some time afterwards but she couldn't remember doing it and claimed she wasn't making fun of my height.

When the dancing finished I asked if I could walk her home. She agreed, and even invited me and Lesley in for coffee. We had a few drinks and I arranged to meet her the next day in the Marquis of Lorne, a pub close to where my aunt lived. It was a family pub, whereas the Wherry was much more a place for trendy youngsters. I arrived fifteen minutes after the allotted one p.m. time, ordered my pint and waited until two. There was no sign of her, so I assumed she had arrived on time, waited for me and then left when I hadn't shown. I decided not to let it lie, and a few days later I cycled round to her house on my dad's bike – one of those very old-fashioned types with round handlebars and a metal cover over the chain – to apologise for my lateness. She cut me short by telling me she hadn't been there at all because she wasn't sure of the time we'd agreed on; she also thought I fancied Lesley rather than her. I assured her it wasn't the case and asked her if she would go out with me that night. She agreed, and we have been together ever since.

I borrowed Dad's Cortina and took her out to the pub for the evening (these were the days before breathalysers). Supper was a bag of chips on the sea front, sitting in the car. It was the romantic thing to do. I turned on Tony Prince on Radio Luxembourg to hear him say, 'The King is dead, the King is dead!' It was the night Elvis Presley died, 17 August 1977. We couldn't believe it. I wasn't particularly an Elvis fan, but it was an historic night nonetheless, and they played Elvis songs for the rest of the evening. How much more memorable can a first date get?

We started going out on a regular basis after that, although one of her friends used to laugh at me because I never wore trendy stuff, even though I could afford it with my wages. It was difficult to impress her friends because they weren't really interested in football. Professional footballers weren't as fashionable then as they are now. And it didn't help most of her friends were hairdressers and I still had the most appalling haircut of all time.

Rita was at hairdressing college at the time, and she invited me to go to their studios to be a model for a free haircut. I refused, so she offered me a shave with a cut-throat razor. While I was waiting for her to make the arrangements she told me how they practised on balloons, and how the balloons kept bursting. I quickly changed my mind. I have still never had one, and I don't fancy it at all. I even find the old razor an enemy when I go to an old-fashioned barber's for a haircut.

Once she'd qualified she went to work for her friend, but soon an increase in my wages allowed her to pack it in. We moved to Ipswich, married, and had three lovely boys, the eldest of them Christopher Charles (the second name of both my and Rita's dads is Charles). He is Chris normally, but if he has done anything wrong it's Christopher, in a very loud voice. The middle son, three years younger than Chris, is Edward John, known as Ed, the John coming from my grandfather. The youngest is Alistair Ian. Ian is my middle name, but he is named after Ally McCoist and Ian Durrant, two lovely guys and ex-team-mates at Rangers.

But back at the start of the 1977/78 season I was still miles away from the first team, with Allan Hunter and Kevin Beattie the two regular centre-backs. There was also Russell Osman and Dale Roberts to compete with, and John Wark was originally signed as a centre-half. Ipswich had ample cover in my position. I was all set to move up to the reserves, but things certainly didn't click into place the way I expected them to. Bobby Ferguson was the reserve-team coach and he demanded absolute perfection and total effort. He was an incredible guy. I love him to bits and still speak to him, but he was a hard taskmaster who wanted the best out of you and wasn't prepared to hang about to see if time would make you a better player. It had to be there and then. Some thought of it as bullying, but though it was forceful, it was character-building, and eventually it brought the best out of me.

But it was tough. It knocked me about to such a point the early part of that second year is a blur. I didn't do very well, I wasn't enjoying my football, and it was a complete change going into a higher standard of football, against better, more experienced players. It was a massive jump for me, and I wasn't coping. A lot of reserve-team football these days both north and south of the border is insipid and played at a very pedestrian pace. There are senior players who don't want to be there, injured players tentatively feeling their way back, and youngsters who may not even have a future at the club. But in the late seventies the standard was high and the competition fierce. Games were played on a Saturday in front of reasonable-size crowds with season-ticket holders enjoying watching the youngsters play. It was the business. If you didn't play to the standard expected you were shouted at or kicked out. There was no sentiment.

My problem was I wasn't aggressive enough. I let people dominate me, let them rough me up. I was six feet four inches tall and wasn't going through to win the ball when I should have been commanding in both boxes. Even my passing, which I prided myself on, was poor. Ferguson was on me all the time, not just during matches but every day of the week, morning and afternoon. I was with the nucleus of the youth team who had also come through, but a lot of them didn't make it and were let go. At the time I wasn't sure whether I was lucky or not because the next step forward was the first team and I was barely coping with being a reserve. I began to ask myself whether I was good enough, was I going to make it. I was full of fear, and my play reflected that. I'd had a good trip away with the first-team squad in the summer, now here I was in the reserves getting nowhere. Russell had progressed to first-team appearances, but I was helping make up the numbers in the reserves.

I was close to telling Ferguson to stick it. Why should I be bothered when I wasn't enjoying myself? It got so bad I spoke to my parents about it. My mother was all for me quitting and taking up my place at Trent Poly, but Dad told me to stick with it. I was in turmoil. I didn't know which way to go. It would have been easy to pack it all in, but Dad persuaded me. He was very strong and explained to me Ferguson was only doing what he did to wind me up, and I was to go out there and show him what I was made of. I had to get the aggression to come out of me and into my play. I didn't know it was there, but everyone else seemed to believe I had it within me.

Big Allan Hunter, an idol of mine, started to pick a fight with me at training one day. He was marking me for a corner during a game between the first team and the reserves, and although I was a few inches taller than Big Al he always seemed enormous to me. He was my idol from the days when I was passed down the Portman Road terraces as a young Ipswich supporter. Allan was playing alongside my mate Russell Osman for the senior team, and they were defending. As the ball came across I went up for the challenge, but Hunter not only barged me out of the way, he also elbowed me in the face. Clearly he was looking for a reaction, but this was Big Al. He could have boxed my ears, punched me, poked me in the eye, done anything he wanted, but he and Kevin Beattie, alongside Bobby Moore, were the two best centre-halves I had ever seen. I revered them, and I wasn't about to fight with one of them.

Al wasn't taking no for an answer. He continued to push me, pull me and slap me across the face, trying to provoke me in his Irish brogue by saying things like 'You're a coward', 'You're a mother's boy', 'You've got no bottle', 'You're useless', 'You couldn't fight your way out of a wet paper bag' – all, of course, liberally sprinkled with expletives. He was clearly trying to wind me up. The other players quickly gathered round, but I was determined not to react, though I would have hit any other player from any other team, even though I wasn't a physical player at that stage of my career. I never got into fights and wasn't interested in the physical battles. I felt I was a footballer.

The coaches on the touchline were deliberately taking no notice and showing no signs of intervening. I have found as a manager that you let players get on with it, as long as there is some passion and some purpose.

They knew it wasn't something that was going to be carried on, and the great English teams of the times – Liverpool, Ipswich, Manchester United and others – would often have bouts like this, with fists flying. But I kept my arms to my side. I looked Al in the eyes but said nothing, and eventually the first team took a goal-kick and the game carried on. Now, whether Al had spoken to Bobby Ferguson about doing what he did I don't know, but they both said later they saw in my eyes indications I could be a warrior. Perhaps this was a calculated attempt to bring the fire out quickly instead of waiting for it to develop.

At the time it was all very intimidating. I was shocked my idol and team-mate should want to rough me up. But it did lead to an incident that proved to be the turning point of my career. The crucial tackle with Russell Osman didn't happen immediately after Al had had a go at me, but in the meantime other players had continued to wind me up. The coaching staff were also giving me stick from the sidelines, telling me to get stuck in. In fact, I received some unmerciful stick, and not just in this game but week after week – far more than my Motherwell youngsters get today. If they had to go through now what I went through they would be in front of an industrial tribunal claiming compensation and would probably be out of the game. It was different then, and if you didn't accept it you knew you were out.

Eventually, I did get stuck in. I didn't realise at the point when the ball dropped between me and another player it was Russell, but it was the moment when a lot of frustration from the game and perhaps years of pent-up aggression were finally unleashed. We didn't slide in gracefully: we went at the ball like juggernauts, and flew into the tackle like two Kung Fu black belts having a go at each other. In fact, the clash was so tumultuous the training staff ran on immediately, fearing the worst. We were both hurt, but neither of us wanted to show it. We jumped up and hopped about a bit until the dead legs started to ease.

It was undoubtedly a pivotal moment – the moment when the Butcher volcano blew its top after years of lying dormant and rumbling only every now and then. The incident reminded me of a day as a kid when I left both a right-winger and a right-back on the ground as I went on a rampage up the left wing. But afterwards I had gone back to apologise and help them to their feet, as instructed by my father. But this was different. This was what I now got paid for, and this was what I was destined to be, for I must admit I felt a terrific buzz, even though it hurt so much. It could have gone either way, particularly if I had been hurt. I had been hurt a little bit, but I knew Russell had too – and he was an English schoolboy rugby union player, a very hard young man noted for his biting and snarling attitude, as well as for being an intelligent player. My shoulders went back and my head went up. There wasn't a flash of lightning or anything, but from that moment on my attitude to defending, to football, to life even, began to change. I hobbled away feeling as though I had arrived at last, and others also seemed to feel the same way. After the incident everything seemed to fall into place for me. I had been tentative because I hadn't wanted to make mistakes, to give the ball away and let the team down. But after the tackle with Russell I suddenly found I had the respect of the senior players, and I rather liked it. The first job as a defender is to assert yourself and make sure the opposition know you mean business. That is what I had done in that one tackle.

Everything began to get better from that moment on, and then came my opportunity to play for the first team. I made my debut on 15 April 1978 because both Hunter and Beattie had problems with their knees. The team sheet went up on Friday, something I still like doing myself, and there was my name. It has always been a big thing for me – it's what you work for – and no one leaves on a Friday at Motherwell until I have put the team sheet up. I can clearly remember the buzz it gave me to know I was playing against Everton at Goodison Park the next day.

We flew up in two fourteen-seater jets from RAF Wattisham and stayed at the Holiday Inn in Liverpool on the Friday night. All the teams stayed there in those days. I was put in a room with David Geddis, the very same player I had battled with when the manager presumably decided I had a future with the club. In my personal life Rita and I had drifted apart, so it was a case of just my parents driving up. The team flew back down after the game and my parents drove back to watch it on *Match of the Day*. Rita remembers watching it in a bar in a hotel. My debut was featured as the main match on the BBC, but there was no fairytale ending as we lost 1–0 to a Bob Latchford penalty after Russell had fouled Martin Dobson. I personally didn't think it was a penalty, but it was one of 30 League goals the Birmingham-born striker scored that season, earning him a prize of £10,000 (taxed, of course) from the *Daily Express*. They were a great family, the Latchfords. Two of Bob's brothers were professional goalkeepers. Peter is now our goalkeeping coach at Motherwell, while the elder brother David was a more than proficient goalkeeper with Birmingham City.

I remember it was a sunny day, but the game passed by in a complete blur. Sadly, I never bothered to keep a tape of my debut. But then I don't particularly like watching myself on television or tape, and neither do I like hearing myself on the radio. All I remember was being absolutely white with fear. In many respects I didn't want to play because I was worried about letting down my club, my team-mates, my family and myself. I had to talk myself into it because this is what I had been aiming for through the youth team and the reserves. Bobby Robson and Cyril Lea were very good to me before the match, telling me just to play my normal game, but I had the shakes from the moment I walked into the magnificent, huge dressing rooms at Goodison Park.

When we arrived the Scousers surrounded the bus, asking for autographs, but no one knew who I was and all they asked me was whether I had any spare tickets. After that it was just a case of doing the routine I was used to, from taking off my clothes to putting on my boots. Everything, as usual, was done in order, and once I had my first couple of touches and my first header I felt a lot better. In fact, it became one of those moments in life I didn't want to end. There were over 33,000 in the ground, Everton were flying at the time, and in Bob Latchford I was marking the best centre-forward in England. The whole experience was awesome. I had my programme autographed by the Ipswich players, and I believe my dad still has it.

When we returned to Ipswich we had a few beers and then went back to Russell's to watch the game on the box. It was something you dreamed about as a schoolboy, being on television and playing in a big match. The only sad thing was we lost. Bobby Robson was great: he didn't say a lot, but what he did say made you feel immense. That's what he does – he makes you feel a special guy.

We flew back up on the Tuesday to play Liverpool at Anfield, with me marking Kenny Dalglish. We managed a 2–2 draw, Dalglish scoring one of theirs and Graeme Souness, one of my future managers, the other, while Trevor Whymark and Mick Lambert were on target for us in front of a crowd of more than 40,000. It was a good Liverpool side, too, with the likes of Phil Thompson, Emlyn Hughes, the super sub David Fairclough, Ray Clemence, Phil Neal, Jimmy Case, Terry McDermott, and even veteran Tommy Smith. They were fourth at the time and we were struggling to put our League season together. It was a big thrill to walk under the sign saying 'This is Anfield', and we started the game well. I remember Geddis whacking Tommy Smith and then getting it back with interest as he lay in a crumpled heap on the ground. The game finished 2–2 but I vividly recall Whymark's goal, a header from eighteen yards he literally bent into the top corner. A tough thing to do with a header, but I swear it's true.

On the Thursday Bobby told me I had done a fantastic job, promptly put me on the train and played me at Bristol City that night for the reserves. Kevin Beattie was back for the weekend, but it was good psychology, bringing me back down to earth. My week had been like a whirlwind.

It turned out to be a phenomenal season because Ipswich went on to win the FA Cup, and although I didn't play in any of the Cup matches we were all made to feel involved. We began to get a feeling about the competition when we reached the quarter-finals and played Millwall at the Den. I was picked as thirteenth man. There was only one substitute in those days, but a thirteenth man was usually taken as back-up in case of overnight illness or injury during warm-up. Generally the thirteenth man was little more than a kit boy, a bit of a 'gofer', but the idea was to take a younger boy along to give him a taste of first-team experience – and what an experience it was! The safest place was in the dugout when the home crowd turned ugly, throwing bottles against the roof above our supporters who were being stretchered out in front of us. It was a war zone, and as we scored more goals so the trouble increased. At one point concrete blocks were thrown at our supporters, who had seen nothing like this back home. Afterwards Bobby Robson, still seething at what had happened, said in the boardroom the hooligans in the crowd should 'have the flamethrowers turned on them'. Unfortunately for him a journalist was present and his comment made headlines the next day. It didn't make Bobby the most popular manager in the Docklands, but years later peace was made when he brought his Porto side to open the New Den – a very different place from their old, intimidating ground.

On the Friday before the FA Cup semi-final against West Bromwich Albion at Highbury I went to the Red Lion at Martlesham with Laurie Sivell, Roger Osborne and our left-winger Clive Woods. We had the usual fish and chips and then went back to catch the bus to West Lodge Park, the hotel England then used before Wembley games. The nerves and the tension were evident, and for a young player it was fascinating to see. I travelled down the next day with the rest of the club to

Highbury, and we were in the stand opposite the main stand. Someone went out and bought some lagers and they were passed along the boys. We were steaming by the end, not just with the beer but with the fact that my team – not just the team I played for, but also the team I supported – had reached the FA Cup Final.

After the semi, everything was geared to the final and the fitness of Hunter and Beattie. I knew I wasn't in the frame because Russell had played in every Cup game up to the semi. He was named thirteenth man for the final. It was never a problem for me because I never expected to get anywhere near the Cup Final Team. I only played three games during 1977/78 – the other was my home debut against Wolves in a 2–1 defeat on 9 May – and we were battling against relegation, eventually finishing a nervous eighteenth out of 22. The biggest problem came in the penultimate game against Aston Villa, which we lost 6–1. Paul Overton, a youth-team goalkeeper, was rushed in for the match because our top two, Paul Cooper and Laurie Sivell, were injured. We also had a talented South African midfielder, Colin Viljoen, but he wasn't popular with the players because he didn't play our style of football. Bobby Robson, however, was keen to play him in the Cup Final against Arsenal and to that end picked him to play against Villa, but there were a few who weren't happy at the thought of him playing at Wembley. A number of players went down with injuries for the Villa match, and those who did play weren't particularly bothered and didn't put in the maximum effort. Poor Overton had a good game but still let in half a dozen goals. It proved to Bobby and his team that Colin shouldn't play in the Final, and in the end they went for a system they had hardly played using Geddis on the right wing. We had lots of good midfield players at the time but no decent wingers. If you were cynical you might think the Villa result was designed to lull Arsenal into a false sense of security. It wasn't meant to, we were just poor opposition that day. You had to feel sorry for Viljoen and for young Overton, because of course Paul and Laurie were both fit when it mattered. I don't think Overton played for Ipswich again. A shame.

I was at Wembley as a fan. It was everything I had ever wanted. I went to the game with the club, but I was there as a supporter along with Mum, Dad and Vanda. It was a lovely day with the wives and girlfriends, sitting just to the left of the royal box, but the more the game went on the more frustrating it was because we were so much on top. We kept hitting the woodwork. Then, when Roger Osborne, the unsung hero, scored the goal, we went berserk. Roger was so overwhelmed he had to come off. It still gives me a tingle now when I think and talk about it. Bobby Robson later called his dog Roger, while Roger called his dog Marty, Bobby's nickname.

I still wasn't back with Rita at the time, so Russell and I teamed up and went back to the Royal Garden Hotel for the reception. Everything was paid for so, needless to say, we tried to empty the bar. We also had these huge Havana cigars. We puffed away, trying to light them, until we were blue in the face, to the amusement of all those around us. Then someone told us that we had to snip the end off first, and then light them. We finally crawled to our beds in the early hours, completely wrecked.

In the morning we were up for the bus trip back to Ipswich, and all the way back on the A12 we saw our fans waving to the players. We were in the second bus in the cavalcade and it was absolutely awesome to see it all happening. We returned to the ground and enjoyed a parade around the town and a reception at the town hall.

Afterwards I went with Kevin Beattie and Russell to a working men's club somewhere in Ipswich. Kevin, who was something of a regular, couldn't buy a drink. I passed on this occasion and didn't drink. I just didn't feel like it after all the booze I had sunk the night before, and I knew we had a game on the Monday for Mick Lambert's testimonial which was going to be a full house as the supporters not only turned up to pay tribute to him but also to the FA Cup, which was to be paraded around the ground. If there had been no game and Mick had simply walked around the stadium carrying the cup, the ground would still have been full.

Then, on Wednesday, I made my long-awaited home debut against Wolves. We were awful because half the team were still drunk. Wolves forward John Richards, my third international to mark in three games, was a lovely fellow. He didn't score, but Bill Rafferty, a much-travelled Scot, did – twice. After the game I bumped into John Richards in the First Floor Club. I was sulking because we had lost. In fact I was absolutely mortified, because I had played in an Ipswich side that had been defeated at home. It had meant everything to me and I was inconsolable. Richards put an arm round me and told me not to worry because it was the end of the season and we had won the Cup. He told me to look to the future. It was a marvellous lift for me, and this after I'd tried to kick lumps out of him earlier.

That summer the first team went on tour to Norway, then on to Majorca. To justify the trip we had to play at least one game, and Norway was the chosen venue. But before I went away I met up again with Rita. We had talked on the telephone a couple of times and the day before we left I asked her about getting back together. She said yes, and it was only then I told her I was about to leave on a two-week trip the next day. Typical male, she would say.

We were still rubbish in Norway, still celebrating. Russell and I couldn't understand it, and we were both embarrassed that we were losing 1–0 to an amateur side going into the last ten minutes. Then we managed to pull it round with two late goals. The difference between the old professionals and us youngsters was marked. They were playing this one for fun, while we were playing to win. We went on to Majorca for a few beers, then I went home to restore my relationship with Rita. It must have been the right decision as we are still together 27 years later.

For pre-season preparation we went off to Holland, and in the final game of the tournament against Belgian club FC Brugge disaster struck. I headed a ball up in the air, and as it went over to the right-back position I chased it, leapt up and headed it away, only to clash with my own full-back George Burley, who barrelled into me, breaking my cheekbone again. I returned to Ipswich and Rita, a pair of sunglasses covering the worst effects. She wasn't impressed with my battered face, and neither was I, because it meant I had to miss the Charity Shield against Nottingham Forest at Wembley – and other injuries meant I would have played. Mind you, we lost 5–0 so I was quite glad to be absent.

This gave me time to look back and consider what a remarkable two years I'd had at the club. I now had a taste both for professional football and success, and I wanted a lot more. I realised very quickly how lucky I was to be involved with my local club, a club I supported. I was fulfilling my dream. My ultimate dream is to manage Ipswich, allied to going to Liverpool and beating them. I have never won at Anfield in the League and only once in a game, which didn't count, when I played for England in the Phil Thompson testimonial game.

I had another operation on my battered face and wasn't available for the reserves, never mind the first team, in August and September. Beattie and Hunter were still around, but injuries were taking their toll on them too, and more often than not it was Russell playing with one or the other.

It was an exciting season to look forward to with the First Division, the European Cup Winners' Cup and all the domestic Cups.

I eventually broke through in October for my first game of the season, a 1–0 defeat away to Forest. Then I had to wait a while for my second game, which was against Spurs at White Hart Lane on 9 December. Again we lost 1–0, and I was beginning to wonder if I was some sort of a jinx with five games and not a single victory among them. I was certainly meeting up with some quality centre-forwards: Tony Woodcock and Garry Birtles at Forest, while Spurs could boast their World Cup-winning Argentinians Ossie Ardiles and Ricardo Villa. On each occasion we were beaten with a goal from a midfield player, Martin O'Neill of all people scoring against us at Forest, and John Pratt for Spurs.

It wasn't until we played Bolton at Portman Road a week later that I won my first game – and I almost missed that. In training we wore boots for games and spikes for sprinting, and after our running I was practising heading but had been too lazy to change my spikes. The inevitable happened: I slipped, spiked my calf, and needed three stitches. Bobby Robson was understandably angry with me for being so stupid, but I was determined I was going to play. Alan Gowling and Frank Worthington were up against me, but it was me in an attacking role which opened up the game as a corner fell to me in the goalmouth. Everyone expected me to poke it goalwards, but as the defenders lunged in I squared it for Paul Mariner to have a tap-in.

That 3–0 victory felt very good, and it was the start of several firsts for me that season. In April 1979 I scored my first goal, against Birmingham City in a 3–0 win at home; I played in my first FA Cup tie, only to lose to Liverpool 1–0; and I had my first games in European competition, against Barcelona, at home and at the Nou Camp. There was another significant first for Ipswich with the arrival of two foreign players, Arnold Muhren from Twente Enschede for £150,000 in August, and in February Frans Thijssen, both brilliant signings. The arrival of Ardiles and Villa at Spurs had opened the floodgates, and Bobby was quick to make his move based on his knowledge and his regular viewing of Dutch football.

It was a good season for me and I enjoyed playing with the two new guys. Muhren had come to the club as a replacement for Brian Talbot, the star of the FA Cup, the local boy made good, who had transferred to Arsenal. No one had heard of Muhren. He was a quiet, shy, studious sort of player with the sweetest left foot, one of the best I have seen. He was also a very good general passer of the ball. I can remember his first game, a 3–0 home defeat at the hands of Liverpool. Arnold came off the pitch shaking his head because he had hardly touched the ball. A lot of our play was to work the ball into channels and up to strikers, often bypassing midfield with the forwards working hard. When Arnold came, everything had to change. We would get the ball to him and he would pick out players. We changed to suit his style, and it was the start of a new era, especially once Thijssen arrived. He was very good on the ball. We called him the Hook van Holland because he could be running in one direction, stick out his right foot at right angles, flick the ball and change direction in the blink of an eye. He had great balance and great movement with the ability to go past people on either side. He wasn't particularly quick, but he would wrongfoot people. Both he and Arnold were great crossers of the ball, and offered different options.

Bobby Ferguson had now become first-team coach; Cyril Lea left with a little acrimony. As players we didn't know for sure what had happened, but what we heard was Ferguson had gone to Robson with the blueprint of how to beat Arsenal in the Cup Final, pinning the full-backs and having a go at them with an extra man coming through from midfield in a 4–3–3 system, and it had worked. It was clear he had a big say in the tactics. Under Ferguson, into the side also came little Eric Gates. Eric had played a peripheral role to this point, but now he became a major cog, playing behind Paul Mariner and Alan Brazil, who had started to establish himself as a regular. We had Muhren on the left, Frans on the right, and Scot Johnny Wark as a holding defensive midfield player. Yet, despite this first-ever 'diamond' formation in the First Division, our defensive midfielder became a prolific scorer both at home and in Europe.

We worked hard on our shape in training, and with Paul Mariner giving us power and aggression up front it worked. Paul was somewhat underrated as he could head the ball with power, had a great touch, and was very quick. It was the end of an era: the wingers were disappearing along with striker Trevor Whymark, and the cup heroes – Clive Woods, Brian Talbot, Roger Osborne – had departed or were going. It was a natural change around a new team and a new system, a system which has been copied and used ever since. It wasn't even called the diamond then, but Bobby Robson maintained that it made other teams think about playing against us and forced them to change their own tactics.

Eric Gates was a clever player who played his role perfectly. If he was man-marked he would go up front and take his marker with him, then the Dutchmen could take advantage of the extra space. Wark was a centre-half when he arrived but revelled in his new position. He scored goals for fun because he could time his runs like Martin Peters and Bryan Robson; they all had the habit of arriving at the right time unexpectedly and without a marker. He didn't have to smash the ball either; he'd just pass it into the net the way Drogba does for Chelsea these days. He also scored a lot of goals with his head, again because of his immaculate timing.

The more you look at the 1978/79 season and analyse it, the more remarkable it is. As I said, I had a number of firsts that season, though for the life of me I cannot remember my very first goal against Birmingham. I can only presume it was a header. I can recall my second goal, in the last game of the season at QPR when we won 4–0 on the grass before they laid down the artificial surface. It was a near-post flicked-on header. It was an interesting season in every respect, for I also had to mark the first £1 million footballer, Trevor Francis, in his debut for Forest in March. We drew 1–1, and I enjoyed playing against him. He was very quick so it wasn't much use trying to kick him; he was also good at turning and twisting, and would go to ground very easily. He was a clever footballer. There weren't many like him at the time. He was ahead of his time, because nowadays even defensive giants like Sol Campbell and Rio Ferdinand go to ground if they feel a touch at the right time. I don't know whether it is deemed good, intelligent play, but strikers can't complain as they began the vicious circle in the first place.

Certainly whenever we played European Cup matches the diving was terrible, particularly South Americans who had come over to Europe to play in the continental leagues, plus the usual villains from Spain and Italy. It was weird with the Italians because they would go straight through you with a tackle but go down screaming and rolling round on the ground at the slightest touch. English crowds didn't like it when their own players started to do it, but now, I'm afraid, everyone has become used to it. To me it's still a form of cheating, and the cheats have won from front to back. Think about other things that have come into the game: spitting, head-to-head contact, elbows. Maybe it's a natural consequence of cutting out the hard tackling. We used to know we had a free first tackle; the referee would always let that go. And some strikers enjoyed the physical side, too, such as Mark Hughes. I remember playing against him when he first came into the Manchester United side. He was wearing funny boots like hockey boots with high ankles, and I wondered, 'What have we got here?' He quickly showed me why. We drew, and he played really well. It was difficult to get close to him as he had good touch and kept the ball on the move all the time.

I always found it hard playing against movement. Give me big, strong centre-forwards like George Reilly or Ross Jenkins every time. You could really have a good tussle with them in the air and on the ground. Allan Simonsen of Denmark was another who was hard to play against. The movement of the Danes made them very difficult opponents to mark. But we also had plenty of our own. Frank Worthington was one who had skill and strength, and he was quick about the pitch too. His mind was sharp and he knew what he wanted to do. He scored a wondrous goal against me in that 1978/79 season, one I'd rather not remember. It was during the game against Bolton at their ground in April. He was juggling the ball on the edge of the area, but as soon as he felt me looking for the ball he suddenly flicked it over my head, raced round me and volleyed it home before it touched the ground. I couldn't do much about it, and neither could Paul Cooper. I keep trying to forget it but he reminds me every time we meet. He has dined out on that goal ever since! He reckons it's the greatest goal ever scored – but then he would, wouldn't he? Still, it was a wonderful goal, and they can't have seen many like it at Bolton. Sometimes it seems I attract stunning goals against me – just think about Maradona in the 1986 World Cup – but then, I can always say they need to score great goals to get past me! I doubt, however, whether I would be believed. Quite simply, I would rather not be involved in great goals at all.

Maradona, of course, was another difficult player to mark. Forget his handball goal against us and his spectacular diving; remember his low centre of gravity and his phenomenal skill. When I played against him I rarely saw the ball because of the twelve-inch difference in height and the way he shielded it. He was very tricky and clever, and rarely caught with the ball. He was good in 1982, but in 1986 he was very much at his peak. If you got near him he could size you up and either go past you or put you out of the game with a pass. I have to admit, despite all the things wrong with him, he was the best player I ever played against. Maybe great players like him and George Best needed to live on the edge;

perhaps it's what made them great players. They just can't be normal people, answering the door, making a cup of tea, sitting down and watching television. Paul Gascoigne was never better on the pitch than when he'd received an early yellow card because it left him on the edge for the rest of the game. He revelled in it. Maradona received his buzz from the fact that everyone expected him to produce all the time, and he was never satisfied until he did. That's why he was paid fabulous amounts of money and was widely acknowledged as a great player.

Not all were like that. Two obvious exceptions were Pele and John Charles, who were rarely in trouble with referees or opponents, particularly Charles who, I understand, was never booked or sent off in his career. Bobby Charlton and Gary Lineker had similar records. But there are certain types of player who, when they want to do their stuff, pull on a mask. As a result, they weren't brilliant all the time. That's why they didn't play more often for their country, or gain more honours, or, in the case of George Best, why some of them didn't enjoy longer careers. It was the way it was ordained. It's the way they wanted to be, and few great players have any regrets when you talk to them about their career in the game. Rodney Marsh, George Best, Stan Bowles, Frank Worthington – all of them had the same sort of devilment in them. Perhaps it was just in their genes, in their characters.

Ipswich's most high-profile opponents that season were Barcelona, and there were great celebrations when we beat them 2–1 at Portman Road. It was my European debut, and it was a wonderful occasion. Even seeing the Barcelona shirt was stimulating rather than intimidating, because it is unique. It makes you want to play well against them, makes you want to beat them. I even went along to watch them when they trained at Portman Road. It was a wonderful experience too. But I remember the disappointment at losing that goal at home. We knew there would be problems. While I had been on the staff, but not playing, we had beaten Barcelona 3–0 at Portman Road but lost the tie on penalties, so we knew it was going to be tough at the Nou Camp. I was marking the Austrian legend Hans Krankl on the night, but it was big defender Migueli who scored the only goal of the game, which put them through on a single away goal.

It was still a fantastic experience for me because it's such a great ground; the changing rooms and everything about it were beautiful. It may sound strange, but there is a smell of importance about the Nou

Camp, a strong, scenty odour that's very Spanish. It stimulates you and makes the nostrils twitch. For me, every ground has its own smell, probably because I have a big nose. They are smells I never forget. The number of people Barcelona had around them was unbelievable, a massive entourage, filling the corridors outside their dressing room and smoking those pungent Spanish cigarettes. It all added to the atmosphere. My one real regret is that I don't have a Barcelona shirt, because in those days you simply did not swap shirts.

I'm not a big shirt swapper anyway, though I do have a bag of them at home. One of them is Platini's shirt from when we played France in Paris in 1984. We lost 2–0 to two incredible Platini free-kicks and our fans rioted. I was running down the tunnel to get away from the fighting when I heard someone calling 'Butcher, Butcher!' with an accent. I turned round and it was Platini, wanting to swap shirts. I still thought he wanted to change with someone else and I looked around to see who else was there. With England we used to be given two shirts, and I liked to keep them both because they meant more to me than any other country's shirts. I could never understand how players could exchange shirts and then put them on, soaked with someone else's sweat. Maybe I'm a bit of a prude, but I didn't want to do something like that. I look now at those England shirts in my bag and I wonder how I got into them, especially the Admiral shirts. They were probably the worst kit I ever wore. They were so small and tight it was hard to breathe, but I guess it was the fashion of the time.

Part of the reason why we didn't swap shirts at Ipswich was because had we done so our kit man, Trevor Kirton, would have gone bananas because it would have left us short. Trevor was a versatile man known as 'Wheels' because he also drove our team bus, a big blue and white thing with a Suffolk Punch on the side. He also drove a bus for a local company, and had two fingers missing (to this day I don't know how he lost his fingers because none of us selfish footballers ever bothered to ask). Being typically cruel footballers, we would shout to him towards the end of a game asking how many minutes were left. He would hold up his hand and we would ask whether it was two and a half minutes or three and a half minutes.

When the club played in Poland against Widzew Lodz in December 1980 we were driving through horrendous snow the day after John Lennon had been shot in New York. We were listening to Beatles songs all the way back to the airport. We were in the bus supplied by the Poles, and

'Wheels' was driving a minibus with all our kit in it. It was so cold that ice was forming on the inside of the windows. Suddenly, through the frosted glass we saw a crash ahead of us with a minibus on its side in a ditch. We continued on the two-hour journey and then saw another minibus on the opposite side of the road, also in a ditch. It transpired that Trevor had been involved in the first crash and had put his right shoulder out as the bus went on its side. They'd managed to right the bus and get it back on the road, and he had gone past us unnoticed, only to crash again on the other side of the road and put his shoulder back in. It sounds unbelievable but there were lots of witnesses and he still managed to make it to the airport.

Ipswich wore Adidas kit in those days, and I wore Adidas boots, so I was happy there was no conflict. Fashion was important then, even though it had not yet become the rage for fans to buy the kit. In those days we wore rosettes or little mascots made out of wool to show who we supported. Supporters used to send them to me when I was at Ipswich, but how often do you see a rosette or a rattle now? Perhaps the only things to have survived are the scarves, but it's the replica shirts that are everywhere. They are, despite what is said, good value, because the kids wear them all the time, even in bed. That represents value for money, whereas if you buy a designer shirt it is worn once or twice a week and then eventually goes out of fashion and to the back of the wardrobe.

Clubs now have three or four kits because of replica sales, but in the first and third years of a contract new strips are produced and if a club changes sponsors they will have four new strips in six years. You can understand why people like David Beckham sell shirts. Kids don't want last year's kit, they want the latest one. The exception is retro kits. Not only kids but also adults buy shirts from years gone by to wear as casual gear. It's some business and makes both clubs and manufacturers bundles of money. Real Madrid, for instance, reckon they have already recouped Beckham's huge transfer fee in shirt sales alone.

The best England shirt ever has to be the red shirt worn in the 1966 World Cup Final, but I love the old white shirt with the badge and nothing else on it, with navy blue shorts and white socks. When numbers on shorts were introduced for the 1982 World Cup in Spain, the kit man from Admiral had to iron them on to the shorts because of FIFA instructions. When we played France in the first game in Bilbao the pitch was littered with our numbers. It was embarrassing – it looked like a

Countdown convention! We had cotton drill tops in Spain, which were far too warm for the middle of summer. In 1986, when Umbro came back, we were given aertex shirts, but they were skin tight too. It was like wearing chainmail, though I suppose you could say there was less for opposition players to hang on to, like the current England rugby shirts.

I was never a shirt puller myself, and I suppose it comes back to my father and his strict ways. Once you have pulled a player back by his shirt you will get into the habit. I would use a stiff arm to block a run, but if you pull the shirt they can still get away from you and it's so obvious. I tell my defenders at Motherwell not to pull shirts. If I see someone doing it in training I will stop play. It's a form of cheating, and it's up to referees to spot it and stop it. In the modern game it is so blatant at corners and free-kicks; a lot of European defenders don't even look at the ball. Referees only need to give a couple of penalties per game and coaches would soon put a stop to it.

My philosophy was I had to be close enough to touch the player, not to hold on to him. If you can't touch him he has got too far away from you, but you also have to keep moving your sight between man and ball because we don't have the peripheral vision to look at both at the same time. It's no use just watching one, you have to watch both. Even I have won penalties because defenders have not done their job properly. When I played against my mate Roy Aitken in the 1986 League Cup Final versus Celtic, he didn't see where the ball was, tugged my shirt and blocked me when I had a free header from a corner. We scored from the penalty and won the Cup because he didn't do his job properly. Of course, sometimes you are going to get beaten, but if it happens too often you won't be in the team.

I find the art of good defending and strong marking has disappeared to some extent. It seems to me a lot of easy, comfortable goals are scored because defenders are quite content to mark their man and not be aware of the space around them or other people's runs. I have never been a fan of zonal marking. It is too easy to exploit. If opponents do it against my teams I will try all sorts of tactics to counteract it. You need to be in control and dictate to the opposition what happens. You have to be cute and clever. Liverpool were very clever when they were in their heyday. They didn't have the biggest forwards but would keep control from a throw-in or a restart. Dalglish or Rush would move out, play a short ball, and form a little triangle in a corner until they could pick out a runner in the box. It wasn't a hopeful ball, but a planned situation.

I can, of course, talk now from experience about the art of good defending. But back in the early summer of 1979, with Ipswich having secured sixth place in the First Division (thus making sure Portman Road would see more European football) and my being selected to go on the England U-21 tour along with the seniors to Bulgaria, Sweden and Austria, I still had a lot to learn.

CHAPTER THREE

THE LONGEST AWAY TRIP

I sat on the bench for England in Bulgaria, and only saw some action once we'd moved on to Stockholm. It was a comfortable trip for me, though, as Bobby Robson was there looking after the B team. Dave Sexton looked after us, and Ron Greenwood, whom we irreverently nicknamed the Pope, was in charge of the seniors.

We won our game in Vasteras 2–1 and were in celebratory mood. The hotel boasted a joke shop, which immediately captured Mr Hyde's attention, and I bought some plastic dog poo for a laugh. It was a beautiful and very expensive hotel, so I placed the poo on the carpet in the middle of the foyer. And who should fall for it straight away but Bobby Robson. He was immediately up in arms.

'I don't believe it,' he said. 'Who would bring a dog into such a beautiful hotel as this? This is disgusting.'

He walked away to complain and I nipped out and put the poo discreetly in my pocket. The last person I wanted to catch me playing disreputable jokes on my first England tour was the gaffer.

There was a good bunch of lads on tour, and almost all of them went on to full honours, the likes of Chris Woods, Kenny Sansom, Bryan Robson, Gordon Cowans, Luther Blissett, Graham Rix, Cyrille Regis and, of course, me and Russell Osman. We ended up going to a nightclub in Stockholm the night before England drew 0–0 with Sweden. We came out of the club around three a.m. and I couldn't believe it – bright sunshine! It was the first time I had experienced anything like it in my life, those short summer nights they have in Scandinavia. It didn't sober us up, but it was a wonderful feeling.

Our next game was in Klagenfurt, Austria, for the 'B' international. It was a long train journey to the foot of the Alps, and we played the match in a vicious electric storm. We were winning 1–0 when the game was called off after an hour as lightning was hitting the pitch. You could hear the ground sizzle on contact. Although we were on top we were only too glad to go indoors, especially when the locals told us that a goalkeeper had been struck and killed in similar circumstances not long before.

With the tour now finally over, we had a few beers after the game and then boarded the train to go back to Vienna. It turned out I wasn't the only player who had made a purchase at the joke shop in Sweden: my mate Russell, who had been left on the bench, had bought some disappearing ink. Joe Corrigan was our goalkeeper and he was a big man, very lovable but very strong. If you took the mickey out of him, as we were inclined to do, he could hurt you. I heard he broke a couple of Kevin Keegan's ribs with a 'fun' punch on one occasion. So Russell took a big gamble when he threw the ink over Joe's spotless white England dress shirt, but Joe did no more than rip the shirt off and throw it out of the train window. Needless to say we had all enjoyed a few more beers on the train, so when Joe ordered everyone else to throw their shirts out of the window a handful immediately followed with buttons flying everywhere. Some of us didn't bother, but Joe was now in full flow and tore off his shoes and socks and threw them out of the window too. It was threatening to get out of hand, and we tried to explain about the vanishing ink. To prove the point, Russell immediately tipped the ink over himself, and after a while, to Joe's amazement, it disappeared. When we disembarked we were a disgrace, half the team wearing blazers and ties but no shirts or socks, though the absence of socks wasn't so bad as it was an American fashion at the time to dispense with them. Personally I wasn't into it, and fortunately Bobby, who was in charge of this B international, was in a separate carriage to us on the way back and was unaware of the whole thing. Just as well.

The next night we watched England play Austria in Vienna in an incredible game that we lost 4–3. We'd come back from 1–3 to 3–3, only to lose the final goal when we looked certain to go on and win. After the game Ron Greenwood gathered all the players together, thanked them for what they had done – namely, winning a big European Championship qualifier in Bulgaria 3–0 – and wished us all good luck for the next season. After the Pope had finished his speech, our two illustrious goalkeepers Peter Shilton and Ray Clemence announced that they had been invited to a beach party. A beach party in Austria where you couldn't be further from the sea? But they were right, for when they came back in the early hours of the morning they were covered in sand. The hotel had thrown a unique party and imported tons of sand. We watched them stagger off to their room arm in arm, trailing sand behind them. They were the best of mates, despite the turnabout in selection policy. But for Clem, Shilts could have gone on to win close to 200 caps.

They were two brilliant goalkeepers. Shilton trained and trained while Clem would do the minimum, preferring to play centre-forward in practice matches. There was little to choose between them until Shilts took over in 1982 for the World Cup. Clem was disappointed, but it was probably the right decision. Shilton was a wonderful player to play in front of – and what a talker! He would be telling you non-stop to close the opposition down, even before the kick-off. He would maybe have one shot in 90 minutes and more often than not he would make a wonderful save, but then he would have a go at us for letting them get that shot in. It was great, though, because it kept us on our toes. Still, Kenny Sansom and I would regularly turn round to tell him to shut up. He would moan off the pitch as well, and if you were caught after he had enjoyed a few drinks he was a nightmare. Even worse was being stuck in the seat next to him on the aeroplane home. He would tell you why you weren't the best player in the world and why he was the best goalkeeper and how he would do things differently when he was England manager. He stopped drinking in 1986 and became a totally different person, much easier to sit next to after a game.

There was a lot of talk around that time that Bobby Robson might be on the point of signing Peter Shilton for Ipswich, but it never happened. We had Paul Cooper, the great penalty-kick saver, and it was after those dressing-room rumours that Paul had his best ever season. He was a clever goalkeeper who made nonsense of his lack of inches compared to other top-class goalkeepers (he measured slightly less than six feet tall). Laurie Sivell was the same, small but brave and very good. He was larger than life off the pitch too. Whenever we drove into Ipswich we'd have farting competitions, the winner measured by how far the window had to be wound down. A full window job was the winner. Stupid footballers. We also got up to high jinx on the way back from training. Laurie was a twitcher – a bird-watcher – and we used to go to the marshes in and around Walberswick near Southwold. There was a bird called the Butcherbird, a redback shrike, which would capture its prey and impale it on thorns the way a butcher would hang up his meat. The first purchase I made with my Access card was a pair of binoculars, and my first sighting was the Butcherbird. Perhaps inspired by the antics of this bird, Laurie asked me during one of our many journeys into Ipswich if I had any ambitions and, strangely, did I really want to hurt someone. I thought about it, and he kept goading me until I played along by telling him I would like to get a big axe and bury it in someone's head. He took me seriously and was apoplectic. He told both Bobby Robson and Bobby Ferguson, and from then on he referred to me as the Axe Man. I didn't get too many lifts after that. Laurie was a lovely guy but a bit mad, like most goalkeepers. The last I heard of him he was selling fish from a van in Lowestoft.

But there's a serious point here. To this day I tell my centre-halves they have to give the impression they are mad and will do anything. That way centre-forwards don't know how to take you. If you are straightforward they know they're in for a fairly easy ride. If I played against someone like Dalglish I'd start out really jovial, asking him how he was, and then, at the first opportunity, I would whack him as hard as I could. Hopefully after that forwards will be looking over their shoulders. I used to shout things too, though mainly to my own players. I wouldn't sledge the opposition on the pitch, only in the tunnel. This started when I was established in the Ipswich team before becoming captain, when I was last in line. I would come out of the dressing room, banging the door, hammering the wall of the tunnel and shouting and screaming right out on to the pitch. It was meant to get my adrenalin flowing, but it was also an attempt to intimidate the opponents with my size and my madness. I loved it all. I liked looking people in the eyes to see if they fancied it. But all this nonsense comes with confidence, when you have earned your place in the team and played plenty of games.

I soon discovered who I could intimidate. Dalglish was clever and very determined and I would always know he would come back at me no matter how hard or how often you hit him. He could hit back, but he would hurt you most by scoring goals. It was what he was best at, but I loved playing against him. Others who caused me problems were people like Stevie Hodge, the speedy, tricky players, unless I could kick them and wing them early on. I remember Steve once leading Forest to a 3–1 win over us at Portman Road (he scored all three). I just couldn't catch him on the day. Mark Hughes was a cagey one and I was never too sure what he would do, while Ian Rush was a wonderful player who took the mickey out of me on several occasions. He would wander around with a blank expression on his face, looking as though he wasn't interested, but it was just to fool you. When the moment came he would react like a panther, and he was in before you knew it.

Having been a manager for a while now, I find it surprising how often you see the other side come out in players like Rush and others of international standing. Look at Rush and the others who live on the edge and they are all winners, obsessed with it, and age doesn't diminish the feeling, it makes you even more determined. I would whack Frank Worthington and he would return the gesture with interest, then say, 'It's 1–1 now. Do you want to carry on, or do you want to play football?' We always opted for football with honour satisfied. Win, lose or draw it was always a great contest with Frank and we would always shake hands on the whistle.

When it came to foreign opposition you didn't know much about what you were going to get, so you'd have to take the bull by the horns. Paul Mariner and I would scream and shout at the top of our voices as we waited to go on to the pitch. This could prove very intimidating, and it could make a difference, as it did once in Belgrade. It was November 1987, and we had to beat Yugoslavia to qualify for the 1988 European Championship. We were in a tunnel of corrugated iron, and as we stood there Tony Adams and I banged on the walls with our fists and chanted 'England, England!' The opposition visibly wilted and we were four up after twenty minutes. They completely caved in. Even now it can work, especially with big lads like Tony and me. Look them in the eyes and you can tell whether they want to play or not. I always knew who I fancied playing against.

Now and again the odd foreign player would have a go back, or they would take the mickey out of you in their own language. You never really knew what to expect. You tried the intimidation, but playing in Europe or for England you knew it was sometimes going to be difficult because these were the best players in the world and they wouldn't be easily cowed because they had confidence in their own ability. Shouting louder wasn't always an option. When we played Cameroon in Naples during Italia 90 I came up against a team who frightened us. Our dressing rooms were right at the rear of the stadium so it was a long hike to reach the field, and Bobby Robson led us through. We were there early, the outright favourites, waiting for Cameroon to arrive. Eventually we heard them coming, chanting in French, 'We are going to win!' I looked back and wondered what was going on. They looked like a Zulu army, glistening with sweat. We wondered if they were on something because they were so hyped up. It made my knees knock. Bobby's scout Howard Wilkinson had earlier reported back a semi-final place was secure, it was as though we had been handed a bye. Bobby had passed the message on to us, and of course we had believed him. But we were 2–1 down as the last ten minutes loomed. I was on the bench, thinking we were on our way home. I'm convinced that Cameroon's tunnel psychology worked. It was really offputting; it throws your concentration and your preparations. And remember, it wasn't just one or two of them, all of them were involved, bouncing up and down, shouting and looking more like warriors than footballers. We were outpsyched and outfought in the tunnel.

I like to see it happen, however, as a player and even as a manager. Not fighting or anything silly, just a bit of mind games. As a manager I wait to see what has happened if there has been a bit of a disagreement. I love to see reactions, in the tunnel and in dressing rooms. I hate to see people just come into the dressing room and silently sit down. I could never have done that. I would throw my boots down, kick a wall and punch a door. Sometimes I would be angry with myself, and sometimes with the referee for something. In the June 1990 game against Tunisia when I threw down my shirt, I was taken off because I was in danger of being sent off. At the time there was a lot of pressure in terms of not being selected to play in the forthcoming World Cup because there were a lot of decent players in defence like Mark Wright, Des Walker and Paul Parker. My form certainly wasn't good. The press and others looked at me and thought I was reacting to Bobby Robson taking me off. Ridiculous. England meant everything to me, and so did the shirt. I threw it down because I was so disgusted with myself.

Yes, I like to see reactions. If a player is honest with himself and has played well then fine, but if he hasn't given his all he should be annoyed. I would never be a good poker player because if I had a great hand I would look too excited; if it was a poor one, again, it would show in my face. I am that sort of person. My Motherwell players are too quiet for me. I try to wind them up before games, but it's difficult. We used to have a huddle. We even outhuddled Celtic at Celtic Park once, but our crowd didn't like it because they thought it was a Celtic thing. What we do now is get together in the dressing room in a circle and put our hands in the centre, like American footballers. The circle is important because it shows unity. We might do it again at half-time, or run on the spot and shout like rugby players do. I believe that rugby and football can learn a lot from each other. I saw nothing wrong in former England rugby boss Sir Clive Woodward wanting to learn more about our game in his role at Southampton.

For two seasons now at Motherwell we have had a psychologist, Tom Lucas, come in before every game to talk to the boys before I do. The mind is so important in football – in fact in sport generally. I am a big believer in it. I was impressed when Steve McClaren's first appointment at Middlesbrough was a psychologist as his number two. The players have to believe in them. It didn't work with Glenn Hoddle and Eileen Drewery because it was new, and like anything new or unusual footballers tend to react by taking the mickey out of it. Psychologists were thought of as 'shrinks' when I was playing; we even laughed at the Brazilians for bringing in people like them, and dieticians. We just didn't want to go there. When I went to Mexico in 1986 a friend of mine, Doc Lewis from Felixstowe, gave me a lot of hypnotherapy tapes. The other players made fun of me, but I learnt to control my adrenalin flow and programme my body to believe when it was hot, I was ice cold inside. Sure enough, when it was hot, I felt cool. It worked really well for me, which explains why I was so keen to have a psychologist in at Motherwell. My players too were a bit dubious when Tom first arrived, but they soon began to focus more effectively on what they had to do. They also benefited from a different voice to the manager's. They are so used to hearing the manager talk that they tend to switch off. It's a good thing for a manager to get away from his players every now and again and let them hear some fresh views.

It was Bobby Ferguson who had introduced Doc Lewis to us at Ipswich. The Doc would take me away in my mind to an imagined desert island, and it was so real I could hear the birds singing and the waves lapping. One day he even put stitches near my eye without any anaesthetic because he had me away on a desert island. I could feel the warmth. Those tapes he gave me were for relaxation and rest, but when it came to games I used to put the tape on. I would don my headphones and go and sit in the toilet at ten minutes to three, and the voices in my ears would tell me my body was transparent and full of fluid, bubbling away because of the nervous tension. Imagine this nervous tension being red. Now look at your fingers and toes, and see them as taps. See yourself turn the taps, and out pours the fluid. The body is now empty, so close the taps. Now, inside, where the heart is, there is one more tap which is where the adrenalin is. When you turn it on you can feel the power, the excitement, and this will get you through the game. Now, turn on that tap and feel your body fill up with the fluid. This is your adrenalin; this is you ready to go on to the pitch; this is you ready to play at the peak of preparation. By that stage I was ready to throw off the headphones, go out and take on the world. I get tingly just thinking about it now.

I try to explain these things to my young players at Motherwell. We arrive at noon for a pre-match meal, and between 12.30 and 1.30, before the team talk, what do the players do? Watch the football on television. I ask them if, after watching, they feel tired or sweaty. If the answer is yes, then the adrenalin is coming through too early. It is wasted. I advise them to read a good book or listen to a tape. Pele used to put his feet up and look as though he was asleep. He was just relaxing until it was time to turn on the tap just before kick-off.

The mind is a wonderful thing but, amazingly, there are still some clubs who don't use psychologists. Even if it helps only one player it has to be useful for the team, and the odds are it will help more than one. Tom picks things out of other sports and from newspapers, taking as examples people like American Tour de France specialist Lance Armstrong and the cancer he overcame to become the world's greatest ever cyclist. I just wish I'd had someone to help me in this way earlier in my career. Bobby Robson had a couple of psychologists come to Ipswich, and they were quite critical of our training and the fear of losing, which were outweighing the positives. Bobby's team talk before playing at Liverpool, for instance, would focus on what we should do when we went a goal down, and that was what immediately got entrenched in the players' minds. It was all about Liverpool. This was the sort of negativity they told us was wrong. Now I try to be positive. I like to say I am not concerned about the opposition. It's all about what we do, how we approach the match. It can be extremely effective. You can win even if you are going to Ibrox, Parkhead, Old Trafford or Stamford Bridge.

Maurice Malpas, my number two, will ask me what I am going to talk about before a match, but I can't tell him because I never know until I am in front of the players, when something always comes to me. I also try to make the talk light-hearted. I have sat through some very long team talks in my time. Bobby Robson could speak for up to an hour and a half, going through his points three times to ensure we had got hold of them. He would then ask us if we had anything to say, and everyone would keep quiet so we could get off for lunch. Then Peter Shilton would stand up and ask a question, and off we would go again for another twenty minutes. Bobby would have meetings to arrange meetings. I can understand it with international players because you don't see them very often, but Bobby used to do it at Ipswich as well. It's not my style.

Bobby absolutely slaughtered me on 8 August 1979 because, to my huge embarrassment, I was late for the opening game of the season against Nottingham Forest. I was moving house at the time and was staying at my parents' home. I drove in from Lowestoft, got caught up in the holiday traffic, and arrived half an hour late for the pre-match meal. To make matters worse, we lost 1–0. I was, quite rightly, fined. Bobby had a saying that went along the lines of, 'If you are catching a train at noon and you arrive at one minute past you will have missed it, so don't be late.' Mind you, this rebounded on him at the World Cup in Italy when we were summoned to a meeting at 12.30. We arrived, but no Bobby. Fifteen minutes, twenty minutes, half an hour, and still no Bobby. Don Howe was sitting with us waiting and shaking his head, and when Bobby finally walked in all the boys mimicked a train whistle and the noise of a train leaving the station. It was repeated whenever he was late with the cry of 'All aboard!' I don't think he appreciated it.

Fortunately, all was forgiven three days later when Ipswich, with me playing left-back again, won 2–0 at Arsenal with goals from Hunter and Muhren. We were up and running, or at least we thought we were. Four days later, a Wolves side inspired by their skipper Emlyn Hughes beat us 3–0. Emlyn was a strange character at times and one of his quirks was to cover himself in Deep Heat, from top to toe. When he ran out he had a big glow around him, just like you see on the Ready Brek television advert. It's sad football has lost such a great character.

By mid-September, with wins over Stoke and Bristol City, we had shuttled our way up to sixth place. We were due to play Brighton away on the 15th, and we'd already seen them play in Holland when we were on a pre-season tour (we used to stay at Zeist, which was their equivalent of Lilleshall). Brighton had just gained promotion so we were quite interested in giving them the once-over. We weren't impressed, so we were looking forward to playing them. Another misjudgement, for they slaughtered us 2–0. It plunged Ipswich into a depression: we won only one of our next nine games and dropped like a stone to the foot of the table. The run included five successive defeats and a 4–1 thrashing by Crystal Palace, the so-called team of the eighties.

It was certainly a strong division at the time, but come December we turned things around in dramatic fashion. After losing 4–1 again, this time at Coventry, on the first day of that month, we didn't lose another match until the final day of the season and ended up third in the League. We were flying. In March we beat Manchester United 6–0, much to the chagrin of my sister Vanda, a Reds fan, who cried her heart out afterwards (no wonder we eventually fell out!). It would have been worse had we not conspired to miss three penalties. Goals were just flying in: we also put four past Manchester City, West Bromwich Albion and Everton. I even weighed in with a couple myself, against Wolves and Coventry City.

The week before we beat United we drew 1–1 with Liverpool at Anfield. We should have lost because I gave away a penalty at the Kop end when I got too tight against Kenny Dalglish and he turned me. Terry McDermott came up to take the penalty, but as he ran up Frans Thijssen threw a lump of mud he had scraped off his boot towards him. Whether or not Terry was distracted by it I don't know, but he missed the penalty and Frans was slaughtered in the papers the next day. We found it hilarious, but we wouldn't have been too keen had it happened to us.

Probably our best performance that season came at Everton, Alan Brazil scoring twice and Gates and Mariner getting one apiece. We had to go back to Goodison Park the following month for an FA Cup quarter-final, but this time they beat us 2–1. Bob Latchford was again a problem. I was marking him, but as a cross came in from their left he drifted off me. I knew he was there and I knew he would score. The sound of the ball hitting our net was horrible. We had had high hopes of winning something during the season because our League form was so good, but we also crashed out of the League Cup to Coventry in the first round, and in the UEFA Cup, after crushing Skeid Oslo 10–1 on aggregate, we lost on the away-goals rule to Grasshoppers Zurich.

In the midst of the League run, on 20 January 1980, I was married to Rita. One of Bobby Robson's friends gave us some scrumpy cider to drink in the coach on the way back from the Bristol City game the day before, and by the time we reached the Post House at Heathrow where we were due to have dinner, we were flying. I had beef stroganoff for my last meal as a single man. The wedding was in Lowestoft with a three p.m. kick-off. We posed for some stupid pictures involving footballs and had our wedding meal at Lowestoft Golf Club (sirloin steak and chips). Russell Osman was, of course, there, and the rest of the team arrived for the evening party. We all had a good lot to drink, and afterwards Russell was stopped in his car in Saxmundham by the police. The constable asked him where he had been and when he told him he said, 'Oh yes, we've had a few cars coming through here from the wedding. When you see the big man [me], send him my congratulations – and be careful how you drive.' It was scandalous really, but that's how it was in those days before the drink-driving laws were brought in. You had to be involved in an accident before you were charged.

Bobby Robson kindly gave me a couple of days off, the Monday and the Tuesday, but we did nothing as my car, a little Datsun 1200 estate, had broken down. Instead we stayed at the Victoria Hotel in Lowestoft. There was a violent storm on our wedding night and the alarm went off constantly. I could hardly sleep! Bobby Ferguson made up for my few days off when I reported back on the Wednesday by running me into the ground in a bid to have me ready for the FA Cup match back at Bristol City at the weekend. The 2–1 win was an added wedding present. Bristol City were a good side in those days with players like Joe Royle, Gerry Gow, Trevor Tainton and Chris Garland.

That April I was struck down by injury again. During the match against Coventry, a match in which I scored, I was up against centre-half Paul Dyson. At one point the ball broke between us on the halfway line. We both went strongly into the tackle and stayed down, but when I climbed to my feet I could feel my calf. I finished the match and played at Southampton the following week, but I knew my leg wasn't right. England had qualified for the semi-finals of the U-21 European Championship and were due in Jena for the second leg against East Germany. It was a trip from hell, miles from Berlin, and it meant going through Checkpoint Charlie. Not only did we lose the game, my leg was still hurting me. Bobby Robson hadn't wanted me to go at all and was quite annoyed when I insisted. He was right to be. By half-time I could hardly walk, and I told the manager, Terry Venables, I would have to come off. When I got back to Ipswich our physio Tommy Eggleston sent me for an X-ray at the local hospital, and it transpired that I had cracked a fibula. I had been playing football with a broken leg. Bobby, needless to say, was furious.

I still went on the Ipswich tour at the end of the season to Israel, as entertainments officer, and then, at last, in June, Rita and I had our honeymoon, in Canada – a trip that meant I missed my chance to become a film star. Bobby Robson came into the dressing room one morning to tell us he had received a call from a film company that was making a football-related picture directed by none other than John Huston. It was called *Escape to Victory* and was to be filmed in Budapest. He explained they wanted volunteers. There was a lot of grumbling until Bobby mentioned Sylvester Stallone, Michael Caine and Pele were in it, and there was money to be had. Suddenly there was a rush. I told Rita about it, but our holiday was already arranged. It didn't take a lot to dissuade me because I wasn't really interested. I felt I was just cementing my place in the team, I was recovering from injury, and I just couldn't somehow see myself as a film star. But Russell Osman, Johnny Wark, Kevin Beattie, Robin Turner, Laurie Sivell, Kevin O'Callaghan and others went out to Budapest. They were well paid and seemed to spend most of the trip drinking beer and vodka, sometimes as early as seven in the morning. Turner and Sivell were cast as Nazis. Another friend of mine, Mike Summerbee, was also in the film. It was, apparently, great fun. We took the mickey out of John Wark because his voice wasn't up to it and he had to be dubbed, while Kevin O'Callaghan had to suffer a 'broken arm' during the action.

It was a busy summer for me, for before the honeymoon, my cracked fibula having healed very quickly, I had to get on a plane to Australia for my England debut. It happened on 31 May 1980, but I'll forgive you if you don't remember a thing about it. In fact, I needed a jog of the memory myself, and as an England fanatic who treasured every one of my 77 appearances it says something that I couldn't instantly recall my very first game. And I'm not the only one. Not even the Football Association carried a report of the game in their official yearbook, leaving a gap between the win against Scotland at Hampden Park on 24 May and the European Championship draw with Belgium in Turin on 12 June. But the team's there in the official lists: Joe Corrigan, Trevor Cherry, Frank Lampard, Brian Talbot, Russell Osman, Terry Butcher, Bryan Robson, Glenn Hoddle, Paul Mariner, Alan Sunderland and David Armstrong, with Brian Greenhoff, Mark Ward and Alan Devonshire coming on as substitutes.

We played on the Sydney Cricket Ground – a rare experience. The actual cricket pitch was raised by about a foot; it was brick hard and right in the middle of the football pitch. It made life very difficult but we eased our way through with goals from Hoddle and Mariner before they scored a consolation late on. The next day we had a trip around Sydney Harbour before flying back in what was a whirlwind trip. There was loads of free booze and the most wonderful spread. Frank Lampard had a prawn as large as a small lobster, and he ate the lot – shell, legs, brains, everything!

We returned to the hotel that night quite drunk. Alan O'Dell, the administrator at the FA, staggered out of the lift and in the short journey to his room managed to take off his clothes, scattering them like a snake shedding his skin. We followed the trail and found him lying on his bed in his underpants, door wide open, dead to the world. Among the clothes strewn down the corridor was Alan's wallet with what must have been a thousand pounds in it, as he was the moneyman for the FA. We scooped everything up, including his wallet, put it in his room, closed the door, and he was none the wiser – probably right up until today when he turns to this page. I will make sure he has a copy of the book because he was a terrific guy who always put the players first.

Another on the trip was former Charlton player and then FA secretary Ted Croker, who took some lovely pictures around Sydney Harbour and sent us all copies. Another great guy who has sadly passed on. I remember him in a lovely hotel in Madrid in 1982 when he and Glen Kirton, the communications manager (among other things), played tennis against Terry McDermott and Kevin Keegan. Ted was always immaculate whatever he did; he had a super-steel racket while Keegan and McDermott were in football shorts and flip-flops. Now Ted took his tennis very seriously, so he was far from happy when, halfway through the first set, a group of the senior players crept up on him, carried him off and threw him in the pool. McDermott watched with amusement before spotting Ted's discarded racket, and with a flash of his arm the expensive racket sailed over the fence and into the neighbouring building site, the irate and very wet official threatening to end every one of the players' international careers. I think people like Croker, Kirton and Graham Kelly are a big loss to the England and Football Association set-up, and it has never been the same since.

My first full cap for my country at senior level was the icing on the cake so far as my 1979/80 season was concerned. It had been a time for consolidation in both my personal and sporting lives. Big Allan Hunter was virtually finished, and Kevin Beattie was missing more games than he was playing because of injuries. My big opportunity to make a mark in football, at club and international level, was clearly coming. It would just have been nice had Rita and my parents been able to see my England debut instead of it being on the other side of the world.

CHAPTER FOUR

THE BEST SEASON OF MY LIFE

I was given a flying start to the 1980/81 season by the somewhat strange first cap for England. It certainly turned out to be the best season of my career, not just because Ipswich won the UEFA Cup, but because of the way we played our football and the way we went about our business. Right from the start life seemed to open up for me. Here I was newly married, newly capped and, I hoped, a regular starter in the team.

After our stuttering start to the previous season we needed to get off on a good footing, but we were handed a tough beginning against a good Leicester side who had just been promoted. It was a really hot day and we were delighted to come away with a single-goal victory courtesy of John Wark – a sign of things to come for the talented Scot as he went on to net a stunning 36 goals from midfield in all matches and, quite rightly, won the Professional Footballers' Association Player of the Year award. To add to John's award, Frans Thijssen won the Football Writers' Award as their Footballer of the Year.

Back in August 1980, though, our system was still in its infancy, and it wasn't quite working in our third game against Stoke City. Alan Brazil was instructed to move out to the left wing. He refused and carried on playing down the middle with the two Bobbys, Robson and Ferguson, going ballistic on the touchline. As soon as we entered the dressing room after the game Brazil was off to the bathroom, taking his place at the extreme end of the communal bath. Ferguson followed him into the room and the two exchanged words, Ferguson threatening to do more than just shout if he could get hold of his centre-forward. I honestly thought Bobby was going to wade through the bathwater after him. It was a game we really fancied ourselves to win, and everyone was furious.

We weren't, however, feeling sorry for ourselves, as we proved by winning our next five on the bounce, including a 4–0 win against Everton which saw a rare Terry Butcher goal, and a splendid 1–0 win over our main title rivals Aston Villa. In fact we went fourteen League games without defeat. The only losses during that time were in the League Cup: a 3–1 defeat at Middlesbrough (we pulled it around 3–0 in the second leg at Portman Road) and a set-back at Birmingham City. It was in that League Cup competition that I suffered yet another head injury when, playing against our local rivals Norwich City, I was knocked unconscious by a flying Justin Fashanu elbow. Deliberate or not I do not know, but it laid me out flat. I went off, was stitched up, brought around and sent back on. We drew 1–1 at Portman Road and then, to my enormous pleasure, beat the Canaries 3–1 at Carrow Road. We began to fancy our chances of an early trophy, but a 2–1 defeat at the hands of Birmingham in the next round put an end to our ambitions.

Our League form remained sound. We drew at Liverpool and at home with both Leeds and Manchester United, beat Sunderland 2–0 at Roker Park, then drew again at home with West Bromwich Albion. The next game, on 8 November, was Southampton away. I never liked playing at the Dell. It was too small and claustrophobic, very intimidating for visiting teams with the crowd right on top of you. To reach the pitch you had to walk down some wooden steps from something like a cottage where we changed. I played left-back with Beattie back in the side alongside Russell. Steve Williams was playing right-side midfield for the Saints. He was a narky guy who niggled away all the time. I had been booked for a previous foul on him, and we were 3–2 up going into the last twenty minutes or so when I made another tackle on him. While he was being treated, Kevin Keegan came over and demanded the referee send me off. Our boys were up in arms and there was something of a mêlée; then, after a long delay, the referee took out another yellow card and I was off – thanks, I am certain, to Keegan's intervention.

All hell broke loose as I trudged off up the long steps to the door of the dressing room that had three slats in its lower part. They went with a bang, followed by my boots, which flew across the dressing room. I sat alone with the radio in the dressing room, listening to comments on why I had been sent off and then to the Saints' equalizing goal from little Steve Moran. I was very disappointed at being red-carded and by the circumstances which led to Keegan needing stitches over his eye after a clash with Russell Osman. All the papers the next day were full of how Keegan had manipulated the referee to have me sent off for the first time in my career. Some said I deserved to be sent off that day, but I didn't think so. My tackles were never taps, they were always full-blooded, and I always tried to get there as early as I could. It's horrible being sent off, the worst feeling in the world. You feel you have let down not only yourself but also your team-mates.

The sending-off meant I missed the Brighton game, which we lost 1–0, though I had the benefit of a nice round of golf and a few beers in Bournemouth while my team-mates prepared for the match. Fortunately we bounced back well with successive victories. Our biggest let-down was a 5–3 defeat at Spurs the week before Christmas. It was a dreadful night of swirling winds, not helped by the fact they were rebuilding the stands, which reduced the shelter. Spurs played really well and deserved to win, but Bobby Robson slaughtered us after the game because we didn't put enough pressure on their injured goalkeeper Barry Daines, who had torn a groin muscle but opted to stay on. In short, we had allowed them to get away with it. And Robson was right. It was games like this that eventually cost us heavily in the League.

Christmas brought the usual weird situation of two games in two days. You never really know how to approach this period as a player. As you know, I love my Boxing Day lunch, with the cold turkey, pickles and bubble and squeak, but you have to do without. It turned out to be a good holiday for us though. On Boxing Day itself we beat our bitter rivals Norwich with goals from Brazil and Wark, and the next day in London we held Arsenal to a 1–1 draw.

We had plenty of distractions in the New Year with both the FA Cup and the UEFA Cup. We started off like a train in Europe with a 5–1 win over Aris Salonika, with four goals from John Wark. Just before the return leg we trained on their pitch where we were slaughtered by a thousand or so Greeks who turned up to watch and jeer us. They threw things at us and mocked us – and this was in training. We started the game badly and conceded a quick goal. Then they won a corner which was headed goalwards towards our captain, Mick Mills, on the line, who chested the ball down and cleared it. But the linesman gave a goal, even though the ball had never crossed what was a very thick goal-line. To say it was a dodgy decision would be an understatement, but we always had the cushion of our big win at Portman Road. This was soon whittled down further when they added a third goal to make it 5–4 on aggregate. The game seemed to be going their way big time, and they needed only one more goal to go through on away goals. Then up popped Eric Gates to turn and score and they were like a deflated balloon. I had been booked in the first game and needed only one more yellow to be banned. I didn't pick one up. It is remarkable how things like that can concentrate the mind.

We were delighted to have escaped, but on the way back to the hotel we suddenly found ourselves under attack from their disappointed fans. The windows of the coach caved in under the pressure so we sat in the middle seats. Despite this we still decided to have a night on the town (it was an afternoon game), and a few of us went out for the traditional meze – a series of small dishes such as taramasalata, tzatziki, stuffed vine leaves, dolmades and the like – with John Wark and his Greek wife Tula's family. We had a delightful time and there were no further problems. It was terrific to see a little of the real Greece. Normally, with a night game, it's in and out straight after the game. We really enjoyed the break.

The next round was against Bohemians of Prague, and again we managed a comfortable win at home. We were coasting two up when the Beat (Kevin Beattie) came on, and with ten minutes to go he hit a free-kick from some 30 yards out into the top corner. As it transpired it was a valuable goal, for when we went to Prague we were again put under pressure, losing 2–0 in freezing temperatures and falling snow. We struggled to hold on.

Next up were Polish team Widzew Lodz, who had put out Manchester United in an earlier round. But we met them at just the right time for us, towards the end of November when we were playing really well, and we turned in one of our best performances of the season, crushing them 5–0. All the usual culprits scored: Wark got three, and Mariner and Brazil one each. In Poland we had to play on an ice-skating rink of a pitch. Nowadays the tie would be abandoned, but when we arrived everyone just put on their tracksuit bottoms, gloves and special boots. The Beat played in long studs, shorts and short-sleeved shirt. The Polish groundsmen had taken off the snow from the previous evening's training session, but we still slipped all over the place, except for Beattie who somehow stayed upright. We lost our third successive away leg, this time by a single goal. It was ominous, as we then had to play the outstanding French team St Etienne away in the first leg of the quarter-final in early March.

Few gave us a chance against a side stuffed with talent, players like goalkeeper Castaneda, Battiston, Janvion, Rep, Larios and, of course, the great Platini, but we produced another great performance. We arrived two hours early to find the ground full of singing Frenchmen. They threw huge oranges at us as we warmed up, but no one took offence, we just passed them round to one another. We were feeling good, and in the tunnel we gave it plenty. You could see in their faces that they were nervous of this team of lunatics. Still, they must have thought they had overestimated us when Johnny Rep, the Dutch striker, put them ahead from a corner. But then we silenced the crowd completely as Muhren picked out Mariner with a cross. We were level with what we thought was an invaluable away goal, but we didn't stop there. I'd started the game at left-back, but I became virtually a left-winger as I pushed the man I was supposed to be marking further and further back. Muhren added a second goal. Later I was in the box for a free-kick and had a shot parried; Mariner tapped in the rebound. Then I crossed for Wark to score.

We were determined to enjoy the flight back, and before the game Russell and I had gone shopping in St Etienne and bought a bottle of Brouilly and a bottle of Châteauneuf du Pape, along with a few cigars. Stupidly, I went into the cockpit and offered the captain and his co-pilot a glass of red wine, and when he refused I offered him a cigar before I saw sense and went and sat down. We flew to Southend, and 'Wheels' drove us back with a carry-out containing all the miniatures off the plane. When we got back Russell's father Rex, an ex-player and manager of the Centre Spot restaurant, cooked us a meal.

For the game at Portman Road the French knew they were a beaten side but they still played all their stars and we beat them again, this time 3–1, with me getting the first and the inevitable Wark and Mariner the others.

It gave us a great lift to give one of Europe's leading sides such a beating, and we looked forward with relish to our next tie against another top side, the Germans from Cologne. They came with all their stars too, including goalkeeper Schumacher, Konopka, Cullmann, Littbarski, Müller, Engels and England striker Tony Woodcock. It was a tight, tough game, full of nerves, and we were left wondering whether we had done enough with our single-goal victory, yet again courtesy of John Wark. Cologne would be even stronger at home, with Zimmermann and Bonhof back to strengthen their team. The most important thing for us was to keep another clean sheet as we did in the first match, but the fixture list and some bad results were conspiring against us.

We were chasing the First Division title at the time, and the club suddenly hit a wall. The more success we had, the greater was the fixture congestion. Bobby Robson tried desperately to postpone at least one of the games, but there was no chance of that. Our schedule around this period read: 28 March, Sunderland at home; 31 March, Leeds United away; 4 April, WBA away; 8 April, Cologne home; 11 April, Manchester City at Villa Park in the FA Cup semi-final; 14 April, Aston Villa (our closest rivals in the race for the championship) away; 18 April, Arsenal home; 20 April, Norwich away; 22 April, Cologne away; 25 April, Manchester City home. Talk about the defining period of the season! Ten critical games in four weeks. And wouldn't you believe our luck, the semi-final in Birmingham went to extra time for the first time ever, and we lost the last two games before the Cologne second leg, to Arsenal and Norwich. Straight after the game, Sir Arthur South, the Norwich chairman and a charming man, flew out to West Germany with us from Norwich airport in what was a fine gesture.

We were ripe for the plucking. We were so low when we arrived in the German city, what did we do? We went to the Cologne funfair and rode – yes, you've guessed it – the rollercoaster, this time for real. It was a clever ploy actually because it relaxed the boys, took their minds off a game everyone now expected us to lose. It was a tense affair, but we managed to snatch an away goal as I headed home a Mick Mills free-kick. It went into the opposite corner to the one I intended, but who cares? When the final whistle sounded we were thrilled that we'd made it through to the final.

We arrived back in England and went straight to Russell's where his dad Rex made us another beautiful meal. Russell also got hold of a case of Holsten Pils so we all went and sat outside in the frosty garden. We were still sitting there in our coats at 6.30 the next morning when a neighbour of mine walked past and without turning a hair at the three of us sitting there sipping beers said, 'Great result last night, boys,' and carried on walking. It obviously did me no harm as I scored the only goal in our next game, against Manchester City, to keep our hopes of a championship alive.

Before the two-leg UEFA Cup Final reached a conclusion in May, we had our last League games against Middlesbrough (away) and Southampton (home). Our fate was still in our hands, and we knew that if we beat Boro, and Villa lost to Arsenal at Highbury, we were only one match away from winning the title. We were 1–0 up through Mariner at Ayresome Park, but then Bosco Jankovic scored twice. Villa lost 2–0, but we had already thrown away the title. The UEFA Cup was all that was left for us in what was still a remarkable season.

In the final we had to play AZ 67 Alkmaar, a good Dutch side with players like Spelbos, Metgod, Peters, Welzl, Kist, Tol and Van der Meer. The first leg, before the Southampton game, we won well, with Wark, Thijssen and Mariner on target, so when we arrived at the Olympic Stadium in Amsterdam we thought we were untouchable, especially when, at one point, we were drawing 2–2 (5–2 on aggregate). But then they switched to 2–4–4 and came right back at us. I had seen the Watford manager Graham Taylor and Holland manager Dick Advocaat do this as well, and it paid off for Alkmaar: they led 3–2 at the break, and then Jonker made the aggregate score 5–4. But with the away goals we had a tiny breathing space, there was no panic, and that's how the game finished.

The sad thing for me was the Dutch stewards did nothing to stop the two sets of supporters coming on to the pitch after the final whistle, which meant we were denied the traditional lap of honour. I missed the moment, especially after having watched my team-mates do it at Wembley three years earlier. Mind you, that UEFA trophy was so big we might have had a problem carrying it around the pitch. We made up for not being able to celebrate on the pitch by filling the cup with champagne, bottle after bottle. Ipswich Town had won the UEFA Cup, losing every away leg except what were supposed to be the toughest ones, in St Etienne and Cologne.

We met up with our families afterwards, but they went back to England on their own while we celebrated and drowned our sorrows in one party. We'd picked up just one of the three trophies we had hoped for, and there was a feeling that we'd been robbed of the League, and the FA Cup, by the fixture backlog. We'd beaten the champions Villa twice in the League that season – after the 2–1 victory at Villa Park in mid-April everyone, including Villa, were ready to hand us the title – and once in the Cup, when I was lucky to escape without a serious injury. I went in to challenge big centre-forward Peter Withe, but as I stooped to head the ball his studs ripped through my shirt and took slices out of my back. After the game Jimmy Hill wanted me to go on television and say Peter had done it deliberately. Whether he had or not – and I don't think he did – I would never have gone on television to criticise a fellow professional. I felt Jimmy, a former player himself, should have known better than to ask a professional to do so.

To compound our problems, we lost the services of our quality full-back George Burley for the rest of the season in the next FA Cup game at Shrewsbury. We disposed of them 3–0 in a replay at Portman Road, and then Charlton quite comfortably in the next round before being drawn with Nottingham Forest at the City Ground. Peter Shilton was in goal and we had a real ding-dong. We put three past him but still drew the match. We were both lucky and unlucky: John Wark had a penalty given against him after a ball had been driven against his hand from two yards away (Clive Thomas was again the referee), then a Frans Thijssen shot which was going well wide was weirdly deflected in for the equaliser with five minutes to go.

Bobby Robson had us in stitches on the way back to Suffolk. Apparently, after the game Forest manager Brian Clough had summoned him to his office. Bobby went along, knocked on the door and was told to come in. But when he opened the door the office was in complete darkness. Clough told him to come in and they just sat there in the dark. The Forest manager was clearly gutted about the draw, but he would have been even more miserable after the replay. Arnold Muhren scored with a right-foot volley and we sat on it, hung on and got tough. Forest were already on the decline after their great years of championships, European titles and cups, but they were still a fine side and put us under tremendous pressure.

Manchester City were next on the list in the semi-final, a dream game for all of us, but of course there was no sort of preparation because of the fixture backlog. Beattie played, I moved to left-back and Steve McCall was on the bench, but apart from George Burley we had a full squad available and thought we would win. It must have been one of the worst games in the history of the competition. The pitch was dreadful and the players were worse, with nerves overcoming ability. John Bond did his job well for Manchester City; their tactics were to stop us playing, and the game limped into extra time. Then we lost Beattie with, of all things, a broken arm. He went up for a header and everyone thought it must be a goal, but he headed it down and the ball shot up off the hard pitch and over the bar. Beattie carried on down and broke his arm as he crash-landed on the solid pitch. Shortly after I gave away a free-kick 25 yards out. Paul Power stepped up and hit it past Cooper for the only goal of the game. We were sick. We poured pressure on them but couldn't score.

The journey back after that defeat was hell. You would have thought our season was over, yet we bounced back to beat Villa in the League on the same ground a few days later – and, of course, to win the UEFA Cup. How do players do it? Where do they find the resolve? It was an amazing performance, yet we just couldn't go on and become First Division champions. We suffered from the usual crop of injuries and we lost seven games out of the last ten. The pressure just became too much. There was no time to prepare ourselves mentally or physically for each challenge. There's no doubt that 1980/81 was a great chance for us to win the League for Bobby, especially after winning six fixtures on the trot in the early part of the year. If we could have kept that run going, who knows? We played Manchester United in the next game and even went one up when Muhren's corner set me up to score, but we lost 2–1.

It was still the best season of my career, despite the disappointments – full, busy and emotional. I played a total of 65 games, including my only appearance that season for England, in a friendly against Spain in March at Wembley. Unfortunately, it was manager Ron Greenwood's first defeat at home. Zamora carved us open before Russell and I had caught our breath, and Satrustegui was left with a simple tap-in for the first goal. We came back to equalise through Glenn Hoddle, but then Zamora beat Clemence to give this new-look Spanish side under new manager José Santamaria what they regarded as a fine win. It was a real education for me to play against such quality players, but my contribution was just the one friendly and I was not to figure again until thirteen months later.

The season was not quite over, of course, because Ipswich players dominated the end-of-season awards. Not only did John Wark and Frans Thijssen come out on top, but we took a one-two-three in both awards – a remarkable achievement never matched before or since to my knowledge. We were all at the Hilton in Park Lane for the PFA dinner. Russell Osman and I went down together and took a room, arriving early so we could prepare ourselves for the big evening ahead. We ordered burgers and chips and asked for tomato ketchup, which was duly delivered. Before pouring it on my burger, I gave the bottle a good shake, as you do. But as a good hotel would also do, the waiter had eased off the top, so when I shook it I sprayed the room from ceiling to carpet, with a big line of red traced across the wall. I had to telephone and apologise for my mishap, and I guess I was lucky they didn't charge me. It was a good thing we were still sober at the time. I must have a thing about those tomato sauce bottles because I did exactly the same thing four years later in the Hard Rock Café in Los Angeles with Viv Anderson after an England friendly against the USA, once again not checking that the top was screwed on. Fortunately, in such a litigious country, I was sitting next to the wall and it sprayed that rather than the customers.

After the awards, Rita and I had a wonderful holiday in Cyprus. England were off playing on their usual summer tour. My turn, I felt sure, would come.

CHAPTER FIVE

NEAR TO DEATH

Bobby Robson must have liked Amsterdam because we were off again to Zeist for pre-season. We'd been invited to play in the Amsterdam Cup, with two games in six days. They knew what we were like when it came to obeying the curfews, and we were in Amsterdam with Frans Thijssen, a local boy who knew everywhere. The temptation was literally to go out and play. We usually finished up at the Sphinx Club on the square, and this was where we met up with the Belgian international Eric Gerets, who showed us around the clubs. I thought it was terrific preparation for the new season. I remember walking back somewhat drunkenly to the hotel one night and coming across this machine in the wall. In return for your guilders, it somehow served you a hot sausage – beautiful after a few beers. Then it was back to the room and a sobering message under the door: 'Meet me in the morning – Bobby.' At the end of these trips we were all given expenses to cover what we had spent. Mine tended to be held back every year, and they were again this time. Once more I had to return home to tell Rita the gaffer had fined me.

We had another tournament before the season opened, in Barcelona, and we finished last – not a good omen. But it was a memorable trip for me. The boys decided, inevitably, to go out on our last night before returning to Ipswich. But I was suffering from a massive migraine and went to my room. I even told Bobby Ferguson on the way up the stairs what I was planning to do. He was impressed, and surprised. When I reached the bedroom I took a call from Rita: she told me she was pregnant and I was going to become a dad for the first time. My migraine disappeared in an instant and I was straight out to join the boys and share my good news. I found them in a nightclub drinking with the

Cologne players, including Tony Woodcock and Toni Schumacher. We staggered back in the early hours and bumped into Ferguson, who slaughtered me for lying to him. I told him what had happened and he grudgingly accepted my excuse.

I was full of confidence after our busy previous season and really felt part of the team. I was beginning to impose myself, to make demands and to talk effectively to my team-mates. In our opening game of 1981/82 against Sunderland at Portman Road I was looking for more from our left-back Steve McCall. I needed him to talk to me, and if he didn't I decided I was going to tell him about it. Steve's a great lad, but he failed to do as I asked and I really had a go at him. This time the normally quiet lad had a go back and I was immediately all over him, grabbing him by the throat and telling him to do as he was told, wagging Mr Hyde's finger in his face. It was, however, sorted out immediately, and there were no afters. He had been an unsung hero in 1980/81 when George Burley was injured and he was a very good young player who won U-21 caps. I never minded players who argued on the pitch, and still don't, if it does some good and there are no grudges. No manager can afford to have his players sulking. There were some great pictures in the papers the next day of me holding McCall by the throat. The commentators were talking about how we were falling out, but it was brief and quickly over as we came from behind to gain a 3–3 draw with a couple of goals from Eric Gates, and John Wark beginning the season the way he had finished off the last.

In fact we drew our opening two games, before going to Old Trafford on 5 September. Three days before the game against United Rita woke up in the middle of the night with blood everywhere. We naturally thought she had miscarried so we rushed off to hospital for her to undergo tests. We were due to leave for Manchester on the Friday so I spoke to Bobby Robson to explain the situation. He was, as ever, totally understanding and told me to wait and see what happened before making a decision. It was just half an hour before the coach was due to leave when I took the call from the hospital telling me that Rita and the baby were fine. It was suggested later that there could have been twins and we had lost one of them, but there was never any confirmation.

What relief I felt sitting on that coach going to Manchester. It all came out on the pitch the next day when I felt like a giant. We won 2–1 with goals from Brazil and Wark, and our season was definitely up and running. We followed it up with a rare win against Liverpool, 2–0 at Portman Road, and began well in the League Cup, beating Leeds United at Elland Road in the first leg of the second round. Before the second leg, however, we played Arsenal at Portman Road, and I picked up an injury. I went into a tackle with Welsh international Peter Nicholas; he clattered into me and gave me a massive dead leg. I somehow managed to finish the game, hobbled in on the Sunday, couldn't train on the Monday, and with the return against Leeds on the Tuesday I felt I had no chance of playing. The leg was sore, I was limping, and there was a massive bruise and a big lump where Nicholas had connected.

I had treatment early on the evening of the game. Ferguson asked me how I was and I told him truthfully it was improving and I was up to about 60 per cent fitness. He then asked me how my running was, but I couldn't tell him. I began to suspect his motives and went for a warm-up and jog. My turning was more sluggish than usual, but Ferguson seemed satisfied and told me to go and see Bobby Robson. It was decided I should play. It was a dreadful risk, but I came through the match without any further aggravation as we coasted into the third round. But obviously there was a lot of residual bleeding inside the muscle. If it is left it calcifies into bone, and to get that bone out, which is three or four inches long, the surgeon has to cut through the muscle. It was stupid of me to play, but if you are asked to play you do. Still, I would never ask one of my players to do the same thing now.

Before we met Bradford City in the next round we played Swansea in the League. John Toshack had gathered a fine squad around him with players like Welsh goalkeeper Dai Davies, Yugoslav internationals Dzemal Hadziabdic and Ante Rajkovic, Bob Latchford, Ian Walsh, Robbie James, Jeremy Charles, Leighton James, Gary Stanley, Alan Curtis, and the ex-Liverpool contingent of Neil Robinson, Colin Irwin, Max Thompson and Ray Kennedy and John Toshack himself. Curtis, Latchford and Stanley scored Swansea's goals in a 3–2 victory. It was a magnificent match which they deserved to win. Bradford then held us to a 1–1 draw and in the replay Bobby Campbell broke my nose in their penalty area. It was all over my face. I was able to carry on and we snatched a win in extra time, but that injury was to come back and haunt me later in the season.

Some indifferent performances in the League followed, but our League Cup run was energizing us, and our tie against Everton really got us going again. We beat them 3–2 at Goodison Park and looked to be back to our best, but once again fixtures were piling up as a result of bad weather and we had a tough three-match spell in mid-January. We beat Coventry City at Highfield Road, beat Watford 2–1 in the fifth round of the League Cup, then travelled to Kenilworth Road to face Luton in the fourth round of the FA Cup. I had a stiff neck and needed a fitness test before I played. I passed it – unfortunately as it transpired.

Luton were top of the Second Division and flying under manager David Pleat. We won 3–0, but the match was a disaster for me. In the first half I was marking Brian Stein, and at one point the ball popped up off his thigh. I leant forward and headed it to Johnny Wark, but as I did so Brian tried an overhead kick and connected flush with my already battered nose. Tommy Eggleston the physio plugged it up and I carried on until half-time when they bandaged and plugged it properly. But I was still bleeding down my throat as we resumed and had to pinch my nose throughout the second half. Everyone was staring at me as I was continually gagging and hacking up blood. As soon as we'd got our third goal I held up my hands, said enough's enough, and left the field.

I went back to the physio's room and had my nose packed again but was advised to go off to the Luton and Dunstable Hospital to have it checked out. Dad was there, so the team left by coach and he took me to the hospital in his car. It was quickly diagnosed as broken and they messed around with it before strapping and packing it yet again. I wanted to get back to Ipswich but I hadn't eaten yet, so we decided to have a McDonald's. As if I didn't have enough problems with my nose, to my embarrassment Dad asked for a knife and fork.

We made the trip back to Ipswich and I didn't feel too bad. That evening Rita and I and Russell went to see Rex at the Centre Spot for dinner and a few glasses of red wine to celebrate the Luton victory. I went to bed early that night but suddenly woke up to feel this pressure behind my nose as though there was a dam about to burst. I woke Rita and told her I thought my nose was going to explode. Rita said I needed to get to hospital but she couldn't drive because she was heavily pregnant, so we called a taxi. I sat in the front of the cab holding a Tupperware bowl under my nose, blood pouring out of it like a tap. The driver drove with one eye on the road and one eye on me. I just about made it to the hospital before it went, gushing like a geyser. I was seen immediately by a Pakistani doctor who was adamant that I had already had a transfusion at the

Luton and Dunstable. I was equally adamant I had not. He told me he had read about it in the newspapers and he seemed more inclined to believe them than me. I was so angry with him I would have struck out if I hadn't been holding the bowl full of blood. It certainly didn't help my stress levels.

They plugged it again and kept me in overnight for observation. The next day it was just a case of taking the packaging out to see what would happen. Clearly I had seriously damaged something in my nose. Sure enough it began bleeding again, and it bled quite heavily for about an hour. I was losing a lot of blood. I was told I would be kept in indefinitely to see what was happening. It was weird, because throughout the next week one minute the nose would be fine, the next it would suddenly start bleeding again. Ipswich had some big games coming up and I was desperate to return to duty, but every time they packed it again it would bleed and the packaging would have to come out.

I was in despair. The surgeon eventually decided to go in and have a look to see what the cause of the bleeding was. They made an incision by the corner of my eye, had a look around, and later told me they had tied something off to staunch the flow of blood. They thought they had solved the problem, but they hadn't. The condition persisted although the heaviness of the flow had been checked slightly. What made it a lot worse was that Ipswich were playing Liverpool in the semi-final of the League Cup and I could only watch as we went out 4–2 on aggregate.

The nose just wasn't getting any better, and not only was I losing blood, I was losing weight as well. It was decided to transfer me to the Ear, Nose and Throat Hospital in Whitechapel, London. I was taken to the East End with Rita and my mum in an ambulance. The specialist was a Mr McKechnie, and when I arrived they wheeled me up to the ward where I waited to be admitted. I was sitting in a corridor bleeding into a kidney bowl. When it stopped, I asked the nurse for some ice to put on my nose. She brought me back one cube of ice, which she then tried to strap to my nose. First impressions not good! I tried to explain that I needed a bag of ice; fortunately it wasn't long before I was admitted.

It was quickly decided I should stay, which presented the immediate problem of how my heavily pregnant wife and my mum were going to get back to Ipswich from London. The only solution was to find them a hotel. Fortunately, Russell's father Rex knew the general manager of the Mayfair Hotel, Herbert Streissleng, and he looked after my mum and

Rita very well, gave them a very good rate and eased one of my growing concerns.

Rita and Mum came up to visit me on the Tube every day. It wasn't the most savoury of hospitals because a lot of down-and-outs would go there for shelter and warmth and there would be empty bottles and all sorts left lying about. I was bed-ridden, still not getting any better, losing a lot of blood and having continual transfusions. It reached the stage where I was having sixteen units of blood pumped into my body, and it was beginning to close down.

I remember Bobby Robson coming to see me. I was by this stage in a private room, its walls covered in cards from well-wishers which I have kept to this day. I was so touched. I had this idea in my head all I needed was another operation and everything would be fine. Mr McKechnie and the other doctors, however, were convinced nature should be allowed to take its course. Well, that was fine for them to say, but I was still bleeding, still losing weight and I had no appetite at all. I had lost about two stone, and my body hadn't been carrying a great deal of excess in the first place. I would try to eat or nibble the food they brought me, but then I would just bleed into the meal. There is nothing more off-putting. Eventually they conceded on the operation front. They went in again, this time up through the mouth. To this day an X-ray will show the pins underneath my cheekbone where the veins were tied off. It looks for all the world like I have swallowed a box of staples.

When I came round I was back in my private room and in a really sorry state. Bobby Robson was now a regular visitor because he was worried about me. He couldn't believe the shape I was in. I had a shaggy beard and looked very gaunt. I was still, however, capable of anger, and I was annoyed when a freelance journalist named Paul Weaver wriggled his way in and did an exclusive for the *News of the World*. That really irritated me. It was the last thing I needed in my condition. Far better was the communication I had with a group of faith healers who sent me a handkerchief. They instructed me to put it over my nose at five p.m. every day, they would all pray for me, and the bleeding would stop. I was at the stage where I was prepared to try anything, so I did as they asked. Incredibly, that was the last time my nose bled seriously. A trickle still came every now and then, but no gushing as it had done before. I'm convinced was the result of the operation, but in the back of my mind I have always wondered. I would certainly never knock faith healing, and if anyone tells me they believe in something different then all I say is good luck. I would never disregard mind over matter in all things.

My recovery began immediately. I still had to spray things up my nose and take pills, but gradually the problem sorted itself out. Mick Mills and Trevor Francis came to see me, and Brian Stein wrote to wish me well. I held no grudge against him because it was nothing but an accident, certainly compared with the previous time I had had my nose splattered over my face. The kindness shown by so many people helped my recovery, and eventually a car was booked to take me home, although I was still taking the tablets, as they say. I was told to drink this awful restorative concoction, but also, thankfully, to consume lots of Guinness as well.

It was a huge thrill finally to get back to the ground after two weeks in hospital, and I felt an overwhelming sense of gratitude as I saw all the familiar things around me. Since then, every time I read of someone catching AIDS or some other disease from a blood transfusion I thank my lucky stars. The odds were not on my side if you believe all you read, and of course I am indebted to all those people who gave their blood to help keep people like me alive.

I began my own fitness programme, and before I made my first-team comeback I played a couple of games in the reserves. One of them was against Spurs, and I was marking little Terry Gibson. We went up for a header together and he just nicked it past me and crunched straight into my nose. It immediately began bleeding and I thought, 'Here we go again.' I was rushed to hospital but was told it was the best thing that could have happened: not only had the knock cleared the passages, the surgeon said it should also give me the confidence to play, knowing I could take a bang and not be in trouble. My heart had been in my mouth until he spoke to me. It was understandable I should be nervous as I had been told had I gone on another week needing more transfusions I would have been in serious trouble, because eventually the body rejects the new blood. My arms were sore from all the injections I'd had. It had been a shattering experience, but as the surgeon said, after the Gibson incident I felt I had come through it.

I eventually returned to the first team as a brand-new father of just six days, Rita having finally given birth to 9lb 9oz Christopher on 7 April. I had missed an awful lot of football, having been out of action during a busy part of the season for a total of three months – with a nosebleed!

Some players return quicker from a broken leg. I had still been playing earlier in the season when we crashed out of the UEFA Cup to Alex Ferguson's Aberdeen side, losing 3–1 at Pittodrie and 4–2 on aggregate. We had meekly surrendered a cup we had worked so hard to win the previous year. I have to admit Aberdeen were a good side at the time, dominating Scottish football above the traditional big two, and a year later they showed the level they had reached when they won the European Cup Winners' Cup. A very good side, in fact. While I was away we had also gone out of the FA Cup, to Shrewsbury in the fifth round, and of course to Liverpool in the League Cup, but in mid-April we were still challenging for the championship. Starting with my comeback game against West Ham, we put together a great run of six wins and a draw, but our title chances disappeared on 15 May when we lost 3–1 at home to Nottingham Forest. Liverpool, who had matched us win for win throughout those final weeks of the season, beat Spurs at Anfield and became the champions; we finished runners-up for the second successive year. I had a torrid time in the match against Forest. They were tremendous on the day with great movement, great passing and great play. In fact, they destroyed us, with Steve Hodge on his debut and Peter Davenport in terrific form. The problem was we never truly believed we were going to win the title as Liverpool surged on.

Not only did I get back into the Ipswich team at the end of that season, I also earned an international call-up. England had suffered a bad time during qualifying for the 1982 World Cup, and at one stage Ron Greenwood had actually quit before being persuaded by the players to carry on. It was Paul Mariner's goal against the Hungarians at Wembley the previous November, when I was in the squad but not in the final sixteen, that finally booked our passage to Spain for the finals. My return to the national side came just a fortnight after my comeback game with Ipswich, against the Welsh at Cardiff where we won 1–0 with a Trevor Francis goal. It doesn't sound a great result in retrospect, but Wales had become something of a bogey team to us and had beaten us twice and drawn twice in our last four meetings. We had to wait until the 74th minute for the winner. I played alongside Phil Thompson, marked Ian Rush, and enjoyed the game immensely. We were happy to come away with the win, and a month later I was privileged to play in the hundredth meeting between England and Scotland, at Hampden Park. These games were crucial to every player because England were selecting the squad to go to Spain. There was certainly fierce competition for the defensive positions with the likes of Dave Watson, Russell Osman, Phil Thompson, Alvin Martin, who had played against Hungary, and Steve Foster, who had enjoyed a great season with Brighton.

We travelled up to Scotland early on the Thursday and discovered the Rolling Stones were appearing at the Apollo in Glasgow. Trevor Francis had been given some tickets so five or six of us went, and we were invited backstage to meet the group before the concert. It was all very relaxed and friendly, and while I was speaking to Bill Wyman, Charlie Watts came up to join us; Mick Jagger and Keith Richard were in the warm-up room, drinking Jack Daniels I guess. Ronnie Wood also shook hands and spoke to us. It was a great experience. I asked Bill what he did to warm up. 'I just go out there and play,' he replied. 'I let all those idiots run around and do their stuff. I just play and come off. It can be quite boring in the end. It's the others they come to see.'

Trevor's contacts were obviously good because we were right in the middle of the stalls in great seats, but as we came in and sat down you could sense the Scots all around us knew who we were, and we felt the hostility rising by the second. Then they began chanting 'England, England, get tae fuck.' I genuinely asked if they were inviting us to go to the front. Well, it sounded a bit like that. The noise was building when an announcer said, 'Ladies and gentlemen, please welcome, the Rolling Stones!' The crowd went mad, and we were saved. As usual, the Stones' timing was immaculate. They were brilliant and played for two hours. Viv Anderson was a big Stones fan and he was in his element. I was so impressed I went off and bought a batch of their tapes.

To cap a great week, we beat the Jocks on the Saturday when, unmarked, I headed against the crossbar and Paul Mariner, following up, slid the ball home. But it was no more than we deserved. I was relieved because I'd had two good chances myself to put us in front before my Ipswich team-mate scored.

It was a great experience just driving to Hampden – a trip I was to make a number of times over the years – through thousands and thousands of fans, so many drunken Scots, some of whom were never going to see the game. It was like a different planet, even though we were playing against people we met regularly in the First Division. The Hampden roar is always said to be tremendous, but in reality, that day at least, it was a disappointment for Scotland never really threatened us.

We caught the shuttle back and we were all absolutely delighted. It was great because we'd kept a clean sheet and I had never been on the winning side for England, apart from the Australia game, which really didn't count in those days.

Because of World Cup selection, we had two more games lined up: Bobby Robson took a B side to Iceland while Ron Greenwood took the full England squad to Finland. This was the last opportunity to clinch a place for Spain. I just hoped I was going to get in the squad. I went to Finland with Alvin Martin and Phil Thompson, but was left on the bench as England won 4–1 to maintain a lengthening winning run. I feared for my place, but when the squad was announced I was in and Russell, who had played in Iceland, wasn't. What do you say in circumstances like those? Mick Mills, Paul Mariner and I were all going to the World Cup finals, and he was the odd one out. It must have been shattering for him as he had always been just ahead of me in the past. It was something I never expected, especially after being out of the game in hospital for such a long time. It was unbelievable.

CHAPTER SIX

OUT BUT UNDEFEATED

From the moment we met up, put all our gear together and posed for a picture on the runway on our way to Bilbao in the heart of the Basque country (where most of the players had been previously to open the San Mames Stadium), the atmosphere among the squad was good. The only drawback was we were beset by injuries. In fact, I would go so far as to say that it cost us a real tilt at the trophy. It was bad enough losing Kevin Keegan and Trevor Brooking for all but a few minutes of the competition; the really hurtful injury, however, was losing Steve Coppell, who had been such an important member of the team.

We took over a lovely hotel in Bilbao, known to the press as Dead Dog Beach after *Daily Mirror* sports news reporter John Jackson went to our hotel in the depths of winter and his photographer took pictures of all the debris on the family beach, including a dead dog which some suggested had been carefully positioned especially for the photo. Of course there was rubbish on a beach during the winter in the north of Spain where the weather was hardly conducive to a bit of quick sunbathing. By the time we arrived everything was pristine, with families sunbathing on a lovely stretch of sand spread out in front of a delightful hotel whose management and staff were wonderful. Each of us was given a bottle of the finest Rioja wine from the year of our birth. Most kept them, but I opened mine. It was truly dreadful. I think it was corked. I certainly couldn't drink it.

The only downside was the amount of time to kill. I roomed with Aston Villa striker Peter Withe – ironic really, because every time we'd played we'd kicked lumps out of each other. But we got on really well and formed a lasting friendship. He was a complete magpie was Peter.

Perhaps the Scouser in him came out, for into his bag would go towels, tissues, soaps, shampoos, shoe cleaner, shoehorns and any other items that were movable. Any spare gear I didn't want he would whisk away for his mates. But on the other side of the coin he was always first up in the mornings to fetch the English newspapers, which were sent over to us. He would also scoop up any food left lying about and bring it to the room.

There was also a problem with smog in the industrial town of Bilbao. If there was a cloud base, it was reputed to be one of Europe's more difficult towns in which to breathe normally. Two British journalists, Jeff Powell from the *Daily Mail* and the late Frank Clough from the *Sun*, had travelled out there earlier and were appalled by the local people spitting at their feet, and by the amount of graffiti on the walls. It really shocked them, and their newspapers dubbed Bilbao 'The City of Hate'. It quickly became evident that spitting was an everyday occurrence as the inhabitants cleared their throats in the dreadful smoggy atmosphere, so other journalists quickly turned the tagline into 'City of Hake', after Bilbao's most popular fish.

The arrangements at our training camp were also good, very carefully prepared. The training was hard and very competitive, and I really worked at it, even though I didn't think for a minute I would play. I desperately hoped I would, of course, so I kept myself fit and sharp. Even if you're not first choice, you never know when injury or illness will change selection policy. I also thought Phil Thompson and I had formed a good partnership whenever we'd played together.

The big squad problems, as I said, were the injuries to Keegan and Brooking. Their continued brooding presence was something of a problem for the rest of the squad, especially when stories broke about Keegan going to West Germany for treatment on his back problem, something he did do eventually in the dead of night in a bid to throw journalists and commentators off the scent. But there was some light relief before the tournament began, notably when we were all invited to an informal cocktail party with members of the press, officials and the touring London Ballet Company, who were due to perform in Bilbao for three nights. We all thought it would be a nice diversion, having a drink with delicate, pretty ballet dancers, but when they arrived they were nothing like any ballet dancers any of us had ever seen before. For a start most of them had large bosoms. A number of them also had quite firm backsides, and there were a few with dyed blonde hair. It began to dawn on us that these girls looked more like belly dancers than ballet dancers, but even so, the party went well and some of the boys, certainly Trevor Francis and Paul Mariner, had their pictures taken with them by delighted English photographers who couldn't believe their luck. Needless to say the pictures appeared in the English papers the next day: England players posing with an erotic dance troupe. Only the lovely Ron Greenwood would have okayed a function like that and still, by the end of the party, believed the guests were what he had been told they were. We had a good laugh about it, and it relaxed the spirits enormously, though I understand a few of the players' wives were not overly impressed with the company we were keeping during our preparations.

Ron announced his team for the opening game against France on 16 June the day before – and I was in it! Alongside me to face a quite rightly fancied French side boasting the likes of Battiston, Tigana, Giresse and Platini were Peter Shilton, Mick Mills, Kenny Sansom, Phil Thompson, Bryan Robson, Steve Coppell, Trevor Francis, Paul Mariner, Graham Rix and Ray Wilkins. A decent side, but still there weren't too many critics predicting a victory for England. I cannot describe how nervous I was. I knew I shouldn't be. Ipswich had enjoyed a great season and I had played my part, despite the long lay-off. I also had a few competitive internationals under my belt. But this was the big one. This was the World Cup.

Before I knew it I was on the coach heading to the stadium on the hottest day of the year – over a hundred degrees was recorded on the pitch. It was so hot out there with those horrible Admiral tracksuits that our feet were sweating, despite the fact that we were wearing flip-flops. The immediate thought is how are you going to survive 90 minutes in a sauna against one of the best teams in the world, but this is offset by the excitement of playing in a World Cup and, on this occasion, the belief we had in our own players. It was a very smart, new stadium, and even long before kick-off it was noisy. We took on lots of water and salt tablets after our warm-up – a brief one in the heat. We had to have cold towels draped over us to bring down our body temperatures.

We had worked on lots of things in training, and one of them was a long throw from Kenny Sansom down the left which I would flick on. We had never tried it on the other side of the pitch with Steve Coppell, but after just 27 seconds we won a throw-in. Coppell took it, I flicked it on, and there was the inevitable Bryan Robson storming in from midfield to hammer a left-foot shot past the French goalkeeper Ettori. It was the quickest goal in World Cup history, beating the record set by the Frenchman Lacombe four years earlier against Argentina. A touch of their own medicine, you might say.

But it left an awful long time for us to hold on. Unsurprisingly, the French equalised through Soler after 25 minutes and we had to start again. He gave me his shirt after the game and I reckon that was as close as I got to him all day. He was very slippery, and for the goal I should have played him offside but he cleverly deceived me on a diagonal ball, spun well, came short and then went long with a great finish to beat Shilts. My fault, and I held my hands up.

At half-time it was a case of cold towels or cold showers. It started to cool down a little in the second half as the shadow of the stand came across the ground and we felt a lot better and began to relax. In fact it was the French who began to look fatigued, especially when Bryan Robson headed home from Trevor Francis. Not long after it was all over when Tresor slipped and my club-mate Mariner scored his fifth goal in five internationals.

It was a great feeling to come away with such a good result, and to have done it without Keegan and Brooking, who were supposed to be our most influential players. But there was plenty of recovery to do before our next game against the Czechs just four days later. Some of our players had sweated off 14lb, and to lose a stone in weight in an hour and a half when you are super fit to start with is stunning. It was the usual stuff back at the hotel, with good words from Ron Greenwood. We were also told dinner that night was free time to eat what we wanted when we wanted. The hotel did a beautiful fish soup, and I had that with a steak, plenty of red wine and copious amounts of lager. It should of course have been pints of water, but not in those days.

It was a great night, and there wasn't much sleep because we were so high. The next day, those who hadn't played went off to training; for the rest of us there was a golf day organised at the local golf club – something else which would be frowned upon now. Eighteen holes the day after a strenuous World Cup match in getting on for a hundred degrees of heat? Tee-off times were right under the midday sun too. Far more attractive was the clubhouse itself with its nice little bar. Each of the players picked up a case of lager and we sat around the club in the sun, some with knotted handkerchiefs on their heads in true British holiday style. The barman also mixed up some sangria for us to go with our lunch, and we enjoyed ourselves until about five p.m.

We went back to the hotel for dinner that evening, and Joe Corrigan, who must have drunk a gallon of sangria in the sun, sat there quietly steaming, looking like a grilled lobster. His back was snow white and his front was scarlet. He had been battering people on the bus as usual, so the lads he had attacked got together once they'd heard he had gone to bed and passed out. Some of them began spraying him with water, and as it landed on his skin it sizzled. But he didn't wake up, so the boys became braver and began to throw other things at him. No one even so much as thought about just how dangerous a mixture of alcohol and sun can be. Doc Edwards, our lovely doctor, simply recommended salt and more salt. Big Joe was in fact lucky to survive – not the schoolboy romp in his bedroom, but the effects of his day off, which did him a lot more harm than good.

Ray Wilkins had also been on great form that day, and on the coach going back to the hotel he slaughtered all the FA members, including secretary Ted Croker, who took it all in good part, coming as it did from one of the most popular members of the squad. Back at the hotel, Butch, tired and emotional, curled up on one of the settees in the foyer and went to sleep. Ron Greenwood gave an informal press conference around the sleeping figure of his midfield player, curled up like a dormouse. He was still there when the smiling press contingent left. Can you imagine what they would have done with a similar story nowadays? It would have been front-page news even then had the newshounds been around instead of the football writers. We were lucky to escape that day without any serious consequences. It was just the British way of celebrating success in those days. Stupid and unprofessional.

We knuckled down and prepared properly for the Czech game back in the same stadium where we had beaten the French. The Czechs were very negative but we continued to batter on their door, and although we lost Bryan Robson with a groin injury, Glenn Hoddle came on and we went on to win, albeit with two decidedly scrappy goals. The first came when goalkeeper Seman (no, not that one) let a Ray Wilkins corner slip through his hands, the second when Barmos put through his own goal as he tried to intercept a Mariner pass. It was a comfortable win and, along with Brazil, we had already qualified for the second phase. The thought began to grow in the back of our minds that Brazil v. England could be the final.

On the bus on the way back to our hotel Ron Greenwood stood up to give us a congratulatory speech, and then he gave us permission to go and get pissed. In those very words. We had no problem with obeying his orders to the letter.

Rita and the other wives flew out to join us before our third group game against the minnows from Kuwait. We met them at the airport, found them a nice little hotel and booked them in – a bit different to the arrangements these days when everything is laid on for their comfort. All went well except I almost missed the bus to the match. I was on the wrong side of the bay and was left with just 45 minutes to get myself back before the team's departure for the stadium. I wasn't playing – it was too risky because of a yellow card I'd picked up against the French – but it wouldn't have looked very good had I been late and kept the team waiting. I managed it by a minute and whipped on to the coach with my bag hastily packed. Rita and the others came to the game, and she of course had Christopher with her, not even three months old at the time. Jack Charlton had flown over with them on the same flight from England and he'd helped her get Christopher off the plane. A great man is Jack. How surreal it was as I sat feeding my son with his bottle while watching England beat Kuwait for maximum points, Paul Mariner's back-heel putting in Francis for the only goal of the match midway through the first half.

We then left our very happy base in the City of Hake and flew to Madrid for one of those regular groups of death in the second round against the hosts Spain and one of the favourites, West Germany. But we were in good humour after our exploits in Bilbao. We were in a beautiful hotel well outside Madrid in the hills, with the training pitch just over the road. Keegan and Brooking were still not fit, and, if I'm honest, didn't look as though they would be, but Bryan Robson was back and so was I.

The first game was played in Real Madrid's famous Bernabeu Stadium on 29 June, and it proved to be a real disappointment. It showed that three-team groups represented poor planning, because neither team wanted to lose, especially the Germans, who had received good reports of our performances in northern Spain. They closed us down and neither Francis nor Mariner was able to get a shot on target. Not even Tony Woodcock, who came on as a substitute for Francis, was able to escape the Germans' clutches, despite playing his football in Cologne where he was used to the same defensive ploys. We might have lost it when Karl-Heinz Rummenigge went past Graham Rix and before I could close him down hammered a shot against the crossbar. But the goalless scoreline was almost predictable and left us both to play hosts Spain for a place in the semi-finals.

It was all a little hard to take in, playing in a World Cup against top teams like France, West Germany and Spain. The Germans were a powerful side. Apart from Rummenigge, they had on show against us players like goalkeeper Schumacher, Kaltz, Stielike, Müller, Breitner and Littbarski. Spain were equally well blessed with talent, and they had the advantage of being at home. We went to the Bernabeu the following week knowing we needed to beat them 2–0 to go through.

Rita was also staying in Madrid, and the Spanish were, to her surprise, making a real fuss of baby Christopher. The wives came out for lunch at our hotel, and afterwards I did some shopping with Rita in town. But once we were on our way to the stadium we knew this was it. When we arrived in the dressing room, we saw physiotherapist Fred Street and his number two Norman Medhurst had put up a big sign in sticky tape saying 'Good Luck, Lads'. The spirit was tremendous, even though we had lost Steve Coppell through injury, but we did, for the first time, have both Keegan and Brooking on the bench, the former having completed his midnight trip to West Germany, returned and trained with us, though not at full throttle. Still, neither of them had played for a long time. They had to be a little rusty.

Both teams had chances to score, but Spain, knowing they had little chance of going through after being beaten by the Germans, were playing for pride and were determined that if they couldn't win, we weren't going to either. The atmosphere inside the stadium was poisonous because of the recent Falklands conflict, and there were constant chants of 'Malvinas, Malvinas!' – the Spanish name for the islands. Keegan and Brooking came on for Woodcock and Rix late in the game, and both might have scored had they been in the groove, Keegan heading wide from a good position and Brooking watching as goalkeeper Luis Arconada made a superb save from his shot. But the game eventually petered out into another goalless draw.

We were all feeling very flat, and after the game we went back to the dressing room to try to see our wives. London journalist Steve Stammers managed to get the wives through to see us, but it was awful because of the Spanish supporters around the doors, still chanting about the war and, worse, throwing things at us. The coach was stoned as we left. It was ugly and horrible, something I will never forget. I said goodbye to Rita and we arranged to see them at the airport for the charter flight back the next day.

We returned to the hotel for a subdued dinner, and then Fred Street threw open the door to the kit room. It was like Aladdin's cave in there. We took all our shirts, shorts, socks and plenty of other souvenirs. I was number 4 because they numbered us alphabetically. The three strips we had were red, white and light blue. Peter Withe must have thought it was his birthday and Christmas rolled into one because he helped himself to everything he could lay his hands on. Some of us swapped shirts – I exchanged with Bryan Robson – and gradually the atmosphere began to lighten. After all, we had gone through the tournament unbeaten, conceding just the one goal, to the French, in the entire tournament.

It was Ron Greenwood's last game as manager, with my club manager Bobby Robson ready to step in ahead of the people's favourite Brian Clough. Ron, Don Howe, Fred, Norman and everyone else were a great group of people. We even got on with most of the press most of the time, at least until they attacked our manager over something, probably the Keegan affair. Considering that Keegan had been influential in having me sent off a little more than a year earlier I found it difficult to feel too much sympathy for him, and I'm not sure his brooding presence was totally good for the team in the circumstances. However, had I been in a similar position I doubt whether my demeanour would have been any different.

For me, that World Cup is still the one that got away. To be part of a team going through a World Cup finals undefeated and not even to reach the final was hard to take. I thought we were good enough to win it. In fact, in the semi-finals West Germany had to go to penalties before they beat the French, while Italy beat Poland in the other semi-final before going on to beat the Germans 3–1 in the final. Could we have done better? I believe so.

CHAPTER SEVEN

THE CHANGEOVER

Before Bobby Robson departed for pastures new at Lancaster Gate, he had arranged a pre-season trip for Ipswich to the USA. The three of us who had played in the World Cup had just thirteen days off before we had to report back for training. We played the tournament and lost in the final. It was a disaster in some respects, for although we were staying at the smart Florida resort of Clearwater and living in the Holiday Inn on the beach, it was very much a holiday hotel rather than somewhere quiet to prepare. I was already at a high level of fitness because of the World Cup, but the others should have been working hard. Instead, we got into the holiday spirit and spent far too much time at the bar. We also had long flights out and back in economy, which offered little leg room and mixed us up with the tourists. It produced entirely the wrong atmosphere as it was all far too relaxed and not very comfortable.

After America we went off to Zeist again, this time to play in a tournament in Eindhoven. Because of all the travelling I had done recently, and the football I had played, I was getting a bit stir crazy. Mr Hyde was emerging from his dark cavern. Bobby Robson was with us in Holland as a sort of farewell trip, and that's when he pulled me to one side and made that comment about my safety valve being alcohol. I wondered what he was talking about because he rarely had this sort of heart-to-heart with me. 'Sometimes you turn the valve and you let off steam, and when you do you let off a lot of steam,' he continued. I told him not to be silly, I didn't have a problem. He nodded wisely then wished me well for the season at Ipswich.

I was taken off after an hour during the last game in Eindhoven to let others have a game, but instead of going to the bench or the stand to watch what was left of the match, I went to the bar and had a couple of sneaky beers. Afterwards it was back to Zeist, which felt like a prison camp in the middle of nowhere. The boys had christened it Stalag 12. They had laid on a cold-meat platter, cheese, bread, custard cakes and some beers for us, and afterwards the two Bobbys wished us goodnight and went off. Some of the players decided to go out and find a club or somewhere to have a late drink, but others, including me, decided to stay in.

In my room I had some Bols cherry brandy and some banana liqueur to take home for Rita. When the beers ran out I could hear the boys screaming out to me to bring them, which I duly did. By this time we were down to just four of us: me, Mick Mills, Russell Osman and Paul Mariner. It was now around two in the morning, and we began to get a little boisterous. We started to stack up the empty beer bottles on the table as skittles and bowl the custard cakes at them to knock them over. It all began gently, but soon the bottles were being stacked up in a pyramid, and instead of rolling the custard cakes we started throwing them like baseball pitchers. Bottles were falling on the floor, and some of them were breaking. This, we thought in our drunken stupor after drinking the two bottles of sweet spirits, was great fun. So we decided instead of the cakes we should use the bottles themselves. Before long we were trashing the room as we grabbed whatever was movable. To be fair to Osman and Mills, it was more Mr Mariner and Mr Hyde who were the main culprits. Those two didn't take too much of an active part, but Paul and I flipped.

When I woke up the next morning I asked myself if I had dreamt what had happened. But then I tasted the bile in my mouth, felt my head, and heard an eruption from downstairs to tell me it had all been very real. Bobby Robson was of course told about what his players had done to the team room, there were meetings after meetings, and eventually word came for us to get our gear and go downstairs for another meeting. Robson was apoplectic. 'Who has done this? What players of mine have done this? I didn't bring you up to do this! I want the people involved to step forward now!'

I lunged forward quickly, followed by Mariner. Although they didn't need to, both Mills and Osman stepped forward as well. Robson immediately dragged us off to another room and absolutely slaughtered us, as he had every right to. We had been totally out of order. Paul and I insisted that Mick and Russell were blameless, and they were excused. But Bobby was boiling. If he could have punched us he would have done. He told us we had let him down, after he had brought Mariner to the club and after he had looked after me. He called us a total disgrace, and the words hurt. He fined us the money we were supposed to be getting for the tournament and told us we would have to pay for the repairs out of our own pockets. What struck home the most was when he said, disbelievingly, this was how we had decided to say goodbye and thank you to him before he went off to manage England – something, don't forget, we both hoped we would still be involved with over the coming months. We apologised. We couldn't have apologised more wholeheartedly. But the damage was done. It was a disaster. Players have been thrown out of clubs for less.

But Bobby hadn't finished with us yet. He took us back into the team room and made us look at what we had done, the damage we had caused. We wanted the ground to open up, and this on top of massive hangovers. He picked up the two empty spirit bottles and swung around towards me. 'Did you drink this?' he said. 'Did you buy this?' I put up my hand. 'I knew it was you,' he continued. 'It's *always* you. This is the safety valve I talked to you about a few days ago. Alcohol. Your safety valve. To drink this stuff! It's rocket fuel!' Then he added, again, 'This is what you think of me? This is my farewell present?'

All I can say in mitigation of my behaviour was that I was gone. The World Cup, the trip to America, the tour to Holland … I was just flat burned out and not looking forward to the 1982/83 season at all. It was Mr Hyde coming out again while Dr Jekyll stood with head bowed, contrite and embarrassed. It was almost worse when the owners of the Zeist sports complex refused to let us pay for the damage. All they did was sweep everything up into a bin and wipe the custard off the walls, ceilings and carpets. Had it been a wild rock group it might have been expected, but not from a football team staying as guests in a foreign country. Luckily, I got on with Bobby Ferguson, the new Ipswich manager, who swept the matter under a carpet – and it needed a big carpet. Neither did the story get out in the media. Had it happened nowadays it would have been splashed across every front page with cries for my head from both Ipswich and England fans. I doubt whether I would have survived.

Still, the feeling of flatness continued. Come the start of the new domestic season, my batteries needed recharging. It didn't help, of course, knowing Bobby Robson had gone, or that Muhren had been sold to Manchester United. There was in fact a general air of departure about the club that season, with Mills, Thijssen and Brazil all leaving at various points, and it showed on the pitch. By mid-September, having drawn three and lost three of our opening six matches, we had slumped to the foot of the table. I wasn't playing well and gave away a goal against Spurs during the run. We even lost to a poor Stoke City side. The club had built a new stand, the Pioneer Stand, with the profits from our success over the last few years and the players the club had sold on. Especially in those early weeks of the season, it felt like a millstone around our necks.

Given my club form, not to mention what had happened in Holland, I was fortunate Bobby Robson picked me for his first game in charge, a European Championship qualifier against Denmark in Copenhagen on 22 September. We drew 2–2 and the press absolutely slaughtered us. Russell and I were the central defenders and we were ripped apart by Preben Elkjaer; but for Peter Shilton we would have certainly started off the campaign with a heavy loss. Remarkably, we had gone ahead through Trevor Francis, but after that we were pressed further and further back until Russell gave away a penalty when he brought down Jesper Olsen, and Hansen converted. Francis put us back ahead again, but Olsen then went past Robson, Russell and me to score an equaliser we could hardly complain about, even though it was so late in the game. This was a good Danish side, although they weren't recognised as such then. The same players went on to establish themselves as one of the world's best teams. They were described at the time by Mike Langley, the football writer for *The People*, as a team of butchers, bakers and candlestick makers. As much as we struggled on the night, he was definitely the one who finished with egg on his face as their reputation grew and grew. They were organised, and their pace was terrific.

Nothing seemed to be going right. In the UEFA Cup, Ipswich were hammered 3–0 by Roma in the Italian capital, Paul Cooper having a torrid time. After the game we went out and found a nice restaurant – difficult not to in Rome – where they served Frascati in jugs. We ordered a jug each, and part of the promotion was that we could keep the jugs. Bobby Robson, who had been invited out for the game, was in the same restaurant, and he must have been impressed when we began to sing into the jugs to exploit the echo effect. We eventually took the jugs back to the hotel and continued our party. There was trouble there, too, with a lady of the night who might easily have got the local police involved after an incident where she was the butt of some very crazy, alcohol-fuelled humour.

We flew back to Heathrow, and when we landed we heard we had followed up our draw against Roma with a League Cup draw against Liverpool – just what we wanted! Before the domestic cup-tie we had the second leg against the Italians to contend with, and for a brief while we harboured great hopes as we led 2–0. The momentum was really with us until they suddenly pulled one back from a free-kick. Although I scored to make it 3–1, it wasn't enough. After several seasons of enjoying the cities of Europe, Ipswich were out. We were to stay out for a long, long time.

The first leg of the League Cup tie was at Anfield, and two mistakes by yours truly led to goals right in front of the Kop. Paul Cooper played a short ball out to me and I foolishly tried to dribble around Ian Rush; then I presented him with a second when I passed the ball to him and he scored. Never ones to miss an opportunity, the Kop burst into full voice, singing, 'There's only one Terry Butcher!' and 'Terry, Terry, give us a wave!' In early October we beat Liverpool 1–0 at Portman Road in the League, and as we'd also recently thrashed Notts County 6–0 we felt we were on our way back. But then came the home League Cup defeat by Liverpool in the second leg and three more League games without a win. The transition from Bobby Robson to Bobby Ferguson was not going nearly as smoothly as everyone had expected. They were vastly different managers. Ferguson was very tactically astute, but this wasn't his team, and when Robson and Muhren left there seemed to be something missing which we never recaptured.

There was the diversion, for me at least, of a couple of England games. In mid-October Gary Mabbutt hit the post early on at Wembley against a new-look West Germany side, but we fell to two goals from the outstanding Karl-Heinz Rummenigge, although Tony Woodcock pulled one back to set up a do-or-die last five minutes. Then, in December, came a nine-goal rout of little Luxembourg. I had the hump in that match after I crossed the ball for Mark Chamberlain to head a goal. He didn't bother to come over and thank me for the pass, nor for that matter in the dressing room after the game. Whatever happened to etiquette? Still, I suppose he was a young man and was too excited at scoring his first goal for his country at Wembley – a thrill I had yet to feel.

In the meantime, Ipswich's League season continued to stutter and stumble along, despite another 23 goals from John Wark. You could tell what the supporters thought of us by April, when a home game with Notts County drew our lowest crowd for ten years, just 15,924. There was no consistency in the team because of the change of players and injuries, though I played in every minute of every match. Russell Osman took over the captaincy from Mick Mills when he went to Southampton, and we eventually managed to finish in the top ten, but there was little joy in the dressing room after such a mixed season, especially after having drawn once with and lost twice to Norwich. Just after Christmas they beat us 3–2 at Portman Road with a goal scored from a free-kick by Martin O'Neill, who never fails to tell me about it whenever we meet. I suppose he would remember it as he didn't score many. But our exit from the FA Cup at their hands was worse because the competition was our last chance of a trophy, and to get back into Europe. I hated to lose to Norwich at the best of times, but this was doubly hard as I was the cause of the only goal. A ball was played down the channel to Keith Bertschin. I tried to nick it in front of him but he turned me with his body. I went careering past him and he went on to score.

The night before the game Sadie, a lovely golden Labrador pedigree bitch whom we had mated, gave birth to puppies. We had paid £50 for the mating, a strange affair which I won't go into here. We waited to see if she had conceived but there was nothing. We even took her to the vet to confirm she was pregnant, but it wasn't positive news. But then she began to put on weight and it was assumed she was having a phantom pregnancy. We shrugged and carried on with our lives, but one day we were sitting in front of the fire and Sadie's tummy began moving around. She was either pregnant or suffering from very large worms, so we took her back to the vet who this time confirmed it.

We had been out for dinner on the night she gave birth. When we arrived back we noticed that she'd had one pup but had rolled on it and suffocated it. It was then a case of making sure she was OK, and we were with her when the remainder of the pups were born. She had nine more, and I was up all night. The only sleep I had was after training on the day of the match. It didn't affect my game necessarily, we just played poorly as a team. The pups survived and I was able to stay in and baby-sit them, because I never went out for three or four nights whenever we lost to Norwich. Poor Sadie. There was one more puppy than teats on her belly, and she had to feed them on a rota. We gave one to our next-door neighbours Bob and Marion Campbell, and they cut a hole in the fence between our two houses so that Butch could look through the wire mesh and see his mum. Not that Sadie took a lot of notice.

We became great friends with the Campbells, and it was with Bob I started up my insurance company, Terry Butcher Insurance Consultants Ltd. We put in £2,000 each and eventually sold the concern to Norwich and Peterborough. I knew nothing about insurance, but fortunately I knew someone who did, and the business took off enormously. The first six months it looked like going under, but then we got the right manager and it went berserk. The company logo was my autograph. I remember once in 1985 going up to the referee before kick-off and giving him one of my cards. I can't remember who it was, but it certainly wasn't Clive Thomas because he would have booked me. Our return on the £2,000 investment was about £80,000 each, and with it we bought two houses in Florida complete with swimming pools which we either used as holiday homes or rented out.

The England season was just as mixed as Ipswich's after our unbeaten run in the World Cup, but I had cause to celebrate in February 1983 when I scored my first ever goal for my country at Wembley, against Wales. It wasn't particularly memorable for any other reason, with a small crowd on an icy night and half the Wembley pitch frozen. It wasn't a good game either. Ian Rush scored early on, I got the equaliser with a volley on the far post from an Alan Devonshire pass, and Phil Neal scored the winner with a late penalty. The pitch was so tricky we didn't know whether to wear pimples or studs. I went for the pimples, which helped when I scored my goal.

We also drew 0–0 with Greece in March on another cold night at Wembley. It was a European Championship qualifier, and they came to defend. The result left us top of the table but needing to beat the Hungarians in April. We did so, after a poor start, with goals from Francis and my old room-mate Peter Withe with a super strike. But it wasn't a memorable match either, and neither was our goalless draw with Northern Ireland a month later. We were in a bit of a trough. I had yet another new central defensive partner in Belfast in Spurs' Graham Roberts, and a debut was also given to a bright young winger from Watford, John Barnes. Roberts had a difficult start and would have marked his first game for his country with an own goal but for a super Peter Shilton save. Whenever we threatened, there was Pat Jennings with those bucket-like hands. He stopped Barnes from scoring on his first appearance.

We were due to play Scotland the following Wednesday so we flew back after the game and Bobby Robson allowed us to have a night off with our families before reporting back on the Sunday night. The plane landed at Luton, and Russell (who hadn't played) and I decided to go to Ronelles nightclub in Cambridge for a quick pint before going home. The beer went down well, and we finally left at around four a.m. I drove back to Ipswich because, if I remember rightly, Russell was banned. It wasn't a good decision. I drifted off to sleep briefly on the dual carriageway, and it was fortunate it was such an odd time and there was little or no traffic on the road.

Next day we went back down to High Wycombe where we were staying at the Crest Hotel. Needless to say, we all met up in a pub opposite Bisham Abbey in Marlow village and had a few more pints. When we arrived back at the hotel there was a wedding party and we were invited to join in. It went very well until around midnight when, suddenly, I looked around and there wasn't another England player in sight. Sure enough a second later there was a hand on my shoulder and Bobby Robson saying, 'I thought you would be here, Butcher. I knew you would be here. Where are the rest of your mates?'

'What mates?' I asked in all innocence.

'So it's just you on your own, is it? I will see you in the morning. Get off to your bed.'

We had a practice match the next day. I was playing in the middle with Russell and we were beaten three or four goals to nil by the reserves. Bobby called a meeting straight away and laid into us. 'You had your chance,' he said, 'but you were all too interested in a disco match instead of a football match.' Oddly, he kept me in for the game, but he brought in Graham Roberts and left Russell out, and Russell never recovered from the decision. He left a few others out too. We went on to beat Scotland 2–0, and I laid on the first goal for Bryan Robson after just thirteen minutes by flicking on a long throw from Kenny Sansom to replicate the goal we'd scored against France in the World Cup. Gordon Cowans scored a second and we had others ruled out from Sammy Lee and Trevor Francis.

Just ten days after we were playing in Sydney, Australia. After a long season it was just what we wanted! We flew in in the morning, slept in the afternoon and trained in the evening. And Bobby trained us really hard because that was what he had been told would help us get over any jet lag. There were a number of players who dropped out, and one or two who appeared and were never seen again. It was a trip Bobby had inherited, and though he approached it professionally it was a few games too far for players who had had a full season. I, for one, had never been so relieved to get home.

CHAPTER EIGHT

BREAKING UP IS HARD TO DO

It's always hard when a very good team breaks up. I doubt whether Ipswich will ever have such a great team again in my lifetime with the way football has gone. It was hard to take at the time, but it's even harder looking back now. I have to question the decision to build the Pioneer Stand to try to bring in more revenue at the expense of the team. We were filling the old ground every week when we were going for Europe and the championship. But would the players have stayed anyway? It's the same at Motherwell, or any other club. Players come in, do well and move on. Our best players at Ipswich went to Arsenal, Liverpool and Manchester United. In the end you are victims of your own success. At some stage you have to decide whether you are going to be a feeder club or a club with a big enough ground and enough income to join the big boys. We fell in between the two. Did Ipswich really believe they could sustain their position at the top chasing trophies, or was it a false premise?

There were no signs of the disappointments ahead when we started the 1983/84 season like a house on fire. We had lost Alan Brazil to Spurs, but he came back to Portman Road with his new club on the first day of the season and we beat them 3–1. We were desperate to show him he was wrong to leave us. I remember going to a party the same evening with Alan and his wife Jill, and how strange it felt now that he was no longer part of the team. We'd come through eight or nine years together.

We won four of our first five and drew the other one to go into second place, but then won only one of our next seven. That's when our season began to go to pieces. One of the worst moments came in early 1984 when we were put out of the FA Cup by little Shrewsbury. It wasn't a good place for us because this was the second time in three seasons they'd put us out of the competition. It was a huge blow. I remember the old coracle in the river which was used to get the ball when it flew over the stand. I tried my best to keep it occupied, but it wasn't enough.

Jason Dozzell, a local boy, played for us the following month. He had a difficult family background but he was a lovely boy and a very good player who, sadly, did not fulfil his potential for some reason. He was still a schoolboy in February 1984 and became the youngest goalscorer ever for Ipswich, and in Division 1 history, when he scored against Coventry City while we were desperately holding on to a narrow 2–1 lead. He was just sixteen years and 57 days old, but tall, strong and lithe. He looked effortless when he ran and he was very comfortable with the ball at his feet. We all thought he was going right to the very top of international football.

Paul Mariner had left us to go to Arsenal, and I found it really difficult to play against him because he was someone I loved and respected. I found it virtually impossible to kick him because we had been such good mates and we had arrived at Ipswich at the same time. We didn't see a lot of each other off the pitch, but we were firm friends. When we played at Highbury in March 1984 he scored twice. Another of our former players, Brian Talbot, also netted in a 4–1 defeat. I just couldn't get my head around being over-physical with him. It was a big lesson for me and for when I became a manager, because I could understand what players were going through when they came up against their mates. It didn't affect Paul. He was the sort who would play well for anyone. He was a super striker and a super bloke, and happily I'm still in touch with him. I saw him in Japan during the 2002 World Cup. We had some great sessions out there, some I can remember and some I can't. He is based in Boston, USA, now, but we talk regularly along with his manager Steve Nicol, the former Liverpool and Scotland player.

A month after Paul left, John Wark was also on his way. He wanted to play for Liverpool, but Bobby Ferguson was disappointed because he was such a good, valuable servant of the club. It wasn't the most pleasant of partings, which was sad after all he had done for us over the years. He helped Liverpool win the League and yet more prizes, while Ipswich continued to struggle. At one stage it looked as if we were going down as we lost an incredible seven on the bounce. Then, at the end of March, we played another struggling side, Watford, and managed to scrape a fortunate 0–0 draw, and gained a little more breathing space by beating their neighbours Luton. We climbed clear of the relegation zone, but it wasn't very convincing.

I did my knee ligaments against Nottingham Forest at home in mid-April and my season was over. However, I remember going up to Old Trafford in May with Rita to watch United play Ipswich. We stayed with Mike Summerbee, who was as pleased as I was when we beat United with goals from South African Mich D'Avray, now a successful manager of Perth in Australia, and Alan Sunderland. Russell Osman and his girlfriend Louise also stayed with us. A treasured moment came when Bobby Ferguson received the Manchester United team line-up. He then made his way to the dressing room and went through the entire team, rubbishing each of their players. When he'd finished, he looked up to see how his players were reacting and saw, instead, United midfielder Remi Moses, one of the players he had torn to pieces, standing in front of him.

'What are you doing in here?' Ferguson asked.

'No,' Remi replied, 'what are *you* doing in here? This is our dressing room!'

The United players had sat there in silence listening to him. They must have been falling about inside. They still lost.

Ferguson also had a thing about biorhythms, and although he swore he never picked a player on the strength of it, he was fascinated by the subject and used to say to me a player could be affected by a knock, or if you scored a goal it could lift you up from a poor reading. He told me one day that he'd looked at my scores and they were so low he felt he couldn't play me, but he did, and I had a stormer. Maybe all the Ipswich players' biorhythms were good in April and May because we finished the season with five wins and two draws in our final seven games which lifted us up from twentieth in the table to twelfth.

As a result of the ligament injury, I also missed England's end-of-season tour, two Home Championship matches and a desperate 2–0 defeat at the hands of the USSR at Wembley. After that match Jimmy Hill said we should cancel our trip to South America to save embarrassment, especially in Brazil, but England went to the Maracana Stadium and beat Brazil 2–0, John Barnes scoring that classic solo goal and Mark Hateley heading home for the second in a comprehensive win. It was Jimmy with egg on his face rather than Bobby this time!

England had begun their international campaign for 1983/84 some nine months before that win in Brazil in exactly the same way as they'd started the last, by playing Denmark in a European Championship qualifier, this time at Wembley. We lost 1–0, though Phil Neal could count himself unlucky to concede the penalty awarded by the Belgian referee and cheered to the rafters by the Danish travelling army of some 13,000. It made them favourites to qualify for the finals in France, even if England won in Hungary and Luxembourg. We kept alive our hopes with a 3–0 win in Budapest with goals from Glenn Hoddle, Sammy Lee and Paul Mariner. I had a hand in Paul's goal, starting the move in my own half. But as we were on our way to our final fixture in Luxembourg in November we heard that Denmark had won in Greece. We were out of the competition. The 4–0 victory over Luxembourg meant nothing to us. Not even scoring with a volley from a yard out (with my right foot) could lift me from my torpor. It was like a dead Test match after the series had been won. We took some stick from the papers, but we had lost out to one of the era's top European teams, as they were to go on to prove.

We were now nothing but cannon fodder for others to test themselves upon, and at the end of February 1984 we played a friendly against France at the Parc des Princes, where Michel Platini scored two wonderful goals. We had probably the smallest, most inexperienced England forward line ever in Brian Stein and Paul Walsh. It was a makeshift team in many senses. That was the day when the Juventus star followed me down the tunnel after the match and swapped shirts with me. It's in a bag under the stairs at home. A Platini shirt from 1984! It's probably worth framing.

We stayed in Paris overnight, and because the English fans had rioted there were police everywhere. As an obvious group of young Englishmen we kept getting turned away from the clubs and bars because they didn't believe we were England players. We eventually explained our problem to a friendly taxi driver and he and his mate took the seven of us to a plush establishment with subdued lighting, luxurious fittings and nice music. We were delighted, even more so when we noticed that very pretty, rather scantily clad girls sipping champagne populated the place. It took a few minutes to register we had walked into a very fancy brothel. The beers were very expensive, and we had the option of buying a bottle of whisky for around £100 – ten times its normal value. We had a whip-round and bought some whisky and beers but were told that if we wanted to talk to the girls we would have to buy a bottle of champagne. Most of us left for the hotel after the beers. In fact, my most memorable moment of a bad night was having a pee on the Champs Elysée.

We were back at the hotel reasonably early because there was just nowhere to go with the riots. Consequently we were also up bright and early to catch the coach to the airport on the Thursday morning, but when the head count was taken we were missing two players – Bryan Robson and Ray Wilkins. Bobby Robson sent Norman and Fred to knock on their door. There was no answer. We were now half an hour late, and Robson reluctantly ordered departure, leaving behind the skipper and his mate. The rest of us were agog, fearing the worst in the newspapers when the travelling journalists discovered that two of England's top players had gone missing. Fortunately, after a while they arrived at the airport, furious at being left behind. Apparently they had drunk so much the night before that they had gone into a deep, deep sleep and nothing could arouse them. They had to travel to the airport by taxi. Their anger at being left behind was somewhat misplaced in the circumstances.

My last England game before injury cut short my season was the Home Championship game at Wembley against Northern Ireland on 4 April. The 1–0 win was so memorable that I had to check I played in the game. I did, partnering Graham Roberts at the back. I tweaked the medial ligament on my left side in that game, and then of course against Nottingham Forest ten days later I did the other knee. If I had been a horse they would have shot me!

So, from a club, international and injury perspective, the season as far as I was concerned was a write-off with only a few memories for me, and most of them were bad. One real downer was the death of former chairman John Cobbold. He and his brother were an institution at Portman Road. They had backed Bobby Robson in his early days when he had battles and even fights with certain players, and also when the fans turned against him. That, of course, was when they offered him his ten-year contract, and he repaid them by building a tremendous side. What that contract did was to settle the whole club down and allow Bobby to work on a long-term plan instead of going for instant glory. The rest is history.

The Cobbolds were great fun, but they were also clever people who were able to assess others. With their public-school background and their time in the forces they were real gentlemen with the right character and the right attitude. I noticed their politeness very early on, but the more they got to know you the more relaxed they became, the fruitier the language, and the more wine was drunk. As players we rarely went into the boardroom because we had our own lounge, but as we got to know them the greetings became more and more raucous. The classic greeting from Mr John was, 'How are you, Butcher, you old c***?' They were an absolute pleasure to be with. The only crisis they had was when they ran short of Sancerre in the boardroom. They loved the trips abroad, whether for pre-season friendlies or for European matches. Before every season either Mr Pat or Mr John would throw a party, and everyone from the club was invited along with their partners. It was a three-line whip – not that it was needed: everyone wanted to go, knowing there would be fabulous food and an abundance of drink. The brothers would wander round with their mother, Lady Blanche, and it was just a wonderful time. No one took advantage of the free drink, they were just fantastic occasions. In fact I have tried to replicate them at Motherwell, working on the theory of getting everyone to mix to feel part of a family. I appreciate it now because it's difficult to do with current Premiership or Championship clubs because of the number of staff they employ. In those days there were only a handful of back-room staffers and administrators. Even the squads were smaller then.

Unfortunately, it was at one of these functions that Mr John fell and damaged his ribs. He was taken to hospital and when he was examined they discovered he was in the later stages of cancer. It was the beginning of the end for the club as it had been.

There are a million stories about the Cobbolds. The brothers got on well with most people, especially at Norwich, but there were some clubs they didn't like, and they would let them know about it. They were politely but obviously ignored. But my great memory of them comes from that trip to Hawaii in 1977 when we toasted the Queen for her Silver Jubilee. We also went to Calgary and then down to Florida at the end of one season. We drank quantities of vodka on the plane, Mr John joined in, and by the time we landed and found our way to a Japanese restaurant he was completely blitzed. But he was compos mentis enough to put his hand in his pocket to pay the bill for the food and drink at the end of the meal. We had to help him to his room when we returned to the hotel.

Having the correct people at the top in a football club is as important as in any other business. I am lucky at Motherwell with owner John Boyle and chairman Bill Dickie, who are both tremendous people. I was also lucky at Coventry with John Poynton, but there are some I have met who

I wouldn't cross the road to shake hands with. If they were on fire, I'd dial 998. But the Cobbolds were real gentlemen, despite their fruity use of the Queen's English.

We felt it heavily when John Cobbold died. Mr Pat was deeply affected by his brother's death, but he rallied round, as did the rest of the board, who were very strong. Mr Pat was still there when I left the club. When I told him I was going to sign for Rangers I had a huge lump in my throat, but he was so nice to me, thanking me for what I had done for the club and inviting me back any time I wanted to come. There were tears in my eyes and I could hardly speak.

One memory definitely worth having from the season was my first taste of club captaincy. Paul Mariner had started off the season as skipper, and when he went Russell Osman took over, though he was promptly sent off at the end of October when we lost 3–2 at Southampton. Ferguson asked me to be captain for the game against Arsenal. We won 1–0 and I was delighted. I had always wanted to be captain and I was very proud to be given the role, even if it was only temporary. I enjoyed being captain of both my club and, when the time came, my country. The worst part of the role was remembering names when I had to introduce them to the celebrity guest. We used to laugh at Bobby Robson for forgetting names, but it was always my mortal fear I too would forget in those circumstances.

One thing lacking in the game at the moment is inspirational captains. There are not many Patrick Vieiras around; perhaps only Roy Keane and John Terry fit the bill, and it's no coincidence they're all from the top three teams in the country. Sure Patrick gets sent off now and again, but he leads by example in the most competitive of areas. I like the Tony Adams type of captain. That's the sort I saw myself as. Gary Lineker always says to me whenever he sees me, 'Caged tigers! Caged tigers!' because it's what I always used to say in the England dressing room. 'Release the tigers!' I would say, and when the cage was opened we would be up and at them, scratching and biting. That's the way I went about it. Shouting and screaming and shaking people. Lineker was the opposite, though Bryan Robson would also snarl and shake his fist. Stuart Pearce was another like me. He liked a scream in the tunnel before and after a game.

Singing the national anthem was also special to me, and I would be careful to have my back straight and my thumbs down the imaginary seams of my pants. I pictured myself doing it as a young boy, singing the anthem and being proud of my country. I still stand when the anthems are played, even if I'm doing commentary. I find it obscene the way certain sections of the England crowd abuse other countries' national songs. They have obviously not thought it through, for all it does is galvanise the opposition into trying harder and performing better. That was certainly my attitude when foreign fans booed 'God Save the Queen'. And if I saw someone in a foreign crowd burning our flag it only increased my resolve.

People think being captain is simply a matter of tossing the coin and choosing the kick-off, but there is a lot more to it than that. When I went to Rangers, one of the first things Graeme Souness told me was that I was to be the captain. It was a great privilege. It boosts your ego and makes you feel special. Even now, when in Scotland I am introduced as the former captain of Rangers and England, even though I was only captain of my country seven times. Bryan Robson was usually captain when he was fit, and when he wasn't it was more often than not Peter Shilton. The most important time for me as captain was in the 1990 World Cup in the quarter- and semi-finals. It annoys me when I look at Sven Goran Eriksson's tenancy and see the armband being handed around in friendly games like a relay baton. He once had three captains in one game. And had I been manager at St James's Park when Kieron Dyer picked the captain's armband up between his index finger and thumb and tossed it at someone, he would never have played for me again.

The captaincy should go to special people, players who deserve it and are respected by their own players, not players who go seeking it for personal glorification. When I became captain I did very little different. I still tried to lead by example, and by voice. There was no special role to fulfil off the pitch, but now I believe the captain should be even more of a conduit between the players and the manager. He should be senior enough to bridge that gap, to be able to speak to both the players and the manager. I like to speak to my players one by one, but everything goes through the captain.

I believe Scott Leitch, my leader at Motherwell, is the best captain in Scotland. I have no doubt about it. He was named Community Player of the Year in recognition of all the functions he attends and organises for the local community. Anything happens and he is always the one to organise flowers, hospital visits and gifts. He tells me how the players are feeling and whether or not they are tired. It should all be geared around creating the best possible circumstances for winning matches, because that's what football clubs are all about. You can have an excellent commercial department, but if the team is at the bottom of the table and no one is watching, how can they operate? Everyone wants to watch a winning team, and a winning team usually has a good captain.

CHAPTER NINE

SURVIVAL

I had to wear plaster casts with hinges on either side of my knee. It was a prototype for the modern braces which are used now, and which are wonderful. My son Chris suffered a medial ligament injury to his knee while playing American football. He was hit by a helmet on the side of his knee but completed two more plays before realizing how bad the injury was. He had it stapled back and was playing again inside a year. Nothing so grand for me, even though it was a much less serious injury and I was fit and ready to start the 1984/85 season. This time there were no more problems, and I played in every League match until the last game against West Ham, by which time we were safe after another desperate season. We started with four successive draws, against West Ham, Luton, Manchester United and Everton, and then had a horrendous run: from October until the end of the year we lost nine out of eleven League matches. From then until April, we struggled in the bottom three.

The light relief in a grim season, made even grimmer by the horrific incident at the Heysel Stadium in Belgium and the fire at Bradford, came in the Cup competitions, and the League Cup in particular. We began with a routine two-legged win over Derby County, and then beat Newcastle 2–1 at St James's Park after drawing at home. Paul Gascoigne and Chris Waddle were playing for their hometown club in those days, but it was before the big revival under Kevin Keegan. This was Newcastle under Jack Charlton, and still with the old stands. We had been underdogs for the replay because a couple of weeks earlier we had been thrashed there, Gazza and Waddle playing out of their skins. They really fancied themselves again, but we surprised them by playing far better on the day.

By the end of the year we were beginning to fancy ourselves a bit for the trophy after beating Oxford at home and then drawing QPR at Portman Road. We believed we were on a run, but we could only draw and had to go to London to play on the dreaded astroturf surface. Few teams had won on this bumpy, lumpy prototype, but once again we rose to the challenge and came through 2–1, even though Russell Osman and Simon Stainrod were sent off in the first half, reducing both teams to ten men.

For the two-legged semi-finals, we drew Norwich City. Ah! we thought, a chance for revenge after important defeats in successive seasons, though the Canaries had a fair side, with Chris Woods in goal, Steve Bruce and Dave Watson in the central defensive positions, and Micky Channon up front. Bad weather messed up the fixtures but we eventually played the first leg at home on a Saturday at the end of February, and won 1–0. We had plenty of opportunities to put it out of their reach but it was still wide open when we went to Norwich a fortnight later. Someone – not me, I hasten to add – had burned down their main stand so we had to change in Portakabins which were placed one above the other. Ours was on top.

My mate Russell had been in and out of the team and he and Ferguson had had a few words, so he was missing for the game. Ian Cranson partnered me in the middle at the back. Ian was known as 'Bull Neck', for obvious reasons. He had no neck at all, really, and could head the ball a mile. He was strong and quite quick, but not as good on the ball as Russell. Truthfully, he wasn't anywhere near as good a player as Russell. I felt Russell could have done a job for us on the day as a defensive midfielder, but he was left out, despite us having a number of injury problems. We struggled. Norwich were very strong and very physical, got stuck in and badly wanted to win. They scored early to set up the game, and five minutes from the end Steve Bruce struck to secure their place in the final at Wembley.

I was unbelievably sick. In the Cup competitions against Norwich we were a disaster. Mr Hyde emerged as we trudged back to our temporary changing rooms. I was one of the last to go in, and rather than push the door open with my hand I gave it a big boot and my foot went straight through the plywood panel. It closed behind me, and a few minutes later Bobby Ferguson came in, saw the damage, and demanded to know who had done it. Everyone stayed silent, but I was sitting there with a piece of plywood sticking out of the end of my boot. A dead giveaway. He looked at it and said, 'I take it that it was you, Butcher?' I could do little else but own up. By then we could hear the Norwich players going bananas after reaching their first final, and the black mood swept over everyone. Norwich went on to win the trophy, beating Sunderland in the final and, they thought, earning a place in Europe for 1985/86. But little did they know then of the dreadful events that were to happen at the Heysel Stadium which destroyed their dream of Europe, along with every other English club, as a result of the blanket ban imposed by UEFA.

In the spring of 1985, however, those grim events were still to unfold, and we still had to go to Norwich in the League in early April. The story of the door had come out in the press by then and my dislike of our neighbours was well known. They even invited me into their trophy room to inspect the cup they had won. Not only did I decline, I also scored one of my two goals of the season as we won 2–0. I wasn't punished, and I certainly did not apologise. I have said sorry for other doors I have smashed, but not this one.

The FA Cup also provided us with a fairly decent run to the quarter-finals. We beat Bristol Rovers, Gillingham and Sheffield Wednesday before drawing the team of the season, Everton. What a good side they had then. They won the First Division title that season and were only stopped from doing the double at the very last hurdle when Manchester United beat them 1–0 at Wembley. They were bristling with good players, from goalkeeper Neville Southall through Derek Mountfield, Kevin Ratcliffe, Gary Stevens, Paul Bracewell, Trevor Steven, Peter Reid, Adrian Heath, Kevin Sheedy, Andy Gray and Graeme Sharp. We did well to draw with them at Goodison Park, just three days after Norwich dumped us out of the League Cup, after taking the lead when I flicked the ball on. It was a real battle as I was marking the rugged Andy Gray, and I wasn't terribly popular with the locals. It was a sometimes brutal conflict as we both gave as good as we got. Once, when chasing a through-ball, I realised he was going to get there first so I decided to take a booking and dumped him in the first row of the stand, missing the ball completely. I took my caution and a couple of elbows in retribution. Andy was a tough player to mark, and a good player as well. He always threatened as he jumped with his arms up to protect himself. But I enjoyed playing against him because it was a good challenge, referees letting us both get away with a lot more than we would now. I don't think modern centre-backs would have stood for it; Andy would have terrorised them – if referees had allowed him to stay on the field, that is. Interpretation has changed so much in such a short space of time. Our left-back Steve McCall received a more than dubious red card in that game, which broke an appearance record stretching right back to February 1981 – some 166 consecutive League appearances. I suppose it was just that sort of season for Ipswich.

We took Everton back to our place on a snowy night. The conditions were such I doubt the game would have been played now, but it turned out to be a good and exciting match. Eventually it was won with a penalty when the ball bounced up off the icy surface and hit Russell Osman, who had come on as a substitute, on the arm. It was a cruel decision. Sharp put the penalty past Paul Cooper and we were out. That left us battling for League survival only. Our revival began in earnest in early April when we won three in succession against WBA, Forest and Norwich. In the last eight games of the season we lost only twice to scramble to safety in seventeenth position, but it was a close-run thing and a serious pointer to our problems, which were not going to go away.

On the international front things were considerably more promising. We were playing for a place in the World Cup finals in Mexico, and we began the campaign at Wembley on 12 September with a friendly against East Germany, winning the game with a late goal, not from our regular strikers Mariner and Woodcock, nor their replacements, the Italian-based pairing of Francis and Hateley, but with a spectacular overhead volley from skipper Bryan Robson. It was his tenth goal for his country. Our first World Cup qualifier came a month later. October was often a month that brought strange results in our international calendar, but not this time as we threatened to overwhelm Finland. Hateley scored twice with Woodcock, Robson and Mark Chamberlain adding the others.

The next match in qualification was Turkey in Istanbul on 14 November. Turkey had not only never beaten us, they had never even scored against England. This, they fancied, was their chance. How different football was in those days. Despite the presence of the usual English hooligans we went to the bazaar in Istanbul after training on the Tuesday afternoon. Can you imagine that happening now? I bought a cheap sheepskin coat for Christopher and was served a cup of tea as we negotiated the price. It was all very civilised. We were staying in the Hilton on a hill overlooking the ground, and when we woke up on the Wednesday morning the ground was already full and seemed to be bouncing up and down, the fans jumping and chanting. It was an awesome sight so early in the day and so long before the afternoon kick-off.

We emerged from the tunnel to a shower of flares and a cacophony of noise. The crowd were really at us; they clearly thought this was to be their day as we had lost both Paul Mariner and Mark Hateley with injuries before the match. Understandably, perhaps, we made a nervous start, but so did they. Then the ball was played to their centre-forward just inside our half. I tracked him and growled a little as he took the ball back into his own half. He hesitated long enough for me to get a foot in, and I poked the ball through to Tony Woodcock. We poured forward, and Bryan Robson got on the end of the cross, as he usually did, to put us ahead after just fourteen minutes. The goal settled us down, quietened the crowd, and made the Turkish team even more nervous. We proceeded to swamp them, skipper Robson going on to score a hat-trick; Woodcock and John Barnes added two apiece and full-back Viv Anderson scored his first goal for England near the end. The crowd turned completely on the Turks and cheered us instead, and we left the pitch to a standing ovation. Quite bizarre, but it was a great win and it took us to the top of the table.

We went on to beat Northern Ireland in Belfast on a very wet Windsor Park pitch to solidify our first-place spot. The game took place in February 1985, and the Irish Troubles were very much alive. One of our Ipswich players, Kevin Wilson, was walking around the ground with Jimmy Nicholl before the game when there was an enormous bang. 'Jocky' Wilson nearly jumped out of his skin and said to Jimmy, 'What the hell was that?' Jimmy rubbed his chin and thought for a moment before answering, 'Sounded like a thirty-pounder to me.' It was a nervous night all round, especially when the stadium was cleared, mainly of English journalists filing their copy to London, when there was another bomb threat. Out in the car park, the waiting journalists watched in amazement as two inebriated locals tried to manoeuvre a cardboard box into the driver's seat of their car and then both got in the back. It took them several goes to get it right, but eventually the car wobbled off down the road. It helped to relieve the tension that had inevitably built up among the journalists.

In May it was Romania in Bucharest and Finland in Helsinki, two crucial away games in our bid to clinch a place in Mexico. Before we met them the FA arranged a fixture against the Republic of Ireland at Wembley. We won our fifth successive international and conceded our first goal in nine hours of international football with a very inexperienced side. Goalkeeper Gary Bailey, Chris Waddle and Peter Davenport made their debuts, while Trevor Steven and Gary Lineker were making only their second international appearances. I had a hand in our opening goal as Hateley nudged on my pass for Steven to score. Lineker added the second before Liam Brady scored a consolation goal. It was a good run-out for us and an excellent result, especially in view of injuries to both Robson and Hateley.

This brought us to our critical game in Romania, played on May Day in the August 23rd Stadium. It was a dour battle in what was then a bleak country in front of 70,000 excited fans consisting mainly of men from the Romanian army. Peter Shilton, winning his 68th cap, had an outstanding game, as did our entire defence, and we came away with yet another clean sheet and a precious draw. It might have been maximum points but for Paul Mariner just failing to take a sharp chance at the end.

When I returned to Ipswich after this match I received a call from a Belgian agent to tell me there was an Italian club very interested in me. What sort of money was I looking for? You have to be very wary in circumstances such as these, particularly on the telephone. It could be a newspaper looking for a line, or another club testing out the water. I simply told him I was contracted to Ipswich, and gave him Bobby Ferguson's number. I never heard another word, and to this day I don't know if it was a wind-up. Ferguson certainly never mentioned it to me, so I don't know if he knocked them back. It was certainly a nice, morale-boosting call as far as I was concerned. Probably a wrong response considering today's values, but not then for a country boy.

England were well on track for a place in the finals, and we expected to beat Finland comfortably again, even on the bumpy pitch at the Olympic Stadium in Helsinki. But you can never take anything for granted. We went a goal down and needed an equaliser from Mark Hateley in the second half to come away with a point. We were disappointed, but it was a difficult game on a bad pitch against a strong, physical side. At least we'd stretched our unbeaten run to eight games, though that came to an end three days later against, of all teams, Scotland at Hampden. Richard Gough scored the only goal – the only time I was ever on a losing side against the Scots. I remember going back through the airport and all the baggage handlers grinning at us and taking the mickey.

We left for Mexico for acclimatisation training and matches soon afterwards. We were put in the Camino Real, a hotel FIFA took over the following year for the World Cup. It was a super place to stay, and as a little bonus it had a bar with several yard-of-ale glasses. This was different to the Australia trip two years earlier as we were to be eased in with a day off after arriving. Among other places, we went to the Reforma Club, which was the home of the Mexico City Cricket Club. I'm always amazed by how many countries around the world have a cricket club tucked away somewhere or another. And after the initial day off, we would have only a gentle training session. The reason for this was not only the long flight, but also the 7,000-foot altitude and the high temperatures – something we were going to have to put up with if we qualified as expected.

On that day off, we decided we would meet up in the hotel bar and each have a crack at the yard of ale. It began to get into a bit of a session, and afterwards a number of us moved into the nightclub within the hotel. It was very dark inside and the tables were sunken. It was almost a 100 per cent turn-out by the players and it turned into a really good night with some of the boys performing on the stage as the evening ran into the early hours of the next day. Unbeknown to us, we had been spotted and reported to the manager. Although it was officially a day off, we weren't meant to go out on the razzle. Nothing was said until we went training the next morning, and suddenly we were put through a twelve-minute run instead of a jog. Robson told us, 'If you lot want to go out and get pissed and abuse your bodies, you will pay for it. I saw you in the nightclub, I saw what you were up to, and now you are going to run, you bastards.' It was page one of the coaching manual, and we were all timed for future reference. I remember Trevor Francis trudging around because he hated long runs. It was just a case of getting it done and sweating out what we had drunk the night before. But there were others, like Bryan Robson, who, despite how much he had had to drink, always breezed the run. It felt good to be sober again, and it brought us together, so no harm was done.

The next day we were due to meet up to watch the European Cup Final from the Heysel Stadium between Liverpool and Juventus. We were numbed and shocked by what we heard and saw. We watched the game (Juventus won 1–0) but I couldn't understand how they could have played under such tragic circumstances. I'm not sure I could have done so. I guess they had to go ahead with it because of the danger of more trouble if they didn't.

The effect on everyone was enormous, especially as our first game was against, of all teams, Italy. Immediate diplomatic channels were opened up, and the senior FA officials who had just flown out were ordered to turn round and fly back to meet angry government officials. We didn't realise the ramifications straight away, but they were brought home to us when we were told to attend a memorial service at midday a couple of days later, the day before the game. It was held at the Italian headquarters, and we dressed up in our official England suits on an extremely hot day. Chris Woods was desperate to be excused, or to be allowed to wear his tracksuit, as his trousers looked as though they'd had an argument with his shoes. But on this occasion there was to be no excuse. He attended, and he wore his suit. If the suits had been smart it would have been fine, but what made it worse was the Italians attended in their tracksuits. There was a distinct lack of communication between the two countries, and we roasted in the hot noon sun.

The service was very difficult, but not as difficult as the match. We were warned in no uncertain terms about our behaviour during the game – positively no fouling and nothing to create problems. The Aztec Stadium, where they were to stage the finals, was a mess. The dressing rooms were awful, there were builders still working on it, and it was hardly recognisable from the stadium we played in a year later. We wore black armbands, though goodness knows where they got them. We wore them over our very tight Umbro aertex shirts, and as we sweated the black dye came out. We looked a rag, tag and bobtail lot by the finish. The Italians had clearly received different instructions from us and got stuck in with an aggressive will. The Mexican supporters in the small crowd were strongly on the Italians' side. A rare mistake by Peter Shilton allowed Bagni's centre to drift into the net late in the game, but we came back to equalise when Hateley headed home Barnes's centre. A 1–1 draw would have been fine, a diplomatic result that would have begun the healing process, but the Mexican referee allowed himself to be conned when Vierchowod dived in the penalty area. Altobelli scored from the penalty spot.

I didn't play in the next game, against Mexico, where, obviously, a larger crowd was again anti-English, as was the referee, the highly rated German Volker Roth, who gave us very little and controversially disallowed a Viv Anderson header which would have given us a 1–1 draw. Again it was not to be, and we lost our third game in a row – the first time that had happened since 1959.

The final game was against West Germany, who had taken a gamble in flying in just before the game in an experiment to combat jet lag and/or altitude. It backfired on them. We were in determined mood as the criticism of Bobby Robson and the team had grown apace with the results. English football stank on and off the pitch. We were fully acclimatised against a German team that had arrived just 48 hours earlier, and it showed. We took the lead for the first time in half a dozen games through Bryan Robson, and any mental doubts we may have harboured disappeared when Peter Shilton saved Brehme's penalty after a fairly obvious foul by Mark Wright on Rahn. As they tired, we took over. I amazingly laid on the second for Kerry Dixon, who also scored the third with a good header from Barnes's cross from the left. I was a bit cross with Kerry as I had run from the halfway line, beaten Augenthaler and taken the ball past goalkeeper Schumacher, only to have Dixon take the ball off my toe, put it into the empty net and run up the field celebrating, leaving me with just an assist and alone in the opponent's penalty area.

On the way back from Mexico we called in at Los Angeles where we played the USA in a friendly. We stayed on Sunset Avenue, Viv Anderson and I rooming together. One of the disappointments was while we were training some of the players' rooms were broken into and a lot of money stolen. On the day in question, Viv and I were on our way to our room in the lift when a small black man got in with us. He was wearing very pointed boots, and as Viv looked from his boots to his face he asked him if he was Little Richard. The man shook his head and introduced himself – singer James Brown. Viv knew he was famous but had got the wrong guy. It was very embarrassing, but my memory was of how small he looked next to Viv and me. He must have felt as I had done in 1983 when I got in a lift with some All Blacks in Australia. Some, did I say? Only three of us could get in the lift. These guys dwarfed even me.

We won the game very comfortably in front of a very ethnic audience, our new strike force of Dixon and Lineker scoring a couple each and Trevor Steven adding the fifth. We even had the luxury of a Glenn Hoddle penalty being saved by goalkeeper Mausser. It was very much an end-of-season holiday romp, and once we were sure of winning a few of the boys were involved in a little side game, playing the ball out towards the photographers on the touchline. Instead of being behind the goals, as they are in England, they were ranged down the touchline, and the majority, unlike our own snappers, were very attractive young ladies. The boys were kicking it out to have a closer look at another of the girls who had been pointed out. There must have been a record number of throw-ins that day.

Talking of girls, Viv and I ended up in Tramp one night where we met a lot of expatriates. One of them had a huge 'pimpmobile' which he allowed me to drive around LA. All I can say is it's a good job I wasn't stopped by the police. I had drunk so much I could still be there now. On the same trip Viv and I went present shopping. We visited a lingerie shop, but feeling embarrassed we asked this helpful young lady to assist us in finding gifts for our wives. She did no more than call up a couple of models while we sat and watched this remarkable display of the flimsiest underwear. We made our purchases and left feeling a lot better for the experience.

As did the whole England squad as we left for home. This trip was to prove a valuable asset in Mexico a year later, even though it had been marred by the Heysel tragedy, which was to leave a scar across English football at both club and international level.

CHAPTER TEN

THROUGH THE TRAP DOOR

The 1985/86 season began badly and finished even worse as far as Ipswich were concerned. I couldn't start the season because I tore the cartilage in my right knee in a pre-season friendly against Notts County at Meadow Lane. I went to charge down a cross and as I blocked it with my right leg the ball hit my toes. My foot moved but the knee stayed where it was, with the inevitable consequence.

What was thought to be a straightforward cartilage operation turned out to be a nightmare. First of all I had a bad reaction to the anaesthetic, then I overdid it with the rehabilitation. I started with hard workouts in the gym, with the result that I did more damage to the knee. There was internal bleeding, and the blood tracked down into my calf, which expanded to a size greater than my thigh. Normally when you push a finger into a calf any indentation immediately comes straight out, but this time it didn't – a clear indication of blood clotting. The result was another operation to clear out all the residue.

I made it back into the team for the game against West Bromwich Albion at the Hawthorns on 7 September. It was only our second win of the season in six games, and we were already struggling near the foot of the table. Then I suffered a second setback and was out for a further two months. After the West Brom game I was due to meet up with England; I had to telephone Bobby Robson and tell him to forget about me for a while. So I missed the start of the season for both Ipswich and England in what was, whichever way you looked at it, a crucial one on both fronts.

I eventually came back from my two operations against Everton in the middle of November. It was a hell of a game, and we lost 4–3. I scored, but it was Trevor Steven who got the winner after we had staged a tremendous second-half fightback to level at 3–3. Incredibly, we also lost the next game 4–3, to Oxford at the Manor Ground. We were three goals up kicking down their famous, or should it be infamous, slope. But Oxford staged an alarming comeback, John Aldridge, soon to go to Liverpool, scoring a seven-minute hat-trick. It was a real six-pointer because we were both down near the bottom, and it was a result that was eventually to save them and send us down. It was that tight. I remember seeing Bobby Ferguson walk off to the dressing room when Slatter put their fourth goal in. I was completely helpless as the right-back's crossing to Aldridge on the far post consistently bypassed my near-post position. I felt I should have possibly changed position and maybe gone man-for-man on the striker.

We lost thirteen matches by a goal to nil during the season and scored only 32 times. In fact, in our 42 League games we failed to find the net in nearly half of the matches. We were tight at the back, but if we conceded a goal it seemed to be all over. We won back-to-back matches in the League only once all season. Some more of our top players left – Gates, Burley and Osman – and I was constantly being linked with a move to Manchester United, regularly encouraged, I have to say, by my Old Trafford-based England colleagues.

I had become a bit of a goalscorer. As well as League goals against Everton, Nottingham Forest, WBA and Oxford, I also scored two in the League Cup in a 6–1 win over Swindon. My winner against West Brom was from fully 45 yards. Some who played in or watched that match will dispute it, but I am sticking by it. It was a right-foot shot I struck following a throw-in received just inside the West Brom half and it somehow flew into the top right-hand corner, beating goalkeeper Stuart Naylor all the way. When I scored against Oxford late in April, in a game we won 3–2, I thought it might yet save us from relegation. It was another right-foot shot, this time a volley I smashed as hard as I could. No rocket science. I had cut my forehead in the game and had one of those bandages wrapped around my head. It was to become my trademark.

Our two remaining games after the Oxford win were away from home, though, the first at West Ham, who were chasing the title that season, and the final one at Sheffield Wednesday, who were also in the top half of the table. We were in with a chance against the Hammers when Kevin Wilson scored, but then, with ten minutes to go, Alan Dickens toe-poked one in from the edge of the box. I have never seen a toe-poke bend, but this one curved round Paul Cooper. Game on. In a frantic finish, little Mark Ward went into the box, a challenge came in from Steve McCall, and Gerald Ashby gave the penalty. Ray Stewart didn't miss many, and he didn't this time. I went berserk. To my mind it was a dive, and with so much on the game I couldn't believe it when the referee gave it.

Mr Hyde reappeared as we walked into the tunnel. The referee's room was on the left and the dressing rooms to the right. I went for Ashby, and had I reached him I would have been banned for life. A policeman with lots of scrambled egg on his hat and arms, along with several stewards and Bobby Ferguson, held me back. I still had my head free and I was trying to head-butt him from a few yards away. I had lost it completely. Ipswich staying up meant so much to me. I was eventually pushed away by the policeman, but when I returned to the dressing room I was so angry I put my foot through the wall right up to my thigh and couldn't extract it. My leg was trapped. I looked a bit like Harry Worth, the comedian who used to introduce himself by raising one leg at the angle of a shop window. I was shouting and cursing, but incredibly, the referee didn't report me. When I calmed down I spoke to West Ham manager John Lyall and offered to pay for the damage. He was terrific and replied, 'It's great to see someone who cares so much about his club. So don't worry about it.' It was a fine response from a gentleman, someone who understood how I felt.

We stayed overnight in Sheffield on the Friday to give ourselves every chance in our final game. We played very well on the day, but lost to a goal from Brian Marwood after Carl Shutt had beaten me for pace down the flank. Paul Hart was the Wednesday centre-half, and he said afterwards how well we had played and how we deserved to stay up. Small consolation. Oxford had lost to Nottingham Forest on the final Saturday, but they still had one game to play against Arsenal, whose season was over. We returned to Ipswich that Saturday. It was an awful weekend, then on the Monday Jim Rosenthal, the sports commentator and a good friend, came round for lunch. He was an Oxford fan. We didn't listen to the Oxford game, just had a good chat and a few glasses of wine and tuned in for the result. They won 3–0, and we were down. I wonder how many Norwich players drank a bottle of champagne that day, because the season before, when they were relegated, I certainly drank champagne to celebrate. This was payback time. When I realised we were finally and definitely down, I was numb, completely numb. It's a horrible feeling, a feeling of intense failure. Even the cup competitions had left no lasting memory: we were trounced at Anfield by Liverpool in the League Cup, then went out of the FA Cup to West Ham in a second replay after extra time.

The day after the season finished I went into the ground to see Bobby Ferguson to talk about my future. We sat in his office and I just cried. I couldn't stop. I had already signed a new contract the previous season and I wanted to stay at Portman Road, despite the interest from Manchester United passed on to me via the players in the England team. Bobby generously said that I needed to move on to further my career, and from the club's point of view they had to let it happen so they could make the final payment for the Pioneer Stand. He then told me to put all thoughts about the following season to the back of my mind and concentrate on the World Cup, promising that the club would keep an eye on the transfer situation.

I was no longer an Ipswich player come the start of the 1986/87 season. It was a sad way to go, but probably the only way I was going to go. It was just a nightmare how we had gone down and down since Bobby Robson's departure.

CHAPTER ELEVEN

NEARLY IMMORTAL

Because of my cartilage injury I had missed the remaining World Cup qualifying games in autumn 1985. The Romanians were ecstatic with their draw at Wembley because Northern Ireland's draw in Izmir before our game kicked off left them in prime position to join us in Mexico. But then Northern Ireland, with the veteran Pat Jennings in superlative form, beat Romania in Bucharest while England beat Turkey, this time 5–0. Jennings, now turned 40, gave another inspired display to keep England at bay in the game at Wembley. It was lucky 13 (November) for both teams as the point apiece was enough to carry both of us through. Any thoughts of an arranged result, suggested by the disappointed Romanians, were swept away by Jennings' solo performance.

I also missed the 4–0 friendly victory over Egypt in Cairo in January, but was back at last to bid for my place in Mexico for the game against Israel at the Ramat Gan Stadium in late February. I roomed at the Tel Aviv Hilton with my fellow central defender Alvin Martin, the Scouser who played for the Hammers. The two of us wandered down to the square for a couple of beers, as you do, but there was nothing excessive this time. No one had played a lot of football at home because the deep freeze in England wiped out so many games, and sure enough I was caught upfield for a corner when they broke and scored through Ohana to go one up. It was hard to break the Israelis down after that and we looked set to be on the wrong end of a shock result until Bryan Robson popped up with a couple of goals, the second from a late penalty after his shot had been tipped away by the Israeli captain who, unfortunately for him, was not the goalkeeper.

Our next warm-up game was another remarkable trip, this time to Tbilisi where we played the USSR, a side that had not been beaten at home for eighteen matches and hadn't conceded a goal, again at home, since 1979. Things began badly before the trip when we lost Bryan Robson to injury; then, at the airport, we discovered Peter Shilton did not have his passport with him. But what a great performance we put in, winning 1–0, Chris Waddle keeping the ball on the right flank when anyone else might have given it up and then whipping a pass into his former Newcastle team-mate Peter Beardsley. The ungainly-looking Waddle then sprinted forward to take the return, and he belted it past goalkeeper Dasaev. It was a phenomenal goal and a well-deserved victory, especially with the Bulgarian referee favouring the home side so strongly. He turned down a stonewall penalty when Gary Lineker was tripped but awarded Russia a penalty when Gotsmanov 'fell over' Viv Anderson's leg. Chivadze missed from the spot.

After the game we discovered, thanks to some advice from a journalist friend, our hotel had a rather excellent little bar-cum-nightclub in the basement. We drank little green cans of Heineken, stacking them on the table as we drained them. You can imagine how many there were with a team of thirsty footballers celebrating a remarkable victory. We had constructed a huge tower of cans and, as usual, I had my back to the door when suddenly the players vanished like the Red Arrows. Once again I felt the hand of Bobby Robson on my shoulder.

'Butcher,' he said, 'have you drunk all these cans? I *knew* it would be you down here!'

I told him I had been with the lads and we had all enjoyed a drink to celebrate our performance.

'Where are they now?'

'They've all gone to bed,' I lied.

'I'm sure they have,' said Bobby. 'Now, get to *your* bed.'

We had been drinking with a couple of the Russian players, including sweeper Bessanov, and I ended up buying half a bottle of whisky which we took up to his room along with a few of the England team who had regrouped once the manager disappeared. He could speak little English and I, of course, didn't understand a word of Russian, so everything was done with signs and smiles. We ended up on his balcony with our glasses full and the radio blaring out Frank Sinatra's 'New York, New York'. Remarkably, Bessanov knew all the words, and we stood there, arms draped over each other's shoulders and a glass of whisky in hand, singing for all we were worth. It was a fantastic experience, but I was like death on the flight back to Luton. Terrific memories, though, and a great performance, on and off the pitch. By a strange coincidence, two years later I was playing for Rangers in Kiev in the first-round away leg of the European Cup, and there was my mate Bessanov. We were warming up when we saw each other. We met in the centre circle, threw our arms round each other and burst into a duet – 'New York, New York' again. Everyone, including our team-mates, the referee and the crowd, thought we were totally crazy. To me it was a special moment. Was it the language of football, or whisky?

Scotland were next on the agenda, in April, before our departure to America and Mexico. The Home Championship competition had now become the Rous Cup and was as fierce as ever, especially with the Jocks on an eight-match unbeaten run. It was an enjoyable physical battle against Graeme Souness and his team, and I was overjoyed to head the first goal after a Glenn Hoddle free-kick had been blocked. Hoddle himself headed the second. I don't know which goal surprised everyone the most, for Glenn didn't score too many with his head. But I was not so pleased when I conceded a penalty by bringing down Graeme Souness. Souness, who was soon to become my manager, stepped up himself and scored from the spot. I was relieved when the final whistle went.

Trevor Francis played that game with a broken cheekbone, desperate to prove himself for the World Cup squad. He had an excellent game, but he wasn't picked for the final 22. He was furious. He was playing in Italy at the time and had put himself at risk to win a seat on the plane to Mexico. Those that did make the squad were entertained at Westminster before we left, and I shared a car to London from Ipswich with the manager, wriggling about after having a hepatitis jab in my backside.

After that we flew off to our training camp in Colorado Springs and the superb Broadmoor Hotel with its man-made lake, two championship golf courses and an ice-skating rink, to mention just a few of its facilities. We had the luxury of flying ambassador class, which made a huge difference from the usual tight-fitting economy section. When we arrived at St Louis airport we all picked up our own suitcases and the individual bags of leisurewear and tracksuits from Umbro, and boarded the bus. Bobby Robson waited by the carousel and saw there were still two bags going round and round.

'Whose are these?' he called out. 'I bet I can guess.'

But I had mine. Eventually he looked at the labels and read out the names Trevor Steven and Peter Reid.

'It's the same old people every time,' Bobby snapped. 'Reid and Steven, where are they?'

We had to remind Bobby that they were both playing in the FA Cup Final at Wembley and were flying out to join us on the Sunday.

I was rooming again with Viv, or Janvion as he was called, after the French full-back. (Viv called me Lofty – original!) We loved the Broadmoor, and it was a great place to relax before a World Cup, but we were rather surprised when, while posing for photographs for the lovable Monte Fresco, we were caught in, of all things, a snowstorm. The sky went black and down it came. I knew it was a ski resort in the winter, but I was astonished to see the white stuff in May.

After a great lunch, we went to the Air Force Academy in the mountains for a swim and sauna. Several of us jumped off the twelve-metre diving board. I must admit when I reached the top I changed my mind, but there was no way down other than into the water. Air Force personnel had to make the same jump, but wearing all their working clothes. We played the Academy team in a warm-up and beat them 11–0, even me getting on the scoresheet with a little header. We also played South Korea and won that 4–1. Tests followed, to ensure we were acclimatizing properly, and they were quite hard. The best of the group was Chris Waddle, who sloped along with stooped shoulders and a permanent haggard look. I was struggling, along with a few others. It felt as though someone had stuck a knife in my windpipe. My pulse rate came down afterwards but I felt very drained. Still, it was a wonderful place to train with great facilities. The sauna was especially useful in helping us to acclimatise.

Before one of those training mornings at the Academy, Bobby Robson left his boots in the hotel. Glenn Hoddle took the same size so he offered the manager a new pair of his to wear. It was a two-hour session, and afterwards Bobby hobbled to the bus and told Glenn he must be mistaken: the boots he had loaned him were more like a six than a nine. Bobby advised him to send them back, but when Glenn looked inside the boots he noticed that Bobby had left the packing paper in the toecaps.

We could feel ourselves becoming fitter and fitter. In mid-May we flew down to Los Angeles to play World Cup hosts Mexico and stayed in a Holiday Inn in downtown LA, one of the worst areas, close to the Coliseum. I am sure we heard some shootings, and certainly there were lots of police sirens at night. We were told not to leave the hotel. Having been there the year before, we were ready both for the high temperatures and a Mexico team playing in front of a lot of their fans. There were an estimated two million Mexicans in LA at the time, and Mexico, playing their eighteenth game in the City of Angels, attracted 63,770 of them, even though the LA Dodgers were playing New York Mets in the National Baseball League the same night. It was a good test because Mexico were the last team to beat us, eleven months earlier and ten matches ago. Mark Hateley scored twice and Peter Beardsley recorded his first goal for his country as we ran out surprisingly comfortable winners. When they attacked they found Shilton in great form again; one save, against Francisco Cruz in the second half, was truly world-class. It was an interesting surface, and though we didn't have the distraction of so many lady photographers this time, we did notice the long jump run-up was just inside the touchline. It was a solid astroturf track just a yard inside the pitch. It was all very dangerous, and not something FIFA or UEFA would ever have allowed in Europe.

Game played, we were back to our base to meet and greet the wives, who had been flown over by the FA. From that point on we would train in the morning and then go out shopping or to the cinemas with our partners in the afternoon. It was all very civilised, and sensible. When we went for a drink in Colorado we were surprised when we were asked for ID cards, and those who didn't have them weren't served. Chris Woods, about 25 then, was constantly turned away and had to start carrying his passport with him wherever he went just so he could have a drink. But it was a wonderful experience, so relaxing, and perfect preparation for the World Cup. It was also good to have Rita with me.

When the girls went home we immediately departed for Canada for another warm-up game in Vancouver, before flying on to our Mexican base in Monterrey. We won our sixth successive game, played in the morning like a youth game for the convenience of television, but it wasn't a thrilling performance. We were probably still thinking about our wives' departure. Mark Hateley kept our run going to eleven unbeaten when he scored on the hour, but the big blow came when Gary Lineker fell awkwardly and damaged his wrist, prompting fears he would miss the finals. Fortunately, it was diagnosed as a severe sprain rather than a

fracture, and there were hopes he would be ready in time for our first
World Cup game against Portugal some ten days later.

After the game we went back for a late lunch, then a group of us
decided to go out to the World Expo Fair. I met up with an old Ipswich
friend of mine, Frank Yallop, a Canadian international who had played
right-back at Portman Road and who now lived in Vancouver. He is a
great lad, and he took me, Viv Anderson, Terry Fenwick and a couple of
others to show us around, but on the way we decided we needed a little
refreshment. We spotted a German *bierkeller* and found a good table with
our steins. There was plenty of music and people there from all over the
world. It was great fun. After a couple of hours of this we decided the
Expo called, but on the way there we spotted another German *bierkeller*,
so off we went again. This time we ended up on the tables singing the
'Birdie Song' and the traditional 'Oom-pah-pah'. We never did get to see
the Expo. In fact, we only just arrived back at the team hotel in time to
pack quickly and jump on the bus for the airport. Five minutes before the
bus was due to depart we suddenly realised we were without two of our
number, Bryan Robson and Ray Wilkins – again! Luckily, with seconds to
go they arrived in a taxi. Their bags had been packed for them and they
were able to jump straight on the bus. Of course it was bad behaviour,
stupid, especially compared to today's careful preparation, and had a
few of us been breathalysed on the bus I doubt whether they would have
bothered taking us to Mexico. But it was how we prepared in those days,
and the one thing it gave us was a great spirit.

I slept most of the way and can remember very little about the flight,
except for two incidents. We had to turn back just before take-off because
a sales rep on the flight looked out of the window and saw that all his
gear was still on the tarmac. We had so much equipment with us there
wasn't room for everyone's luggage. He got off to reclaim his bags and
we left without him. Then, when all I wanted to do was sleep, a couple of
hours later we suddenly dived dramatically and landed at Tijuana, a
sleepy little airport and a totally unscheduled stop, which had everyone
guessing at the reason. Drugs? The official story, and probably the right
one, was that we needed more fuel because the plane was so heavy. But
we did notice them bringing some extra baggage on board. Why would
they do that if it was an unscheduled stop?

We eventually arrived in Mexico, and a few of us gave interviews to
the local media before going off to our hotel in the back of beyond in

Monterrey. It might have been isolated but it was a great hotel with a lovely swimming pool. BBC and ITV were both there as well as some of the regular press boys who we knew well and were comfortable with.

There was a lot of talk around the squad of players' club movements after the World Cup. The biggest whispers surrounded Graeme Souness, who was off to Glasgow Rangers as player-manager. He wanted to buy in top English players, which ran totally against the grain. We knew a player had signed for Rangers from our squad, but no one knew who it was until I discovered much later that it was Chris Woods. Woods was on to me about moving up, but I was still hoping Manchester United would come in for me. I spoke to Bryan Robson and he said to sit in and hold tight because they definitely wanted me. But one of Graeme Souness's great friends, my co-author Bob Harris, had told me of Rangers' interest in me and another couple of the England squad members. Both Bob and Chris were very persuasive as they highlighted what Souness and the board at Ibrox wanted to achieve, and I have to admit it sounded very exciting. But I still had this hankering for Manchester United. Although they hadn't won the title for a while they were still the glamour side of English football. But then, I had been constantly in touch with Ipswich and Bobby Ferguson, and they reported that nothing was happening on the transfer front.

The seed had been planted. At least it was nice to know I was wanted somewhere. If anything, the seed grew more in Rita's mind. She quite liked the idea, and she ultimately was the one who was for it, even when other clubs in England began showing an interest. She has far more common sense than me and saw it as a great opportunity for the family. Souness was in America at the time with the Scottish team, and I had no doubts about the veracity of either his approach or the people who were telling me about it. But at the time it was really a case of concentrating on the World Cup. And I have to be honest and say I thought Chris was a bit mad to go for it. Was he going to put himself out on a limb? What would happen to his England prospects if he was playing in Scotland?

I had to put it all to one side, for the opening match of England's World Cup was close, against a side everyone expected us to beat, especially in our current unbeaten form. The journey from the hotel was a glorious ride through the Sierra Nevada mountains where they had filmed the Humphrey Bogart film *The Treasure of the Sierra Madre*. It was said there were still bandits up in the hills, but they would have done well to stop us as we had a convoy of police cars plus helicopters every time we made the trip.

We had to attend a function in Monterrey along with the other three teams in our group: Portugal, Poland and Morocco. When we looked around at who we had to play we really fancied our chances. Then, on 3 June, came the Portugal game. Before the match there was a blow when Doc Edwards, a lovely man from Watford, suffered a heart attack. He was one of the most popular men among the backroom staff. But he was really ill and was replaced by Arsenal's Doc Crane, with the ITV doctor, a very pretty lady, stepping in to fill the gap before the Gunners man arrived. We trained at the Monterrey stadium, and I can vividly remember looking around this strange ground with its little privet hedges, only part of it covered. It was weird, nothing like you would imagine a World Cup ground to be.

On the day of the game it was very hot after days of English-style drizzle, and it was a poor match. Lineker had an opportunity when I put through a long ball but he just failed to make contact with a Waddle cross. We began to think it might not be our day when Gary beat goalkeeper Bento only to see Oliveira chase madly back and hack it clear off the line. Then, fifteen minutes from time, with a goalless draw looking inevitable, Diamantino eluded Kenny Sansom and crossed in between me and Terry Fenwick for the unmarked Carlos Manuel to steer the ball past Shilton. I was criticised for not going out to the wide player and closing him down, but I felt with three England defenders in the box and one forward we should have been able to handle it. I was wrong. I was also booked for a tackle on Paulo Futre, so, just as in 1982, I was on a caution from the opening game for a bit of extra baggage.

It was the worst possible start, with no goals and no points. The next day Bobby Robson took us to a monastery on top of the hills, away from the clamour and the press. We were well looked after and able to play tennis, read and generally relax. We had a barbecue lunch and talked about what had gone wrong in the Portugal game. We even had a few beers, but not to excess.

Then it was back to training and preparation for the Morocco game. Morocco had shared a goalless draw with Poland in the first game so we were firmly at the bottom of the heap. The North Africans were underrated, for they proved then, as they have done since, that they produce some very high-quality players. Everyone assumed we would win, and Bobby Robson kept faith in the same team, but disaster followed disaster. There had been a problem with Bryan Robson's right shoulder after an accident in his bedroom in America. During the game, he damaged the injured shoulder while chasing a ball in their penalty area and was replaced by Steve Hodge; then Ray Wilkins was sent off for throwing the ball in the general direction of the Paraguayan referee, earning himself the distinction of being the first Englishman to be dismissed in a World Cup finals. With the temperature in the hundreds we had already been struggling to contain their top forward Bouderbala, but we had just seemed to have settled when we lost Robson and Wilkins. It showed up the inconsistency of the refereeing in the competition – something that was to raise its head in an even more serious matter later in the tournament. It also meant for the first time in English football history we had three captains: Robson had passed the armband to Wilkins, who in turn had had to pass it on to Shilton. (Sven, you are forgiven! Perhaps not.) Even then it wasn't a question of hanging on, and our ten made the running against an unambitious side who were happy to record their second goalless draw, even though they later proved their strength by winning the group.

After the game the England fans turned on us, and quite rightly so. We hadn't played up to the standards we had previously set. With one game to go we were staring elimination in the face having started as one of the favourites.

The bus ride back and the trip up to the monastery the next day weren't very good at all. Then we started to see the English papers from the first game. They were awful, so we knew what was to come after the Morocco game. And we took a lot of stick. The late Emlyn Hughes did nothing to help when in his ghosted column in the *Daily Mirror* he said he was ashamed to be English, which was well over the top. We ended up playing a game of cricket at the monastery where John Barnes and Glenn Hoddle proved themselves to be more than useful bowlers. Ray was distraught as he was banned for two games, and there was major doubt over Robson's participation in the rest of the tournament. We faced the realistic proposition of going home after the third qualifying game. Bobby Robson had given us a list of dates when we could go home, and this was the first date for the aircraft to leave.

The manager announced the side to play Poland on the morning of the game. He used the flip chart, turning over the first page to reveal the team. Until then we had played 4–3–3, but this was a 4–4–2 and it came as a major shock. It was a radical change as Wilkins, Robson, Hateley and Waddle from the previous match were missing; Peter Beardsley was playing up front with Gary Lineker, while Trevor Steven, Peter Reid and Stevie Hodge came into the midfield. We hadn't done any work on the system and the team had never played together. How much of a gamble was it? It looked a major risk on the face of it, but the manager and Don Howe knew their players. The remarkable thing was Bobby remained very upbeat and confident. He always wore his emotions on his sleeve and he could be really downbeat as well as positive. But he was serene and very bright during that team talk, and it was probably the best he had ever given. He was funny without meaning to be, telling us not to worry about the other results, just to concentrate on getting a win against Poland. It made sense, but then he turned over to the next sheet on the flip chart and all the other results and combinations of possible scores were laid out in neat, clear rows. It was just like being in a bookmaker's. Everyone laughed, and it broke the ice.

One of the biggest joys about the Poland game was the privet hedge was a thing of the past as we moved to a different stadium. As we drove to the ground we all knew we could be flying home the next day. It was a question of bayonets fixed and up and at 'em! Judging by the press reports, the whole of England had given up on us. It was backs to the wall, but the manager and the staff were tremendous, as were the players who had been left out, especially Robson and Wilkins. The stadium felt good to us, and as we went in we played Simple Minds singing 'Alive and Kicking', a record I will always associate with that game.

The Poles were a pretty useful team with the dangerous Boniek, the red-haired striker who was popular in Italy, playing up front. They had a couple of chances early on and were certainly up for it. I managed to toe-end a pass back to Shilton who punted it upfield, and from it Lineker scored the first of his three goals. We had great balance to the team, with Hodge on the left and Steven on the right. They played really well, and the whole team performed, with Gary Lineker at his best. He had completed his hat-trick nine minutes before the break and we were able to conserve our strength through the second half with few scares, other than Boniek hitting an upright. We could see by their body language at the break that they were a beaten team, whereas we were in the dressing room, cooling down under cold towels and ready to go over the top again

November, 1987: Rita comforts me after I had broken my left leg against Aberdeen in a challenge with Alex McLeish. [© Bob Thomas Sports Photography]

With Rita and the boys – Alistair, Christopher and Edward. [© Daily Record & Sunday Mail]

Living up to my surname as a young professional.

At the PFA Awards dinner with my Ipswich team-mates. John Wark won the trophy with Frans Thijssen and Paul Mariner second and third.

Outjumping FC Cologne's English striker Tony Woodcock in a UEFA Cup semi-final in April 1981.
[© Bob Thomas Sports Photography]

Larking about with my team-mate and friend Russell Osman in a mask I frequently wore unchallenged through customs control.

Proudly awaiting the singing of the national anthem before the World Cup quarter-final against Argentina in 1986 at the Aztec Stadium in Mexico City. [© Bob Thomas Sports Photography]

Defeat in that game – and the manner of the defeat – was tough to recover from as I sat on the turf after Maradona's solo goal. [© Bob Thomas Sports Photography]

Yes, that really is blood and not red dye! Stockholm, 1989 after the 0-0 draw with Sweden.

They patched me up – not a pretty sight.

TOP: *It was a proud moment to open my hotel for the first time.* [© *Daily Record & Sunday Mail*]

MIDDLE: *Outside the hotel with my family and staff.* [© *Daily Record & Sunday Mail*]

RIGHT: *Cooking up a new career with chef Paul McGurl.* [© *Daily Record & Sunday Mail*]

Let's rock!

Fully armed, and ready for battle! In the Rangers tartan. [© Jim Moyes]

Signing for Graeme Souness at Glasgow Rangers was a very proud moment for me.
[© Glasgow Herald/Evening Times]

As you can see, playing for Rangers gave me some of the most enjoyable years of my career.
At Tannadice in 1990 after clinching the League title.

if necessary. Boniek, in his broken English, sidled up to me during the second half and said, 'Give me just one goal – I need one goal.' My reply was two words, and the second of them was off. A clean sheet meant more to me than a goal to Boniek.

We were through, and we had won back the fans so completely they were loving us again and doing a conga around the terraces. It's not often you know at international level that you have won with 45 minutes still to play. We went straight back to the hotel where the staff went mad and celebrated with us, and we were off to the monastery again the next day. My song memory for the day was 'The Sun Always Shines on TV' by A-ha, and it has become one of my all-time favourites because of the circumstances.

By then we knew we were on our way to Mexico City to play Paraguay, but after our great hotel in Monterrey we were billeted in a dreadful hotel by FIFA on the junction of two highways. To make matters worse, my bed was too small for me. At least we got to train at the Aztec Stadium, which had gone through a complete transformation since our appearances there a year earlier. It was immense and very impressive. Hung high across the pitch was a cable which carried the mobile camera. A typical British footballer's warm-up was to try to hit the camera with the ball. If today's coaches could have seen us they would have gone berserk. The pitch was surprisingly soft, quite heavy, and if there was a divot the groundsmen would come along with a machine to take out the old sod of earth and replace it with a new one. It was such a change from the previous year.

We were still unhappy with our noisy, traffic-polluted hotel though, and we eventually had a word with the gaffer and asked if we could change as we weren't getting the rest we needed. The FA staff moved into action immediately and we moved out near the airport to a Holiday Inn where Italy were based. We saw the Italians and admired their usual smart gear and their laid-back attitude. And we were set to remain there longer than them as they lost the day before we played. While they were there, it was interesting to see the differences between the two countries. The main thing I noticed, inevitably I suppose, was that there was always wine on their dinner table.

It was lovely to wave goodbye to them as we prepared to play Paraguay. We retained much the same team, with Alvin Martin coming in to partner me in place of the suspended Terry Fenwick. They had a sharp striker, Canete, who was more European than South American. He had terrific balance, and before we scored our first goal he might have had two himself when he latched on to Fenwick's headed clearance and forced Peter Shilton into a flying save; then I hopelessly miscued a back-pass to put him in again. I hadn't seen him and I raced back to tackle him and save the situation. I almost had to go off and change my shorts. I was lucky to get out of it, and my unaccustomed speed over the ground was a result of pure fear.

Once we scored we took control of the game. It was Gary Lineker again who slid the ball in from a Steve Hodge pass, but as we got on top so Paraguay became more and more physical. We didn't get a lot of protection from the Syrian referee al-Sharif. They did everything to unsettle us, from spitting to elbows in the throat, and everything in between. Remarkably we were able to keep control, and it was absolutely crucial. The second goal came from a right-wing corner. It reached me on the far post, I controlled the cross on the edge of the box, shot, and the goalkeeper Fernandez saved but spilled it. I like to say it was a world-class save, but in truth it was purely routine and nothing more, but at least when Peter Beardsley tapped in the rebound I could honestly claim an assist in a World Cup goal! Spurs' Gary Stevens, who had come on for the injured Peter Reid, provided the cross for the third, and Lineker scored again.

We were very strong and very powerful in the end. There were a few sore players, but we had survived, and we were now due to face Argentina in the quarter-final. This was a tasty one, with memories of the Malvinas fresh in their memories, as was our last World Cup meeting at Wembley in 1966, when their captain Rattin was sent off. We, of course, talked about Maradona a lot before the game – after all, he was reckoned to be the world's number one player and we all knew he could win a match on his own, such were his talents. But there were other players who could not be ignored, notably for me the man I was down to mark, Valdano, who was a different sort of player, much more of a British type of centre-forward. He went on to become general manager of Real Madrid, but that day he was my direct opponent and I knew I would have my hands full without worrying about Maradona as well. Still, we had to keep an eye on the little Argentinian, slotted in just behind Valdano, and Burruchaga, who made darting runs from midfield. The biggest problem, however, was we were to play at midday in the heat of the Mexican sun. We knew we had to prepare properly, take on plenty of fluids and, in those days, salt tablets – something you wouldn't do now. I also wore sweatbands on my wrists, which I quite liked doing (it seems to have come back into fashion now). Despite all this, we felt we could beat them.

The build-up to the match is something of a blur, because before a game where the stakes are so high you are simply focused on what you have to do, who you have to mark and how you are going to play. There was no over-the-top excitement that morning. All the talking, about how we would take care of Maradona and the rest with the 4–4–2 formation we had retained from the previous two successful games, had been done the day before. The system worked well, for it not only helped us combat opposition strengths, it also gave us a platform from which we could spring forward with our attacking full-backs Gary Stevens and Kenny Sansom. Ray Wilkins was available again after his suspension, but Bobby stayed with Peter Reid, Glenn Hoddle, Steve Hodge and Trevor Steven, who had done well against Poland and Paraguay. We also had the likes of John Barnes, Chris Waddle and Mark Hateley on the bench should we need the attacking options.

The dressing room was quiet before the kick-off, and I was lost in my own thoughts. We were nervous because of the importance of the game to the nation and the prospect of the intense heat and certain dehydration. Noon was a frightening time to play, a real ordeal, because in those days if you went for water during the game you were considered weak – completely the wrong way to regard things, as we discovered in later years. We were playing in white shirts with pale blue shorts and socks – probably the only time England wore the kit.

If I had one major concern on my mind before the kick-off, it was my knee. I had strained the medial ligaments in my left leg against Poland and it felt sore and niggly. It was certainly nothing to keep me out of a game as big as this, but I was aware of it nonetheless. But I was so intent on doing well that even the national anthem, something I am always well up for, also passed in a blur, and before I knew it we were into the first half. That passed by in a flash too, and we came into the dressing room at half-time feeling no one had really played in the first half. The Argentinians probably felt the same. It was bound to take off in the second half, and it did, thought not in the way we wanted.

Maradona broke the ice when he scored his infamous Hand of God goal. Steve Hodge miscued a high ball back towards our goal, and as Peter Shilton went up to catch it Maradona beat him to the punch, literally. I have to hold up my hands and admit I didn't see the punch until I watched it on television afterwards. But I do remember thinking there was no way this little fellow Maradona could have got up so high, above Shilton's raised arms. It was a weird moment. I felt I was on the outside looking in, almost as if I were watching it on television; while my movements were in slow motion, others seemed to be rushing around. Sure enough, Peter Shilton, Terry Fenwick and Glenn Hoddle were rushing past me to complain to the Tunisian referee. We looked towards the bench, and Robson clearly knew what had happened. Since then I have, of course, seen the replay and the handball, but it wasn't until I saw Shilton racing towards the referee slapping his hand repeatedly on his arm while screaming and shouting that I realised it might not be a valid goal. As they were claiming handball, I joined in, without giving it my full commitment. But we were never going to change the decision.

It was a huge blow, because the first goal is always vital, especially in such a big match. It gives the scoring team a massive boost and knocks back the team on the receiving end, not only because they're behind in the match but because they also feel aggrieved. The world's best player had resorted to underhand – or should that be overhand? – tactics to give his team the edge, and then, to make matters worse, he popped up to score the second.

If I never saw that goal again I would be happy, but I live in Scotland where it is shown with great regularity. Indeed, straight after the match Argentina shirt sales rocketed in Scotland. It fills me with complete dread. As much as everyone says it was probably the best World Cup goal ever, it was not nice to be on the receiving end, especially as Maradona is very condescending in the way he speaks about me. He always says I was trying to kick him. Well, I would have kicked him if I'd got the chance. I remember Glenn Hoddle losing possession in the centre circle and Maradona coming at the back four. Peter Reid was breathing fumes, absolutely knackered – that's how dehydration can affect you – and couldn't get to him. Soon the Argentinian had the momentum as he barrelled towards the heart of our defence. Terry Fenwick was first in line, but he had already been booked and couldn't bring him down for the risk of a red card. Then Shilton came out at him while I was trying to get back the way I'd done against Paraguay. As Maradona went past

Peter he came within my line of vision, and I thought 'Gotcha!' I still felt my big legs against his little legs gave me an advantage, but I couldn't see the ball because his body was in the way. I just lunged at where I thought it was. It was so close a number of people thought I had scored an own goal. It was an o.g. I would have gratefully accepted.

Maradona wheeled off to the corner flag, leaving me on my backside thumping my shin pads in anger because I felt we should have stopped him. At that moment I felt completely distraught. I had let the country down. I had been mugged and abused. It was horrible.

From then we could only go for it. Chris Waddle came on for Peter Reid, and then John Barnes replaced Trevor Steven. John made a great impact and turned the game on its head. Suddenly it was all England. Barnes produced a great left-wing run and cross, and there was Gary Lineker again to put us right back in the game. 'Digger' did it again a few minutes later, but this time Gary appeared to miss the chance. I still don't know how, but we have to give credit to the defender who did really well on the line to hook it away. The combination of Barnes and Lineker produced a third chance, only for it to go just behind our striker who had now scored six World Cup goals, enough to eventually earn him the Golden Boot. This, sadly, was not to be the seventh.

The Argentinians were definitely rocking, and we had further chances to take it into extra time where we might have won as the momentum was with us. But Argentina had the sucker punch on the day, and it's these lucky breaks that can win matches at this level. The handball was decisive. It was hard to take, and I didn't want to shake hands with Maradona afterwards. To this day if I see an Argentinian shirt I feel physically sick, not because of the people but because of what they did to us in that quarter-final. They are not a nice team to play against, they pinch and pull and tug, although I have to say I didn't have any problems with the man I marked, Valdano, who was perfectly fair.

Afterwards there were feelings of frustration and hurt, but more because we hadn't played well for 90 minutes than the fact Maradona had cheated. We felt we had let ourselves down. We only played to our potential in the last quarter. But there was no doubt Maradona had been the difference between the two sides, especially the handball. You can ask why the officials didn't see it, but on reflection it was rather well done. He hid it brilliantly, and if you are going to do something like that you have to do it well. What grated most was his after-match quotes: he refused to accept he had handled the ball into the net and has continued to do so ever since.

It was even worse in the doping control room after the game. After the final whistle I was selected in the tunnel for a drug test along with Kenny Sansom and Gary Stevens of Everton – three defenders. Two Argentinians also came into the test room, leaping about and hugging each other, and then who should walk in but Maradona himself – the last person in the world I wanted to see. However, it was interesting to see his face as I had spent most of the match chasing after his backside. He looked over, waved to us and came across to shake hands. I couldn't speak Spanish or Portuguese so I tapped my hand and then my head to ask him how he had scored. He lied and indicated it was with his head.

We grew increasingly angry because we wanted to be alone, not with these three celebrating South Americans. I thought it showed great disrespect to the three English players in the room. And we had to wait before we could pass water after being totally dehydrated by the midday sun in the thin air of Mexico City. There was just nothing there. We asked for some beers but they wouldn't give us any, so we had to drink water. It was ages before any of us could urinate. By this time I was ignoring the opposition completely. The team had long gone by the time we had done our duty, and we went back to the hotel by car where we had a meal and a meeting with Bobby. Once again the kit door was thrown open on the special gear reserved for the semi-final and final.

The players were rolling down an emotional hill, plummeting. The more you think about a defeat like that, the worse it gets. It's hard for anyone who hasn't been in an identical situation to appreciate. You feel absolutely drained, not just within yourself but for your country. We had shattered so many people's dreams, not just our own but Doc Edwards', back at home after his heart attack, the manager's, the coaches' – everyone connected with the team. We had been building up for this for two years, long years of pain, sweat and tears. A lot of effort was put in by everyone, from the clubs through to the FA. We'd even started to make plans for the wives and families to come out for the semi-final. We were so sure we could do it this time. We knew we were capable, and I can remember the hairs on the back of my neck standing on end when Bobby Robson made his rousing pre-match speech, telling us we could all become immortal. It made us feel special. Even now I get a tingle when I recall his words. It took weeks to get over that loss.

My opinion of Maradona and Argentina was coloured for ever, for the worse. It has nothing to do with the Falklands: that, for me, is a separate issue. This was because of the way they had beaten us. I still say Maradona is the best player I have ever played against, but I have no respect for him at all. The pictures of the handball are conclusive, yet he never acknowledged it. Would an Englishman have done the same thing? I guess so, but he would have tried to get there with his head first; had it hit his hand it would have been more by luck than judgement. Certainly it would have been admitted afterwards.

We flew home the next day thinking about what might have been as Argentina prepared to face the tournament outsiders Belgium for a place in the final. At Heathrow I went straight to the TAP ticket desk because all my family were out with my parents in Portugal. I waited around for a bit, then jetted out to Lisbon where there was another six-hour wait for the plane to Faro. I was completely wrecked with jet lag and bitter disappointment, and the only salvation I could see was in a bottle of Ballantynes whisky at the airport bar. I admit I was in a state of disrepair by the time I reached Val de Lobo. All I wanted to do was forget, but there was no chance of that because although Portugal had gone out in the first round they had beaten us in the opening game and every Portuguese person I met wanted to remind me. Added to that, all I had with me on holiday to wear was my England T-shirts and casual gear. I watched the World Cup Final between Argentina and West Germany on television in Portugal, still thinking it should have been us there. Two years of hard graft had been finished by a handball and a spectacular goal, probably the best of this or any World Cup. I was gutted.

CHAPTER TWELVE

DOUBLE TOP

I arrived back in Ipswich after the holiday (though not into pre-season training because of the World Cup) with my club planning life in the Second Division. Manchester United had still not come in for me despite more calls from Bryan Robson telling me to wait and do nothing with anyone else. Then Graeme Souness called to tell me he had made an official bid of three quarters of a million pounds in cash, which had been quickly accepted by the club.

In the meantime I had been invited to play in Los Angeles for the Rest of the World under the management of Franz Beckenbauer against the Americas, captained by a certain Diego Maradona, for UNICEF. Gordon Strachan from Scotland and Pat Jennings from Northern Ireland joined me. Why me? Perhaps a good few had pulled out. I was very surprised but delighted at the honour. We were to play the game in the Rose Bowl Stadium in Pasadena. We trained beforehand a couple of times and I found myself in goal after Pat had saved a couple of shots, decided he'd done enough and gone and sat in the sunshine. I put on his gloves and they were like frying pans – massive.

Before the game we met up with Danny Kaye, the great American actor. He was involved because of his work for the charity and he had the most bizarre pair of shoes I have ever seen in my life. I thought he was having a joke, and it was all I could do not to laugh. They looked like the sort of shoes the Munchkins wore in *The Wizard of Oz*. I wondered if he had flown in on a magic carpet. But he was a lovely man, and what a mega star.

On the day of the game Beckenbauer told us he would change the team round at half-time, but I started along with little Gordon. We soon won a free-kick on the right-hand side, and I lumbered up as usual, but what wasn't usual was Strachan's perfect strike flew straight on to my head and I scored for the Rest of the World. We then went two up, but the Americas' fitness kicked in and they pulled back to 2–2. Then, of all people, Maradona won it for them from the penalty spot. Still, the result didn't matter. It was just a wonderful occasion, marvellous to be part of.

After the game there was a party high up in the hills in a Hollywood mansion, and we all went up to the glamorous house. Gordon was good company, a really funny guy, especially as by this time we were having a few scoops. We were enjoying ourselves when, all of a sudden, it was show time. Everyone moved into this huge wooden hallway and the host's wife, who had obviously been practising, began this Greek dance with a man I assumed was her instructor. We all looked on in amazement, wondering if this was what they did every night in Hollywood. It was a complete showstopper in the middle of the party. We looked on for a few minutes at the surreal scene, shrugged, then went back to the kitchen for more beers.

When we returned to the hotel I was just subsiding into a drunken slumber when the telephone rang by the side of the bed. It was Graeme Souness. We exchanged all the niceties, including him asking me what time it was. As it happened, it was three a.m. He had probably been trying me all night, but I didn't ask. He told me he wanted to meet me at Heathrow when I returned so we could discuss the transfer, now the clubs had agreed a fee and he could speak to me officially. He told me the name of the hotel, I said yes, and went back to sleep.

The next morning I woke up, tried to recall the hotel Souness had mentioned, and went to the airport to catch my business flight back to London. I went straight to the Holiday Inn at Heathrow, sat there, and waited for him to show. I waited and I waited, but still no Souness. There were, of course, no mobiles at the time, so I telephoned home from the front desk and asked if there had been any messages for me. There hadn't. I was baffled. Then the telephone went on the desk and the porter asked if there was a Mr Butcher present. I took the call, and it was Souness calling me from the Sheraton Skyline Hotel. I'd got the wrong hotel. But, I strongly claim, it's easy to get the two names mixed up, especially when you are 5,000 miles away, half asleep and much the worse for free drink.

Souness rushed over to the Holiday Inn and said, straight out, 'Let's get sorted out. There's a flight waiting for us to Edinburgh.'

'Hold on a minute,' I replied, 'I don't even know what's happening here. Shouldn't we talk it through first?'

But he was adamant he wanted to take me to Scotland to show me the ground and everything else.

We piled on to the shuttle just before the doors closed and flew to Scotland. We drove to Glasgow, looked around the ground, then went back to Edinburgh and the Norton House Hotel, owned by David Murray, the man who would eventually put his money into Rangers. The Commonwealth Games were on at the time, and in the hotel was heavyweight boxer Frank Bruno. Perhaps he had been deliberately put in the bar to impress or intimidate me – I don't know. Souness and I talked terms, and everything was pretty well agreed. I was to go to training the next morning to meet the lads. I probably sold myself short with the money I accepted, judging by what others said later, but I was happy at the time as they gave me what I asked for.

But I was still wondering about Manchester United. There had been no word from them at all. The only club to have come in for me was Spurs, and their manager David Pleat wanted me to fly back to London before I put pen to paper with Rangers. Rita arrived the next day and still thought Scotland would be a good move for us all. The first two days I was there the sun shone, but when she arrived the rain came pouring down, so it could hardly be said that the weather had clouded her judgement. I made one last call to Mr Pat and he told me there had been nothing from Old Trafford.

I thought the whole thing through. Rangers had been fantastic to me, but still, had Manchester United come in at the last minute I would have changed my mind and gone there. I suppose after three years of being in contact I had come to expect the move to Old Trafford. Big Ron Atkinson, their manager at the time, is a great guy who I would have enjoyed playing for, though he wasn't destined to be there for much longer. I heard later it was Bobby Charlton who did for me. Big Ron blamed me for getting him the sack because he went to the board to try to persuade them to give him the money to buy me but Bobby indicated that they already had good enough players in my position. End of story. As for Spurs, they hadn't even agreed a fee or made me any sort of offer. They had wanted me to fly down on spec. David Pleat is very persuasive, and had he matched or bettered the Rangers bid I might have gone to White Hart Lane. As it was, it was too much up in the air for me, so on 1 August 1986 I signed for Rangers.

I have to say I saw Scotland at the time as something of a backwater. It was, I felt, a lesser league than England's, as it still is. But as I advised Paul Gascoigne, don't knock it until you have tried it because it's a fierce competition, much more so than in England. I didn't really know what I could expect by signing for Rangers, other than new grounds, new players and a different environment. But United didn't want me and there was no continental team making an offer, so I suppose going to Scotland was as close as I was going to get to moving abroad. It was a shock to the system, but I quickly realised it was a big country with a good road system and a fantastic way of life. It was easy to travel to games and to get to and from training in the morning.

By a strange coincidence, the very next game Rangers played after I signed for them was the next day in a testimonial at, of all places, Spurs. I sat it out but was stunned by the sight of 10,000 Rangers fans turning up for a pre-season friendly in London. It spoke volumes about their passion for the club. We drew 1–1, and I was introduced to left-winger Ted McMinn. What a strange man he was. He would beat six players, get to the dead-ball line, fall over as the ball trickled out for a goal-kick, yet still receive a standing ovation from the Rangers fans.

Despite everything, it was a massive wrench to leave Ipswich. It was my home, all my friends were there, and I had lots of fantastic memories connected with the club. I knew I had to move on both for the club and myself, but Scotland was a long way away from our parents. Still, Edward had been born in 1985, and from a family perspective it was a good time to move with the two boys.

I had also made sure by talking to Bobby Robson that playing in Scotland wouldn't affect my England opportunities. For those of you who have wondered how I kept my place in the England team for a decade, I can reveal now that before the move to Scotland I had a house very close to Bobby Robson's in Ipswich and we regularly used to meet while taking our respective dogs for a walk. We would just stop and chat. Even the dogs got on well. We also used to share a car together, whether it was to Luton airport or our hotel for home games. So how could he drop me? I was the teacher's pet! As I said, I talked it over with him and he was fine about the move, though I understand our two dogs weren't very pleased.

I had spoken to Rangers left-winger Davie Cooper before I signed and asked him if he thought the club would win the League. He had said definitely. It was a sweeping statement because Rangers hadn't won it for a stunning nine years and there was good-quality opposition in the Scottish Premier. It wasn't just the champions Celtic, who had clinched the title in the last game of the previous season beating St Mirren 5–0 Aberdeen and Dundee United were strong too, as were Hearts, who lost both the Cup Final to Aberdeen and the League itself on the final day. At the time it was a twelve-team League with a 44-match season, though primed for a change of format as the Scottish Football Association searched for the best approach to the limited quality in the country. It was a close and even scene, not a race between the two Old Firm teams, as many believed south of the border.

My first appearance in the blue shirt of Rangers was in a friendly on 5 August against the Germans Bayern Munich at Ibrox in front of 36,000 people. We did well until ten minutes from the end, when we began to run out of steam. We made a couple of substitutions but eventually went down 2–0. But what a wonderful stadium it was to play in, completely different to Portman Road, and so noisy. It was a great feeling, and despite the result the fans made me feel as though I had made the right decision.

I had missed much of the pre-season preparations, but I was straight in at the deep end four days later in the first League game at Hibs. Both Graeme Souness and I were staying in Edinburgh at the Norton House Hotel until we found suitable family accommodation; Chris Woods had already earmarked a plot of land in Dunblane for a new house to be built. We went off to the ground on a beautiful sunny day. The Hibs pitch sloped lengthways in those days, and we were a goal down after a scrappy first half when all hell broke loose in the centre circle. The Hibs centre-forward George McCluskey had gone into a tackle with our player-manager; Souness had seen him coming, and in an act of destructive self-preservation he had gone higher and tried to remove George's cartilages with his studs, slashing his knee in the process. Souness was sent off, but before he went everyone was tussling in the centre circle, though pushing and shoving rather than fighting. The only person not involved was Hibs goalkeeper Alan Rough, who sensibly stayed in his own area.

Our goalkeeper Chris Woods ran 50 yards to join the mêlée, and I tried to hold him back on the edge of the circle. It was neither the best of sights nor the best of starts: Ally McCoist scored from the penalty spot, but we went down 2–1. It was a fraught day altogether. At one point their other centre-forward, Cowan, chased me towards the corner flag; although I was in front, he was pulling at me all the time. There was no whistle, so I took the law into my own hands and tried to elbow him away, with both arms. The result was my first yellow card in my first game. Afterwards, the SFA decreed everyone involved in the fracas would receive two penalty points, so, with my other booking, I managed to pick up four disciplinary points on my League debut. A nice quiet start!

After the game Souness, having been sent off in his first game and having lost to a fired-up Hibs side, was a nightmare. We went out together in Edinburgh that evening to drown our sorrows, but he almost finished up in a fight in a bar. A guy was trying to be smart and clever. I tried to placate him, but Graeme, fed up of his attitude, told him to fuck off. Time to get a taxi back to Norton House and some sort of sanity before something worse happened.

We entertained Falkirk at home in the next game and struggled to beat a team we were expected to whip. We just about made it with another McCoist penalty. So we had hardly won many friends in our opening two games, but three days later we had an opportunity to make amends when we welcomed Dundee United to Ibrox. Rangers started brilliantly and were two up at half-time with two McCoist goals. We were playing the way we knew we could, and were expected to, but then we fell apart in the second half. Two goals from Gallacher and another from Redford gave Dundee United a 3–2 win, putting them on top of the table and leaving us trailing in a distant seventh place.

Something was wrong, and it needed putting right very quickly. One of the problems was training on Friday mornings, having a pasta lunch at the ground, and then traipsing off to the Grosvenor Hotel in Glasgow where we would sleep in the afternoon, have dinner in the evening and return to the bedrooms to watch television and sleep again. It was a system Souness had picked up while playing for Sampdoria in Italy, but while it worked for them because it was part of their traditional build-up, I wasn't sure it was working for us. We would say goodbye to our families on Friday morning and not see them again until Saturday evening, and this was every week, sometimes twice a week if there was a midweek game. The players found this very difficult, especially as the distances to away games were so slight. After a few games and a few well-chosen words in his ear from the lads, Souness saw reason, realised we weren't in Italy, and changed things.

And after those two early defeats we embarked on a good run. We had a good win against the difficult Hamilton Academical, and it was the result we needed before meeting Celtic at home on the last day of August for my first Old Firm derby. Nothing can prepare you for this unique game of football. It was such an immense fixture, and I told journalists afterwards it was one of the reasons why I went up to Scotland. I didn't yet fully appreciate the religious fervour and rivalry, but the atmosphere alone was stunning.

The changing rooms at Ibrox in those days were huge, with wooden panelling and all mod cons. The visitors were treated in the same way – not always the case with the other Scottish dressing rooms. We weren't allowed to warm up on the pitch before the game in case it inflamed the fans. We could do it at Parkhead, but only because there was nowhere else to go. At Ibrox we warmed up under the stand, both teams a little way apart. The Rangers fans could see us warming up and would give us encouragement, and at the other end the Celtic fans did likewise as they made their way to the enclosures.

We came out of the tunnel together and, as captain, I walked out alongside Roy Aitken. In the contract talks with Souness, one of the first things he had said to me was that I would go to Rangers as captain. I'd asked how it would stand with the rest of the players and he'd responded he didn't care. A man of few words was Graeme! So I was club captain even before I arrived. Perhaps it wasn't justified, and I would still have gone to Rangers had I not been offered the captaincy, but it was an honour. Fortunately there was no resistance at all from the players. Some people thought I was already captain of England, though I hadn't had that honour yet. Anyway, as Roy and I emerged from the tunnel, the noise hit us like a wall. It was immense, and I loved it. We had a good team with a nice mix of young local players like Derek Ferguson and Ian Durrant and a few with a lot of experience at international level. We won the game 1–0 thanks to a bit of magic from Davie Cooper, one of the best players I have ever played with. He played a delightful reverse pass to Durrant, who smacked it past Packy Bonner. It was a great result and performance, and our delirious fans forgot our bad start in an instant. I left the ground hoping it was always going to be like this. As captain in my first Old Firm game it was an incredible feeling. It gave us a lot of confidence, and we won six of the next eight games, moving up to third place. We often lost games when we were clear favourites, to teams like Motherwell, Aberdeen and Dundee, whereas against Celtic we won three, drew one and lost one in my first season. The fans loved it after the barren years.

The football in Scotland, I was now able to note, was far quicker than in England, played at 100 miles an hour. I felt it suited me because they had big centre-forwards and big centre-halves – just the sort of thing to make me feel comfortable on the pitch. It was a standard of football I was enjoying very much because there were fierce battles all over the park. But they weren't used to ball-playing central defenders; they expected you to boot it forward. The players weren't as good as in England and they lost possession more easily, but that just meant the game became more end-to-end, thrilling and exciting. It was how the Scots wanted their football played. In England there was a not nearly so frenetic build-up with teams holding on to the ball for longer. It took a while to bed down into this new style, but because the football was played at such a pace it kept me sharp, bright, eager and on my toes, ready for international football.

On 20 November, the Butcher family moved into our new house. The owners of Rangers at the time were in fact a building and construction company, John Lawrence Ltd, owned by Lawrence Marlborough, a descendant of the original owners. David Holmes was the chief executive of Rangers and John Lawrence Ltd, a man I didn't meet until a lot later one. He had a certain aura about him, a very powerful but very nice gentleman. He obviously sanctioned the moves for the players to Rangers. But it was through another contact in the building trade, Jimmy Marshall – the owner of Gateway Builders in Bridge of Allan, a supporter, and now a very good friend of ours – that we got the house. Jimmy had written to the club to say he was selling his property and asked if I would be interested in it. When we drove up to have a look we were immediately impressed. The house was in a beautiful situation overlooking the Forth Valley, Stirling, the Wallace Monument and the castle. It was in Kenilworth Road, and it was called the Hawthorns. How English was that? It boasted four bedrooms, was clad in beautiful sandstone and had servants' quarters underneath, which I converted into a snooker room. It even had its own little bar. Everything was perfect for me, and it was ideal for Rita and the children. Their school, Beaconhurst, was in the same road.

We played in Aberdeen two days after moving in, and our central defender Dave McPherson was sent off after a tussle with Davie Dodds, known affectionately as the 'Unacceptable Face of Scottish Football'. The dismissal came after a free-kick had been awarded on the left-hand side. Before the kick had been taken, Dodds slumped to the floor and McPherson was sent packing. I raced straight over to Dodds and told him he was a cheat, then turned on the referee, telling him Dodds had dived. The referee looked at me and said, 'Before you say another word, look at him.' I did. Poor Dodds had his nose splattered right across his face, and it certainly wasn't self-inflicted. It was a dangerous elbow and a definite red card. We lost that day in every way, the final score 1–0 to the Dons.

But after that defeat we embarked on a nineteen-match unbeaten run in the League. One of the highlights was our win over Celtic on New Year's Day – always a very special, highly charged occasion. Graham Roberts had joined us from Spurs and had gone immediately into a bonding session, the players' Christmas party. There was a good turn-out, plenty of booze, and the inevitable Ally McCoist rap songs. We'd beaten Dundee United on the 27th, and went on to beat Celtic by the same score, 2–0, with the same two goalscorers, McCoist and Robert Fleck. What's more, we played really well. The game ended with Souness endearing himself to the Celtic fans and players by taking the mickey with lots of back-heels and flicks. He wasn't playing much at the time because of calf trouble, but when he did he was always influential one way or another.

It was an incredible run, our only defeat a 3–1 loss at Celtic Park in April. I gave away a penalty for the second goal when I fouled a certain Mo Johnston as I slid in to tackle him in the box .He flicked the ball over me and clattered into my leg. It was clever forward play, but I was unimpressed and promptly booted the ball straight out of Parkhead – a fair effort in those days. There was a very intimidating atmosphere at Parkhead which always used to fire me up. It has all changed tremendously now, but I used to love the warming up and other preliminaries at Celtic. The changing rooms were painted in a sickly green with the Celtic crest in the bathroom; we counterbalanced that by taking two pictures of the Queen into the dressing room and placing one at each end. They were our pride and joy, and we took them carefully away with us after each game. Before the game I would run straight across to the far side to warm up in front of the area called the Jungle. It was where the real diehard Celtic fans gathered, and I took terrible stick from them, at least according to the bits I understood. I used to do my groin stretches with my back to them to show them my backside, and when I wanted to clear the phlegm I would spit in their direction. Once the ball was introduced, if it ran off the pitch towards them I left it. There was no way I was going to go anywhere near them. It was an odd atmosphere, absolutely unique and special. We deservedly lost that April game and they remained neck and neck with us for the title.

In our remaining five fixtures we beat Dundee, Clydebank, Hearts and St Mirren while drawing at Pittodrie, a difficult ground to play at with equally fervent supporters. We stayed the night before just outside Aberdeen and I was stunned so many of our supporters had made the trip in case we won the title on the day. It looked unlikely as Celtic were at home to Falkirk; they were odds on to win that match and take the race into the last game of the season. Not everything went our way as player-manager Graeme Souness was sent off for the second time that season. We were down to ten men and playing for the title. Halfway through the first period we won a free-kick 35 yards out and I strolled up, making eye contact with Davie Cooper, who was able to put a ball on a sixpence. I made my move, he delivered the ball straight into my path, and I redirected it into the net. I celebrated behind the goal, and suddenly I was faced by thousands of Rangers fans who had bought tickets from Aberdeen supporters and had infiltrated the home area. It seemed as though I had the entire side on my back as all my team-mates jumped on me. It didn't matter: at that moment I could have lifted the world. Brian Irvine equalised just before the interval, and during the break Souness told us to hold fast and dig in, which we did. Towards the end, news started to filter through the predominantly Rangers crowd that Celtic, who had started their game five minutes earlier, had lost to Falkirk and we were champions. The score in our match didn't matter any more, but Graham Roberts and I were determined we weren't going to let Aberdeen score, and when the whistle went we just embraced each other. It was an incredible feeling to win a title. It was the first I had ever won and it was very special.

When the game finished our thousands of fans poured on to the pitch. It took us twenty minutes to reach the sanctuary of the dressing room. Once we had checked no one was missing, we came out to greet the crowd. All the Aberdeen supporters had left, but Rangers fans without tickets had come in and completely filled the ground. I carried

Ian Durrant around on my shoulders on the very ground where a year and a half later he was to suffer a serious injury which all but finished his career.

The next most important issue was to make sure we had enough beers on the bus for the journey back to Glasgow. The players went back to the Aberdeen hotel while Graeme Souness, nicknamed Champagne Charlie by a journalist friend in his Liverpool days, lived up to it by buying champagne for all the staff. Mike Summerbee had once told me if I ever won a championship I should sit in a bar, drink champagne and remember it for ever. I made do with a Tennents lager, but I wasn't complaining.

The bus journey on the way back to Glasgow was brilliant, as we sprayed each other with beer. The boys were singing and jumping about so much the coach almost turned on its side. It was just a great feeling, one of the best ever in my entire career. The return journey was two hours, but it passed in a flash. The road to Aberdeen in those days wasn't the best and we had to stop every now and again because of the football traffic. The punters wouldn't leave us alone: farmers in the fields were waving wildly, the police were putting their thumbs up, and every car was beeping its horn. Locals were stopping the traffic in front of us so they could come to the coach to shake hands with the players. Indeed, some even tried to get on and join the party.

When I got back to Bridge of Allan, Rita and I went with Chris Woods and his wife Sarah to a restaurant called Kipling's where we drank champagne before heading for Stirling's Rainbow Rocks disco. I finished up behind the disc jockey with a pint of lager and a bottle of champagne. I don't think I bought a drink. No one realised how much it meant to our supporters to win this particular title.

We still had to play St Mirren, though the outcome didn't matter. We were presented with the championship trophy in front of a full house. St Mirren had a good team and were due to play in the Scottish Cup Final the next week, but we won 1–0 with a Robert Fleck goal. Afterwards, three of us wore T-shirts reading 'McRoberts', 'McButcher' and 'McWoods' – the English connection.

The only cloud on the horizon was that there were no bonuses organised for winning the League. I asked Graeme Souness about it and he brought in David Holmes to join the conversation. He finally decided that they couldn't pay bonuses, but that we could share the takings from the St Mirren game, which had attracted a good crowd of 43,150. It probably worked out to about £10,000 each – a considerable sum then.

I missed just one game all season, because of suspension: I had picked up the two bookings in that first game and then three more quick cautions and was out for a match as early as September. My final tally was 55 club matches played and three goals scored. Most important of all was the fact we had sorted out the defence by mid-season, helping Chris Woods to set a new record of 1,196 minutes without conceding a goal, including eleven clean sheets.

That record had been set during a Scottish FA Cup tie against Hamilton Academical, which we went on to lose. But we were much more successful in the other domestic Cup competition. We easily beat Steinhousemuir 4–1 in the opening round of the League Cup and then drew East Fife away. They had the smallest dressing rooms in the world and a hard, bumpy pitch with a slope. We were very poor on the night. Striker Colin West, another of the English signings, suffered a bad knee ligament injury which put him out for the rest of the season, and we were taken to extra time and penalties. We had no plans for who took the penalties on these occasions. I hated the thought, but I realised as club captain I should volunteer, so I took the third one against Gordon Marshall, later to be my goalkeeper at Motherwell. I picked my spot to the right of the goal and opted for power with a natural curve to take it away from the keeper. I told myself to hit it hard and low. But as I was running up I glimpsed Marshall moving towards the very corner I was aiming at and I made a split-second decision to go for the other corner. I stubbed it goalwards, it bounced three times, but it went in. I have never taken a penalty since, and I admire greatly the people who do. Still, I can always claim I have a 100 per cent record from the spot!

We won that penalty contest 5–4, Woodsy saving a spot-kick to earn his money. We then beat Dundee at home, drew Dundee United in the semi-final at Hampden Park, beat them too, and ended up facing Celtic, again at Hampden, at the end of October. We had played them only once at that point of the season and had beaten them, but they were flying with a great deal to say for themselves.

The dressing rooms at Hampden Park in those days were very old-fashioned, with individual cupboards so high even I needed stilts to get to the top shelf. In the middle of the room there was also a huge metal-rimmed table which people climbed over because it was so much in the way. You certainly couldn't call it luxurious. To reach the pitch you had to go down some concrete steps, and on the way I slipped on them in my studs, almost banging my head on the stone lintel at the top of the tunnel.

The occasion was fantastic, and it was a tense game, very open with opportunities at both ends. We scored the first goal with an Ian Durrant volley in the second half. Our fans were ecstatic, but fifteen minutes later Brian McClair equalised as I failed to get across to him in time. Then, with only five or six minutes left, we were awarded a free-kick. I charged upfield into the box, and as the cross came in I felt it was mine: I had half a yard on Roy Aitken, my marker and opposing captain. As I started going for the ball he grabbed hold of my jersey, but I kept going. The more he pulled the more determined I became. I was sure I was going to score, but he was just as adamant I wouldn't, and with a last desperate effort he hauled me to the ground. It was a stonewall penalty. If there is one person to take a penalty under pressure, it was Davie Cooper. He had taken the crucial penalty against Wales which took Scotland to the 1986 World Cup finals, and he nonchalantly stroked it past Packy Bonner. Celtic became more and more desperate for the equaliser until Mo Johnston completely lost his head and tried to butt Stuart Munro. That was it. The final whistle went, and in a blink of an eye half the stadium emptied.

When I walked up the steps to receive my first trophy for the club, it was to Rangers supporters only. There wasn't a green and white scarf or flag to be seen. I was supposed to pass the trophy down the line, but instead I legged it down the steps and on to the pitch. I would have loved to do a full lap of honour, but the ground was only half full so I felt slightly deprived. There was no point showing the cup to concrete terraces devoid of people.

Afterwards it was into the changing rooms and back to Ibrox for a reception. There is a supporters' social club right next door to the stadium, and after the celebratory meal we took the trophy next door to show the fans and to sing songs with them. It was too good a night to stop, so when the festivities had finished at the club we departed for an establishment called Panama Jacks in Glasgow along with our wives. Just as we were leaving Ibrox I thought it would be a good idea to show the cup to Glasgow, but as I was leaving I felt a hand on my shoulder.

'Where do you think you're going with that?' Souness asked.

'To show the fans, Gaffer.'

'No you're not. Give it to me.'

'OK. Goodnight, Gaffer, see you tomorrow.'

You didn't ever argue with Souness.

Off we went to the club on the banks of the Clyde. Bad mistake. I was all right with Rita and Chris Woods' wife Sarah, but there were some Celtic fans inside and they started to give us stick. Rather than stay and make a show of it I gathered everyone together and off we went home. It was a bad experience, and it put us off going for a night out in Glasgow again because it was simply too provocative and dangerous for the girls. It's hard to explain to English players and supporters because this thing went far beyond football, and sometimes, I thought, far beyond religion. It is more than a passion, it is a way of life, and there is nothing like it down south, not even at Manchester United, Arsenal, Chelsea, Millwall or anywhere else you care to name. It can be very intoxicating as well as weird, spooky, strange and scary.

Initially it was just a question of getting used to it. Rangers and Celtic have hundreds of supporters' clubs all over Glasgow, Scotland and the world, and as the season comes to a close they all have awards ceremonies for their own player of the year. If you couldn't attend in person – and there were so many it would have been impossible – they were allowed to come to the ground to make the presentation before matches. It was all very good public relations, but on some Saturday nights at the end of the season you would have to go to perhaps three or more of these ceremonies. Each one would ask what present you would like. More often than not I opted for Edinburgh crystal, which gave them a wide range of gifts from which to select. When they didn't ask I received some very strange awards, among them a red, white and blue golf umbrella, a number one iron and several golf bags. Perhaps they all thought I needed the practice. They were such warm, generous people. They would want to give you presents just for turning up, whether or not you had won an award. But it was difficult because you couldn't just go for an hour and then move on. It was two or three hours in a very smoky environment with your eyeballs getting sore from all the flashlights. There were flute bands too, and they would have you up on the stage singing the usual party songs, which I learnt very quickly. The first Rangers supporters' club I went to was in Larkhall, a district where was one Catholic family, ironically Celtic and Scotland player Paul McStay's; conversely, if you went to Croy, it was all Catholic with no Protestants. At Larkhall I was asked to sing a Rangers song. I tried to explain that as I had only recently arrived I hadn't had time to learn any. There was only one thing I knew about Glasgow Rangers. Allan Hunter at Ipswich had taught me the phrase 'No surrender', and with those two words I brought the house down.

People in business had to play it much more carefully than the supporters' clubs in order not to alienate a large section of their clientele. So, if a garage forecourt or a shop needed opening they would make sure they invited someone from both Rangers and Celtic. Not only was it politically correct to do so, it also ensured the picture would definitely be used in the Scottish newspapers. Consequently, Roy Aitken and I would get invited to a lot of places together. Miss World came to Glasgow once for a function and our families were invited to join her. If a clothing store opened they would invite both teams and give us all vouchers to spend. The idea was always to get us 'united', but it rarely happened, and in the pictures Rangers would be on one side and Celtic on the other. The players would not mix as they genuinely disliked one another. You would never see a Rangers player change shirts with a Celtic player after a game. A pity, I think. Had I thought about it at the time I would have changed with Roy after an Old Firm derby because it would have been an unbelievable gesture. It would have been greeted by silence, but I think it would have been one of the best things that could have happened.

When I first went to Rangers, I was warned against wearing anything green, and as it was one of Rita's favourite colours she had to leave her dresses in the wardrobe. Davie Cooper once told me if I wore anything green he would personally rip it off me. Supporters used to approach me and say things like, 'How old's your granny?' I would say that my grandparents were dead, but they would insist, 'No, how old's your granny?' I discovered later if I said she was 78, it would mean I was a member of Lodge Seventy-Eight. It was a Masonic thing. I got so dragged into the culture I very nearly joined the Masons, but Rita was really against it, saying we shouldn't have secrets and she wasn't happy with the idea. I believe I was one of only a couple of Rangers captains who wasn't a Mason. But you still got the secret handshakes. I haven't a problem with the Masons at all; it seemed to go with the territory. Rangers were such a massive club and it made you feel very special.

Of course Celtic, too, had a huge fan base. You had to accept when you played for one of the big two in Glasgow, as well as taking the plaudits and the compliments you had to take the stick and hassle. And it wasn't solely the football fans on match days. In petrol stations or in the cinema, people would pass sectarian comments. It doesn't end once you've left the club either. Recently in Glasgow, at nine o'clock in the evening while I was going for a meal with Rita, a group of Celtic supporters behind me started chanting 'Hun, Hun, Hun!' If you are a Rangers player you are a Protestant and a Hun, and will be for ever in their eyes.

There were lots of things I'd had no clue about in my previously sheltered life that I learnt by experience, simple things like your name. Ted McMinn's given name was Kevin, but that was considered a Catholic name so he called himself Ted. When you signed an autograph and it was to a Steven, if you asked which spelling you'd be told with some umbrage the Protestant way was with a 'v'. You soon learnt to stop asking. I didn't sign many for Josephs, Timothys or Seamuses! It's not everyone, of course, but it is a vociferous minority. If you are a Glaswegian they know by your surname which school you went to and what religion you are. I can recall one incident at Ipswich before a reserve game when I crossed myself, something I had seen Alan Brazil do. Big Allan Hunter was sitting in the stand, and after the game he grabbed me and asked me if I was a Catholic. I told him I wasn't. I was an English Protestant. Why, then, he asked, did I cross myself? I told him it was for luck, but he told me to remember I was a Protestant and warned me never to do it again; if I did, he would really sort me out. I quickly forgot about it, but my arrival in Scotland soon reminded me ... and then some. In my naivety I had thought the sign of the cross was something to bring you good fortune, like crossing your fingers.

It was all very wrong, but I, like the others, was sucked into it. I was married in a Church of England church and frequently used to attend the Methodist church too, but I had never forced my religion on anyone else. The problem was you wanted to be a part of it, to share everything with the fans. We were drawn headlong into it and ended up being stupid about it. I am not the sort to dip a toe in the water and see how it feels; I am the sort who dives in head first with anchors around both ankles. It took my wife Rita to see it, and she told me to have a good look at myself in the mirror, because I would have a few beers and would just start singing the songs. She pointed out I was English, and hadn't been born a Rangers fan. I had to be shaken to realise that I had gone too far, I had to just step back and play for Rangers – play football the way it's meant to be played.

I remember when I moved to Coventry it was as if a huge weight had been taken off my shoulders. I swore I would leave it all behind and not bother with religion in football again. I am now the patron of Nil By Mouth, which is against sectarianism and bigotry, and I am proud of it. There is even a wrist bangle of green and blue to denote support for the Kick Racism out of Football campaign. They have sold a lot of them too. Nowadays, though, the atmosphere is a lot saner. What amazes and pleases me particularly is Rangers now play with a great number of Catholics. A lot of the credit should go to Souness, who was determined to break down the barriers by signing a Catholic. He searched diligently, but more than one got cold feet and turned down what would have been a great move for them, most notably Irish international Ray Houghton, who was born in Glasgow. He was playing for Oxford United but went to Liverpool in the end. When it became known he was going to sign he received death threats, and he pulled out because of his family.

After I left there was a time when I had an ache and desire to be at Rangers, to work at Rangers, a real emotional gut feeling. I would have crawled over broken glass for the club. But as time moved on the club changed, and so did I. As manager of Motherwell, I now want to beat Rangers as much as I want to beat Celtic and everyone else. Back in the late eighties I would never have thought it could happen, because Rangers were everything to me. As I said, you just got sucked right in. Some Rangers fans might not understand my change in attitude, but to me winning is everything. Just ask Sir Alex Ferguson how much he wanted to beat Rangers, a team he, too, used to play for.

One place where you never found religious bigotry was in European competition. Rangers took part in the UEFA Cup in 1986/87, though we didn't stay for long in the competition. In fact, it was a disaster. We comfortably beat Ilves from Finland at Ibrox with enough goals to cushion a 2–0 defeat away, and then beat Boavista home and away. Next up was the powerful German side Borussia Mönchengladbach. We drew 1–1 at home and then 0–0 away, losing the tie on the away-goals rule. I vividly remember Graeme Souness during that second leg when time was running out and we were down to ten men, having had Dave McPherson sent off. One of the Germans slid in on the touchline and played the ball back to his goalkeeper in front of Graeme, who then stood on his thigh and twisted his foot as if to move off. Everyone was watching the ball and no one saw what happened, but we all heard the German's piercing scream and his leg was in a terrible mess as he was carried off. Souness was a very hard man. He was the one man you would want in your team when he was at full power. He could win games on his own. He had such a reputation when he was at Liverpool that he rarely got in trouble because no one would go near him. Just imagine lining up against him and Jimmy Case. What a frightening thought. They could handle themselves and play, as could Leeds United in their pomp with the likes of Billy Bremner, Norman Hunter, Johnny Giles and the rest of the crowd. Souness and I fell out badly when things came to an end at Ibrox, but he was an incredible person, a real winner.

There was no religious fervour on the international scene either. Bobby Robson was as good as his word. My first game for England while I was at Rangers was in Stockholm against Sweden on 10 September. And we had the usual problem at that time of year: our team was just starting the new season while the Swedes were coming to the end of theirs. The spotlight was on me, with doubts over whether I could cut it in internationals while playing in Scotland and seemingly not performing at the highest level. Bobby Robson told me to ignore the press comments on the subject. But it has to be said we didn't play well on a bumpy pitch, and Ekstrom beat me to score the only goal of the game.

But Bobby stuck by me, not only selecting me for the European Championship qualifier against Northern Ireland a month later, but also making me captain for the following game against Yugoslavia, another crucial qualifying match. We beat the Irish 3–0 at Wembley, with Gary Lineker back in the side scoring twice and Chris Waddle getting the other. We needed such a result before playing Yugoslavia at Wembley on 12 November. With Bryan Robson injured, I was chosen as skipper, and my biggest worry, as I've said, was making sure I remembered all the names during the introduction to the guests of honour. I was never so glad as when it was over. It was far more nerve-racking than the game which, I have to say, was a tough one. Gary Mabbutt, back in the side after a three-year absence, not only filled in for Robson but also followed his example by scoring. Viv Anderson, of all people, added the second, and Chris Woods, making his first Wembley appearance for England, made a super save from their golden boy Zlatko Vujovic, who then went on to squander two great chances. At times they murdered us, and we were lucky to come away with a win.

The next game was not until February – Spain in the Bernabeu Stadium. The day before the friendly I met a very good friend who had owned a restaurant in Essex but had moved out to Spain. Fernando and I got together on the Tuesday afternoon, and he took me to a tapas bar where I sat sucking the heads off prawns 24 hours before an international. I must have been mad. It was a stupid thing to do because of the risk of food poisoning, but I loved it, and afterwards he took me to a china shop where I bought a huge, beautiful piece of Lladró, Fernando haggling the amount down well below the advertised price. It was a great idea at the time, but not brilliant taking it home on the plane after the match. It turned out to be a great match too. We won 4–2, with Lineker, who was playing for Barcelona at the time, scoring all four. Those goals took him to eighteen in 21 matches, while our victory was Spain's first defeat at home for three years. It was also Tony Adams' debut, and a significant start for the Arsenal defender.

I earned my 50th England cap in Belfast on, of all days, 1 April, but the game was no joke as it was another European Championship qualifier and we needed a win to keep us on track. Elton John was in the tunnel before the game, shaking hands with the England team, and it was such a surprise to see him I forgot to pressure the Irish with my usual shouting and screaming. Bryan Robson was back after injury, and typically scored the opening goal when I headed on a huge throw from Gary Mabbutt for the skipper to run on to. Chris Waddle added the second, and we were so comfortable the manager was able to withdraw Peter Shilton, who was suffering with the flu, and send on my team-mate Chris Woods.

In May, the Rous Cup against Brazil and Scotland replaced the Home Internationals. The week before we were due to play the Brazilians at Wembley, Bobby gave Chris Woods and me time to go on Rangers' end-of-season trip to Israel. This was one of our manager's old stamping grounds from his days with Liverpool, and stories abounded of what they had got up to on their trips. For most it was simply an end-of-season jolly, but when we lost the friendly I was gutted. Few seemed to be bothered, though, and afterwards physio and fitness coach Phil Boersma, who followed Souness everywhere, was by the poolside sampling the local brew. It was quite cool outside and he moved on to drinking champagne out of a Babycham glass, effing and blinding in a very embarrassing fashion. The other lads were enjoying a few beers too, and as Phil went off to the pool, still cursing, we were muttering under our breath, 'He's going to drown.' Ally McCoist was sitting by the pool picking his toenails while this was going on. He calmly gathered up the clippings, put them into Phil's glass, filled it up and passed it to the former Liverpool player in the pool. All the boys went 'Cheers, Phil, down the hatch!' He did as we asked, and didn't notice a thing.

I loved the trip, apart from the result, and the place itself. Liverpool were there at the same time, and among them was Zimbabwe goalkeeper Bruce Grobbelaar, a great character and great fun to be with. He had this trick where he pretended to take the top of a beer bottle off with his eye socket. He told our youngsters Ian Durrant and Derek Ferguson how the men used to do this in South Africa, the tough men of the Veldt. Unknown to the youngsters he had taken the top off in the normal fashion and then gently pressed it down on top of the bottle. The kids watched wide-eyed as Brucie pretended to lever the top off, letting out a totally believable hiss between his lips as he did it. The two kids were excited by this, claimed they were men too, and promptly jammed bottles into their eye sockets with the inevitable consequences. Everyone was falling about on the floor, but the kids kept on trying, with blood running down their cheeks. I loved Bruce, and met up with him a couple of times after that trip, at Heathrow and in America with his family. I got on with him really well, and he was always up to something.

After less than a week in Israel we flew back for the Brazil game. It was a good match in front of a capacity crowd. Peter Beardsley played well and laid on the goal for Gary Lineker, who scored with a spectacular diving header. But a minute later Mirandinha pounced as Peter Shilton made a save, hitting home the rebound to level the scores. A certain Stuart Pearce made his first appearance in that game, becoming the 999th player to pull on an England jersey.

Then it was off to Hampden to face Scotland. This tie was fascinating for me to see what sort of reception I would receive from the crowd, many of them Rangers fans. I fancied I would be favourably greeted by the majority. How wrong can you be! I was pilloried from the moment I appeared. It was a dull match to begin with, and not a lot happened in the first half. It improved in the second period, but still no goals. I was again surprised by the lack of atmosphere in this renowned stadium, by the treatment of me and by the poor quality of the football. Still, I have to say the barracking didn't bother me then and it doesn't bother me now.

I was feeling good anyway, as all in all it had been a great year for me.

I had completed my first season at Rangers, convinced myself I had made the right move, picked up silverware, captained my country and hadn't jeopardised my prospects with England. I was even placed second in the Player of the Year award in Scotland, behind Brian McClair – an honour for an English defender. Ipswich had been a great side in the late seventies and early eighties, but they'd won only two trophies. I'd already won two with Rangers in just one season, and it felt like there was lots more to come.

CHAPTER THIRTEEN

GOLDILOCKS AND
THE THREE BEARS

I should have guessed from the start that the scales of life were tilting in the opposite direction for me. After so many good years, everything suddenly started going dramatically wrong. Season 1987/88 was my own personal annus horribilis.

It all began as early as pre-season when we travelled to Switzerland, and instead of the usual hard training Souness decided we would regain fitness from playing matches with a little training in between. It wasn't the best of preparations, we felt, nor did we enjoy it. All we wanted to do was return home and get on with the proper job. Even that was frustratingly delayed as, in a hangover from the previous season, Graham Roberts, Souness and I were all suspended. Rangers did not start off very well at all, with one point from three games.

I came back for the third of those games against Aberdeen on 15 August, which we lost 2–0, and then at last we got our season off and running with an Ally McCoist hat-trick in a 4–0 win over Falkirk. I picked up an injury, a twisted back, and I was out for another couple of games. When it failed to respond to treatment I tried all sorts of things, including manipulation. That eventually seemed to work, and I was back for the Dunfermline game on 12 September, a 4–0 win with yet another McCoist hat-trick. In fact, Ally scored three hat-tricks in the opening two months of the season, and though the team wasn't playing well, he certainly was. Maybe it was the arrival in the summer of Trevor Francis from Atalanta in Italy and Marc Falco from Spurs that galvanised him into action and an incredible tally of five hat-tricks in a season and

42 goals in all matches. It may have been fun for Ally, but it wasn't for me. Poor form and bad injuries seemed to be the order of the day, but before I could feel sorry for myself worse was to come. Our climb up the table into the top four would prove to be something of a false dawn, as, personally, was our progress in the League Cup.

That autumn we also embarked on our long-awaited tilt at the European Cup. We didn't have the best of draws in the first round as we had to travel to Kiev where the Russian army turned out in force to bolster the crowd. It's a long, long way to Kiev. I will always be reminded of the flat, uninspiring landscape of the journey from the airport to Dynamo Kiev's ground whenever I hear U2's album *The Joshua Tree*. We took the precaution of taking our own chef, and we should have taken our own music as well, for crowd noises were played over the loudspeakers to pump up the atmosphere. We lost a close game 1–0 but we fancied our chances in the return in Glasgow.

The Russian champions may have pulled a few strokes with the canned cheering and their rent-a-crowd, but Souness topped them by unexpectedly narrowing the pitch for the match, bringing the sidelines right in. We didn't know he was going to do it and we didn't even train on it. We could only assume he had decided to do it after Kiev had trained on the normal full-sized pitch. It had been a controversial few months for Souness, for apart from starting the season suspended he had also been sent off in the first of the Old Firm games against Celtic – his third red card in twelve months. But his ploy worked well. New boys Francis and Falco played their part in the 2–0 victory. The first goal was the result of a complete hash of a goalkeeper throw-out: the ball hit his own defender and bounced for Falco to tap in. We knew if they scored we were in trouble, but we defended well, backed by a terrific crowd on the night. We eventually went ahead overall when Francis broke down the right and crossed beautifully, as he could; Falco knocked the ball down for McCoist who completely misheaded his effort and sent the goalkeeper the wrong way. Ally will tell you he did him with a dummy and sold him with his eyes. I know the truth. They bombarded us for the final ten minutes but we held out. It was a sensational result. After the game I was so drained mentally and physically I went straight home to bed. For one of the few times in my career, I did the sensible thing.

That win should have kick-started our season, and to some extent it did as we beat Gornik Zabrze 3–1 at home in the next round and held them to a 1–1 draw in Poland, courtesy of an Ally McCoist penalty. Unfortunately, in those days there was then a break in European competition for the winter, and it wasn't until March that we crashed out of the Cup at the hands of Steaua Bucharest – but by then my season was long over.

The League game against Celtic on 17 October was a total disaster. Celtic were going well in their centenary year, a big occasion for them, especially with us winning two trophies the previous year and St Mirren winning the Scottish Cup. They had to win something for their fans, and to help them achieve their goal they had signed Andy Walker from Motherwell, Frank McAvennie from West Ham and centre-half Mick McCarthy. We knew we would have to be up for it, but we weren't. The first couple of balls into our box Chris Woods had taken comfortably, but on each occasion McAvennie had gone in late, and on the second he bundled Chris into the net for an obvious foul. We were all angry with the ex-West Ham striker; his strong-arm tactics were over the top even for an Old Firm game. Then a third cross came in under the bar, and this time McAvennie boxed Chris's ears, tapping him about the face, not so much to hurt as to irritate. Chris took the bait and grabbed McAvennie round the throat with one hand while keeping the ball in the other. McAvennie tried to slap him away, then I came over and pushed McAvennie in the chest. He stumbled away a good ten yards. I was really angry and, like any defender, wanted to protect my goalkeeper. Graham Roberts followed up, and though I didn't see it, apparently a punch was thrown, or some sort of contact was made. McAvennie went down in a heap. The referee arrived at about the same time as everyone else, and although there was no fight there was a lot of pushing and pulling before a red card was shown to both Chris and McAvennie. Graham Roberts had to go in goal, we made adjustments at the back, and got on with the game ten versus ten.

Ten minutes later a ball was played over the top. I ducked and let it run on before playing it back to Robbo, in the days when that was still allowed; but instead of rolling it along the ground I lofted it over our substitute goalkeeper's head for a spectacular own goal. Had I been in goal I could have headed it away, but Graham wasn't as big as me. Disaster followed disaster as Celtic scored again, and we went in at the break two goals down.

I had been booked for my push on McAvennie, but whatever the circumstances we had to go for it and I was going forward for all the dead-ball kicks. I was constantly in their box contesting every ball with their goalkeeper Alan McKnight, and on one occasion he and I fell with our feet locked. As we went down we both had a little kick at each other. McKnight promptly rolled about clutching his face. I was shown a second yellow then a red, and I was on my way as all hell broke loose around me. It was the second time I had been sent off, and I sat in the dressing room inconsolable, especially as I was the captain of Rangers and we were playing our bitterest rivals at home. As I sat in the bath I heard a huge roar to signify a goal for us. Then, as the 90-minute mark approached, I heard another huge roar, much louder than the first and building in volume like an aircraft taking off. It transpired that McCoist had scored the first and Richard Gough had grabbed a late equaliser to snatch the most dramatic of points.

Everyone came into the dressing room jumping around, but I couldn't bring myself to join in because I had let them down. Souness came into the bathroom and told me I had to be big and strong. He told me he knew how I was hurting but I had to go out and be big for my team-mates and for him. It was an astute, inspiring conversation, the sort of thing Graeme was always capable of producing. He didn't say a lot, but when he did, more often than not it made a lot of sense. I was quickly out among the boys, covering up my own disappointment.

What made my mood truly black was having been sent off, Chris and I were going to be automatically suspended for the next game, which was the Scottish League Cup Final at Hampden against Aberdeen. On top of that blow there were the usual whispers that the police were going to take action, but I was more concerned at the time about missing the showpiece. I didn't even want to watch, but we had to show our faces and go along as spectators. It wasn't ideal, but it was a great game: 3–3 after extra time, and then we won 5–3 on penalties, so, despite not having had a good start to the season, we had won a trophy. Three out of four for Souness at this stage.

I was banned for three weeks, so I decided to go and see my parents in Lowestoft. It was while I was in England I received a call from Chris Woods telling me I had to report to the police at Govan police station, back in Glasgow. When I got there Alistair Hood, the Rangers operations officer, and solicitor Len Murray joined me. It was obviously quite serious. We were shown into a small room where the policeman was brief and to the point: he told me I was to be charged with behaviour likely to cause a breach of the peace; what did I have to say? I was stunned, but answered, 'Not guilty.' I was still dazed as I walked out because there had never been any threat of crowd trouble during the match. It had happened on a football field, no one had been hurt, no one had even been injured. But there was much talk of potential riots and the disgraceful behaviour of the players. In football terms, the build-up to the match had been intense: we had won the title the year before, but Celtic had already established a good lead in the championship. There were no fences at the ground and the worry was always there that there could be a surge on to the pitch by spectators. After the game it was very much a case of making an example of players who had behaved irresponsibly.

Although I was suspended from League games, I was still able to play in the return leg in Poland against Gornik Zabrze, and in internationals for England. I had missed England's season opener on 9 September, the 3–1 defeat at the hands of West Germany in Düsseldorf, but I was back by mid-October for the European qualifier against Turkey at Wembley. This time the Turks really fancied their chances, but when John Barnes scored after only two minutes we, and they, knew we were on our way to another big win against them. Lineker (twice) and Barnes had made it 4–0 by the break; further goals came from Bryan Robson, Peter Beardsley, Gary Lineker (thus completing his fourth England hat-trick) and Neil Webb.

Then, on 11 November, came the big one: a tie with the highly talented Yugoslavians in Belgrade we knew we had to win to be certain of reaching the finals. It was one of the most defining games of my entire career, coming as it did at the end of a trying and frustrating period. On top of that, a certain journalist from *The Sunday Times* questioned my involvement in the game and whether I was good enough any more to play for England, but Bobby Robson showed great faith in me and it was very much a case of wanting to go out and prove to everybody, including myself, that I could still make an impression, find some sort of form and serve my country well.

It had been a foggy day in Belgrade, and there had been some doubt over whether the game was going to be played. I remember I was reading a book about Robert the Bruce and how he had had to overcome so much to become king of Scotland. I, of course, read it very quietly, trying to put out of my mind the fact that the game could be delayed. I say to my players now that they should read in that hour and a half before the game to save the adrenalin and focus on something else. Then, when the match is about to start, they are fresh with an adrenalin rush that can have an effect. I'm not sure any of them take any notice of me, but they play cards and do other things to distract themselves. The *Sunday Times* journalist Brian Glanville was always very scathing in his criticisms of me, describing me as a veteran and well over the top. I used to rip out his articles and use them as bookmarks. So while I was reading the inspiring story of Robert the Bruce, I was also glancing at the bookmark, gradually becoming more and more fired up. Frequently I would go on to the pitch in order to ram his words down his throat. Perhaps I should have dedicated this book to the man who unknowingly motivated me so much. Thank you, Brian, for criticising me so badly and so often.

We knew it was going to be a hostile atmosphere. The stadium was in a bowl with the dressing rooms at the top. When the evening arrived it had turned mild and misty, and there was a beautiful grass surface to play on. We were held up in the tunnel – something to do with the mist and flares being let off – so I just started hitting the corrugated walls of the tunnel. I liked to be last out with England, and Tony Adams was just in front of me. We were two huge guys and must have looked intimidating standing there waiting for the signal. I was feeling impatient, and I started to shout, as I usually did, all the while hammering my fist on the side of the wall. It made a good echoing noise, which I rather liked, and Tony soon joined in with me. The Yugoslavs must have thought we were two escaped lunatics. It was a wonder they didn't ask the referee to search us for concealed weapons.

When you are backed into a corner, as we were for this game, there are no half measures. I had been loud prior to games before, but this was the first time I really went for it with England. The Yugoslavs, a much smaller side than us, looked over nervously and started to give some sort of response, but it was pathetic and we laughed at them. Then we shouted and banged even louder. We were using all the usual England supporters' chants, including 'Caged tigers!' You could see in the Yugoslavs' eyes they were petrified. We knew we had rattled them even before we set foot on the pitch. We were bursting to get out there, and when we did we tore into them and were four up after about twenty minutes: Peter Beardsley scored inside three minutes, and John Barnes, Bryan Robson and Tony Adams added others. It was all over by the break. Katanec's second-half goal was nothing more than a consolation.

I loved every minute of it; I could be in that tunnel for ever. Bobby Robson was behind us and loved hearing us getting worked up, and as a manager now I encourage my players to look their opponents in the eyes when they are in the tunnel waiting to go out and play and see if they are up to it. In the changing rooms after the game, knowing we had qualified for the finals in West Germany by beating Yugoslavia home and away, Woodsy and I were singing the Rangers songs in the showers with the rest of the squad looking at us as though we were mad. Bobby Robson put his head round the wall at one point and said, 'Shut up! You are getting on my nerves now, Butcher!' So I sang even louder. But Bobby loved it because it was one of the best results of his international career against a very talented side. It was one of the highlights of my international career too. Such moments I want to hold for ever, cradle and cherish, because there are so many setbacks in the game. For me it was the peak of my season after a wretched time. It was a complete release.

But as I got closer to home my troubles reappeared. I was facing a possible court case and its ramifications. We flew back to Heathrow and I stayed the night there, flying back to Glasgow the next day. The Welsh squad were in the same hotel and were on a real low because they had lost in Czechoslovakia and were out of the championship. We had enjoyed our usual good drink on the plane to celebrate our victory, but the Welsh were drinking to drown their sorrows. We soon linked up with Ian Rush, Peter Nicholas, Leighton James and Mike England and had a really great night. Their defeat brought home fully what we had achieved by reaching the finals.

Six days later I was back from suspension and lining up against Aberdeen at home. Rita was late to the game, and she had only just taken her seat when a corner was put into their box and the ball came arrowing straight to me. I thought it looked like a good chance and swung my left foot, but, as I did more often than not, put it high over the bar. Alex McLeish had come in to try to block it with a strong but fair challenge, and it was a complete and utter accident as I caught him while following through. I finished up on the deck. I had taken plenty of blocks of a similar nature and usually the blow was numb for only a few moments, so I waited for a few seconds, but instead of it wearing off I felt a searing pain up my leg.

Physio Phil Boersma came on and even then I told him I was fine. He helped me to my feet. I thought it was easing, so I stamped my foot to check. Bad mistake. I knew then it was broken because I felt my tibia move. I collapsed to the floor again. I don't know whether they believed me, though, because I wasn't stretchered off, I was carried off – not just off the pitch but right round to the dressing room. The pain was almost unbearable as I was laid out in the treatment room. I could feel every little movement as they pumped up the yellow sock to enclose my leg. Then I received a jab to kill the excruciating pain. Rita arrived and we went down to Ross Hall Hospital in Glasgow. They took an X-ray, plastered me up and kept me in overnight. I heard we had lost to Aberdeen – another big knock to our hopes of retaining the title. But for me, the broken leg had brought the season to a shuddering halt. I had managed to play just eighteen domestic games. Goals? Just the one, against St Mirren.

The next day the club sent a big limousine to pick me up so I could stretch out my leg in the back. I had to enter Ibrox by the tradesman's entrance as the press were waiting. The pain was so bad I was in tears as I hobbled up the stairs on my crutches, a full-length plaster encasing the damaged limb. I had plenty of visitors, including Graeme Souness and other players, but I was depressed, worrying about the possible court case and whether or not I would be fit in time for the European Championship the following June. But it was only the tibia, not the fibula, and the prognosis was that I would be ready by then.

I eventually received a message from the club's solicitor informing me that Chris Woods, Graham Roberts, Frank McAvennie and I would all have to get together on a certain date to be arrested and formally charged. A policeman came to my house, as I was lying in bed, unable to move. He was a Rangers fan and told me how he hated having to do this. It was confirmed on his walkie-talkie that all four policemen were with the four players, and I knew then that it was going to go all the way. A date was set for a trial – 12 April 1988.

In the meantime, I was determined to push hard from the outset to secure my place in the European Championship squad, and went to the national rehabilitation centre at Lilleshall to do my rehab under Graham Smith, who has since become a good friend. There were some wonderful people at Lilleshall, including the patients, and there was a fantastic spirit and camaraderie. One of the games we all had to play was sit-down basketball, which was great fun. We did it at the end of every session. On a Friday we had what they called a Grand National with a circuit of 24 activities. We went three times round and then played sit-down volleyball with hands and heads. It was a foul if you raised your backside off the floor. The winners got to shower and go home straight away, while the losers had to pay a forfeit of a five-mile bike ride to and from the main gate, with the last leg all uphill. It made the games fiercely competitive and the atmosphere generally hyper. I was there with people like Brendan Ormsby of Leeds United and Mark Aizlewood, and Kevin Blackwell, manager of Leeds United as I write. When Rangers were playing Steaua Bucharest in the second leg at home I asked BBC producer Geoff Byrne at Pebble Mill in Birmingham if we could watch the game live. A group of crippled footballers made their way into the studios to watch, among other things, a horror tackle from our player-manager Graeme Souness. We won 2–1 on the night, but went out on aggregate.

It seemed like only days later that I found myself in the dock at Glasgow Sheriff's Court before Sheriff Archibald McKay. We were there all week from nine a.m. every morning. The three Rangers players, all of whom lived near to one another, would go into Ibrox to shave, shower and take a sauna, ready to go into the dock. We sat with McAvennie, but we didn't talk to him because as far as we were concerned he was the reason the four of us were there. If he hadn't boxed our goalkeeper's ears none of this would have happened. It was a real media circus both inside and outside the court. The evidence was brought forward about crowd incitement, with the referee's report a key factor. It was completely rigged as far as I was concerned. As I said, we listened to this evidence for a week. It was very humbling, and I felt like a criminal. Because I wasn't training with the lads day in, day out I felt somewhat isolated as well, with far too much time to dwell on likely consequences.

When the crunch came, Frank McAvennie was up first to be given his judgement. He was found not guilty, and as he had been the aggressor and the one who had initiated the fracas, we thought we were in the clear. Graham Roberts was next up, and when his case too was found not proven Woodsy and I turned to each other with another look of relief. After all, Robbo had struck Frank, not us, and he was free to go. Then I was called up and the sheriff announced, 'Guilty.' I couldn't believe what I had heard. I didn't even hear how much I was fined, I was so stunned. Chris Woods was also found guilty and fined £500, twice as much as me. We were not happy bunnies.

The only footballer I can think of who has been dragged through court because of what happened on a football pitch is Duncan Ferguson, who was sent down for butting an opponent. Others, like Tony Adams and Jermaine Pennant, have been given time, but for matters not related to football. For someone as law-abiding as me, and with a father who was a prison officer too, it was horrifying to think I had done something on a football field which led to me being branded a criminal. Then my thoughts turned darker. Why me? I wondered. Why not McAvennie? Why not Roberts, the most aggressive of the three of us? It just didn't seem fair. I had done worse things on a football pitch and not found myself in court. Why this time?

The media, both in England and Scotland, were sympathetic. Naturally it was an immense story in Scotland and they gave it the full treatment, but there was always this air of disbelief about the case. I believe there's every chance it was a political decision taken way above the heads of the clubs, the police and even the courts. I think it was a decision made by the government to put football in its place. Prime Minister Margaret Thatcher hated football, hated its reputation, and loathed the way its hooligans had tarnished Britain's image abroad – it was only two years after Heysel, remember, and English clubs were still banned from Europe – and to this day I have a strong feeling that Woodsy and me, as high-profile players, were used as an example. I can think of no other reason for such expense and pomposity over an event on a football field. It's purely guesswork, of course, but I spoke to the legal people and they also suspected another agenda. Just consider the events on the pitch at Easter Road during my first League game for Rangers – much more likely, I would have thought, to cause a riot than the brief flashpoints in what was, after all, an Old Firm derby. What would they have done in a similar political climate after the more recent Arsenal and Manchester United mêlées? Put them away for life? As someone commented, it was a case of Goldilocks and the Three Bears, and they didn't want Goldilocks (McAvennie with his blond hair) but the three bears (the three Rangers players).

Souness was in a flap because he was really worried we were going to say enough was enough. David Holmes also said if we decided we had had our fill of Scottish football and Scottish justice, the club wouldn't stand in the way of our leaving. But I told them immediately I wouldn't be forced away. It was a sick joke as far as I was concerned.

Chris Woods was concerned about his England place and contemplated a move, but Graham Roberts also said he would remain, not knowing he was going to be released in the summer anyway. Naturally we put in an appeal, but it was turned down. I wondered again about some of the deliberate fouls and unprovoked attacks I had witnessed in my football life, some of them not even punished by the referee during the game, never mind later in a court of law.

So I finished the sorry episode with a criminal record, and to pour salt on the wound I was then told my leg had not healed properly and I wouldn't be going to West Germany that summer. Peter Scott, the specialist, called me in and told me the bone had not bonded well and there was evidence of a crack not strong enough to withstand any impact. The safest thing, he said, was to forget all about the European Championship. Easy for him to say. I had pushed myself to the limit at Lilleshall to make sure I was ready.

I went off to Florida on a family holiday and tried not to think about the finals. I watched only bits and pieces on a Spanish-speaking television channel. It was, I think, the right thing to do rather than watch it at home and mope about. It was my second time in Florida that year, because the club had sent me there in January when I was a bit low and not healing particularly well. We stayed at the Fontainebleau Hilton, which was spectacular, though I was taxed on the perk and every member of my family was ill at different times. But both breaks gave me a great lift when I really needed one. I hoped I would return fresh, fit and ready, mentally and physically, for the challenge of a new season.

CHAPTER FOURTEEN

BACK TO ACTION

The 1988/89 season was a crucial one for Rangers because Celtic had won the double in their centenary year. We had an influx of new players, such as the much-travelled Ray Wilkins, winger Mark Walters and yet another striker, Kevin Drinkell. Graeme Souness took us to Sampdoria's training ground in Il Ciocco, in Tuscany. Before we went we had three hard days' training at Bellahouston Park near Ibrox under the pace-making of Phil Boersma who, despite his capacity for alcohol, was a very fine runner. We didn't see a ball for three days; it was just 20-, 30- and 40-minute shuttle running, hill climbs, pyramid runs and body circuits, with two sessions on the Thursday and Friday and one long session on the Saturday before we flew out to Italy on the Sunday. The running was really hard, and at the end of the sessions we would run back to Ibrox along the streets, then up and down the steps at the back of the stands – probably 150 of them in twos and threes at a time, carrying people up them too, and even hopping up on one leg.

In Italy it was warm and the food was beautiful. We would start at nine a.m. with some ball work and finish around two hours later before going back down the windy road to the hotel. There was a running track and a big pitch there, exclusively for our use. We would have lunch and then go back in the afternoon for another session. After a sleep, there'd be more running at five p.m., still working on our stamina, before eventually moving on to the short, sharp stuff. In the midst of all this we might do a few lengths in the pool in the afternoon. By the evening we were too tired to do anything else other than have dinner. Even if we went to the bar it was for water, because we were there for one reason only – to get fit. We had just the one night off, when we were bussed down to the town for a wild meal with copious amounts of wine and beer. Souness was there and he loved it as we bonded with songs and jokes, all together in one restaurant. When the meal was over and Souness thought we had drunk enough, we were whipped back to the hotel. It eased the pain of training – in fact, we could feel virtually nothing by then!

The trip back up to the hotel was about twenty minutes, and Chris Woods and I would stand back to back in the narrow aisle of the coach and invite everyone else to come and fight us. The only rule was no headshots. All the young guys like Durrant and Ferguson would want to have a go, and despite the rule there was a closed eye and a few nicks about the nose by the time we finished – though far less than in the average Old Firm game. The kids kept coming back for more. There wasn't a lot of damage done because of the confined space between the seats, which restricted us to short, sharp jabs, but those brave enough to have a go knew about it.

We were at the camp for ten days and played just one game, against the local amateurs. When we returned to Scotland we were supremely fit and couldn't wait to start the season proper. I thought it was wonderful preparation, and when I was manager of Coventry I thought seriously about doing the same thing.

We started off with a comfortable win at Hamilton and a disappointing goalless draw at home to Hibernian. Celtic were next up – always a grudge match, but after losing our title to them the previous season we were well up for this meeting at Ibrox. I led the team out next to the Celtic captain Roy Aitken, who was followed by Ian Andrews, an English goalkeeper recently signed from Southampton. I looked at him and saw his eyes were glazed. I turned to Woodsy and told him his opposite number was all over the place and we would win this one.

We couldn't have had a worse start, however, as we went a goal down to, of all people, Frank McAvennie, who I still blamed for some of my problems the previous season. But we came back at them strongly and led 2–1 at half-time, with Mark Walters, Kevin Drinkell and Ally McCoist in outstanding form. We scored three more in the second half. We had done our job and were happy to see out the game, but the fans were going mad demanding more. I couldn't understand their reaction for here we were, hammering the reigning champions, and they were having a go at us. I later discovered the reason: Celtic had beaten Rangers 7–1 in the League Cup many years earlier and they wanted us to match or better the score. They were annoyed we had shut up shop when they felt we should have gone for the throat. Even beating Celtic 5–1 was not enough for them! We didn't know about the history and were more concerned about putting down a marker for our clashes over the rest of the season – four more of them, as it happened.

The result gave us a terrific boost. We won the next five games and didn't lose a game in the League until we went down at Aberdeen in October, when Ian Durrant and Neil Simpson clashed. Durrant was a brilliant, young, athletic player already ensconced in the national team and looking as though he would stay there for many years. He had lots of skill and was a bubbly character in the dressing room too. There was no hint of the problems to come when former Aberdeen player Neale Cooper put us in front. A free-kick was then awarded just inside our half, and the whistle had only just gone when the ball fell to Durrant. Simpson, who is still at Aberdeen as a successful community officer, carried through with his tackle and bent our youngster's knee backwards from the front. Everything went – cruciates, cartilages, ligaments, everything. Few people, including the referee, had seen the incident because attention was focused on the previous foul. The first we knew about it was Ian's piercing scream. He was stretchered off, we were forced to reorganise our team, and we finished up losing 2–1 after a late Charlie Nicholas goal. Chris Woods was at the changing-room end in the second half and as we came off he told me all he could hear was the screams coming from Ian Durrant. He was out for a little more than two years and was never the same player when he came back, eventually moving to Kilmarnock.

Was it deliberate? A lot of people said it was. I didn't see the incident, but I have to say it would have been completely out of character for Simpson. He just wasn't that kind of player. His career suffered tremendously afterwards because wherever he went and wherever he played he was always reminded about that challenge. He had to carry the baggage around with him for the rest of his career. He has hardly ever talked about it since. I have had plenty of rushes of blood to the head in my time, but none of them ever had such an ending. As it was knee-high and late, it suggests it was, at best, a serious misjudgement. Ian had nipped the ball away and Neil was presumably committed to his challenge. The saddest thing of all was the whistle had gone, so there was no need for either player to play the ball.

The shock of the incident prompted the almost inevitable on-the-pitch brawl, and afterwards everyone was raging about the tackle. I was so annoyed I booted the first thing I saw, which was the referee's door. My foot went halfway through it and then I was dragged away to our dressing room. When I came out after showering I was summoned by the police and charged with vandalism and a breach of the peace. Here we go again, I thought.

I tried to push it to the back of my mind as I was due to go out for dinner the same evening with Aberdeen favourite Willie Miller. The Millers had flown out to Florida at the end of the previous season on the same flight as the Butchers; we had made friends with him and his family and enjoyed a really good holiday together. We remain friends to this day. Prior to the Aberdeen game we had arranged for Rita and I to stay with Willie and his wife Claire, so after being told the bad news by the police I went through to the players' lounge where Rita and Claire were waiting. We went out for dinner at the beautiful Invery House and then went back to Willie's house. I sat with him having a few beers until the early hours of the morning. After being charged for a second time by the police I was seriously contemplating chucking it all in and moving back down south. I felt enough was enough. Willie and Claire were fantastic and helped me to make the decision to stay on.

During the drive back to Glasgow on the Sunday we received a telephone call from Jimmy Marshall, from whom we had bought our house in the Bridge of Allan. He warned us that the press were besieging our house because they had heard about the police action. It was no use avoiding it; I had to face them and get into my house. It's all starting again, I thought, but later in the week I was told charges were not going to be pursued and I wasn't going to face another court case. I was surprised because it was a done deal: there were plenty of witnesses who saw me boot the door and I had been officially charged. At the time I could only assume that someone, somewhere, had put in a good word for me, and later, of course, it transpired that Alex Smith had done just that. I was, however, charged by the Scottish Football Association for bringing the game into disrepute. I pleaded guilty and was fined £500 – a lot of money then and now. I was livid at the hearing when the Aberdeen secretary Ian Taggart said on oath I had aimed a kick at the referee as he stood in front of his door. Had that been true it would have led to a much more serious charge. At the time Louis Throw, the referee, was a long way down the tunnel, having seen the last of the players off the pitch. Fortunately he backed me up, stating he had been nowhere near the incident. I was left stunned once again by how far things had escalated.

I go back to Aberdeen regularly and they still haven't replaced the door, they've just patched it up. I guess they use it as part of the guided tour of Pittodrie. They must tell the punters it's one of the many dressing-room doors Terry Butcher kicked in during his career. Perhaps I should autograph it for authenticity.

We regrouped and readjusted after the loss of Durrant, and went back to Parkhead on 12 November to face Celtic. We were top and they were struggling in fifth place in what was now a ten-team division. We got off to a flyer with a Mark Walters penalty, they equalised, and then they went in front with an own goal – mine! And not just any own goal, but one of the best I have ever scored. It started with a free-kick from Celtic's left. I was on the edge of the box and I thought I had it. I flung myself full length to head it away at waist height only to watch it bend round Chris Woods into the top corner – the opposite direction to the way I had wanted it to go. It helped Celtic to a 3–1 victory. Own goals were something of a speciality for me. It's a fact that during Souness's reign at Ibrox no opposition striker scored more goals past Chris Woods than I did. It was odd Celtic had scored first in our first game and we had won 5–1, and this time we had gone in front with a goal only for them to win. The pattern continued in our next match on 3 January when they scored first and we went on to beat them 4–1. Happy New Year!

Early in December we lost another two games, on the trot, to Dundee United and Hearts. We bounced back to beat Hamilton, then came the New Year drubbing of Celtic, and then it was off to Motherwell and another defeat. They were always one of those teams that would beat us once a season, and I suppose it was good for the game in Scotland, even though it was rare (I certainly think it's good for the game now I'm at Motherwell!). But it was only a slight blip, and a win at Aberdeen – in what was for me a grudge match after all the police nonsense – set us off on another run of a dozen League games without defeat until we met the Dons again in the last game of the season at Ibrox. But the title race was over by then and we finished six points clear of the Dons and ten ahead of Celtic. We'd virtually clinched the championship at Celtic Park on April Fools' Day with goals from Drinkell and McCoist. The title was only officially ours, however, once we'd thrashed Hearts 4–0 at Ibrox, Mel Sterland, another English import, and Drinkell scoring two each. Mel was with us for half a season, and he too bought a house from my friend Jimmy Marshall, who seemed to have a good thing going with Rangers players. I have to say winning the title in 1989 didn't mean nearly as much as the first one, even though this time we won it in front of our own fans.

It was our second piece of silverware that season: we'd already secured the League Cup at Hampden before Christmas with a 3–2 win over Aberdeen – something the great Liverpool team used to do with regularity, winning the first trophy on offer so they were sure of something. As for our Scottish Cup run, that had begun towards the end of January when we drew Raith Rovers away. Souness promised us when we won he would take us away to Eilat in Israel for a few days' break. It sounded splendid – sunbathing on the shores of the Red Sea and staying in the fabulous King Solomon's Palace. But try as we might we could only manage a 1–1 draw. Raith played really well on the day and our sunshine trip in the middle of January was cancelled, much to the disgust of the manager. We beat them without difficulty at Ibrox, then put eight past Stranraer. Next up was Dundee United, who had a top striker in Kevin Gallacher who always used to give me problems because of his style of play. I hated playing against him. The tie went to a replay, and they clearly fancied their chances, but we played well and won 1–0 for a place in the semi-final against St Johnstone, who were in the division below us. The game was at Parkhead and everyone said Rangers need only turn up to go through to the final. We turned up, but we didn't go through. They could easily have won the goalless match, and you can imagine how angry Souness was afterwards. He never really spoke much in terms of tactics, and this time he was very short and to the point about poor standards and being bad professionals. Few words, maybe, but pointed and very true. We scored an early goal in the replay, settling everyone down, and we romped home 4–0.

Suddenly we were on for the treble. As Rangers captain I was desperate to do it. With just a few League fixtures of the season left I was only one booking away from a suspension, which would have kept me out of the May cup final, so I was rested for a couple of games. I returned to the side for the final League game at home to Aberdeen, when we were to be presented with the championship trophy. The occasion fell flat as they comprehensively beat us 3–0. I think one or two players were looking forward to the final. It was a warning we should have heeded.

We played Celtic on a hot Saturday afternoon, and we had one or two players struggling with fitness as well as having Ray Wilkins missing through injury. The truth was the final was coming at the end of a long, hard season, and Celtic were up for the game: they were on a mission to stop us taking all three trophies, as well as needing to win something themselves. The pitch looked green and good, but it was rock hard. We never really got going, and we looked a tired, lethargic team. Halfway through the first half we won a throw-in inside the Celtic half, but big Roy Aitken, who had chased the ball out, picked it up and threw it in, and with everyone on the back foot referee Bob Valentine waved play on. The ball was pumped forward, Gary Stevens failed to control it as he tried to play it back to Chris Woods, and little Joe Miller nipped in to score. It was an appalling error by the officials. Then, late in the game, there was a long throw from Gary Stevens and I managed to rise above Pat Bonner to head what I thought was the equaliser, only for the referee to blow his whistle for a foul by Davie Cooper on the goalkeeper. I watched it afterwards and obviously I didn't think it was a foul.

It's a strange thing, but whenever I played for Rangers we always felt everyone was against both Celtic and ourselves. Now I'm on the other side, as it were, with Motherwell, everyone thinks Rangers and Celtic are given everything. It's just the way things are. My doctor at the time (he still is), Iain Cathcart, was also a grade-one referee and officiated in a lot of European games. We talked about my problems with referees' decisions, and having refereed me he was taken aback by how much I argued with officials. He told me it straight, and I listened, though whether I put his wise words into practice is more difficult to say. He is still at it now: he sends me text messages when I criticise officials during my Radio Five commentaries. He keeps an eye on me like my conscience. And he was right, because I was booked a lot for dissent and slamming the ball down when I didn't like a decision, or when I was asked to move too far back for a free-kick.

Despite the disappointment of the Scottish Cup defeat, it had been a great season for Rangers, and from a personal point of view: I had more than made up for my quiet 1987/88 with a total of 51 games and four goals, two of which had come in a UEFA Cup first-round game against GKS Katowice of Poland. We had scraped a 1–0 win at home and were favourites to go out in the return leg in the harsh Polish city, but we won 4–2. What was really memorable about the match happened afterwards when a local fan came up and asked me to sign a book I had co-authored. I couldn't believe it had turned up there. It was more of a thrill for me than my two goals, for not many copies had been produced. Still, losing in a Cup Final to our biggest rivals in such controversial circumstances was a real downer. After the match we picked up our loser's medals and trudged back into the dressing room, listening to the Celtic celebrations. When Graeme Souness came into the room, he took his medal, threw it in the bath and said, 'I don't take loser's medals home with me.' It wasn't the only thing thrown about the dressing room that day. Later, little George Soutar, our kit man and a very nice old man who looked like the cartoon character Mr McGoo, pulled the plug out of the bath and right at the bottom of the plughole was Graeme's medal. Souness still didn't want it, so George took it home.

Once Bobby Robson had survived the threatened and much-called-for axe following the disastrous showing at the 1988 European Championship, it also turned out to be a decent season for England. I was fit and ready for the first game, a friendly against Denmark in September, though only 27,000 turned up at Wembley after the summer's disappointments. Robson brought in young Arsenal midfield player David Rocastle to play alongside Neil Webb, who scored a goal made by Bryan Robson. It was a good one to win, and I for one was relieved, because at one point I'd given away the ball to Elstrup, just managing to make up my ground to stop Laudrup as the Juventus striker was about to pull the trigger. During that match, too, there was a late arrival from our bench, a cocky young lad by the name of Paul Gascoigne who had just moved to Spurs from Newcastle for a fee of £2 million.

October brought the first of our qualifiers for the World Cup in Italy. We didn't make the greatest of starts against Sweden, our biggest rivals in the group, and it ended in a turgid goalless draw. Naturally we took some stick from the press for failing to win our home game, Gary Lineker missing the best chance of the match and Chris Waddle unlucky not to be awarded a penalty when goalkeeper Ravelli brought him down. Pressure began to build on Bobby Robson again, particularly after a 1–1 draw in Saudi Arabia which prompted the *Daily Mirror* headline 'For the Love of Allah – Go!' It seems it was a good one for me to have missed.

It was crucial we achieved some sort of result in our first friendly of 1989, when we met Greece in Athens. It didn't start as well as we might have hoped when, inside the first minute, Samaras broke through between Des Walker and me and tumbled to the ground when I tackled him. Saravakos scored from the spot. Fortunately for England, and for me, John Barnes levelled with a twenty-yard free-kick seven minutes later, and towards the end we converted a great deal of pressure into a winner from Bryan Robson.

The next game, our second World Cup qualifier, was a trip into the unknown. The time we spent in Tirana in the very communist country of Albania was an education. Thousands at the airport welcomed us and we were surprised to find the streets gridlocked, not with cars but with people and horses and carts. There were no public-service vehicles at all on these beautiful wide roads. All the men and women looked the same, with their dark hair and their short, stocky build. It was a very unusual place.

We had nice big rooms in the best hotel in town. We were in the middle of the capital city, but our windows looked directly out over a farm. The problem was the farm had a noisy donkey and an even noisier cockerel, who decided he would be our personal alarm call first thing in the morning. Gascoigne was sharing a room with Chris Waddle, while Chris Woods and I were next door. On coming back from lunch we heard a racket from their room, wondered what Gazza was up to this time, and decided to take a look. Waddle had lifted a shutter on the window and was holding it open while Gazza hurled blocks of red carbolic soap at the cockerel some 50 or 60 yards away. We were winding him up as he kept missing, so I went to hold open the window too so he could take a flying run at it. Just as we were fancying our chances, Bobby Robson suddenly appeared and demanded to know what Gazza was up to. He told him honestly he was trying to hit the bird that had been keeping him awake at night. Bobby, instead of being cross, said, 'Go on then, Gazza. The bugger has been keeping me awake as well.' And with that he walked over and helped us prop open the window to give Gazza as much space as we could. Incredibly, Gazza eventually hit the bird with a piece of soap, though it bounced a couple of times first. The bird limped away to the cheers of the hotel room. We quickly shut the window and pulled down the shutters, wondering aloud what the farmer would think when he came to harvest his crop of red carbolic soap.

When we got to the training ground for our 'private' training session we discovered they had let in about 5,000 spectators who seemed determined to put us off. At the end of the session Gazza took Shilton's gloves and went in goal. He started doing imitations of all the England goalkeepers and fooling around. Someone would take a shot and he would dive over it like local Albanian hero and British comedian Norman Wisdom. The crowd loved it, and the more they cheered the more Gazza played up to it, with spectacular saves followed by chronic mistakes. It was wonderful entertainment for a quarter of an hour; he had the crowd in the palm of his hands. It was a great public-relations exercise.

The next day we played our game on a very bumpy pitch. John Barnes scored the first and made the second for Bryan Robson. Shilton, once again, came to the rescue as I didn't have one of my best games, but 2–0 was a good result at a difficult venue. We had them back at Wembley in April and beat them 5–0 to get right back on track for qualification. Lineker had gone seven internationals without a goal, but he settled himself and the team with an early header. His strike partner Peter Beardsley scored a couple, Chris Waddle also put his name on the scoresheet, and then, to the delight of the 60,000 crowd, substitute Gazza, making the longest appearance of his international career so far at 24 minutes, netted the fifth two minutes from time.

Come May and I was back in Scotland, at Hampden for the third time that season, lining up against Scotland in the Rous Cup. As usual, we stayed in Troon at the Marine Hotel on the golf course. I had a great friend who lived in Troon, the late Scotland rugby player Gordon Brown, and he and his wife Linda had indicated they would like to meet up. Rita had also telephoned me to tell me she was pregnant, with Alistair. The news came out of the blue as we hadn't been trying for a third child. I was thrilled. I immediately telephoned Gordon and his wife and sneaked out into the night to meet them for celebrations at nearby Piersland House Hotel. I had a nice few beers before getting back in the early hours of the morning, much the worse for wear. I was with Chris Woods and we were totally out of order again, but this time we weren't caught and any noise was covered by the fact that a number of the press were staying at the same hotel and they were rolling in at all times from their nocturnal research. Sorry, Bobby!

I was still very much on a high the next day, even when I suffered the usual jeers and boos from the Scots. We were without Lineker, Barnes and Beardsley that day; there weren't any Arsenal or Liverpool players because of their crucial final League game on which the title depended. John Fashanu started up front with Tony Cottee, but it was Fashanu's replacement, Steve Bull of Wolves – something of a rarity in an England shirt because his team was, at the time, in the (old) Third Division – who struck the decisive second goal after Waddle had opened the scoring. It was Steve's 54th goal of the season in 62 competitive matches.

It was a sweet win for me; in fact, it was one of the most pleasurable games of my life. I really enjoyed both the game and its aftermath because it really shut a few people up and it was nice to prove a point about the English in Scotland. After the match we drove home, Chris and me in the back with a few beers and our wives in the front. We took great delight in gesticulating the score at the Scottish fans we passed in their buses.

Mo Johnston played that day, even though previously he had claimed he'd had enough of Scotland and had moved away to play in France. There was a lot of talk about him coming back, and there had been pictures in the paper of him wearing a Celtic top and signing for Billy McNeill. I was determined no player, especially Mo, was going to score against England, so during the match I was chatting to him. At one point I asked, 'So you're coming back to Scotland next season?'

'Yeah,' he replied. 'I will be with you next season.'

I responded, 'Yes, and I look forward to giving you a good kicking.'

He looked at me a little quizzically. 'No,' he said, 'I will be playing with you.'

Had I been really sharp I would have picked it up, but I dismissed it as the typical ramblings of a centre-forward trying to put me off my game. But several weeks later, on 12 July, a big day in the Protestant calendar (it's the anniversary of the Battle of the Boyne), Mo Johnston signed for Rangers to become the club's first Catholic player. He must have signed the contract with Celtic in invisible ink.

At that time it was still a very strong principle that Rangers did not sign Catholics. Celtic, however, were prepared to sign players regardless of their religion. Players such as Danny McGrain and Kenny Dalglish, and their legendary manager Jock Stein, for example, were all Protestants, so Celtic had the pick of everyone. Graeme Souness was no fool and quickly realised he was damaging his chances by having only half of the football's population to choose from, and he was particularly anxious to break the mould. He had played in Italy and in Liverpool and knew the only way to be successful was to encompass everyone. His only concern was signing good footballers, regardless of their chosen god. When I'd signed he was desperate for me to be a Catholic, but I wouldn't tell him what I was. I remember in my first few weeks at Ibrox there were all kinds of rumours going around, and regularly I would be asked by Rangers fans what school I had been to and what my parents' names were. I didn't say. I simply told them I was an English footballer. It eventually came out in the newspapers. They pointed out my marriage had taken place in St Peter's, a High Anglican church and therefore very similar to Catholicism. My son Christopher also attended a nursery called St Mary's, which increased the rumours, but eventually they became convinced I was C of E.

Souness wanted to smash these ridiculous self-imposed restrictions, but in Mo Johnston he not only signed a Catholic, which was controversial enough, but an ex-Celtic player who was reviled by the Rangers fans. No one could believe it when he signed; we thought Souness was off his head. Certainly sign a Catholic, but not one who was hated as well. The fact he had only recently posed for pictures with Celtic holding a green and white shirt having ostensibly signed for them meant he was also hated by the Celtic fans for letting them down. It was a typical Souness signing, and I would love to do something as brave as that as a manager.

Sixteen years later, Mo Johnston is still a topic of conversation with football fans and his signing remains one of the most controversial moments in Scottish football history. It still rankles with both sets of supporters to such an extent that when an old Old Firm match was staged for charity recently Mo was going to play one half for Celtic and one for Rangers, but there was such a furore from both sets of supporters the organisers had to ask him to step down altogether to avoid trouble. That is how serious it is still taken. The raw nerve will not be healed.

After the Scotland game there were still two England matches remaining, including a really crucial World Cup qualifier against Poland at Wembley on 3 June. Despite the lateness of the season it was one of those great days at Wembley: the sun was shining on a full house as we beat them 3–0 to take a massive stride closer to Italy.

It would have been nice to be free to drift off on holiday after that, but we still had to play Denmark four days later at the Idraetspark in

Copenhagen. It was completely unwarranted as it was only a friendly and could only have been a reciprocal arrangement because we had played them earlier in the season. So after the Poland game we went back to the hotel, had a few beers, then wandered down to the Black Bull in Bisham where Gazza was in top form, even though he was still only a peripheral figure in the team. There was one customer at the pub wearing a very obvious wig. In fact it was the worst wig I had ever seen, and to make matters worse he was sitting at the next table to us with a woman he was clearly trying to impress. Gazza couldn't contain himself. Cries like 'Syrup straight!' filled the air. I have to say the guy took it really well as he was being slaughtered.

We went back to the Burnham Beeches Hotel that evening in quite good shape, and on Sunday Bryan Robson, Chris Woods and I decided we would have a lunchtime drink while the substitutes were training. We went down to the local at midday and ended up going way beyond last orders at 2.30, staying until about six for a six-hour session. We made it back to the hotel for dinner, trying our best to look sober, which we certainly were not, then got straight back to the pub, though like good professionals we left at closing time, despite invitations to stay on for 'afters'. But when we arrived back at the hotel we walked straight into a party. We were asked if we would like to join in. It would have been churlish to refuse, and we stayed until one a.m. This time there was no tap on the shoulder from Mr Robson, even though we knew he was about. Perhaps even he realised the Denmark friendly was a game too far.

In that match Peter Shilton surpassed Bobby Moore's England international record of 108 caps before being replaced by Chris Woods. In Denmark's goal was Peter Schmeichel, and for the first time in my career a goalkeeper threw the ball over my head as I stood just inside my own half. Despite our awful preparations, we managed to preserve our unbeaten record for the season. Gary Lineker scored his 29th goal for his country, but then we gave Lars Elstrup too much room from a corner and he made us pay for it. It was the first goal we had conceded in nine and a half hours' play, and as I made my way home for a well-deserved break I hoped I could be just as tight at the back for my club in the forthcoming season.

CHAPTER FIFTEEN

BLOODY HERO

Over his years in management Graeme Souness has proved himself to be as spiky as he was as a player, and those who fall out with him don't hang around for too long. Such a case in point was Graham Roberts, who we saw go during the close season. There was undoubtedly some friction between Roberts and Souness, who had blamed him for a couple of our defeats because of individual mistakes he had allegedly made, particularly in the last game against Aberdeen. After that game Roberts had said a few things about Souness after being rollicked loud enough for others to hear. They had more words, with a few good old Anglo-Saxon terms flying across the dressing room, until Souness said, 'Are you telling me to fuck off?' To which Roberts answered, 'Yes!' End of story – the final nail in Graham's coffin. In the pre-season Roberts did not go to Italy; instead he was sent with the reserves on the Highlands tour with instructions to the coaching staff he was to strip as a substitute but not be used in any of the games. It all finished with a move for Graham back south of the border.

The last time Rangers won the championship I had been suspended for the first game of the season and had to present the chairman's wife with a bouquet of flowers and sit in the stand as the champions' flag was unfurled. Then I watched as we lost. This time I was available for the ceremony, but once again we started off on the wrong foot, losing at home to St Mirren by a single goal, Kenny McDowall, now the reserve coach at Celtic, scoring the one that mattered. Once more we had shown no sense of occasion, losing a game we should have won.

We were due to visit Celtic at Parkhead for the third match of the season, and we couldn't have gone there in much worse shape as we also lost our second game, at Hibs, by two goals to nil. Celtic were top by the time we arrived, but any concerns we had were quickly brushed away when Trevor Steven, another of our England internationals, took a right-wing corner and I rose above my marker Paul Elliott and got my head to the ball. Elliott took me down so I didn't see the ball hit the net, but I heard the swish as the ball struck home amid the complete silence of the Celtic fans massed behind the goal. What a pleasant feeling that was. I've scored, but what do I do now? I decided to take off with my fist raised and ran the length of the silent main stand to our supporters at the other end, who were going berserk. Dziekanowski scrambled an equaliser, but we were delighted with our first point of the season.

A feature of that game was the appearance of Mo Johnston who, remember, had supposedly signed for them before joining us. Needless to say the Celtic fans screamed abuse at him whenever he was near the ball, echoed by some of our own fans who from the start showed their disgust at having a Catholic in their Protestant ranks. Mo was reviled by the Rangers fans particularly for head-butting Stuart Munro during the League Cup Final in 1986, for which he had been sent off. He was second on the Rangers hate list only to Peter Grant of Celtic, who had long been top of the charts, and he was constantly threatened. Not only did he have a bodyguard, he was also staying at Souness's home in Edinburgh for his personal safety. He eventually moved out to his own flat in Edinburgh. We all knew what a great player Mo was, but none of us realised his strength of character and purpose. I have to say, the reaction of our own so-called supporters was disgusting, with scarves being burned and season tickets sent back by the diehards.

As I said, as a group the players hadn't believed he was going to sign for us until he actually put pen to paper hours before we departed for Italy on our pre-season trip. The news soon arrived he had joined the club and was flying out on a private plane straight away. It was, as far as I was concerned, a fabulous signing for the club because Mo was such a good player, while Souness had achieved his ambition of beginning to break down the sectarian barriers at Ibrox. Our only doubt was we knew he was fiercely proud of being a Celtic fan, and we wondered how he would settle with us. We need not have worried. He was terrific.

Next day the club wanted the English and Scottish players to hold a press conference to tell the media what a good signing he was. There was no problem as far as Ray Wilkins, Chris Woods, Mark Walters, I and some others were concerned, but the Scottish players Davie Cooper, Ian Ferguson, Ally McCoist, John Brown and the rest declined because they had received so many telephone calls from friends back home telling them not to become involved. Jimmy Bell, our kit man, didn't want to become involved at all. Mo roomed with Ally McCoist, as he had done for the national team, and it was Jimmy's practice to put fresh kit outside everyone's room for the next day. But he refused to do so for Mo, just leaving Ally's, forcing Mo to go down three flights of stairs to the kit room to fetch his gear. Mo did so stoically and without complaint; in fact, in the end he made a joke about it. But this was a complete upheaval for the club. Even at meal times there were a number of Scots who would not sit with him. What had happened to the moral high ground claimed by Rangers? They always used to say it was Celtic who were intolerant and unable to cope with the mixing of religions. Wrong. There were no such difficulties for the English players, of course. All we knew was that we had signed a good player who was going to help us retain our title.

In early September I returned to Glasgow from international duty in Sweden after a few beers at Heathrow. My head was still bandaged – more about that later – but I didn't expect nor get any sympathy when Souness met me. He congratulated me on a decent result and promptly told me to get it into my head that I would be playing against Aberdeen on Saturday. He wasn't going to get any argument from me. I wasn't, however, in the best of shape, and I had to cancel a personal appearance for my boot sponsors Nike the day before the game because I felt faint, I suppose from the loss of blood (either the blood or the beers!). It had all got to me, and I slept from lunchtime right through to the next morning, when I showered, re-bandaged my head, and went out and helped beat our old rivals Aberdeen. Mo Johnston scored for us.

Immediately after that Aberdeen game we faced Bayern Munich at Ibrox in a European Cup tie. We shocked them by going a goal up with a Mark Walters penalty, but then they scored three. Kogl, Thon from the penalty spot, and a wonderful 25-yard strike from Augenthaler undid us. We held them to a goalless draw in the return leg in Bavaria but we were never really in with a shout of turning over that first-leg score.

Johnston continued to ignore the taunts from his own fans and carried on scoring goals for us, against Hearts, Dundee United, St Mirren and Hibs. But the real turning point came on 4 November when he scored against Celtic at Ibrox. He'd had a quiet time against Celtic in the first game, but the entire stadium erupted when he scored the winner a few minutes from time. He finished as our leading goalscorer in the League. Now everyone loved him – well, nearly everyone!

We were on good form, and I even scored with a left-foot volley against Dunfermline as we enjoyed a run of success spoilt only by our usual defeat against Aberdeen at Pittodrie. We beat Celtic again at Parkhead with a goal from another of our ever-growing English brigade, Nigel Spackman, and then for a third time at home on April Fools' Day. I crossed the ball for Kevin Drinkell, Anton Rogan stuck his hand up to concede a penalty, and Mark Walters converted as usual; Mo and Ally, with another penalty, completed the scoring. The title was clinched at Tannadice Park on 21 April with a goal from Trevor Steven, and afterwards, in the very small changing rooms at Dundee United's ground, we sang the Rangers songs, including the 'Sash'. As we were going at it hammer and tongs a BBC crew came into the dressing room and relayed our rendition of the songs to the nation, which did little to narrow the religious divide. After that it was back to the Swallow Hotel to celebrate our third title in four years – but still the first one remained the best for me, as it was my first championship honour and it broke a nine-year barren run for the club.

Our only defeat of the season at the hands of Celtic came in the fourth round of the Scottish Cup. We had beaten St Johnstone 3–0 but we lost at Parkhead to a scrappy goal in a scrappy game. As we came off, Billy McNeill, the Celtic manager, was being interviewed live, and as I came through the door I smashed it against the wall. I was, if I remember rightly, chasing referee Brian McGinlay at the time. I thought no more about it as I showered, changed and moved off to Ibrox to pick up the car. Woodsy and I would often go off to the Rising Sun, a neutral pub in Bridge of Allan where club colours were banned. It was very much a male preserve, and when we walked in there was a round of applause and cheers from the Rangers fans. That was unusual for this establishment and I couldn't understand it – we had lost the game after all – but it was explained they had shown the match live on BBC along with the post-match McNeill interview. While they were watching, the door crashed back and I came through shouting and swearing, McNeill cringing in the corner, all captured live on television. That, naturally, is another door that gets a mention when tours are taken round Celtic Park, even though the ground has changed. *Doors I Have Smashed* by Terry Butcher could possibly be a sequel to this autobiography. I'm ashamed to say it's a never-ending story, but I suppose it's better than kicking people around the stadium.

Unfortunately, having reached the League Cup Final for the fourth year in succession, we lost the match – to Aberdeen. The first person I saw after the final whistle was Willie Miller. I was pleased for him as he is a good pal. We had beaten them twice before, so this was third time lucky for them. We received our medals then ran across to our supporters, and I threw them my shirt. They were special shirts to commemorate the match, but to me it was a loser's shirt and I had no wish to keep it. It wasn't the brightest thing to do, however, as there was a massive battle over who was going to take it home. I ran back across the pitch in shorts and socks bitterly disappointed we had missed out on what would have been the first trophy of the season.

So we finished with just the one Cup, but it was the one we wanted the most. And to make things better for us Aberdeen also beat Celtic in the Scottish Cup Final, 9–8 on penalties after a goalless draw. Celtic won nothing in 1989/90, Alex Smith had led Aberdeen to a double, and Rangers were the champions of Scotland – again.

England were involved in two World Cup qualifiers during the first months of that season, both were away, and both were crucial. The first, as I've already mentioned, was in Stockholm against our biggest challengers Sweden, and I finished it bandaged up like a mummy after splitting open my head. It became my moment of true fame. Despite all the games, the trophies and everything else, I am still best remembered for my fifteen minutes – actually, that should be 90 minutes – of notoriety for cutting my head. These days I doubt whether I would have been allowed to continue as my white England shirt turned as red as the bandage around my head. Now there must be no blood, either on the face or on the kit, because of the problem of AIDS.

It was a big game for us, and with Bryan Robson injured and Peter Shilton wanting to concentrate on his goalkeeping, I was asked to skipper the side. We knew we needed a result. I had suffered a disaster against them the previous year when we could only draw 0–0 at Wembley, so we were really under pressure. During the first half a cross came in and I thought I would head it back into their half with some interest. But as I was about to connect their centre-forward Ekstrom nipped in front of me and flicked it on, leaving me to crash my forehead into the back of his head. There was a crack, and I knew it was going to be a sore one. I put my hand to my head right on the hairline and immediately felt very thick blood, not the usual thin variety. I knew I was in trouble, and I was having difficulty stemming the flow until Fred Street and Norman Medhurst ran on to bandage it up.

We weren't playing well, and it was a bumpy pitch. It was clearly going to be a battle to qualify in the second half, but I had no time to share my thoughts with Bobby Robson at half-time as I was whisked off to the treatment room. Doc Crane laid me down, wiped away the excess blood, and started to stitch me up. Bobby popped in to see how the ten stitches he was told I needed were progressing, but there was no mention of me coming off. When the bell for the second half went the doc had only completed seven of the stitches. He insisted that I needed at least two more, but I insisted time had run out, so he quickly wrapped another bandage around my head and gave me a clean shirt to replace the now bright red one I had already taken off.

So my problem was the cut had been left partially open and the blood was still pumping, helped by the flow of adrenalin. Every time I headed the ball I could hear a distinctive and unsettling squelching noise, a wet sound of leather on bloodied flesh. Every player on both teams had some of my blood on them, either on their shirt or somewhere on their body as they came into contact with either the ball or me. The biggest problem was for Peter Shilton, because the blood made the ball slippery. I remember him looking at this speckled, slimy ball and then at me, as if to say, 'What are you trying to do to me?' But it didn't affect him too badly. Right near the end Des Walker made one of his rare mistakes – perhaps the only one he made in his international career – but Shilton produced a superb save to preserve our share of the points. A goalless draw doesn't sound like a great result, but believe me it was. They were a very strong team and didn't often drop points at home.

But the only story afterwards was me as I came off covered from head to foot in blood; pushed very much to the background was the fact that Neil Webb had also been injured, far more seriously, with a ruptured Achilles. I have a tendency to do the mad eyes for the photographers, and this expression mixed with the blood made me look like a complete lunatic. The picture made most of the papers across both countries.

I went straight in to see Doc Crane to have the final stitches inserted.

He cut away some of my hair, then dressed the wound with a plastic bandage so I could have a shower. It took me ages to scrub off the dried blood as it was matted in my hair and all over my body, and then I noticed I was still bleeding, only this time from a cut over my eye from another collision. Back I went to see the doc to have more stitches inserted. When I eventually emerged I was greeted by the press, who already had a quote from the manager: 'People have been awarded Victoria Crosses for less.' The comment, I felt, was a little embarrassing. It seemed everyone was being carried away by the sight of a bit of blood. But it just happened to be me, and I believe any member of the team would have done exactly the same thing. Whether they would have enjoyed the rest of the match as much as I did is another story, but I found in it something that drove me on. I had played through injury before for Bobby, at Ipswich, and my desire was always to continue until it was physically impossible to do so. I was caught in another scrum at the airport when the English press again surrounded me, eager for quotes.

The head knock must have been worse than I thought, because I remember buying everyone a drink at the airport, even Brian Glanville. I stayed the night at Heathrow with Gary Stevens and Woodsy before returning to Glasgow in the morning. When I spoke to Rita she told me journalists had been ringing her up to ask her what she thought of her husband being a hero. She'd known nothing about it because Scottish television wasn't showing the England match; the first she heard of my injury was when the first journalist to ring told her, and she'd immediately tuned in to the radio to listen to the rest of the game. We'd worn an all-white strip for the match, and when I got back I showed her the shirts and shorts covered in blood. Almost as we were looking at them I took a telephone call from a company called Radion who made a washing powder; they asked if they could use my bloodied kit for a television advert. We got six months' supply of their detergent for our co-operation. Both shirts came up spotless, and one of them is in the museum at Hampden Park.

I have signed hundreds of pictures of me in the bandage and bloodied shirt since then. In fact, Motherwell are fed up of having these photos sent to them. The incident became so well known I even took part in a re-run during the build-up to Euro 96 with Skinner and Baddiel for their irreverent feature 'Phoenix from the Flames'. It was a real good laugh with two personable lunatics. We re-enacted it at Hendon football ground, and Steve Hodge came down for it. Skinner and Baddiel took the Michael out of the Swedish presenters by wearing woolly-type jumpers. We had a team line-up to start off with, and everyone who was famous for wearing white, from Randall in *Randall and Hopkirk Deceased* and Elvis in Las Vegas to the little chap from *Fantasy Island*, was included. Even the Pope was in the line-up in his white robes. I went into the changing rooms to put on my England gear and there were all these famous lookalikes talking with Cockney accents. I was kitted out with a bandage with a tube extending from it to a bucket of mock blood; I had to chase the presenters with blood literally spurting from my head. Two more buckets of blood were thrown over Steve Hodge and the 'Swedish presenters' as I went running past. Needless to say, it was all well over the top, but it was hilarious. Skinner and Baddiel were also going to include a reference to the cut head in their 'Three Lions' anthem, something about Terry Butcher going to war, but the Football Association made them cut it out because it was considered politically incorrect. It was a pity because I loved the song, even more so because the Scots hated it. When I was commentating on the England–Spain quarter-final during Euro 96, it made the hairs on the back of my neck stand up when it was played at the stadium after the penalty shoot-out, with all the fans joining in.

But back to England, for we still had a qualifier to play, possibly needing a point to be sure of our place in Italy. We were completely outplayed by Poland in Chorzow that October, but managed another goalless draw. There is no doubt that Peter Shilton saved us; they even hit the crossbar towards the end, though Peter claims he saved that one as well. Still, we were through, having finished a point behind group winners Sweden but four points clear of the Poles. After the game we had to wait on the plane for the journalists who had to file their copy. By the time they arrived Bryan Robson and I had consumed a full bottle of champagne and were in an exceptionally good mood. We were both very available for any quotes.

Over the next seven months we played seven warm-up friendlies, six of them at Wembley. Against Italy in November we recorded a third successive goalless draw, but the goals came back in December when Bryan Robson netted twice against Yugoslavia, over whom we seemed to have the Indian sign. Bobby Robson tried out a whole batch of new players in the game, including Paul Parker, Palace's Geoff Thomas, Tony

Dorigo and David Platt. In March 1990 I had the honour of captaining my country against Brazil at Wembley, and a 1–0 victory courtesy of a Gary Lineker goal made it a perfect day. We were playing for a trophy called the Varig Cup, and I had to climb the famous Wembley stairs for the first time in my career to collect it – a great thrill. It's the only time I finished on the winning side against the Brazilians.

A month later we beat the Czechs in a match that will be remembered by a lot of supporters because of the performance of Paul Gascoigne. It was one of the best games you could ever wish to see, and it was a huge pity only 21,342 people turned up to watch what turned out to be a cracker in which Gazza really pushed himself to the fore. He scored one of the goals, Stuart Pearce with his fearsome power added another, and Steve Bull also scored – twice. There had been a huge press campaign to have Gazza in the side, something which was never certain because of the number of quality midfield players England had available to them at the time. But Gazza did so well that he kept his place against Denmark in May, and again we recorded a good win. A week later we lost to Uruguay in our final Wembley game, but it was our first defeat since the 1988 European Championship and we were in good heart as we left for the World Cup.

CHAPTER SIXTEEN

NEARLY IMMORTAL AGAIN

The cruellest cut of all in football has to be when a preparation squad for the World Cup is finally trimmed down to the last 22. The decision was made only days before we were due to leave for Italy, and it must have been a hard choice for Bobby Robson and Don Howe. But it had to be done, and midfielder David Rocastle, striker Alan Smith, centre-half Tony Adams (all from Arsenal) and goalkeeper Dave Beasant were left out. It was a nightmare saying goodbye to guys you had been working so close with, but I have to say all four of them were great. There was no sulking and no one threw his toys out of the pram. Still, it was clearly a damn sight harder for them than it was for us.

We met up at Luton towards the end of May, which was when the news came through that Bobby Robson had decided he wasn't going to stay on with England after the competition. He had not been offered a new contract by the Football Association and, with Graham Kelly's permission, had signed a contract to manage PSV in Holland for 1990/91. There was the expected over-the-top explosion from the media, who claimed the manager should go now because his mind could not possibly be on the important task of managing England in the World Cup finals. Clearly they did not know Bobby Robson as well as I did, for there could have been no doubt at all over his commitment, or of those players for whom this tournament was also a last throw of the dice. We were determined to give it our best shot, not just for ourselves but for our manager.

Our base was the beautiful island of Sardinia, and we had our wives or girlfriends with us for the first week as we relaxed in the resort hotel Is Morus. It was a great week with the girls, and a special occasion for the

Butchers as it was Rita's birthday while we were out there. The team received lots of guests, among them Nigel Kennedy, who played his violin for us, and Mick Hucknall, who showed up to wish us well. It was a good way to prepare.

In early June they watched us leave to take a short flight to Tunisia for a final warm-up match, then flew home themselves. I was in the starting line-up in Tunis on a really horrible pitch under the hot African sun. My place, according to the critics, was in doubt – there were others, like Mark Wright and Paul Parker, emerging on the scene to partner Des Walker in the heart of our defence – and I didn't particularly enhance my reputation with my performance on the day. We were soon a goal down after a horribly sliced 40-yard pass from Paul Gascoigne opened us up, and from that point on we were chasing the game. I was having my own problem with the striker I was marking, who was a bit quick. I was becoming frustrated, particularly when I went up for free-kicks and corners. The player marking me would hold his arms in front of my chest while facing away from his goal, and I couldn't get past or get away from him. I eventually told him to keep his arms down or he would get an elbow or worse. He ignored me. Gazza was on the dead ball, and I gave him the nod to find me. Sure enough my marker was standing stock still in front of me with his arms ready to gather me in. I put my head down and ran at him like a bull. I knew I would make contact if he held his ground, and I caught him under the cheekbone, knocking him spark out. Their players went potty while I protested my innocence. I was surprised when the referee cautioned me because before I made my run I had checked he was not in eyeline – as you do!

Bobby wasn't best pleased, although he wasn't sure what exactly had happened, and he eventually replaced me with Mark Wright. When I was substituted I took off my shirt and threw it at the dugout because I was so annoyed with my performance. But it was misinterpreted as anger aimed at Bobby Robson for hauling me off, and was reported as such. Total rubbish. I respected the man so much I would never have dreamt of doing such a thing. Sure I was cross, but only because I thought I had played myself out of the World Cup team. Bobby defended me to the press, then looked at the video. My head butt stood out a mile, and as they watched all the players applauded. But not Robson. 'I stuck my neck out for you, Butcher!' he stormed. 'I've gone to the press and batted in your defence, but looking at this tape you've got no defence whatsoever!'

Steve Bull saved us from an embarrassing defeat with a goal a minute from time, but the draw meant that over the next few days my beard grew longer: through some silly superstition I had convinced myself I mustn't shave until we won a match. Bobby was still niggly with me, and after a scrambling win over a Sardinian side he came up to me and asked what I was doing growing a beard. I told him that until we won a match I wasn't going to shave. 'Don't be so fucking stupid!' he said. 'Shave it off now!' And as he walked away he added, 'What's more, you are fucking ugly, Butcher!'

Robson used my example to stress the need for good behaviour on the pitch to the others, and left me in no doubt that he expected better of an England captain. He certainly didn't expect to see anyone throw an England shirt on the floor again – for any reason. All in all I was thoroughly chastised, and, worse, seriously concerned for my place in the team. But right through that week Bobby stood by me. The BBC had isolated the frame of me colliding with my marker and had asked the Football Association what they were going to do about it. Even the *Star*, for whom I was writing a column, demanded I should be sent home. Thanks to Bobby, I survived.

There is always a danger of boredom in training camps, where there is little to do but eat, sleep and train. After a while you also run out of conversation with your room-mate, in my case Chris Woods, and to break the monotony he and I took a trip into the local village of Pula to replenish our toiletry stocks – or so we said. What we really wanted was a couple of pints. It was our secret little treat. Whenever we went out we were driven and escorted, but there was never a problem and the guards would leave us to do our shopping or whatever and take us back afterwards.

Word got out among the chaps about the success of our little foray and a few of them decided they would like to join us. It was also suggested that rather than during the day we should go up together one evening. It was three days before we were due to face the Republic of Ireland when we gathered a little group which included me, Woodsy, the skipper Bryan Robson, Steve Bull, Steve McMahon, Chris Waddle and, of course, Paul Gascoigne. It was a bit like *The Great Escape*. We formed an escape committee and organised a post-dinner route: past the ping-pong table, turn left at the pool, and out through a gap in the fence. The cars were all organised too, and down to Pula we went. The locals were very surprised to see us in their bar but they joined in the fun. Chris

Woods had a bit of an arm-wrestling contest with one of them, we sang some songs, and the drinks flowed. Before we knew it it was closing time, one a.m., and instead of a couple of pints we must have enjoyed at least seven or eight.

We followed the same route back, sneaked into our ground-floor rooms and dived into bed, thinking we had got away with it. But at eight a.m. there was a loud knock on the door summoning us to a meeting with the gaffer. Had we been rumbled? Were we in trouble? Robson was raging as he sat waiting for us with Don Howe at his side looking like a wet Monday. The manager slaughtered the players, telling us we had let down our country. He then informed us that the captain was laid up in bed and almost certainly out of the World Cup because we were more interested in alcohol than we were in serving our country and playing in football's greatest competition. He finished by saying, 'I am going next door and I want those responsible to come to me personally and apologise for letting down yourselves and your country.'

We were then left to it, and the talk was that those of us who had gone out were going to be at best suspended and at worst sent home. Chris Woods was going frantic. He had played second fiddle for so long, and now that Peter Shilton was about to retire he could see his great opportunity going up in smoke. In fact, we were all panicking. Gazza and Chris Waddle were first in, and Chris was additionally chastised for not looking after his impressionable young room-mate. Bobby told Gazza he was as daft as a brush – neither for the first nor the last time. Then I knocked on the door, and as I walked in Robson gave me a withering look.

'I thought it would be you, Butcher!' he shouted. 'I knew it! You were the first person on my list. You are a disgrace. You are *always* like this. I warned you back in 1982 about your safety valve and you continue to do it. You are a joke.'

Unbeknown to him, Gazza and Waddle were enjoying my discomfort outside Bobby's eyeline, Gazza pulling the most extraordinary faces at me, so much so that eventually I began to snigger.

Robson's anger went up a few notches. 'What are you laughing at, Butcher?' He demanded. 'It is no laughing matter. You have let down your country. The captain of our team is in bed now and may be out of the World Cup thanks to you. Why is it always you, Butcher? Every time it is you! And another thing, Butcher: you are fucking ugly!'

At which point Waddle and Gazza collapsed in unrestrained laughter, the manager turning on them and screaming, 'It is nothing to laugh at! Now fuck off out of here!'

It transpired that Bryan Robson, instead of sneaking into bed as I had done, had decided to go to Gazza's room. Gazza had by this time climbed into bed, so the skipper picked up the bed to tip his team-mate out on to the floor, but as he lifted it up the opposite side of the bed slipped along the tiled floor and took off his entire big toenail. There was blood everywhere. The panicking Gazza told him to put his foot in the bidet, but instead of turning on the cold water the mad Geordie turned on the hot tap, leaving Bryan screaming for him to turn it off. Things got so bad they had to call the team doctor, and he, of course, was obliged to bring in the manager. Gazza was then asked what had happened, and inexplicably he said Robbo had caught his foot on the bidet. Gazza had had to think very quickly and had not thought this situation through, so he wasn't anticipating the follow-up questions, such as what was the skipper doing in Gazza's room in the early hours of the morning, and why the hell would he have his foot in Gazza's bidet? Answers on a postcard, please.

All this happened 72 hours before our opening game of the World Cup. From that moment on I was completely banned from going anywhere. Unbelievably, the story did not surface before the game; even more miraculously, I found myself in the team, as did the skipper, who had to play with only a sliver of nail on the big toe of his left foot. I was marking Tony Cascarino in what was a very British match played in very British conditions. Gone was the balmy sunshine, and in its place we had black, rolling clouds illuminated by flashes of lightning. The temperature plummeted in Cagliari, and it felt more like Ipswich on a November evening than a summer's night on a holiday island.

The Republic were a difficult team to beat under Jack Charlton and they had brought their usual support with them, including lots of Celtic fans who wore their traditional hooped jerseys. But our training had gone well, apart from an article involving one of the Italian hostesses who helped with administration and logistics. A British freelance journalist sold a story to the *Sun* about player high jinks with this girl. The relationship between the press and ourselves was already poor because of the flak Bobby had taken over going to PSV, and after this latest piece broke we decided that, apart from those of us who had contracted to write columns, we would no longer talk to the press. As a result we developed something of a siege mentality, which can often help when you are all thrown together in a situation like this.

But the game against the Irish was not the best. It was as scrappy as the unseasonal weather. We were playing against the wind in the first half and took the lead when Gary Lineker converted a Chris Waddle cross. Strangely, the wind dropped at the interval and some of our advantage was gone, but we should have killed it off when Waddle was brought down by Kevin Moran for a clear penalty, ignored by the German referee Aron Schmidhuber. John Aldridge was then lucky not to be sent off for a crazy tackle on Des Walker a yard off the pitch. We held on until the last fifteen minutes, when our substitute Steve McMahon gave the ball away and Kevin Sheedy scored with a tremendous cross-shot. We should have won the game with the number of chances we created, but it wasn't to be our night.

I enjoyed my physical battle with Cascarino. At half-time I had to have an ice pack under my eye to bring down the swelling where he had elbowed me in the face, and after the game another pack on the other eye following another accurate hit. I guess he had one or two bruises as well. I could even have won it right at the end when a free-kick came in from the left. All I had to do was head the ball across Pat Bonner in the Irish goal, but I went for the near post and saw it end up in the side netting. Had I scored I would have run right into those Celtic supporters, even those in the upper tier.

There were lots of problems on the day, not least of all for poor Gary Lineker who was suffering with a stomach upset before the game. Instead of clearing up, it persisted. During the game he tried to break wind and suffered an uncomfortable accident instead. He literally had to sit on the halfway line and rip off the slip under his shorts, leaving them lying on the edge of the pitch. No one appreciated what had happened until afterwards. It did, however, sum up the game, and the world's media slaughtered us afterwards – and not because of our dirty laundry. We were seen, as always, to be in the group of death, and they generally reported what an awful game it was. We socialised with the Irish players afterwards around the dressing rooms. They all had beers but we were banned from drinking because of what had happened three days earlier.

The next game, on 16 June, was against the Dutch, and they were favourites to progress. They had a powerful side, with players like

Koeman, Rijkaard, Gullit, Wouters and, of course, van Basten, who had done us serious damage in the past. There was lots of talk in the media about the senior players having approached Bobby Robson and demanded a change of tactics. It was not true. Any tactical adjustments made during the World Cup were made only by the manager and Don Howe. One of the biggest points under discussion was the introduction of a sweeper system. In fact, the senior players were against the idea rather than arguing for it as we had played a practice match a few days before the Holland game and we were all at sea, losing 2–0 to the reserves. Eventually it was all sorted out and I was to mark the big blond centre-forward Kieft; Des Walker was to pick up van Basten and Mark Wright was to sweep with Stuart Pearce as left wingback and Paul Parker as right wingback. Bryan Robson, Paul Gascoigne and Chris Waddle would make up the midfield with Lineker and Barnes up front.

In the end all our careful preparations were torn apart as Kieft was on the substitutes bench. I was now set to mark Hans Gillhaus, but the principle remained the same. I knew Gillhaus well because he played for Aberdeen and I had tussled with him several times. He was small but quick and played virtually on the left wing, so I had to follow him out wide, almost playing as a right-back. I doubt whether we touched the ball ten times each before he was taken off and replaced by Kieft, a more orthodox striker. At corners, I was designated to mark Ruud Gullit. I have to say he wasn't hard to pick out with his long dreadlocks, but for their first corner I was on the near post and lost him when suddenly there was a waft of Armani and this apparition appeared. Arnold Muhren and Frank Thijssen had kindly taught me a few choice words in Dutch so I was able to pass some comments to him, causing him to laugh his head off. Every time I marked him I used foul Dutch language, far too bad even to quote with asterisks here. He continued to fall about with laughter and I suppose in a bizarre way I nullified him as I had done Gillhaus.

But I could almost have sat in the stand and watched the game in comfort. It was a close, dour, goalless game, with Walker doing a fine job on van Basten. Stuart Pearce had a goal from an indirect free-kick disallowed when it screamed through the defensive wall without getting the necessary touch by anyone, and we probably enjoyed the best of the few chances made, including one by substitute Steve Bull with his first touch of the game. The only problem for us was that Bryan Robson limped off early in the second half to be replaced by David Platt, with me taking over the captaincy. Not bad! Captain against Brazil, and now Holland.

Everyone was drawing in the group, so we needed a win against Egypt in the final game in Cagliari to be sure of qualification. The biggest menace until then, as ever, was going stir crazy, so we organised a little diversion for one of the routine meal times. Fortunately we got on particularly well with the waiters and they were willing to join in when I suggested that our table, with Woodsy, Chris Waddle and Gary Stevens, should have a back-to-front meal. We all dressed back to front, walked in backwards, started with the coffee followed by the ice cream, then the main course and the soup. The lads found it hilarious, but we could see Bobby prodding Don and asking him what we were up to. We even walked out backwards, to the applause of the boys.

It was so successful we decided on the eve of the Egypt game to give it another go. I arranged with the waiters to fill old wine bottles with sparkling water and put them in an ice bucket on the table along with some wine glasses. This time Woodsy declined the invitation, leaving just the three of us dressed in our England blazers, white shirts and official ties. We gelled our hair into spikes and put on sunglasses, jockstraps, socks and shoes. We made sure we were into dinner before everyone else and sat at the table with the long tablecloth covering our bare legs. We pulled our ties slightly askew, filled up our glasses, and pretended we were on the wine. Gradually the other lads came in, wondering what we were doing. We were very loud and cheerful, shouting greetings not only to them but also to Don Howe and 'Rebounds' Kelly, the goalkeeping coach. Norman, Fred and the Doc then arrived, followed by Bobby.

Bobby had dropped me for the Egypt game, for the first time in our long association, so he must have thought I had let myself go as a result. He kept nudging Don and asking, 'What's Butcher up to now, Don? Has he been drinking wine? They've got wine, Don.' Don told him to relax. He had already guessed we were pretending and told him it was probably water.

We were getting louder and louder in our pretence of being drunk. Everyone was laughing when all of a sudden in walked the entire FA international committee led by Graham Kelly. Bert Millichip, Jack Wiseman and the rest were a great bunch of characters, but we hadn't planned on them being there. Still, we decided to stick to our strategy. We enjoyed the main course, and when we had finished the three of us stood up, toasted the English players and Bobby Robson, and walked out, to the astonished stares of everyone. It was all very Monty Python. Once again the boys loved it, and as we walked up the stairs and out of the restaurant we stopped, lifted our shirts and showed our backsides. That was rewarded with a standing ovation.

Perhaps it was just what was needed, for we won the match playing 4–4–2 with a goal from my replacement Mark Wright. We topped the group too as the Irish and Dutch shared yet another draw, so we knew we were in the second round against the solid Belgians in Bologna. Our first target had been achieved. We were ready to move on and get our teeth into the real competition. We liked our new hotel in Bologna, and one day it was thought to be Gazza's birthday because of a misprint in the team biographies. ITV certainly believed it, and their commentator Jim Rosenthal presented him with a cake from the company as we sat around the pool. Chris Waddle pushed the gooey chocolate cake into Gazza's face, although we suspected he had told Chris to do so. Certainly Gazza seemed to enjoy it more than we did.

I was back in the team on 26 June for my 75th cap and named as captain as the manager juggled his team again after losing his regular skipper. Bryan Robson had had to go home to see a specialist about his dodgy Achilles tendon. Sadly, it was the end of his World Cup. Steve McMahon came in for him and we were back to the 3–5–2 formation we had used against the Dutch. We weren't the better team, but we did have goals by John Barnes and Gary Lineker disallowed, television proving the Barnes' strike was a cracker and quite legitimate. The talented Enzo Scifo hit the woodwork for them twice, and there was really nothing in it. David Platt eventually came on for the tiring McMahon, but the odds were heavily in favour of a penalty shoot-out as the game went into extra time. Then, with only seconds remaining, full-back Eric Gerets fouled Gascoigne. Gazza took the free-kick himself and Platt spectacularly hooked home over his shoulder. We piled on top of him and then got ourselves together for the last few seconds.

Once the whistle had blown it was celebration time. Waddle and I went over to our fans who were singing 'Let's all do the disco!', which we promptly did. I had kept on my England shirt and wouldn't swap it with anyone. It meant far too much to me. Back at the hotel, I thought as I was captain it was up to me to set up some sort of celebration. I telephoned room service and ordered a trolley full of beer and wine, though, in consideration of the quarter-final to come, no spirits – very professional thinking. Most of the squad found out about it and joined in, so much so we had to order another trolley. I didn't feel too guilty as the gaffer had said we deserved a drink, though just one. Whether he meant one beer or one trolley I'm not too sure. He had also told us to go to bed, as we had to travel to Naples. But I don't think he would have been surprised to discover we had enjoyed a little secret drink in our room that night. As a manager I have discovered you always know when a player has been drinking, even if only by the smell of his breath. If Bobby knew, he wasn't letting on.

We were put in a beautiful hotel outside Naples halfway up a mountain, with the press further up at the top. Gazza, as was his wont whenever we went to a new hotel, went straight to the bar and ordered a cappuccino into which he slyly got the barman to put four or five Bailey's.

Howard Wilkinson, who had watched our next opponents Cameroon, said in his report they were so ordinary it was as good as being given a bye, but Bobby Robson would not have this and told us their ancient centre-forward Roger Milla was on fire and they were a very tall, strong and athletic team. But we did fancy ourselves after two successive wins; we had a good shape and everyone was very confident. We even relented on our war with the press. Until then anyone who had spoken with a journalist had had a polystyrene cup bounced off his head, but as I said, those of us contracted to do columns had continued to do so, which made a bit of a mockery of the entire thing. Still, we spoke only to the people we wanted to speak to, not to those who had let us down. One of the problems was every paper had sent out news reporters on the hooligan watch but, Bologna apart, the supporters had been reasonably well behaved so the hacks turned their attention to us. Had they been a bit smarter they would have had one or two very good stories about drinking and singing, but they weren't as good as they thought they were and called us yobs because of an incident after training when some water was thrown in their direction. Still, it was amazing how different the attitude was now we were in the quarter-finals, with lots of journalists converging from the other countries who had been knocked out.

As captain, I also talked to the manager about the possibility of bringing our wives out. The FA had agreed beforehand that they would be able to come out for the latter stages, but Bobby, understandably, hadn't wanted to tempt fate by pre-organizing anything. Now, the FA needed a list of names to prepare. My parents had already been out to Cagliari on a supporters' package trip and I had been able to see them for lunch a couple of times. I had also seen Rita before the tournament began, of course, so I was quite relaxed about it all, though it did need sorting out.

While we were outside Naples a few of the lads managed to sneak off to one of the bars down the hill, but for once I wasn't involved – not because I was captain, but because nobody had bloody well told me. Probably a good thing in the circumstances. I wasn't a big fan of Naples anyway: to me it seemed like a dirty city with a lot of criminal activity, full of people who loved their adopted son Diego Maradona.

We were happy that Bobby was going to keep to the same system, with David Platt starting in place of Steve McMahon, and we went off to the stadium aware a place in history was within our grasp. West Germany were already waiting for us in the semi-final, and reaching the last four of a World Cup was something no other English team had ever achieved abroad. Still, we knew there was no such thing as a comfortable passage at this stage of a World Cup. I got myself ready to go out with my captain's armband on and a shield to give to the Cameroon skipper at the toss-up. It was quite a long walk to the tunnel, from one side of the stadium to the other, and we were lined up ready to go some minutes before our rivals. Then the Cameroon players bounced in, chanting. It was, I admit, a fantastic sight to see these physical players in brightly coloured shirts that could barely contain their rippling muscles, and for the first time in my international career I felt our team were cowed by their very presence. Bobby Robson took one look at them and said, 'Don't worry, lads, they might be able to sing, but they can't play.' I thought to myself 'Oh no!' as the Cameroon captain caught the aside and passed it back along the line. Then the barbed-arrow stares started coming our way, and suddenly we didn't have a quarter-final on our hands, we had a virtual war. It wasn't nice feeling that for once we'd been outButchered.

Despite being up against it from the outset we started well, scoring when David Platt came in at the far post to meet a Stuart Pearce cross. But Cameroon did not succumb; indeed, they came at us even harder. Peter Shilton was again forced to make several good saves and we were on the back foot with the entire world, outside England, backing the underdogs to beat us. For a while it looked as though they would, and at half-time Robson had some warning words for us. It didn't help when we lost John

Barnes with a groin injury and he was replaced with Peter Beardsley. We should have had a penalty when Platt was brought down by their keeper N'kono, which would have made it 2–0 and probably made us safe, but referee Codesal Mendez of Mexico inexplicably waved play on. Worse was to follow in the second half when he awarded a penalty against us. Gazza, of all people, had stuck out a leg and Milla had thrown himself over it. What the hell was Gazza doing back there in the first place? Kunde scored from the spot, and three minutes later the Africans took the lead when substitute Ekeke latched on to a Milla pass.

We were reeling. It was difficult to see how we were going to get back into the game because at that stage they were undoubtedly the better team. Bobby Robson had to go for it, and in a bid to salvage the game he took me off and sent on Trevor Steven to revert to the old shape of 4–4–2. The catalyst for the swing in fortunes was Paul Gascoigne. For an hour he had been anonymous, maybe overwhelmed by the occasion, but suddenly he began to play and things began slowly to go our way. But still problems dogged us, and when Mark Wright split his eye we were in trouble as we had used all our subs. Des Walker was limping, and Beardsley was unable to get into the game. As a ten-man team we hit the post when David Platt latched on to a defence-splitting pass from Gazza, then a patched-up Wright came back on.

Time was ebbing away. I had just turned to Chris Woods on the bench and said at least we would be back home tomorrow to see our families when suddenly we were given something we hadn't received for five long years – a penalty! Another Gazza pass had put Lineker through, and he was brought down. Lineker doesn't miss penalties, and his goal sent the match into extra time. But could we cope? We'd gone through a mind- and energy-sapping extra period against Belgium just five days earlier, and here we were again. But it was the Africans who ran out of steam first, although Trevor Steven did have to execute a miraculous goal-line clearance. We were now not only the strongest but also the best team on the pitch, but we still needed a break. We got it when the goalkeeper again brought down Lineker. As Bobby said afterwards, 'Two penalties in eight years and now two in twenty-three minutes!' All it needed was for Lineker to finish it, and he did. The ball hit the back of the net and we were through. It was a great feeling, but Cameroon must have felt very down because over two hours they had been the better team. Perhaps they even deserved to win. We hadn't played to our potential, but now we were set to face the Germans in just three days' time. It was now all non-stop action.

We hadn't a clue about the hysteria back home; we just concerned ourselves with looking after the walking wounded, making arrangements for our families to fly out, and taking a long, hard look at our opponents. We arrived back at our hotel very late that night after having had no more than a couple of beers, mainly due to exhaustion. Unfortunately, some of the boys discovered their rooms had been rifled by the cleaning staff at the hotel. We lost shirts, jewellery and money.

It was nice and warm in the morning so, as we weren't due to leave for Turin until the following day, we went down to the pool. As I sat reading my book, Bobby came down. I was hardly taking in the words in front of me, thinking only about being in a World Cup semi-final. Bobby put a towel down and we talked about team shape and other things managers and captains talk about at such times. He asked for my opinion on our approach to the Germans and I gave him a fairly long, considered answer. When I'd finished I looked across at him. He was fast asleep and quietly snoring. I still don't know whether it was the late night or my long, boring answer which tipped him over the edge. No one goes to sleep when I'm talking, I thought, and I walked to the far end of the pool, ran its length and dived in just by Bobby's sunbed. The water splashed all over him and woke him up but he hadn't a clue who had done it as the pool was fairly busy and no one said it was me.

By the time we left for Turin we knew our families would be joining us, along with everyone connected with the FA, right down to the England women's football team and a variety of politicians. It was a fantastic feeling being the centre of all this attention. We trained at Juventus's complex in Asti – only light sessions because of the two long games and two helpings of extra time. Everyone was hanging on the team announcement, but it was pretty much as expected, with three at the back and usually me playing spare.

Boredom once again reared its ugly head. In Bologna our hotel room had overlooked a café. At one point Gazza had appeared at our door telling us to fetch him a cup of water. Then he'd opened the window, thrown out the water and closed it quickly as the elegant people sipping their mid-afternoon coffees below suddenly wondered where the rain had come from. The sequel came in Turin. Bobby Robson had a friend coming along with his secretary from Ipswich, Pat Godbold. We were in a room overlooking reception and I thought to myself here's an opportunity, so I tipped a bucket of water over Bobby's friend. Stupid thing for a captain to do and not something I am particularly proud of. My only excuse was the players were doing it to one another all the time, and it was only water, nothing more damaging. The quieter side of Mr Hyde, but still Mr Hyde.

We all watched the other semi-final, Italy versus Argentina, on television knowing that one way or another, either in the final itself or in the third-place play-off, we would meet one of them. The locals were desperately hoping for the hosts to go through. The game went into extra time and then to penalties before Argentina won, though they finished with injuries and yellow cards. They would be short of four players in the final, including their star striker Caniggia, while Maradona was a shadow of his former self. We were convinced a win in the semi-final against the Germans would make us favourites to win the trophy for the first time since 1966. What a thought it was!

We trained at the ground where we were to play, and it had big dressing rooms, a beautiful surface and the now familiar suspended camera. Once again we tried to hit it, but this time it was too high. They must have heard we were coming. Everyone was nervous before the warm-up, but once we settled into a routine we went into game mode. It was the proudest moment of my life when I led the team out and stood for the national anthem. The usual trick of trying to pick out my family in the huge crowd helped pass away those nervous minutes prior to kick-off.

We started very well with a good shape, and we hit the post. It was goalless at the break, but they took the lead fifteen minutes into the second half when Stuart Pearce was, I thought, unfortunate to be penalised for a foul on Hassler. Brehme took the free-kick, which struck Paul Parker and looped over the groping Shilton. I thought Shilton would have reached it under normal circumstances, but it did take a massive deflection. Now Bobby had a problem, and he resolved it in the same way he did against Cameroon, by taking me off and reverting to a more familiar 4–4–2. I enjoyed my time on the pitch, and I know I did all right because I saw a tape of the match in 2004. I was delighted when John Motson in his commentary went into raptures about a little back-heel of mine. I tell people I was England's secret weapon – take me off and we scored. It worked again, as Parker put in predator Lineker for a superb goal.

We thought we would win it, even as we went into our third successive bout of extra time. We gave everything, and the lads were superb. Waddle hit the inside of a post and Shilton made a couple of superb saves as the game surged and heaved with a life of its own. Then Gazza was booked for bringing down Berthold and he knew, whatever the result, he would be out of the next match. Lineker looked towards the bench and warned the manager that Gazza, tears streaming down his face, had gone.

The game ran its course, and it was penalties again. I could do nothing. I was rooted to the bench by regulations; I couldn't even go out and talk to the players. It was almost like watching it on television as both Chris Waddle and Stuart Pearce missed their penalties. I went on the field to console Gazza. I was impressed with the way Franz Beckenbauer, the German manager, came across and offered his condolences to all of us. A terrific gesture, but we were numb. Sports minister Colin Moynihan and Graham Kelly came to offer their sympathies too, but they were the last people we wanted to see in our grief. I had to pull myself together to do some interviews with the press in the mixed zone, but we had given our all and there was nothing to be ashamed of.

The bus to take us back to the hotel was parked side by side with the German bus. The Germans were obviously delighted, while we sat quietly with a hidden case of beer. Suddenly, someone started singing, and everyone joined in. We were hit with the realisation we had given it our best shot and had had a great time. The volume grew and the bus began rocking as we launched into 'Blaydon Races' and 'Knees Up Mother Brown'. The Germans were looking at us in total amazement, shaking their heads. You could almost hear them saying, 'The English, they are mad. They think they have won!'

The party in Asti that night was a combination of celebration and commiseration as we tried in vain to drink the hotel cellars dry. The fact we were out didn't completely hit home until next day when we went to meet our families. The punch in the stomach suddenly arrived, and there were lots of tears as we met up with our wives and parents. Peter Shilton had announced he was to retire after the game, but I had no intention of giving it up despite a sore knee that had given me problems throughout the tournament. I decided to give the play-off in Bari a miss, so unbeknown to me at the time, I had played my last game for England. We lost to Italy 2–1, but my fourth-place medal is one of my proudest possessions.

We went back to the hotel after the game to say our farewells to Bobby Robson, who was now finished as England manager. He shed tears, as did others at the end of the adventure. The international committee presented him with a painting, and I gave him a Wedgwood dinner service on behalf of the players. We then levered him outside where he was to be thrown into the pool. He had time to give his medal and his watch to Fred Street as we hemmed him in, but what I didn't realise was I was to go in as well. Bobby and I were suddenly rushed towards the pool, and Bobby's head missed the diving board by a millimetre as we fell. Others, like Barnes and Waddle, came in as well. Bobby hadn't told us, but he'd broken a rib in an earlier pool accident. The dunking must have been very painful, but he came up laughing. After that it was – well, what do you think? Lots and lots of alcohol before preparing to set off for home the next day.

We drank champagne all the way back. I was wrecked by the time we arrived at Luton airport. I was grabbed for a press conference, but to this day I can't remember what I said. I was too drunk. We knew we had an open-topped bus ride back to the hotel, though we didn't know what the full arrangements were. The streets of Luton throbbed with thousands of people. We had our children with us, and as we drove through the town people were passing up burgers for them. I was wearing sunglasses and an air stewardess's hat. Suddenly, someone grabbed me and I fell to the floor just as we passed under a bridge. It would have decapitated me had I remained where I was – though I probably wouldn't even have felt it! After that it was into a car and off to Heathrow with the other three Scottish-based players for the flight home.

Italia 90 was, without doubt, the most significant time of my football career, a truly fantastic adventure. It was a wonderful team, full of character. We missed John Barnes though, who didn't reproduce his Liverpool form through injury, and Bryan Robson when he went home. Robson was, without doubt, the best player I ever played with. When we had him in front of our defence he would either save goals or score them. He gave me some terrible rollickings but he was the boss on the pitch and I never took offence. He was immense, and always made sure the lads were looked after.

The same goes for Bobby Robson. I have told some tales about him, but I would never have a go at him because I love him. All the other players did too. We all admired the way he grew into the job after trying to cover every base as a newcomer. He was an excellent England manager, second only to the man who won the World Cup, Sir Alf Ramsey – and both of them Ipswich managers of long standing. Think of the preparations these days and they don't compare with our lead-in to big international games, when we played huge First Division matches a few days beforehand. They wouldn't even let Bobby appoint a full-time assistant in Don Howe. How things have changed. It was a very limited backroom team in those days, with the wonderful medical men doing the kit as well. Everyone had to chip in. We also had the major problem of having our clubs banned from European football, which robbed that generation of players of the opportunity of testing themselves more regularly against the best.

Alistair had been born in January 1990, and with such a small child a long flight was not on, so the Butchers went to Jersey after the World Cup for two weeks. I was only there for a week, however, because I got the call to go into hospital for an operation on my knee – nothing to do with the ligaments I damaged in 1984, or the cartilage the following year, just simple wear and tear. After that it was simply a case of considering my international career under new manager Graham Taylor. He came up to see me, Woodsy, Gary Stevens, Trevor Steven and the other Scottish-based England players, and it was then I made a decision and told him I was retiring from international football. I felt I couldn't play at the highest level any more after my knee problems. Actually, if I'm honest, I have to say I was hanging on in Italy. Taylor wasn't surprised, and it was actually quite nice to be in the position of being able to announce my own retirement rather than be thrown out by the new gaffer.

I won 77 caps between 1980 and 1990, scored three international goals and played in three World Cups. In those days the FA didn't give caps for individual matches in tournaments. Instead they gave each player a lovely light blue cap with gold braid, the England badge and a tassel on the top. In each segment were the qualifiers you played in and the matches in the finals itself. I count myself lucky to have three of these World Cup caps, and proud too: I had a lovely cabinet made by a Scottish joiner in Bannockburn, and they're all displayed in there.

CHAPTER SEVENTEEN

SENT TO COVENTRY

Having undergone knee surgery, I surprised even myself by being ready to play in the second round of the League Cup on 21 August against East Stirling, who we beat 5–0. In fact, there were no signs of the upheavals to follow in this dramatic 1990/91 season as Rangers began the League campaign with wins against Dunfermline and Hearts and made further progress in the League Cup, beating both Kilmarnock and Raith, a game in which I scored twice. I remember it well. We were leading 3–1 when I scored a spectacular own goal, then promptly went up the other end in my anger and frustration and netted a 35-yard screamer. My celebrations were muted.

On 19 September, four days after drawing 1–1 with Celtic at Ibrox, we went to Malta in the European Cup and beat Valletta, a poor side, 4–0. Three days after we played Dundee United. It was to be my last game for Rangers. It was 1–1 when I scored my last and best own goal. The Dundee United goalkeeper Alan Main launched a clearance down the hill at Tannadice, and as I ran back I thought I needed to get a head to it. I did, and it sailed over Chris Woods into the back of the net. The ball never touched the floor from keeper to net. Graeme Souness wasn't impressed, as he showed during preparations for the semi-final of the League Cup against Aberdeen. On the morning of the match we trained, and afterwards Souness pulled me in and told me he was dropping me because of my form.

I was totally shocked. I had been hurried back into the team after my operation and I hadn't trained the whole time with the squad, mixing it with rehabilitation work on the bike and weights in between. My sharpness and pace were undoubtedly lacking at the time, but it was still a hammer blow. I was distraught, in tears. I didn't feel able to face the players, and I told Graeme not to make me substitute because it would not be good for the team to have me moping about on the bench and in the dressing room.

It made big news on both sides of the border. I took the dog for a walk to think about my future, and then I had a chat with Rita, telling her there were two ways out: either I asked for a transfer or I fought to get my place back. I was determined to fight back, especially as Rangers beat Aberdeen with a Trevor Steven goal and were once again in the final to face Celtic.

I worked desperately hard to regain my form and fitness and played a couple of games for the reserves at Dundee United and at Hibernian. Then came a bid from Howard Wilkinson, the manager at Leeds United at the time. Rangers accepted it, and my agent Johnny Mack told me it was only a question of tying up a few details before the move. It was clear Souness was ready to let me go no matter how hard I worked.

The day before the League Cup Final, 27 October, I played for an hour in a reserve game and afterwards Souness approached me, told me John Brown was an injury doubt and asked me to play the next day. I said no. I told him I was not the same player any more because I knew he wanted me to go. I had already started to think of playing for another team. I watched the game from the stand and I didn't go to the celebrations at Ibrox later. I just didn't feel part of it any more, and I knew I had to leave.

Things became spiteful between Graeme and me. Souness had been banned from the touchline again for things he had said in the press, and he had been caught on camera by Scottish Television talking to his assistant Walter Smith as he walked down the tunnel – somewhere the Rangers manager shouldn't have been while banned. He immediately stopped all the players from speaking to STV, but when news leaked out that my name was on the transfer list they caught me outside the ground and asked me about it. When Souness heard I had spoken to them he went bananas. He told me I had stuck it up his backside by talking to STV and now he was going to stick it up mine. He then gave a press conference to tell people exactly why I had been left out of the team, and why I was leaving the club. He was shaking with emotion, anger or both as he faced the cameras; normally he is very relaxed in front of the media. He gave a generally slanted version of the situation, obviously in his favour. I told him that as he had had his say, I would throw a press conference of my

The English connection – MacWoods and MacButcher – celebrate victory over St Mirren, May 1987.

"I love you, Woodsy, I really love you!" [© Bob Thomas Sports Photography]

When in Rome … trying curling for the first time.

Suitably attired, taking the salute at the Highland Games at the Bridge of Allan in 1988.

There were seven – just count them – Englishmen in the Rangers squad for the pre-season tour of Switzerland and West Germany in July 1987: [from left to right] Graham Roberts, Neil Wood, Mark Falco, myself, Chris Woods, Jimmy Phillips and Trevor Francis. Absent through injury was Colin West, making eight! [© Bob Thomas Sports Photography]

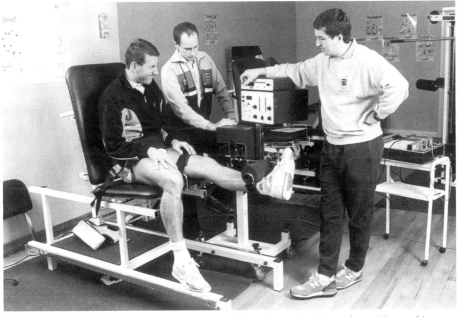

January 1988: being put through my paces on an isokinetic muscle testing and exercising machine by Graham Smith [right], the director of the FA Rehabilitation Centre, and his assistant Phil Newton. [© Bob Thomas Sports Photography]

LEFT: *Rangers versus Celtic, Hampden Park, Skol Cup Final, October 1986: the penalty incident with Celtic skipper Roy Aitken holding my shirt.*

MIDDLE: *Something of a tête-à-tête with Dynamo Kiev, September 1987. [© Glasgow Herald/ Evening Times]*

BOTTOM: *Ref! I got the ball. Honest I did! Jock McStay was feeling the pain after a challenge in my return game after breaking my leg.*

Rallying the troops for Coventry City in November 1990 in my debut against Liverpool.

Watching my Coventry team from the bench, January 1991.

It looks like a sending off but the ref is sending me away after a foul playing for Sunderland against Charlton, February 1993. I was playing with a broken bone in my right arm.

With Walter Smith in the Sunderland dug-out in pre-season before the 1993/94 campaign.

Going through the hell that managers must endure, August 2002.

Getting a point across to the lads, July 2004.

Dreaming of winning the CIS Cup, but it wasn't to be.

Celebrating the last-gasp victory over Celtic on the last day of the SPL's 2004/2005 season.

own to give my version, but he responded that if I wanted to move to another club I should forget about it. There was an impasse between us. Neither of us was going to back down.

A fee was then agreed with Leeds United, in some haste. I agreed terms with Howard Wilkinson and had shaken hands on the move, but before I put pen to paper Coventry City chairman John Poynton got in touch and asked me if I would like to be his player-manager. It was a bolt out of the blue. I had never even considered managing and playing. But it was something to think about, especially as my knee was still not right. Howard knew about the knee but wasn't troubled, saying they would get it right for me. I told Howard that I needed to speak to another club before I signed anything. He was reluctant to let me out of his office, but the next day I went to the Hilton at Manchester airport where I met John Poynton, who had flown in from his home in Jersey. They were ready to stump up the £400,000 fee and pay me more money than Leeds; in fact, it was a very good salary. But what he was offering me most of all was a job as a manager, something I had aspired to for some years.

My mind was so confused. Instead of driving up the M6 to Scotland I drove across England on the M62. If I hadn't stopped I would have driven straight into the North Sea. I had to divert on to the northbound A1 east of Leeds in order to get home – the long way. I talked to Rita and Johnny Mack and decided the time had come to put my foot on the first rung of the ladder of management, even though I was only 31. It was hardly starting at the bottom either: Coventry were in the top flight in England and had been there for some years. I told Howard I had to take the Coventry offer, and I wished him all the best. He said likewise, then asked me where I was going. I told him, and his response was, 'All the fucking best!' He clearly thought I would face an uphill struggle.

I went straight back to Ibrox to pick up my gear. I didn't see Souness, Walter Smith or any of the upper echelon as I returned to the ground for the last time to pick up my boots and bits of gear, which I put in a black plastic bag. I said my goodbyes to those who were there, and as I walked out I saw Willie Waddell, one of Rangers' greatest ever managers. He was using a stick by then but he took the trouble of shaking my hand and thanking me for all I had done for the club since I arrived. He wished me all the best and left me with a big lump in my throat.

It didn't take long to make it up with Souness. He didn't make it difficult. If he didn't want to speak he wouldn't have done so, and now, having been on the same side of the coaching network, I can understand why a manager comes to such decisions. It is never easy. For him, once a decision is made he carries it out with the minimum of fuss, and moves on.

In hindsight, I was wrong not to play in the League Cup Final. I was still employed by Rangers, I was reasonably fit, and I had been asked by my manager. The only way I can justify my refusal is at the time Souness was making moves to sell me on. On the one hand he wanted me out, while on the other he needed me to play in the final. But it was out of character for me, as it was the sort of game where I would normally roll up my sleeves and go out to prove everyone wrong. Maybe deep down I just thought I couldn't do it. Emotion plays a great part in my football, and I felt my heart had been ripped out. I no longer felt the same about the team. And if I had played and suffered a bad game, Souness would have been in the right. Hindsight is a great thing, but the best thing to do would have been to play the game. As it was, it was a poor and very disappointing end to what had been a great time of my life, full of adventure and trophies. Ibrox is a wonderful place to play football, and Rangers is a great club. I suppose you don't know what you have until you lose it. I played 176 games for them and scored a dozen goals (and almost as many went into my own net).

Rangers went on to win their third consecutive title, in addition to the League Cup. But things weren't as straightforward as they seemed, for on 16 April Graeme Souness walked out on Rangers to take over from Kenny Dalglish at Liverpool. Not surprisingly, the club's League form slipped. Walter Smith took the reins with four matches remaining and the title was only clinched in the last game when Mark Hateley scored twice against Aberdeen at Ibrox, breaking the deadlock which had seen both teams level on points and goal difference going into that final game.

But that was all now a million miles away for me. At Highfield Road I had succeeded John Sillett, a legend in those parts after helping the Midland underdogs win the FA Cup in 1987 against David Pleat's odds-on favourites Spurs. I had no coaching badges or any experience whatsoever but I was straight into it in the middle of November, flying down on my own with my boots in a carrier bag. The one remaining worry was the medical, and I was surprised I passed with the bad knee.

The first item on my agenda was to speak to the players. The atmosphere was not good, and I discovered later exactly why. Sillett had promised his job to not one but several of the players when he left. He had told Trevor Peake, Cyrille Regis, Steve Ogrizovic and Brian Kilcline they were all managers in waiting. Coventry were something of a dads' army, filled with good but ageing players. Unbeknown to me, there were precious few kids coming through the ranks, but the fan base was rock solid. One of the other problems was the backroom staff left behind, people like youth-team coach Colin Dobson, assistant manager Dixie McNeill, reserve-team coach Terry Payne and others, all of whom wanted to know what was going to happen to them. I hadn't a clue because I hadn't given it a thought. I was too busy sorting out my own position. I wanted to play, but Kilcline was the man in my position, supported by Peake. It hit me hard. One minute I was a player, the next I was a manager, and I had to make decisions not only about myself but other players as well. I hadn't called anyone to talk about it because I had been sworn to secrecy by the club until the announcement was made to the media, so I hadn't had the benefit of any advice. I would have liked to talk about it to mentors like Bobby Robson and Bobby Ferguson. I have no doubt had I been able to seek advice I would have been told to play on for as long as I could, but this was too big a chance. Coventry were a solid club, not doing well, but with potential. But I should have looked at how many managers they had worked their way through before my arrival – five over a nine-year period – for a better idea of my prospects. My only knowledge of Coventry City was going there as a player some years before, and I remembered enjoying playing at Highfield Road – probably because we won.

My first priority was a good number two, and after some thought I asked former Coventry manager Dave Sexton, but unfortunately he was in Saudi Arabia. He told me he would love to do it but couldn't break his contract. Others I wanted were still playing, so I kept Dixie and Terry until the end of November, when I appointed my old Ipswich captain Mick Mills. He had telephoned me a few times and pushed himself forward as a number two – a role reversal from our days at Portman Road. He had been at Stoke City and done a good job there, so I took the decision to bring him in. I knew him well, knew his character, and he knew the ins and outs of management. He was a safe choice, but there was never the same chemistry between us as a management team as there had been when we were players. Mick and I got on well as mates, but it was some time since we had played together and so much had happened to both of us since. Still, by bringing in Mick I thought I would be able to play on and leave him to make the decisions in terms of substitutions and whatever else needed to be done. I also brought in Brian Eastick, who had been at Coventry before and was recommended by Mick. Sadly, that appointment didn't work out too well either. We just didn't gel as a management team. I wanted to play after a four-year absence from the First Division, but player-manager is a difficult job and you need an outstanding number two, like Gary McAllister had, ironically when he was Coventry manager, in Eric Black.

I have to say that Coventry had super training facilities, with two pitches. I also had a nice little office at Highfield Road where I could invite opposition managers and coaches in after games. It was a super set-up, and to be fair to John Poynton and the board they gave me money to go out and buy players, which was a good thing considering the high average age of the side and the fact that, as I said, there were few in the reserves and youth team I could bring through with any confidence. But my main concern for the remainder of the 1990/91 season was to keep Coventry in the division – they were sixteenth when I took over – and look for good Cup runs.

It started off well enough for me. We lost to Liverpool on 17 November, but only through a sensational piece of individual skill by Peter Beardsley. As luck would have it we then had to play the team I almost joined, Leeds United. I played in the game and Lee Chapman, the man I was marking, scored for them while Kevin Drinkell netted ours. My third match in charge was a bizarre match against Nottingham Forest in the League Cup: we led 4–0, were pulled back to 4–3 by the break, and then to 4–4 before we won 5–4. Kevin Gallacher scored a hat-trick for us, and Nigel Clough also scored three for Forest. The victory put us through to the quarter-finals.

My knee wasn't improving, but because of the workload in the office I had no time for the remedial work or the treatment I should have pursued. I was doing just enough to get by, as I was getting back late from the office and not resting. I played only half a dozen matches and we didn't win a League game until we beat Spurs 2–0 on Boxing Day. It was a very sweet result, but even sweeter would have been a win over Manchester United eleven days earlier. We had led 2–1 going into the last five minutes, but Danny Wallace popped up with the equaliser. After the Spurs win we also beat Norwich City, a game I really enjoyed. I was trying to change the team around during this period – I moved Gallacher into the middle with Cyrille Regis, for instance – and we were playing some nice football. Before those two important victories we were either drawing or losing games narrowly.

In January in the League Cup fifth round we went out to the only goal against Sheffield Wednesday, and it was before the rearranged game that my knee flared up again. I wanted to play because we had injuries, but it was a critical error. The knee was badly swollen so I told the doc to draw off the fluid and strap it up. He took out a staggering ten syringes of fluid. The knee was bandaged, I went home to bed, I woke up in the afternoon and felt really good, and decided to play. As we chased the game after Wednesday scored, my knee began to fill up again. My play was very laboured, and the knee felt completely wrecked. It was a stupid thing to do, and it was the last time I played that season, but the team was doing well without me. It was very satisfying to beat our local rivals Aston Villa at home. We had our usual pre-match meal at the training ground and then went by bus to the ground. For the pre-match talk I gathered everyone around the pool table. I used the pool balls to show how I expected Villa to play, but when I came to our shape I didn't have enough balls and had to ask the chef for some tomatoes. We won the game 2–1, and I told the press afterwards that the tomatoes had swung it for us. Better, I suppose, a tomato than a turnip.

Just before the transfer deadline I signed Kenny Sansom for £87,500 from QPR, which I thought was a tremendous signing, and Robert Rosario, a big striker from Norwich, for £525,000. Robert had played well against us and I fancied he would fit in. We also brought in young Andy Pearce from non-league Halesowen and Ray Woods from Wigan, for a quarter of a million. I enjoyed the wheeling and dealing. That January I also moved Steve Livingstone and Tony Dobson on to Blackburn for a combined fee of £750,000, and I sold David Speedie to Liverpool. I had enjoyed having David in my team, despite everyone telling me he was a handful. I can honestly say I never had a scrap of trouble with the man. On the last day of a busy month Steve Sutton was signed on a month's loan from Nottingham Forest, as well as Stewart Robson from West Ham. I had also tried to sign Peter Atherton, but he declined because his father was ill. I signed him later on, and he was to become something of a local legend as he won England U-21 honours.

The influx of new players was designed to prop up our decent form and lift the club well clear of the relegation area, and it worked. We had a great win against Manchester City in March, then drew 2–2 at Spurs despite having been two up after twenty minutes. On the first day of April we beat Chelsea at home, then drew away with Norwich and Liverpool. It was all promising stuff, and we hauled ourselves right up to ninth place in what was a tight mid-table when we beat Derby County 3–0 a fortnight later. We were now nicely safe, but with the pressure off we took only a single point from our last three games and slipped to sixteenth by the end of the season. Micky Gynn was a key figure in those crucial games. He was only five feet five inches tall but he scored in five out of the critical seven games as we hauled ourselves up the table. He was from the Fens and was a very good midfielder. He's a postman now – just the right height to reach the letterbox. He was a very deep person and difficult to understand, like all Fen people, but on the football field he certainly did the business for me. The great escape was complete, and Coventry would again be in the top division for the 25th successive season – a remarkable achievement for a club with limited means.

Our last game of the season was against Arsenal at Highbury, where they were to be crowned champions having already clinched the title. We were late arriving at the ground because there was so much traffic en route. I had agreed to let the players go away to Fuengirola for a week in the sun in recognition of their successful run, but we were hammered 6–1, Anders Limpar scoring a hat-trick, and I was so furious with the performance I went for them in the dressing room and was an inch away from cancelling the trip abroad. At the post-match press conference, rather than talk about how bad we were I offered to talk about how good Arsenal were. But before I started I asked about Rangers playing in the title decider against Aberdeen at Ibrox. When I was told they had won I was delighted for Walter Smith, especially as after Souness left Walter had got in touch with me to ask if I wanted to go back to Ibrox as his number two. I'd told him if he could match my wages and pay the compensation, I would be delighted. But I was on £200,000 a year – a lot of money in football in those days – and it was too much for Rangers' purse.

I relented with my players after my huff at Highbury and we went to the Costa Brava, but when I returned I was back in the ground every day (apart from a couple of weeks away with my family in America), sitting by the telephone and hoping someone would ring to enquire about one of my players so I could raise some more money for the transfer market. But it was a complete waste of time because everyone else was away. It was a stupid idea, but I'd had a difficult introduction into the management game and I was anxious to improve what had been a decent enough start. My record for 1990/91 was won eight, drawn eight, lost ten, with 31 goals for and 34 against. As a manager I generally add together wins and draws and put them against the losses to avoid a negative reading of the equation. I felt it was a solid beginning.

I did sell one player during that close season: Brian Kilcline moved on to Oldham for £440,000 – a good result, as I already had Andy Pearce and myself to play at the back. I also decided to release Cyrille Regis. I now had Rosario, and although Cyrille had been a crowd favourite and a great servant to the club, I thought it was time we moved on. Cyrille promptly signed for Ron Atkinson at Aston Villa, our closest rivals. I had suffered the same sort of decision as a player, and now it was my turn as a manager, but Cyrille took it very well and landed himself a good contract. There was no animosity, and we still speak now, as he is an agent.

After his loan period, Stewart Robson signed on a free, and he was a big success for us. For a boy from a very good background he was a hard player and a fine professional, but unfortunately he suffered problems with his back. There was also a young lad from Zimbabwe named Peter Ndlovu who had been scouted by the previous manager and who had now secured his work permit. He was a talented player, and at £10,000 was an absolute bargain. I also brought Paul Furlong out of non-league football. He was at Enfield and was being chased by Watford, but they offered less than we did. I was told someone at Enfield had warned Furlong that if he didn't move to us he would be involved in an unfortunate accident! We picked him up for a total of £140,000. He was a good, strong, left-footed striker who has lasted well in the game. I made a mistake, however, when I signed Martin Hayes on loan from Celtic. I had seen him play in Scotland and I thought he could be good for us, but he was so poor in training I ended up not selecting him for a single game.

For pre-season preparation we played a series of games in Scotland followed by a tournament involving Rangers, Sparta Rotterdam and Kilmarnock. We were staying at my old international stamping ground, the Marine Hotel in Troon. Trevor Peake, midfielder Lloyd McGrath and

Kenny Sansom went out on the town after one game and had a little too much to drink. There was a row in the hotel on their return, and on Mick Mills' advice I bought three tickets for the train back to Coventry, sent them home, and told them they would be fined two weeks' wages and placed on the transfer list. In hindsight it was the wrong thing to do, especially for a poacher-turned-gamekeeper, but I was a young manager trying to make a mark. I should have done what Bobby Robson used to do with me and given the errant players an opportunity to atone instead of humiliating them in front of the other players and their families. I was too hasty, too ready to listen to advice. I felt I needed to prove myself and make a stand, but it wasn't the right time to do it.

Kenny Sansom twisted his ankle anyway and missed the first game of the season, a loss at home to Manchester City. We beat Luton 5–0 in our second match, Rosario scoring his first goal for the club, and a draw at QPR and a home win against Sheffield United moved us up to sixth place, but this was one of those topsy-turvy seasons. Two defeats were followed by a remarkable 2–1 win at Arsenal, one of the goals scored by the blossoming Ndlovu. We withstood a storm as they fought back and I was proud of our defensive qualities, especially after having lost so badly a few months earlier.

I was trying to get myself playing again, but we were going so well my absence wasn't a major problem. When we beat West Ham away on 5 October we moved up to the dizzying height of fourth place. I eventually made my return against Aston Villa in the Zenith Data Systems Cup, but unfortunately I was sent off for a professional foul, and we lost the game. Afterwards big Ron Atkinson came waddling into my office with half a dozen of his cronies. There was hardly any room for me.

At the end of October, somewhat incredibly, we registered a second win over Arsenal, this time in the third round of the League Cup, but our League form was dipping dramatically. Then, on 9 November, John Poynton resigned as club chairman and Peter Robbins, the son of life president Derrick Robbins, took over. I learnt about the change at a club dinner and dance at the Hotel Leofric in Coventry to celebrate our 25 successive years in the top division. We were having a good night when John called me and Rita over for a chat. He told us the club had been taken over and as from tomorrow he would be out and Robbins would be in. He was also passing on a message from the new chairman who wanted to talk to me at the ground the next day, but he assured me my job was safe. It was a complete bombshell, totally unexpected. I had just announced that I was to retire from playing, so we drove home that night with our minds in turmoil. Fortunately I was completely sober.

I met Robbins and he assured me all was well, but a week or so later he came to my house and told me he didn't like Mick Mills and Brian Eastick and he was letting them go. He asked me if I wanted him to wield the axe, but I preferred to take the responsibility as I had appointed them. Mick took it remarkably well, but at the same time he warned me to watch my back. Eastick left the club ranting and raving. As for me, I was left having to find a quality replacement as my number two. I plumped for my old England trainer Don Howe, who lived just up the motorway, and he agreed to come to Highfield Road.

Coventry's first game under the new regime was at Norwich on 23 November. We lost that 3–2, and followed it up by going out of the League Cup to Spurs at Highfield Road. It was a big disappointment to everyone at the club in front of a 20,000 crowd. We were then slaughtered 4–0 by Manchester United at Old Trafford. As I was walking back to the coach from the old dressing rooms, bemoaning my ill fortune, a car came by and ran over my foot. It hurt like hell and I was lucky no bones were broken. I never did find out who was behind that wheel. Had I done so I might well have introduced him to Mr Hyde. This disaster was followed by another dreadful game at Luton where we lost to a Mick Harford goal. The new chairman had now seen us lose four games out of five, a win over Southampton the only reprieve, with tricky matches coming up against Sheffield United and Wimbledon. He must have been highly impressed.

I was under pressure, and things really started eating into me. I was drawn, I was tired, and I was worried about my job and my family, who had of course by this stage moved down from Scotland. We lived in a beautiful village called Hunningham, complete with a pub and church. The house itself was sixteenth-century with five bedrooms, a huge inglenook fireplace and, outside, orchards and a swimming pool. During lunch on Christmas Day I was so preoccupied with the team that I was moving salt and pepper pots around the table, thinking about the game and ignoring all the usual routines I had always enjoyed so much. I knew something was wrong because I was off my eating! We travelled that night to Sheffield for the game on Boxing Day, and we played really well, comfortably winning 3–0. We followed that up two days later with a 1–1 draw at Wimbledon. Stewart Robson scored for us in both games, and suddenly we were up to thirteenth with a little breathing space. I went up to the Wimbledon boardroom after the game and the two sets of directors sang 'Happy Birthday' to me. It was only then that I realised it was 28 December.

On New Year's Day we lost to Spurs, then drew with John Beck's up-and-coming Cambridge United side three days later in the FA Cup. On the Monday morning following the game I was called to meet the chairman at the ground at ten a.m. We were on a day off so I had Christopher and Edward with me. I took them into my office where they could draw and watch television. As I approached the boardroom I was wondering what sort of future plans the chairman might want to discuss, but when I opened the door I saw that there were two pieces of paper on the table. The first was a statement to the press saying my position had been terminated with immediate effect and Don Howe was taking over as caretaker manager. The second piece of paper questioned the validity of my contract; lawyers had been instructed to look into all aspects of it. It appeared, I said to the chairman, that not only was I being sacked, the club was also trying to get out of paying me any compensation. I should have known it was coming. They had already tried to persuade me to take a reduction in wages because I was no longer playing. I wouldn't do it because I knew it would make it easier for them to sack me when the time came. I'd simply told them I wanted to see the job through. I kept my dignity by thanking the chairman for all the club had done for me in giving me my first chance in management, then went off to see Don Howe and Colin Dobson and to say goodbye to my secretary Jenny and all the staff.

I was a man out of work, and it was hard to take. I found a cardboard box, and the boys helped me to clear my desk as I telephoned my wife and my agent. We then went home, where the press besieged me. The next day I went to see the lawyers in London with Johnny Mack and was told I had to sort the matter out through the courts. It took me two years to get any compensation out of Coventry. A couple of days after that I went on television with Sky Sports as a summariser as I was determined not to hide away from anyone. I also went to a reserve game at Villa Park. Villa chairman Doug Ellis took me into the boardroom and wished me well for my future, saying how pleased he was I was out and about. How nice coming from a man about whom negative comments have been made in terms of the way he treats people. I certainly have no complaints about him.

My overall record at Coventry was played 61, won 20, drew 14, lost 27 – not bad for a young manager trying to turn a club around with little money to play with, and better than the record of Don Howe, who won only three of his nineteen games, though that was small satisfaction. This was the last season, remember, before Sky money came in, and everyone was chasing the promised pot of gold in the new Premier League. Coventry were in a lot of debt at the time so relegation would have been a disaster. They finished just one place and two points above the trapdoor. Don had signed an eighteen-month contract, but by the start of 1992/93 he had gone too and Bobby Gould had taken over.

When Bobby was appointed, it jogged my memory. Earlier that season, when Mick Mills and Brian Eastick were still there, Bobby had suddenly appeared at our training ground at Ryton. He arrived just as we were going to lunch, and naturally I asked him to join us. We had a convivial chat, and when he had gone I asked who had invited him in. No one had. His appointment less than a year later made me wonder what was going on. It was all very strange, what with the change of chairman and everything else.

CHAPTER EIGHTEEN

THE MANAGER MUST GO

After leaving Coventry in January 1992 I decided I was going to get myself fit. Rita bought me a mountain bike for fifty quid and I went out cycling for two or three hours a day every day, doing twenty or more miles around beautiful places like Leamington Spa, Stratford upon Avon and Warwick, getting my suspect leg strong again. Not only was I becoming fit, I was also working hard to earn my coaching qualifications and badges at Birmingham University.

My old England team-mate Trevor Francis was manager of Sheffield Wednesday at the time and I asked him about the possibility of training with the club, as it was only an hour up the road. He agreed to let me train for a couple of days a week with the first team. They were lovely people, and I knew a few of them, including Chris Woods who had moved there from Rangers. I even played a couple of reserve games, at Newcastle and Rotherham, both of them wins. It was a real good workout for me: I not only enjoyed it, I also proved to myself I could still do it. I wasn't paid for playing but I did do some scouting for the club, watching games and writing reports. I travelled in the Peugeot I still had from Coventry. I once went to watch Watford and ran over a rake in their car park. My front tyre caught the prongs and flicked it up in the air, and it came down on top of the bonnet. I didn't realise how it had happened at first; I thought it was raining rakes. I eventually had to give the car back, complete with the satisfying little dent in the bonnet, but there was at that time still no money from Coventry so I was grateful for the bits and pieces from the television work and my scouting.

During this time I became friendly with Fran Burke and her family from Warwick. She needed a bone marrow transplant and I was asked if

I would help her and the Anthony Nolan Trust with some publicity for a charity bike ride from Scotland to Portsmouth. Instead I offered to do the ride on one of three tandems. I made sure I was at the front to shield the team behind me, and we cycled for seven days. It was hard on the posterior – several jars of Vaseline were used to keep me in the saddle – but I have to say I enjoyed it, and we raised a lot of money for the charity. When we arrived at Portsmouth there was a band waiting for us and I felt a great sense of achievement. It also helped me because it gave me a target just before the start of a new season when I hoped to find myself back in the sport I loved and missed so badly.

For season 1992/93, ex-Ipswich boss Bobby Ferguson had been appointed number two at Sunderland. Despite spending the entire season in the bottom half of Division Two, Sunderland had reached the 1992 FA Cup Final, and Malcolm Crosby, a lovely man who had been caretaker manager, was reluctantly given the manager's job as a reward. Bobby had asked Rita what I was doing and she had given him the thorough CV, telling him about my fitness levels, my bike riding and my games for Sheffield Wednesday reserves. Bobby was clearly impressed and told Rita to tell me to come up for a trial if I fancied it during pre-season. I was worried the knee might blow up again, but I iced it continually and did well. I didn't do everything the other professionals did, but things felt good, and I was once again enjoying football with no responsibilities as a manager.

In the midst of all this pre-season work I went to Japan on a coaching assignment. First Wave Management, with Frank McLintock and agent Graham Smith, had arranged for Bob McNab, Chris Nicholl, Paul Taylor and me to go out there for a week, earning good money coaching kids. Sunderland wanted me to play in their opening fixture of the season on 15 August away to Swindon Town, so I flew back for the game and went straight to the hotel to join the rest of the team. On the day, another of my former England colleagues, Glenn Hoddle, who was player-manager at Swindon, put us to the sword by scoring the winning goal, but I was relatively satisfied with my performance. In fact, I went on to play some 38 League games during the season, 42 in all.

After Swindon we lost 3–2 at home to Huddersfield in the League Cup, a game in which I scored my only goal of the season, and went out of the competition in the second leg on the away-goals rule. It was a struggle for us in the League as well, and after a draw with Bristol

Rovers at the end of September I was out with injury until early November, when I returned as subsititute for the game against Peterborough at London Road. As I warmed up right up tight against the Posh supporters they started singing, 'You're not famous any more!' It was very funny and I was laughing along with them. 'Who are you? Who are you?' they chanted.

We lost that one 5–2, and there was further embarrassment in the next game at home to Leicester City when I was marking an unknown youngster named Julian Joachim. Over a twenty-yard chase he gave me an eighteen-yard head start and still beat me. What a flying machine he was, and to make matters worse the game was televised live. To rub it in even further, Joachim scored twice. But we won our next three games, the first of them against a Derby side featuring Marco Gabbiadini, an old Sunderland favourite. It was a very wet day at the Baseball Ground, and after the match I gave Malcolm Crosby a big hug to celebrate. He was singularly unimpressed as I was rather muddy and he was in his best suit. I, of course, did it on purpose. We followed this with another away win, at Southend, who had a certain Stan Collymore playing directly against me – he was a handful, but rather lacked support on the day – and a 2–1 victory at home to Barnsley.

But it was a false dawn. We slipped back down, and after four games without a win Malcolm Crosby was sacked when the pools panel decreed another defeat away to Tranmere in a postponed game (I wonder if Malcolm is the only manager ever to be sacked on the verdict of a pools panel). That left a vacancy, of course, and on the first day of February 1993 I filled it. With hindsight, I shouldn't have done it. It's very difficult becoming the manager of a side with whom you have already built up an understanding as a player. You know all, or most, of their secrets. The experience turned out to be worse than at Coventry, because at least I'd gone to Highfield Road as a stranger.

My first game as player-manager of Sunderland was at home to Swindon on 6 February, and again we lost by a single goal to Hoddle's team. I challenged for a ball at one point and as I fell I put my hand down to cushion my fall, but broke a finger in two places, which meant I had to wear a light cast for games. It was my right hand, too. I couldn't even write. That first month was a bleak spell. During it we found ourselves up against West Ham United at Roker Park in the Hammers' first game after Bobby Moore's death. The minute's silence was stunning, not a sound. It was very emotional because he had been my hero, and there were tears all round. It was a difficult game to play, and the best thing would have been to call it off. The 0–0 result said everything about it.

Relegation was fast becoming a big threat. At Leicester on 10 March we lost after leading 1–0 and 2–1. They pulled back to 2–2 when a long ball was played into the box. I was picking up big Steve Walsh, but as I came forward to head it clear my own player Gordon Armstrong was coming back and he flicked the ball into Walsh's path. The final result was 3–2 to Leicester, simply because neither Gordon nor I had shouted. And television again caught us on a bad day, this time losing 2–0 away to Barnsley. The cameras also caught me rugby-tackling a spectator who ran on to the pitch. I passed him on to the police. It was probably my best challenge of the day.

The bad run continued, and Sunderland toppled from fifteenth place to twentieth, right on the cusp of relegation in the 24-team division. I gave away the goal that enabled Wolves to beat us on 27 March, and in the next game Southend's Collymore wreaked his revenge on us for keeping him quiet in our first game. It was a particularly bad result as they were second from bottom at the time. Collymore on his day was lethal, and although he only scored once in the 4–2 win, it was he who tore us, and me, apart. It was his goals more than anything else that lifted Southend to safety. I had another bad moment at Brentford three days later when a group of Sunderland supporters came down the terraces to have a go at me. I wasn't in any sort of mood to be hassled so I swore back, and had to make a humble apology later.

The crunch came on 25 April when we lost to Kevin Keegan's Newcastle United at St James's Park. Before this televised derby I had taken the players away to Turnberry for a few days. The big Ayrshire hotel had suffered a last-minute cancellation and I was able to get a really good rate, to the delight of the club. We trained hard, had a few drinks for bonding purposes, and were up for the big game. It poured cats and dogs on the day, and I doubt whether it would have been played but for the cameras. Scott Sellars scored the only goal to keep Newcastle firmly in top place, where they had been since September, and it was my foul on David Kelly which led to the goal. The rain had been so heavy there was a big dip by the side of the track which had filled up with water a foot deep and a good ten feet across. I gave Kelly a gentle shove as we ran for the ball and he went head first into the pond. Newcastle's success simply magnified our struggles at the other end of the table. The Sunderland supporters found it too hard to shoulder, and they wanted to blame someone. I was the obvious target.

With three games remaining we knew we had to win at least one of them and perhaps draw another. The first of the trio was at Roker Park against a Portsmouth side going for promotion. It was the day it all came together: we played really well and won 4–1. I remember the day vividly because Bob Murray, the chairman, met me in the boardroom after I had spoken to the press. It certainly wasn't a dry boardroom. Murray had me on the Chablis and, on top of playing and having nothing to eat, it went straight to my head. I somehow managed to drive the five minutes to my assistant Bobby Ferguson's house, and he and his wife Anne promptly took my keys and drove me to my hotel in Washington, where I was staying on my own before Rita and the family moved up. In fact, I was so drunk he had to help me to my bedroom. When I think now about how I drove to his house, I shudder.

We lost our final two games, but struggled home in 21st place because Brentford lost 4–1 away to Bristol City and Cambridge United went down 2–0 at West Ham; Bristol Rovers, the third team to go down, were already relegated well before those final matches. Needless to say, our attendances dropped by around six per cent while up the road Newcastle swept all before them, compounding our failure a hundredfold. In May, Bobby Ferguson resigned. He had simply had enough and was sickened by the poor quality of the players he had to work with. It was enough for me too. Both the team and I had been dreadful, and I also decided it was time to call it a day.

But only as a player, for that summer, with my manager's hat on, I saw an opportunity to regroup and add players to the team. I brought the squad in for two days straight after the final game in order to go through my plans for Sunderland's future. I told six players – Gary Owers, Gordon Armstrong, Tim Carter, Anton Rogan, Tony Smith and Peter Davenport – they weren't going to be part of those plans, and I asked them to speak to their agents to find new clubs. My problem was they didn't move on, as not a single offer came in for any of them. Owers and Armstrong had had offers over the previous couple of seasons so the club thought they had a value, but nothing happened. In the end this came back to haunt me, and again with hindsight it's something I shouldn't have done, but I felt I owed it to them to be honest. That's how I would have wanted to be treated myself. The problem is when they stay and you play them, you make those who aren't getting a game even unhappier than them. I had imploded. Shot myself in the foot. I was too honest.

I was given some money, though, and I signed Derek Ferguson from Hearts, with John Colquhoun going in the opposite direction. I knew Derek well from my Rangers days and knew what he was capable of, even though his career had naturally been affected when he and his wife Carol lost their newborn son. I also signed Northern Ireland striker Phil Gray from Luton, Ian Rodgerson from Birmingham for the right side of midfield, and Oxford's Andy Melville to go into the central defensive position. In all I spent about £1.75 million.

I took the players off to the Stirling management centre for pre-season work and some practice games. It went very well, despite the fact I still had the six unwanted players. Later, Walter Smith kindly agreed to bring Rangers down for a testimonial for Gary Bennett, and we attracted a big crowd. We lost 2–1 but we played well. Ferguson was immense, and the crowd fell in love with him immediately. We then played Middlesbrough away at Ayresome Park and won 2–1. We looked very useful, there were good vibes all round, and my new signings were working. After the game the team went back to Roker Park by coach while I drove to Darlington and my new home. Derek Ferguson had his car at Roker Park and gave a lift to Phil Gray, Andy Melville and Ian Rodgerson. Derek came out of the ground and ran into a wall of traffic, almost literally. He was going too quickly to stop, so he tried to be cute, went round the outside of a roundabout the wrong way, and hit another car head on. Gray, who had been sitting beltless in the front passenger seat, went through the windscreen and landed outside the car; Melville was concussed; Rodgerson, who had been holding on to the arm strap, had damaged the ligaments in his shoulder; and Ferguson, who was strapped in, was considerably shaken up. The police were called along with an ambulance and Gray went to hospital for an emergency operation on his eye.

I was at home relaxing with a glass of wine and reflecting on how promising the side was looking for the new season when I was called and told my players were in hospital. Phil had had an operation, which was a complete success, and Ian Rodgerson was out for three months. The season was in turmoil before it had even started, and I had to reshuffle for the season-opening trip to Derby County, although both Derek and Andy played when perhaps they shouldn't have. The incident affected the entire team. We were humiliated 5–0 and got off to the worst start possible. It really felt as though we were destined for another season-long struggle, but almost immediately we bounced back, beating Chester in the League Cup and thrashing Charlton 4–0 before August was out.

A bad run of results followed, but by mid-September I had Phil Gray back after the crash, and we got a great result against Leeds in the League Cup, beating them 2–1 at home. It was our best performance of the season so far. Draws with Watford and Grimsby and a win against Peterborough followed, then we went to Elland Road for the second leg of the League Cup tie and beat Leeds – a Premier League side, don't forget – by the same score again, oddly with the same scorers, Phil Gray and Don Goodman. That was one of the best performances of my managerial career, and it lifted everyone at the ground. Our undefeated run stretched to six games on 9 October when we beat Birmingham City to move away from the bottom of the table. Despite a setback at Middlesbrough in yet another televised game, we continued our climb up the table to eleventh place.

The beginning of the end for me came in the third round of the League Cup against Aston Villa. We outplayed them at Roker Park at the end of October – and lost 4–1. Even Villa boss Ron Atkinson was moved to admit the best team lost on the day. 'They murdered us 1–4!' he said dryly. Everything they hit went in, and I came away scratching my head, wondering just how we had lost. It hit the team even harder than me and our form went out of the window. We lost the next five League games and we were in a mess. The chairman began to demand better results for his investment and our relationship started to disintegrate. He was angry that we had too many on the staff, but we just couldn't shift the players I had earmarked for transfer and I didn't want to break up the players I had brought in because I thought we could put it back together.

On 11 November, two nights before the visit to Tranmere where we lost 4–1, I went to a supporters' club meeting and they asked me about my relationship with the chairman. I told them it was as wide as the Wear Valley. Inevitably it appeared in the press, and I had to speak to him before the game at the hotel. Surprisingly, the meeting went well, and I began to think of building bridges, especially when we started so well at

Prenton Park and were deservedly a goal up through Goodman at the break. But we completely collapsed in the second half with some incredible defensive errors. We performed badly again the following Saturday at Roker Park against Southend.

I spoke to the board and, amazingly, there was no mention of resignation or being sacked; instead they were very keen to help me out and do what they could after six defeats on the trot. I told them the best thing to steady the ship was to make a statement to the press and tell them I wasn't going to be sacked. They agreed straight away.

I waited all week, but there was no statement. Still, there didn't seem to be a problem as I worked the players hard in a bid to improve levels of fitness for the game against Nottingham Forest on 27 November, talking to the board and the chairman throughout the week. On the Friday morning before the match I was a little bit late arriving at the ground and I heard on my car radio there was going to be a statement on my future by the Sunderland board. At last, I thought, they were going to do what we had planned. The radio man surmised it was going to be the sack. I smiled to myself and thought I was going to enjoy the day.

The ground was besieged by the media. I was asked about my future and I told them I was still manager and intended to be so for some time yet. I went into my office and my secretary Moira, someone I am still friendly with now, was in tears. She knew I was going to get the sack because the chairman had asked her to write the statement to the press. Earlier that season I had taken on Ian Atkins as my number two, but chairman Bob Murray had also been keen for me to appoint a reserve-team coach, and had recommended Mick Buxton – someone well known to Murray as it transpired. I looked out of my office window and saw that someone had let in the press: they were all gathered around my door inside the corridors at Roker Park. There was a knock on the door and it was Ian and Mick, along with one of the directors, John Featherstone. He asked me to step into the boardroom, leaving Ian and Mick in my room. There was no Bob Murray, just Mr Featherstone and Mr Wood, another director, who told me they were going to sack me. Circumstances, they said, dictated I should go. I asked about all the positive stuff that had passed between us during the week and they just shook their heads. Ian Atkins was also to be dismissed, but Mick Buxton would take over the club on a caretaker basis. I asked about my compensation, having already had my fingers burnt at Coventry, and they told me it would be sorted out. I reminded them I expected Ian to be looked after as well. I then asked why the chairman had not told me himself, and I was told he had stepped down and was no longer in control. After that I put on my dignified hat, thanked them for all the help I had received while I was manager, straightened my back and walked out.

It was left to me to tell Ian and Mick what was happening. I told them I was going back to see my wife and children. Mick asked me where I would be for the rest of the day and I told him I wouldn't be moving from my house. He promised he would ring. I am still waiting for him to call twelve years later.

I went outside and talked to the press. I did all of them – papers, TV, radio, national and local – to get it all out of the way in one hit. I didn't have the chance to say goodbye to the players as Mick took them training. But what would I have said anyway? I never have been good at fond farewells. I was out of work again. After two sackings I did not expect to be a manager again, and I wasn't at all sure I wanted to be after what I had been put through. In some ways it was almost a relief.

The Butchers decided to go home for Christmas, back to Lowestoft. I got my bike out, dusted it down and again worked on my fitness, just for myself. As usual when things hadn't worked out, I punished myself, pushing things to the limit, thinking hard. I not only faced a bleak Christmas but also a very uncertain future. I had to ask myself the question, was I cut out to be a manager at the top level? Did I have what it takes? But the questions weren't entirely selfish for I was well aware the family was facing another major upheaval. Was it fair to keep putting them through the hoop every time I lost my job? Christopher and Edward were doing very well at Barnard Castle School, where former England international and deep thinker Rob Andrew coached. It was, needless to say, one of the best rugby schools in Great Britain. Alistair had just started at Hurworth Preparatory School near Middlesbrough's current training ground. We all really enjoyed Darlington – we still have friends there – and it was going to be a wrench for all of us to leave the area. But where would we go, and what was I going to do?

CHAPTER NINETEEN

MORE WHINE, SIR?

I had had two stabs at managing and two major disappointments, so Rita and I reached the conclusion we should invest our time and money in something a little different. Eventually we decided to go into business with my sister Vanda and her husband Nigel, who were in the catering trade. They had the experience, having managed and looked after pubs and golf clubs in Essex. I had always wanted to set them up in their own business and I thought this was an excellent opportunity both for them and us to move back to Scotland, our first choice as a family. The boys loved Dollar Academy in Clackmannanshire, and I had a better and bigger name there than in England.

In the meantime the courts had set a date for my case with Coventry to settle the contract dispute from 1992. The solicitors, who had been recommended by my agent Johnny Mack, had been working on a brief to gather all the information before passing it on to a barrister. I had meetings in London, and early in 1994 a week was set aside at the High Court in Holborn. I travelled down on the Sunday to be prepared for a Monday morning start. Johnny Mack sorted out a hotel for me, but when I arrived at the Mayfair it was a stunning £300 a night. What if I lost the case? I wouldn't be able to afford my bill! I spent one night there before moving into the far more modest Strand Hotel, within easy walking distance of the courts.

The first day was spent with the barristers, outlining the case and talking about the legal arguments. It hit home for the first time that I could lose a great deal rather than be paid what I thought I was owed if the club could prove their actions were justified. When I left Coventry I had been given two documents, remember, the one a press release and

245

the other questioning the legally binding nature of my contract because I had played only eight times due to injury. Essentially, they were claiming I hadn't fulfilled my contract. They knew I would have to put my house and savings on the line to prosecute the matter. It was all very intimidating, especially as going to High Court is an expensive business.

The night before I was due to be cross-examined I didn't sleep at all. I was so worried about what was going to happen. I had it all worked out in my mind and was ready to tell them I had been available to play but wanted to concentrate on getting the managerial side right because it was all so new to me. When you see your thoughts in black and white it is very sobering. In the morning I walked along the Strand to this famous court and prepared myself to go into the dock. I was terrified. I have never been so scared in my life. I was due in court at 8.30 a.m., and I was asked if I was ready by my lawyer Allan Henderson, a top man and still a pal, as he talked me through it. We were all ready to go in when the clerk of the court came out looking for us and told us there was going to be a delay. The defence counsel wanted to speak to the plaintiff's counsel.

Suddenly, after all this time, Coventry's legal team wanted to talk, with the suggestion that they were ready to settle. I continued to prepare myself for the dock as the talks dragged on, but after an hour and a half I was told that a compromise could be reached. At around 11.30 they thrashed out a deal: I was to get what I wanted – not all I was due, but a sum I had already indicated I was ready to settle for. I went into the chambers and enjoyed a glass of sherry Rumpole-style with the people who only hours earlier had been getting ready to tear me apart. Talk about putting on a business face! They were far more Jekyll and Hyde than ever I was. It was all very jolly and pleasant. They also told me Coventry would pay the legal fees, amounting to some £58,000. I don't think that until the last moment they ever thought I would take them all the way, but I had to. I was adamant. I wasn't just fighting for my pride, but for my family. We were talking about a great deal of money. It seemed clear to me they'd known all along they had no case, and had expected me to fold. They obviously didn't know me, or appreciate the quality of my legal team.

We went back to court to sign all the papers, and I met Mr Richardson, the new Coventry chairman. We had a chat and shook hands, and he told me I was welcome to go back to Coventry whenever I wanted as his personal guest. I only went back once, when I was covering a Sky game. I didn't go anywhere near the boardroom, though, and didn't speak to anyone from the club. Only recently I received a letter from chief executive Graham Hover asking me if I would attend the last match at Highfield Road before the club moved. I was going to reply I would rather gnaw off my arm, but Graham and his wife Julie are super people and I didn't want to hurt their feelings. Fortunately I had a game to attend, but I really don't think I could have gone, especially as there was another gala ball following the game. I remembered only too well what occurred at the last Coventry function I had attended.

The victory celebration was held at one of Fleet Street's most famous hostelries, Ye Olde Cheshire Cheese, one of my favourite haunts when in London. I confess I drank a great deal and could have flown back to Scotland without the aid of the aircraft. People don't realise what a case like this takes out of you unless they have been through one. Rita was also hugely relieved at the result because she knew as well as I did there had been no guarantee. We could have lost the lot. I flew back to Teeside airport and drove to Darlington where the celebrations continued, but only after Rita had told me what she thought of me for driving back in my condition.

To add to the money from Coventry I now had a pay-off from Sunderland – again not the full sum but a monthly amount agreed through gritted teeth. The fact that I had won the case against Coventry helped, but I have to say I felt the Professional Footballers' Association weren't much help. The situation was unusual in that I had two contracts. With Coventry I signed on non-contract forms as a player as my main job was as manager with playing duties, but for Sunderland I signed as a player before becoming manager and signing another contract. I was still registered as a player when Sunderland sacked me, but the PFA were very slow to back me up. They were in both camps, but they had a duty to me as a professional footballer and they did next to nothing. At the time there was no League Managers' Association so I was left to my own devices.

Despite my reservations about continuing in management, I bought myself a typewriter and started writing letters to clubs. I enclosed a CV and said I was prepared to work in any capacity at any level. But I only had replies back from one or two clubs and no offers at all. I appreciated I had suffered two strikes at Coventry and Sunderland and chairmen would be wary of me, especially as I hadn't yet completed my coaching badges, but it was all very depressing. There was only one thing for it: I got out my trusty bike and went off cycling around Darlington and North Yorkshire. I went out to Barnard Castle and other places of interest, doing a steady 30 or 40 miles a day, cranking up my levels of fitness and feeling really good about things again.

I started to look towards Scotland with a view to doing some television work and newspaper articles, and especially to 6 June when we were due to take over the Old Manor Hotel. It was a place we knew very well from our days living in Bridge of Allan; we'd often enjoyed Sunday lunch there. It had seven bedrooms and nice grounds, the sort of place you could go for a few beers and lunch with local friends. It held good memories of being a homely hotel with a good reputation. The previous owner had split from her husband and the hotel had proved too big for her to run on her own. We made a good offer for the property and the land in a very sought-after place. It had become a little run down, but I thought it would give us a good base and my sister and her husband something they had always wanted. In our inexperience, however, we hurried things through without having a really good survey done on the property, something I would advise every prospective owner to do. We quickly discovered a lot of faults and a number of areas where a great deal more money needed to be spent. Had we known this we wouldn't have gone in with such a big offer.

I made my sister manageress and her husband manager. There were stables alongside the hotel dating back to the early eighteenth century, and I moved my family in there, despite the damp and the general lack of facilities. For Vanda and Nigel we bought a big mobile home and hoisted it over the hotel and into the back yard with a huge crane. It was a tight squeeze, but it was a matter of necessity as every one of the seven bedrooms in the hotel needed money spent on them.

We were away on holiday when the move was finally made, and returned two days later. We walked into a disaster. Everything needed doing, from the plumbing to the electricity. It was so bad we should have levelled it and started from scratch. We took advice from a lot of people, including Ken McCulloch, well-known owner of One Devonshire Gardens and the man who founded Malmaison Hotels. He looked at the place and recommended we spend a lot of money on it and theme it in the 'Butcher' style with everything chunky, from chips to furniture. But we wanted the hotel to be a little more upmarket to suit the area, something with a little more class.

We began spending money on the place straight away, with lots of work being done on the bar, the restaurant and the kitchens. Then we started renovating the bedrooms upstairs. Even the televisions in the bedrooms were ancient, and in some rooms there was no central heating. Think of any problem that could beset an old hotel and we had it. The lot. The only thing we didn't have was a vermin problem. I don't think we were good enough for them with so many other nice properties in the area!

There was so much work to do, and with no hotel experience we left it up to my sister and her husband. But it was our names above the door, Terry and Rita Butcher. My reputation was at stake, and we wanted it run in a certain fashion. Unfortunately my sister had her own ideas, and they were very different to mine. Gradually, a rift developed between us in terms of the direction in which each of us wanted the business to go.

Outside the hotel things were going well for me. As soon as I returned to Scotland I was offered a very good fee by the *Daily Express* to write a weekly article, while Radio Clyde gave me a job as a pundit on Saturdays and Sundays. I also landed some television work with STV. I was soon building up quite a good portfolio and was more than happy to stay in touch with a game I loved so much. After games I would enjoy going back to the hotel and chatting to the customers in the bar and the restaurant, playing mine host, especially for the people who had come to the restaurant simply because it was mine and they felt they might meet me there.

But after a while it all began to wear a little thin because of problems with the kitchen or complaints about the food. It was difficult, because there could be 99 perfect meals out of 100 but the one single complaint I would take personally. It would weigh on me far heavier than the many compliments we received. The developing situation with Vanda and Nigel wasn't helped by me being away more and more through my media work, leaving Rita to cope with any problems with menus, staff and the many other things the hotel business throws up. Rita wanted to be involved as it was our investment, but there was an obvious conflict there because Vanda was the manageress. Resentments snowballed until everything came to a disastrous head.

Before the explosion I had taken to playing in the odd charity game here and there. Cammie Fraser, who I had played with at Rangers, talked to my old Rangers team-mate Davie Cooper after one of our games, and he called me in for training on Tuesday and Thursday nights at Clydebank where he was player-coach. It was brilliant. I loved every minute of it, especially when manager Brian Wright offered me a month-long contract because of a couple of injuries to both their main central defenders. I was delighted to say yes, but because I hadn't told my sister before it was announced on the news it prompted another big row. She felt affronted because as a business partner I hadn't confided in her first.

I wasn't really fit after so long out but I was delighted to be asked to play again. My first game was at Dunfermline, and we lost 4–1, but I felt I did fine in the unusual circumstances. I was better when we went to Dundee, although we lost again, 2–0. Then we played Raith Rovers at home. They were a good team, I had a particularly bad game, and we lost 3–0. I wasn't at all impressed with my performance but I took note of Raith and said in my *Express* column the following week that I wouldn't be surprised if they upset Celtic in the forthcoming League Cup Final at Ibrox. I pointed out they were a well-organised team and manager Jimmy Nicholl had got them playing good football. Stevie Crawford, who went on to Millwall and Plymouth and played for Scotland, led the line well and was always likely to score goals. I was commentating on the radio for the Final, and lo and behold Raith backed up my prediction with a win, after penalties, against all the odds. Pity I'm not a betting man.

That appearance against Raith Rovers on 19 November 1994 was my last professional game. I was quite rightly not picked for the next match, and by the end of the month the injured players were back and I was out. I didn't mind at all, for the three games had done enough to remind me I should quit. I had just been helping out the club and an old friend. Sadly, Clydebank are no more. There is no more Kilbowie, the first all-seater stadium in Britain. Sadly, too, Davie Cooper is no longer with us. Davie, who began his career with Clydebank, played 377 games for Rangers, winning three League titles, three Scottish Cups and four League Cups, and 22 times for his country. While attending a coaching school at Clyde's Broadwood Stadium in March 1995, he died suddenly. He was only 38 when he passed away, but I will never forget him. A true genius.

That last game for Clydebank coincided with the beginning of the end of the relationship between us and my sister and her husband. There were too many rows and I was worried about my investment, which included their wages. I wanted a say in what was going to happen to my business, but Vanda and Nigel had their own ideas. We'd been planning for Christmas since the middle of summer, but when it arrived the problems continued to escalate. We tried to give Vanda and Nigel days off but all that did was lead to confusion for the staff, with the owner saying one thing and the manager another. It reached a head at Christmas when Mum and Dad were due to stay with us for the holiday season, and close friends Ian and Rita were to join us for the New Year celebrations. It was my birthday on 28 December, so after a good Christmas Day Rita and I decided to go away for a couple of days to celebrate with some friends in Darlington. We stayed at the Marine Hotel in North Berwick and were delighted to get away from the hotel's worsening atmosphere, especially Rita who felt like the piggy in the middle, with me pulling one way and Vanda the other. We had to get away, even though it did not delight my parents to see their son vanish a few days after they had arrived. But we thought it would give them time to be with Nigel and Vanda and help solve a few problems.

When we returned on 29 December the situation was poisonous, hardly ideal as we went into Hogmanay. We had a family meal on the 30th and I told Dad I was committed to working at the Partick Thistle game the next day, but Dad turned round and said he and Mum weren't going to stay because the atmosphere was so bad. They had already told Vanda and Nigel. I went back to the Stables with Rita and decided there and then we had been through enough. The next morning, New Year's Eve, I called Vanda and Nigel in and sacked them. I told them it would be best for everyone if they were to go home with Mum and Dad. It was completely the wrong thing to do and I treated it much too much like a football sacking. I should have done it in a completely different way – at least waited until after New Year's Eve. But that would not have been me. I had made up my mind and it had to be done there and then. Still, to this day I cannot justify sacking her. There was no gross misconduct. We should have just agreed to part amicably on the basis it wasn't working out for either of us.

They eventually left, and we haven't talked since. Our only contact is through my parents, and we send cards to the respective children. It's all very sad, and says something about the potential difficulties of becoming involved in a business with family members. The affair understandably upset my parents hugely. Dad threw the keys at me and told me he didn't have a son any more. It was just too hard to explain to him how the situation had developed. They hadn't been there for the arguments, the animosity, the evil looks and everything else that went with it.

We had put a lot of money and commitment into the place and we had to carry on, particularly that evening of 31 December which went a long way towards paying holiday wages and other necessary bits and pieces. There was a seven-course banquet and everything was laid on for a wonderful night. I took Ian to the Thistle game, left the two Ritas to cope, and rushed back in the evening to help with the dinner. I had just about enough experience to take over, and with the help of the chef, Paul McGurl, and staff we had a great night. I had explained to them what had happened, and they helped to make the evening go perfectly. The only sour note was my sister and her family were still in the trailer. Mum and Dad had driven off, leaving them on their own.

They stayed in that mobile home for about a month. Rita babysat their children one day while Vanda and Nigel posed for pictures outside the hotel to go with the tabloid story she had sold – 'How my brother stabbed me in the back!' After that we gave them what little money we had spare and they went back to Norfolk. It was an unbelievable situation, and horrible for everyone involved. As I said, I don't regret they left the business, but it could have been done so much better, and at a better time. But how can you ever sack your sister subtly? There are lots of regrets and no little hurt, but I still love Vanda deep down. One day I hope we can resolve our difficulties.

From January 1995 it was simply a case of pitching in and doing it ourselves. We worked very hard and never took out any money from the business because all the accounts had to be looked after first and there was nothing left for us. We started the year with seven full-time staff plus part-time staff, bills to pay, mouths to feed, and still lots more work to do on the building, the car park, the bedrooms and the kitchen extension. Chef Paul McGurl, a lovely guy who I interviewed for the position myself, was one of our greatest assets. He stayed with us for two and a half years and built up the reputation of the food in the hotel. I remember that when Paul first went to look around the property he went to open the fridge door and received a massive electric shock because the appliance had never been earthed. That was the state of the place when we took it over. All they had were domestic fridges and a very small kitchen. We trebled the size of the kitchen and installed a huge walk-in fridge. The summer of 1995 was a hot one, and we used to stand inside the fridge for a few minutes to cool down. There was, of course, no air conditioning.

The renovation of the bedrooms was particularly hard work. I walked so much around the buildings during that period that I lost a lot of weight. Eventually we decided to bring in a manager to look after the day-to-day running – Jonathan Wengel, a big Rangers fan whose parents owned the Fox and Hounds in Houston, near Paisley. He was wonderful for us and built up a good understanding with Paul to produce some very good menus. Another good friend, John Morgan, who ran an advertising agency, designed the menus, cards, stationery, brochures and everything else. We built the hotel up so much we managed to get into *Taste of Scotland*, a very creditable Scottish good food guide at the time. We also had three crowns from the Tourist Board. As a result, you couldn't get a table on Saturday night. High teas were also popular, with steak and kidney pies, fish and chips and scones, rather than the cucumber sandwiches, cream cakes and pots of Earl Grey favoured south of the border. We all chipped in, and I would serve our speciality, the Old Manor Mixed Grill, myself. It was a huge meatfest for two served on a carving plate with a couple of sparklers. I would make a big entrance from the kitchen and carry it to the table.

As far as events were concerned, John Morgan ran, for the Burns Club, the Old Manor Burns Night. We could seat 72 people, making it a bit like school dinners. We used to pass the food – soup, haggis, steak pie, cheese and biscuits – down the table and it went on until the early hours of the morning with bottles of whisky on the table instead of wine. The 25th of January is a raucous night anyway in Scotland, and it was always a huge success. I had to twirl the bottles of whisky behind the haggis in true traditional style as the bagpipes played. Those nights made us good money, even though they required a lot of hard work. We also used to do weddings for up to 70 – very good for second- and third-time marriages when the guest list is usually more refined. And in 1997 the Rangers convention, which travelled round the world, came to Scotland. Some of the participants came to our hotel, and I made a speech. The hotel always made good money out of my Rangers past. In the hotel I frequently took meal orders, waited on tables and served wine, but some of the Rangers supporters didn't like it when I served food or cleared up plates. They thought that as a former captain of Rangers I shouldn't be doing such menial tasks. They would ask for one of the other members of staff to serve and clear their tables.

It was the hardest I have ever worked in my life, and Rita worked even harder. It was especially tough when, out of the blue, someone would complain: the story always made the national newspapers because of who I was. Once, a moth was found in a steak and kidney pie. But how is that possible when the pies were hand-made in the kitchen? There were no moths in our kitchen. But the hardest time was when Paul McGurl left us after two and a half years. Employing a good new chef was as hard as getting a star centre-forward. They were either lunatics or alcoholics, and when we did get one we really liked we were already thinking it was time to get out of the hotel business.

Everyone thought we were making a fortune, especially at Christmas, but you put in a lot of hours, you have to pay staff overtime and a half, you have lots of overheads and you need to buy in specialist food. And at the busiest times there were many drunken revellers who would cause a great deal of damage, all of which had to be repaired. At the front of the hotel we had four cannons, about a metre long, monstrously heavy and sitting on carriages. They were ornamental and beautiful, but they were always being stolen, mainly by students from Stirling University. We were part of what they called the Stirling Bridge of Allan golf course. We were a par one while other bars and hotels were designated par two or par three – only in this case the pars were for the number of drinks to be consumed. They would start with us and eventually finish with us. The problem was they, like a lot of students around the world, would hunt for souvenirs from the hotel and the grounds, and our heavy cannons were a prime target. It would take two prop forwards from the rugby team to carry one of them off on their shoulders. We could see and hear them disappear, and we used to chase after them, sometimes but not always recovering our property. We also had long wooden signs at the entrance which advertised our high teas, bar lunches and dinners; these would vanish too. Apparently the students used the noticeboards as ironing boards. It became so bad that whenever we had a group of students in we would know things would go missing. I regularly used to ban them and was often the butt of their comments. I even banned all students completely at one stage because they were stealing far more than they were spending.

At times it really was the hotel from hell. Staff turnover also threw up its own problems. Bringing in expensive temporary chefs is a financial and logistical pain, and then when a permanent chef arrives there have to be new menus and a complete change around. I would interview a chef, but until he cooked you could have no idea how good he was. Who eats references? Hotel jobs are transient as far as staff are concerned. Paul McGurl once took on a kitchen porter, the worst job in the kitchen and a rapid changeover job, but after just a few days Paul told me the new employee couldn't come in on the Friday because he was due in court. It was something, he said, to do with his daughter. We never saw him again as he was sent down for three years as a paedophile. The next day I drove through the town to see the newspaper billboards proclaiming 'Ex Rangers Captain's Hotel Employs Paedophile'. I was slaughtered for something I really had nothing to do with.

A lot of friends laughed at our regular predicaments, comparing me to Basil Fawlty and the hotel to Fawlty Towers. Sometimes it felt exactly like that. All hotels have the potential to be the best or the worst, and it's quite frightening how narrow the dividing line is between the two extremes. Our favourite bolthole is the Crinan Hotel by Lochgilphead out in Argyll. It overlooks the Isle of Jura and is blessed with great walks for the dog while the service is good and homely and the seafood is straight out of the sea and wonderful. It is just how I would have liked our hotel to be. But it was a valuable learning-curve experience for us, particularly in terms of the appreciation of good food and wine. We can now go into a restaurant and sense instantly whether or not it's a happy restaurant, and we know the difference between good and bad service and good and bad food.

By mid-1998 we felt we had had enough. It was too much of a slog, much of it at unsociable hours. In the evenings I used to do the bills, and on Saturday night I would get to a stage where there were one or two tables left at around one a.m. When they finally went I would go into the kitchen and make a huge tray of sandwiches for all the staff. I didn't drink during the night, so I would set myself a target of a minimum of two pints of lager before I went to bed. That was a real buzz and a good wind-down at the end of a long and busy day for everyone. Often on a Saturday night we would serve over 200 covers and it was a good feeling, especially knowing Rita and I were off the next day. It was a time when we could talk to the staff and listen to any problems.

We sat down as a family and decided to tell everyone we were going to close the hotel, and on 1 November 1998 we did. We called in a Falkirk-based company, Central Auctions, run by a family called the Penmans who we knew socially, to sell off the hotel equipment and the pictures of my Rangers days. There were quite a few of them on the walls, and it was always funny when Celtic supporters came in by accident, not knowing who ran the hotel. They would order a pint, look around at the pictures, and disappear in record time. On one memorable occasion a lad came in with his fiancée to talk to Rita about a wedding reception. When they sat down he looked around at the pictures, turned to his wife-to-be and announced they had to go. When she asked him why, he replied, 'Because it's a Rangers shrine.'

We were living in the stables while the people looking after the sales and the viewing were in the hotel for ten days. At the time I was at Dundee United – more about that in the next chapter – and I'd gone out for a Christmas party with the staff of the club. When I returned I found our steam cleaner had been stolen. We found it six months later in Falkirk, but no one was prosecuted. They had obviously cased the joint well because the laundry room was the only one not alarmed, though it was locked and bolted, and they were unable to access any other part of the building. Rita hated the experience, mostly because the people running the auction were extremely intimidating; they even had the nerve to tell me she was upset because she was having a nervous breakdown. In the end I'd had enough and I told them to take the sale items away and to get off my property. They charged us a huge, grossly overpriced commission, including items not sold. We were in a tight corner because they had taken all the money and refused to give it to us until we paid their inflated prices.

We had already refurbished the stables beautifully while living in the trailer, so when we closed we were able to sell the conversion straight on, to a lovely family. We even sold part of the car park, to Bobby Halliday, a local architect, as a plot on which to build a house. It was then a case of converting the hotel back into a house, one of the oldest in Bridge of Allan. The five of us and the dog moved into the house. The dog was a necessity as well as a family pet, to keep away intruders. The main road, the old A9, ran past the hotel and the outside wall was chest high, which meant that anyone could look over into the Old Manor. That was fine when it was a hotel and we wanted potential customers to be able to see us, but it wasn't so good when we were living there as a family. I had the wall built up to over six feet high to give us some privacy, but you could still hear the comments and the remarks of the students as they went past on a Saturday night. I became a real Victor Meldrew as I complained about rubbish thrown over the wall – bottles, cans, fish and chip paper, road signs, For Sale signs and worse.

Still, our boys loved it because each of them had his own ensuite; there was also a bar, a games room for pool and a 52-foot-long lounge. It was a magnificent house, but even with the three boys and the dog it was too big for us. It was an ideal place for parties, though, as the boys discovered when we were away. Before long, Chris went away to university, which left just Rita, me, Edward and Alistair in this enormous house. We rattled around inside it. Eventually, in 2002, we sold it. The proceeds of the sale, together with the money from the car park and the stables, meant that we just about got our money back.

I was glad to sell it in the end because apart from all the good memories there were too many bad ones, the break-up of the family being the main one. Then there was all the hassle and aggravation, particularly with the staff. Worse than the turnover was the absenteeism. Staff would fail to turn up with not a word to us, and one night even the head chef didn't show. With a full restaurant booked that night, at lunchtime he packed his knives and departed without a word to anyone. How can anyone do that? Rita had to cook for everyone with the junior chef while I went out front to try to explain to everyone what had happened.

The biggest lesson I learnt is there is no easy, cheap way to quality. It is a long, hard road, and you have to invest not only in bricks and mortar but in people as well. I would never go back into the business. A restaurant maybe, but I certainly don't want to relive the nightmare of running a hotel.

CHAPTER TWENTY

THE DOTCOM REVOLUTION

While the hotel business was still ticking over, I continued to harbour a deep desire to get back into football. Alex Smith, who had been manager of Clyde and St Mirren when they won the Scottish Cup in 1987, lived in Bridge of Allan. When Alex went to Raith Rovers in the late summer of 1997 to join Jimmy Nicholl, who I also knew from my Rangers days, I wrote to Jimmy and asked him if I could come in and help with the coaching. They invited me in for a couple of mornings a week. I enjoyed working with the young kids immensely. It was an hour's run across country in my car to get there, depending on the weather, but I didn't mind as Raith was a lovely club, in the First Division at the time but trying to get into the Premier Division. Eventually they took me on full time at the princely sum of £12,500 a year, with the bonus of a regular tank of petrol. I started as youth-team coach, eventually moving up to the reserves. John Brownlie took over as youth-team coach, and the four of us worked with the team, even though Raith had no money to spare at all.

At the same time I joined the BBC to summarise for England games in the build-up to the World Cup in France. It was good for me to be involved with coaching full time and with England matches, not to mention my other media work. It all added to my experience and my CV. The money was moderate, but it was a lifesaver, and good publicity and involvement for me.

Slowly John Brownlie, the other coach at the club, began to get things going on the coaching front. Raith had some good youngsters coming through, and Jimmy and Alex were building up a great atmosphere within the club. For lunch the boys used to go out and get their own stuff, but, as we discovered, they were eating rubbish. So we decided to feed them. The only problem was there was no budget for food. We tried to find meals that were both cheap and nutritious, and decided on baked beans or spaghetti on toast with lots of brown sauce and pots of tea. I brought in a great big pot from the hotel and we went to the supermarket to buy bread and huge tins of spaghetti and beans. We managed to feed up to 40 players for an incredible £7.50 – around 20p a head! What's more they loved it. The players who are still there talk about it today. They actually looked forward to it. It really was good wholesome food, although the dressing rooms weren't always the most pleasant place to be after training and lunch.

Jimmy Nicholl would hold afternoon quizzes with the kids. It was so successful I do it myself with youngsters at Motherwell. Jimmy used to have his *Rothmans Yearbook* and a pile of cream cakes by his side, and the players would break into pairs ready to answer his questions. As each player answered a question correctly he would be allowed to take one of the cakes. There was always one cake fewer than players present, thus giving matters a strong competitive edge. There would also be a forfeit to pay for the last one. They were always funny, something like singing a song naked or giving a half-time team talk, taking off Jimmy or Alex. Jimmy would give them a scene-setter for these talks, something like being four goals down with three players sent off. Some of the youngest would come in and go berserk, grabbing me by the collar up against the dressing-room wall and telling me I was a 'fucking disgrace'. One or two bottled it, but for most it was great character building, and all credit to Jimmy who is now doing a great job at Aberdeen.

The atmosphere was so good within the club the team did well where it mattered, on the pitch. I loved it, and I enjoyed coaching the reserves. It was something I had never done before. I had only been a first-team manager, but this was my opportunity to fill in the gaps, to learn things I had bypassed the first time round. I will forever be indebted to Jimmy and Alex for what they did for me at a time when I really needed it. They helped with my football education for a whole year, and I say without hesitation they are two of the best guys in the game.

I couldn't have been happier when I started off the new 1998/99 season with the club and the players, but then came an opportunity too good to be missed. Tommy McLean had just been appointed at Dundee United, and he asked me to help out with the coaching, though without specifying what job he was offering me. He also doubled my wages, which was a massive incentive as it came at the time when Rita and I were winding down the hotel business. When I left Raith there were no hard feelings. We had the club's coaching staff and their families round for a meal to say thank you for all they had done. Alex Smith still talks of the night when he thought Rusty Nails were on draught.

When I first went to Dundee United I was still unsure about what exactly I was supposed to be doing at the club. There was already a coach, Gordon 'Stubby' Wallace, but Tommy McLean used to do a lot of the training himself. I took the kids for a couple of sessions, then Stubby would take them. On my first weekend with the club, at the end of August, they played Motherwell away. I sat on the bench with Tommy and Stubby as we lost 1–0. We were woeful.

The following Saturday England were playing Sweden in Stockholm in their first qualifier for the 2000 European Championship, and I went away with BBC Five Live. I had only been at the club a couple of weeks, but as I was playing such a minor role I thought nothing of it. Then, the day before I left for Sweden, Tommy called me in and told me he had had enough and was going to quit; he had put forward my name as a candidate for his job. I was pretty bemused by this as I had given up a job I enjoyed at Raith to join him. The way football operated, I could suddenly find myself out of work. The news of Tommy's departure did not break until after the international, so I returned to Scotland wondering what was going to happen with my career. I soon discovered St Johnstone manager Paul Sturrock, a former player with the club, was being named as the new manager, with John Blackley as his assistant. I was made youth-team coach, Paul telling me the position would be reviewed after three months.

With such a short time in which to prove myself, I got my teeth into the job, enjoying the fabulous scenery while driving to and from the training ground. I went to Largs to gain my youth coaching licence – one of the hardest things I have ever done in my life – and began to really enjoy being with the youth team, then the U-18s. A lot of the youngsters Dundee United looked after then are still around, but a great deal of the credit for that must go to Graham Liveston, the youth development manager, who was based in the Holy Cross School near Glasgow. He provided a conveyor belt of top-quality youngsters and worked constant miracles.

Dundee United was a lovely club with an intense rivalry with their neighbours Dundee. I began to build up a very good relationship with Maurice Malpas, who was coming to the end of his first-team career. He still played in the first team but also took the reserves. I worked with him and he helped me with the kids. It was such a tight club that Maurice also used to do the laundry. He would pack the hampers the night before an away game, play, return, unpack the skip and put the washing in to sort out the next day. He was often also the best player on the day – a great tribute to his professionalism and his character. Can you imagine one of today's players washing socks and shirts after a hard 90 minutes?

We had a training ground just over the road called the Gussie where we played a lot of the U-18 matches. New turf had been put in with an artificial surface with little rubber pellets underneath, making it really bouncy and not hard and flat like the previous synthetic surface. We also parked our two minibuses and a trailer at the Gussie garage. Every night we had to take our portable goalposts into the garage for security, and Maurice and I were the only ones who could back up the trailer without halting the traffic for a long time. We had a small kitchen facility at the ground too, and sometimes I would help our dinnerlady Maureen prepare the lunch and do the washing up for her afterwards. We used to feed up to 60 people with pasta and the like, but the big day was Thursday when we served battered fish with baked beans, tomato and tartare sauces, toast and tea. It was my favourite day, and I could eat the same meal now. It makes my mouth water just thinking about it. We used to have all the youngsters up for training on Thursday nights, the fifteen- and sixteen-year-olds as well, as we looked for the next intake. We would play the local men's teams and we never lost a single game. Why? Because our youngsters passed the ball better than the adults, who would run with the ball and not pass it. It wasn't long before I could clearly see the route through for the youngsters, and the progress they were making. I began to wish that I had gone through such an instructive period first, not gone straight into management after playing.

On match days, when the youngsters weren't playing, I did the warm-up for the first team. I enjoyed that too, and consequently I built up a relationship with the players, and soon they started to come to me with their problems. I could see that being back at his former club wasn't proving easy for Paul Sturrock. There was a great deal of politics, and Paul was clearly somewhat uncomfortable in the job. And Sturrock and I weren't a particularly happy marriage, in part because I felt he was unsure about where he was taking the club, and also because his son Blair was in my youth team. I was afraid the lad wasn't going to be as good as he thought he could be, and this was a problem. What made things even more inconvenient was Paul would go home in the middle of the afternoon and leave me to take his son home, which was somewhat out of my way. What could I do? At least Paul never told me I had to pick his son, though I played him anyway as he was a big, strong centre-forward who, at the level we were playing, was reasonably effective. As I write this now, Blair Sturrock is at Kidderminster. Had he not been the manager's son, I would undoubtedly have released him.

I worked for Paul for some eighteen months, and during that time, towards the end of 1999, the Butchers went on one of the best holidays we've ever had, in the French skiing resort of Val Thorens. I had never tried skiing before, but the boys and Rita had and they'd loved it. We had a fantastic time. The knees were a bit sore, though. Earlier that year I'd been to see Dundee United's specialist, and he'd told me I had the knees of a 70-year-old. His immediate prognosis was that both needed replacing, but I'd have to wait ten years. Despite the soreness, I felt I was in my element on the slopes. I suppose I was tailor-made for the sport: I am built like a snowplough, and being knock-kneed I only had to push the ankles out a bit to come to a shuddering halt. I took lessons in the morning and in the afternoon and soon began to get the hang of it. We saw in the new millennium while we were there, and enjoyed ourselves so much that we have been back since. If I had my way, I would go every year.

In early 2000 I was casting an eye around for other things to do. Ian Redford, an agent in Scotland who used to play for Dundee United and Rangers, spoke to me about a new venture he was embarking on with another agent, Murdo Mackay. I knew of him because he was looking after Gary Stevens and Chris Woods. I said I would listen to what they had to say and after a meeting at my house I rather liked the idea of a website to be called insidesoccer.com, with the company named Inside Soccer. As well as a functional football site, it was to encompass the grass-roots aspects of the game. Everyone was trying to become involved with the dotcom companies which were taking off in a big way and earning a lot of people a great deal of money. There was already Planet Football and 365 with Danny Kelly and other big names involved. It meant coming away from football, but I had been involved with the media since returning to Scotland and I could see a new career developing. I liked to write about games, and after the meeting I stayed up all night writing down ideas for tactical pages and myriad other things. The scope, it seemed to me, was limitless. The fact that they were prepared to double my wages was another factor. Rita was all for it and Paul Sturrock said the club would not stand in my way.

So in March I went to work with the holding company Inverplan. There were a couple of girls in the office, Mackay was managing director, and the operating officer was Tom Graham, a man who had come from the hotel business and, in effect, was my boss. For the first nine months my directive was to work on the website and gather information and people who could link in to become part of a grass-roots page concerning itself with women's football, schools football, handicapped football, keeping racism out of football, Sunday leagues, five-a-side teams and the like. I worked through the organisations listed in the *Rothmans Yearbook* and I often travelled down to London to meet various people, including a company that looked after schoolboy football who were keen to link up with us. We also spoke to administrators in women's football and the Football Association, who were keen to explore the idea. I was generally sifting through the information on my own, apart from when Murdo took me down to London for meetings. He was dealing with venture capitalists and potential sponsors while I grafted at a lower level as a business development manager.

We had ideas for other projects too, like Power Ball, where we had a confined area and a goal with holes in it. One team would defend the goal and the other would attack it, and the attacking team scored points through the holes. We had a prototype set up at Bath University, who worked with us on the development. They worked a lot with other sportsmen too, and we were talking to them about setting up an academy. The ideas seemed like great ones to me, and I was hearing from the top that there was plenty of interest in investment. I had no reason to think otherwise as we would always stay in good hotels in London. I was even given a C180 series Mercedes as a company car, with all my petrol paid, and there was a health plan and all the other perks associated with big business.

The only problem at this stage was I couldn't get a start date for the launch of insidesoccer.com. When I joined in March 2000 I was told it was going to be up and running in June. Then it became July, and then August.

I could never get a firm date. By then another website, onefootball.com, had launched, and we went down for talks with them. There were other sites starting too, and with broadband on the horizon it was becoming exciting and more practicable. Eventually we were told the idea had to be put on the shelf because the company didn't have sufficient funds to pursue it. I was disappointed to say the least as I had put in nine months' hard work by that stage and made a lot of promises to people who trusted me on the basis of all the information I had been fed.

It became a bit of a nightmare, and I began to feel a little uneasy. Murdo then brought in Eric Black, who had recently been sacked by Celtic along with John Barnes. Eric was brought in at the same level as me on the same money. I knew him slightly, but our friendship began to take off when we worked together. We began to progress a player-recruitment business idea to start paying the bills and the wages. The investment in the dotcom business was apparently there, but nothing was coming into the company in terms of income. We were to be called Inside Soccer Recruitment, and were eventually to be online. Murdo explained we would be like a normal recruitment agency but connected solely with football. On the strength of this I asked my mate John Morgan to become involved. It was a mistake because he ended up, like the rest of us, losing a lot of money. Sorry, John! Anyway, he helped us bring out this glossy brochure about what the company could do in terms of filling in vacancies for clubs, including, of course, footballers. If a team needed a left-back, Eric and I would draw up a list of recommendations; if the club acted on our proposals, they would pay us a fee.

The big snag was the players didn't belong to us, so we would have to approach their agents first – a major hurdle to overcome. There were so many drawbacks and imponderables it was difficult to see deals through to their conclusion. So Murdo, an agent himself, tried to get agents tied in with us; they would therefore have to pay a fee for us to push their clients. It was slightly restrictive, but at least we could recommend players knowing we could deliver.

I had to go out to the clubs and sell the idea to them, helped by our excellent brochure, which opened many doors. Then came the hard part: I had to persuade the clubs to sign a terms-and-conditions contract to pay us fees. None would sign up, and I couldn't blame them. I felt I wouldn't have signed it myself in their position, which made me feel uncomfortable. It was a tangled web. First of all we tried to get clubs to pay to use us; then we tried to get agents to pay; the only other revenue we could get was if we actually completed the transfer of a player, but even that was a gamble because there was no guarantee of being paid. We had no recourse in law if the agent simply claimed it was his player and walked off with the fee.

We did manage to bring in some cash through Eric Black because he had a lot of contacts from a spell in France. The advantage lay in the fact that we would be introducing new faces and new names. He also had a good relationship with the agents involved, and they were prepared to split the money with us. I improved my French working with the fluent Eric, and I was able to talk to the French players he brought over with some success. But I was becoming more and more ill at ease with the company. It was making me feel poorly. I felt I couldn't go on because I couldn't see how it was going to work, especially as I was going to clubs trying to sell a project I had little or no belief in.

I then became involved in a sort of scouting role. We would build up dossiers for every player at every level in every club. Murdo brazenly claimed he had a deal with the Press Association whereby they would pay to use the information. I got together a group of seven or eight scouts including Nigel Brown, who was chief scout at Wigan at the time and had done some work for me at Sunderland. He was a hard-working man, and we began to develop the base for our library material.

But clearly the company was struggling to make money, because Murdo approached me, Eric and another business development manager, Stewart Brown, and asked us to invest in the company in return for a one per cent share. He told us he had been offered millions for the business but did not want to sell it. As a result, I invested £37,000 while Eric put in almost double. Rita had told me not to do it and went crazy when I drew a cheque and paid it over. And what did I get in return? Nothing. No shares, not even a receipt for the money paid. It almost certainly disappeared into the cash flow to pay the wages while Murdo continued to drive around in his big Merc with personalised number plates and telephones, and to take his family on luxury holidays.

We continued to develop our players' bible for the scouts, an easy-reference guide that would cut out the hours of writing and make reports easy to compile. It was a good system, totally computerised, and I enjoyed working on it as I was able to scout games live and on television. Eric was still doing deals with players, bringing them from France to

Scotland and England, but we knew we weren't bringing in enough money to pay us, never mind to keep the company afloat. I repeatedly asked Murdo to return my money, but there was always some excuse for not doing so.

In October 2001 Eric, a first-class coach, was suddenly offered the job of manager of Motherwell. He had already been looked at by several clubs, but now he told me about Motherwell and asked if I would be interested in going to Fir Park with him as his number two. I immediately saw the opportunity as a parachute out of the difficult situation I had become caught up in. We had discussions with Pat Nevin, the football director at Fir Park, and chairman John Boyle. The only difficulty was we had to be released from our current contracts, and when we told Murdo he went ballistic, threatening to sue us. He told us he had spoken to Michael Buckley, his main backer, and Michael was coming to talk to us for a big clear-the-air meeting.

It was arranged for Buckley to meet me at 9.30 a.m. at the Hilton at Edinburgh airport before going on to talk to Eric in Glasgow. Then I received a call from Murdo saying that Michael's plane had been delayed but he would be there himself to meet me and we would wait together for his arrival. Murdo tried to talk me round as we waited, but I told him point blank I thought the company had no future and I wanted to go back into football. It was a bad meeting. He then took a call, and told me it was Michael who had said he was now going straight to Glasgow to meet Eric. On my way home I telephoned Eric and told him I thought there was something fishy going on. We had actually met Michael on a few occasions and had got on well with him, so Eric decided to call him direct. Michael said he had no knowledge at all of any meetings with either Eric or me. Eric immediately telephoned Murdo and told him we were out of there. But we had to leave without our money. It was an expensive lesson in business for a couple of novices.

Sure enough the company went into liquidation at the end of the year, owing a great deal of money. The good ideas had never been turned into fact, and there was no revenue stream. And it wasn't just me and Eric who lost out: several big investors, including Victor Chandler the bookmaker, saw their cash go down the pan as well. Murdo Mackay has tried to telephone me a few times since, wanting tickets for games and other things, but I won't entertain a man who still thinks he can be my friend after taking my money in exchange for false hopes.

Incredibly, he was director of football for Derby County but has subsequently left the club.

Several times I sent recorded deliveries to try to recover my money, but my calls and letters were never returned. I had never been able to see how the company was going to make money anyway, unless Eric discovered a player who was worth millions, thus netting the company a big commission. But then the top sides would already have earmarked such players. Agents' fees are gradually being phased out anyway, and I feel clubs have a point. The only person who should pay an agent is the player himself.

I worked for the company for about eighteen months, and worked for nothing when the money I put in is taken into account. Everything there was hired, from the desks to the wastepaper bins. When Tom Graham and Murdo were absent we played football in the office with a futsal ball, which had been sent to me as part of a promotion for the new competition being played mainly on the Continent. We would have 20- or 30-minute head-tennis sessions and were happy doing that for a while, but later we started smashing the ball around this big open-plan office. We used to chip the balls into the thin metal bins, often taking leaves off the hired plants standing next to them. The bins weren't very strong either, and I guess we destroyed at least half a dozen of them. At least we got rid of our pent-up frustration.

The longer I was with Inside Soccer the more I switched off, with Radio Five in particular coming to my rescue. Whenever they asked me to do anything I was only too happy to help. I also turned my hand to all sorts of things. I went out to Hong Kong with a friend and took former England goalkeeper Peter Shilton. My old friend and England team-mate Dave Watson arranged for Rita and me to go on a cruise with former players Jim Pearson and Martin Chivers plus commentator Tony Gubba, playing football on the deck and talking to the punters as we cruised around the Mediterranean. I also took Dave McPherson out to Singapore to do some coaching, though Inside Soccer had the cheek to ask me what possible benefit the trip could be to the company. It was certainly of no benefit to the company, but it was to me personally in several ways. Firstly, it was during that trip that I was able to explore places connected with my birth and early life. Secondly, Dave put me right about Murdo, his agent, when he told me about problems with his testimonial and the delay in being paid his money.

It was yet another interesting passage of my life. It was an expensive one, certainly, and when it all ended my confidence was shaken and I became seriously bitter. But I learnt a great deal too, and besides, had I not gone there and met Eric Black I would not have gone to Motherwell. As soon as they beckoned, I was off. For me it was a great escape, and I was glad to get out before things really hit the fan because you can be sure that had I still been there it would have been my name plastered all over the newspapers.

CHAPTER TWENTY-ONE

JUMPERS FOR GOALS

Eric Black and I arrived at Motherwell on 16 October 2001 to face the press as the new management team. Also present were George Adams, the youth development officer from Celtic, and Chris McCart, the U-15s coach and a former Motherwell captain. After the press conference we booked a table at Hermann's in Stirling and got plastered. Not the wisest thing the day before starting a new job.

It was really nice to be back in the fold, back in football. Eric took the big office at Fir Park and I was next door in a smaller room with Chris McCart – a room I occupy today, with my assistant Maurice Malpas, as I still see the big room as Eric's. I was quite happy with my number-two role behind someone I respected as much as Eric, but Motherwell were in real trouble at the time. They had won only twice that season, were near the bottom of the SPL, and had big financial problems. There were more than 50 players at the club, many of them on big money, £4,000 to £5,000 a week. Eric and I looked at them, and some were simply not worth their places. Actually, I don't think Eric knew how bad a financial state the club was in. The owner, John Boyle, had put in a great deal of his own money, up to £11 million, chasing the dream of being the third force in Scottish football behind the Old Firm. Big players had come and gone, and he wasn't left with a great deal at the end of his spending spree. Fortunately for him Motherwell was only a small part of his conglomerate, Hamilton Portfolio, for it was the major loss; they consistently had to find the cash for the club to pay the wages every week. That was fine when the stock market was doing well, but as it slipped the cash flow became a problem, which eventually resulted in the club going into administration.

But we were not to know all this at the time, and in the autumn of 2001 we concentrated on rebuilding team spirit. Eric is an excellent coach. Sometimes he told me what he was going to do, and sometimes he didn't. I would get the balls, put the cones out, do bits and pieces and speak to players. I would then take the younger players in the afternoons, or the U-21s as they were called. I felt it was important to have a team you were identified with. It gets rid of anxieties and frustrations because you know you are in charge of something.

Our first fixture was on 27 October away to, of all people, Dundee United. We drew 1–1, coming from behind. We won only two of our next eleven games, and then on 5 January we crashed out of the Scottish Cup at the first hurdle, beaten 3–1 by Dunfermline. It was a low point because we played really dreadfully. After the game a furious Eric Black began to have a go at the players, but when he turned on one of the youngsters, one of the senior players, David Kelly, had a go back at Eric for shouting at the young kids. He questioned Eric's tactics too, and things soon got out of hand. David called Eric a prick, and when asked to repeat it he did so. I then jumped in to support my manager and asked David who he thought he was, having a go at the boss in front of everyone. He then turned on me and called me a prick, and when asked to repeat it again there was no hesitation. I went for him but was stopped just in time by two or three people diving in and holding me back. I don't know what would have happened had I reached him, but in the mood I was in I would have probably been finished in the game. Eric immediately ordered everyone back to the ground, and this on a Saturday night. By he time we got back to Fir Park everyone had calmed down, so Eric addressed the players again, having already sent David Kelly home and suspended him for his outburst. Eric told the rest if anyone felt the same way he would move them on. There was talk of Kelly being sacked, but his contract was terminated and chief executive Pat Nevin paid him off. We were furious at the decision as we felt it undermined Eric.

That January we began to restructure. A few players moved on, some were shown the door, and the squad was reshaped. Eric was again using his contacts in France and brought over several French players for trials. Some could speak English and some couldn't, which left me talking to players in my basic French. One useful Frenchman was little David Ferrere. He was so small we thought he was a mascot, but he came on as a half-time substitute during a home game with Hibernian in early

February and immediately won the fans and us over with a second-half hat-trick in a 4–0 victory. That was the end of Hibs manager Frank Sauzee. Eric turned up quite a few gems in his time, and results generally weren't too bad. Gradually we were turning ourselves into a hard team to beat.

We got through Easter, and Eric started looking at his budget for the following season. It had already gone down from £2.5 million to £2 million, and even that wasn't definite. He was continually going to Pat Nevin to ask for assurances. Then we received the dramatic news that John Boyle felt he could no longer carry on underpinning the club financially. He was faced with two options: going into interim administration and cutting staff and wages, or going into liquidation, shutting the doors and closing the club down. The main asset was the ground, but even Fir Park wasn't worth as much as John had lost. It was felt the only way forward was to go into interim administration, which guaranteed redundancies on and off the pitch. The club really had to cut back to a workable level. When this decision was taken there were only two games left to play. Motherwell's place in the top division was assured, but Eric felt he could not continue, especially as he had signed players and made promises to them. Pat Nevin, who believed the answer to the problem was another big injection of cash, joined him in his decision.

PKF were appointed as administrators, with Bryan Jackson in charge. Eric and Pat asked me to take control as manager of the club. With Eric resigning on a point of principle I almost felt beholden to join him, but he persuaded me to stay on. As I knew the players I said I was prepared to see the season out, which meant an away fixture at Kilmarnock, a home game against Dundee and a friendly against the Italian side Chievo. Chris McCart and I picked the team for the Kilmarnock game on 27 April and we went there with a massive following of fans. They were showing they wanted the club to survive; they even set up a trust. They were magnificent. We won 4–1 as the players went for it, thinking it might be their last game together. It was a tremendous performance.

We told the players to have the Monday off and come in on Tuesday when the club would talk to them. Those were my instructions, but the situation changed over the weekend and I had to ring round to get the players in on Monday after contracts had been studied by the administrators in conjunction with the club. The players met in the Davie Cooper Stand behind the goal in private boxes. Some would stay with wage cuts, others would be made redundant with immediate effect. It was terrible waiting for the players to arrive that day. A total of nineteen of them went, young and old, a lot of them had their pay slashed, while others were kept on as assets. They joined what was a very long list of creditors. It was an extremely black day. I gave everyone two days off after that, telling them to come in on Thursday to prepare for the Chievo match. Remarkably, with a much-changed team we managed to hold the Italians to a 1–1 draw, having taken the lead. Then we played Dundee at home on the Saturday, winning 2–1, seventeen-year-old centre-back Willie Kinniburgh making his debut. We literally had no one else to play.

Hull City came in for one of our players, Northern Ireland international Stuart Elliott, who had joined us from Glentoran. He was a very religious young man and had only agreed to join us because there was a branch of his church in Motherwell. He was a nice guy, quick, and did well for the club. Hull's healthy £235,000 bid was a great bit of business for the administrator and he would not let us turn it down. Everything was finalised, then Elliott suddenly had second thoughts. He only eventually agreed to go when he found out there was another of the sister churches in Hull. The later money from the sales of James McFadden and Stephen Pearson went into the pot too, to help pay off the creditors at something like 25p in the pound – a bonus to the zero they might have got had we tried to carry on.

I was now in charge of the team over the close season, but for six of those weeks I was due to be in Japan for the World Cup with Five Live. Had I been in Scotland it would have been hard enough to get players in to a club in administration that had just sacked nineteen players and were paying a far lower average wage than before; to have to do it from Japan was some task. I spoke to a lot of agents and contacts, trying to bring on board people I knew I could trust. I had a nucleus of good players, but in the main they were very young.

One of the problems when it came to persuading players to join me at a club that was broke was we had no training facilities. We trained at Dalziel, a school in Motherwell with its own sports grounds including three football pitches. Every season we were paying £43,000 plus VAT for use of the facility. It was now out of the question to pay so much money, and we had to look around elsewhere. So poor were the training facilities for Motherwell in 2002/03 that we had to be careful what coaching theme we worked on, whether it was shooting, crossing, defending, set-pieces or whatever, because it would depend on where we trained. Only once we knew that could we decide what we were going to do with the players. It's hard to believe, but we used jumpers for goalposts, just as we had done as kids. We had poles, cones, markers and balls, but no portable goals. Eventually we persuaded the club to invest in a set and we put them down at Smithycroft, an undulating public area where dogs would be walked and geese fed. Incredibly, we weren't the only club to make use of it: Hamilton Academical used to train there as well, along with other junior teams in the early evening. As a public area, it was more than a little dodgy to leave our new goalposts lying around. They were supposed to be portable, but they were so heavy they were hard to shift. The only way we could protect them was to padlock them together, but the local youngsters would come along and superglue the locks so we couldn't get them open. If we didn't padlock them, sometimes we would arrive at the ground and find Hamilton using them. Then we'd have to say, 'Can we have our goals back, please!'

There was another training ground we used where a junior team used to play before disbanding. It was overgrown and full of litter, and our groundsman Gus had to go out there and clean it up so we could use it. When it was wet it was boggy, and when it dried it would be rutted. How we didn't suffer any broken limbs or a drowning there I will never know. We also used to go to Glasgow Green where they had excellent pitches, but they cost £150 to hire. To save money we used to train in between the pitches on a 50-yard-by-50-yard area. The only trouble was Clyde trained there as well, as did Celtic U-21s, so if we weren't there early we wouldn't get the best areas. Even then it would cost us £70 to hire that bit of ground between the pitches. It was ludicrous for a professional club. We were a Scottish Premier League team and I felt we shouldn't be struggling for somewhere to train, but when I checked I found the problem was the same for the majority of the clubs. At Raith, the most important piece of equipment was a shovel for dog crap – not only unpleasant but also dangerous to the health of young footballers.

We certainly saved on the £43,000 every year we'd been paying for pitches, but you couldn't get a quality area any more and our performances reflected it. If our form improved, one of the reasons was we used Dalziel from time to time, which was infinitely better. On the parks grounds you couldn't work on your passing, touch, crossing and shooting; in fact, we hardly ever did crossing and shooting because we didn't have the facilities or the room. It was like telling the players they could wear only one boot to play in. They were, however, very professional. They didn't moan or groan, just got on with their jobs.

We also used the facilities at Shotts, one of the highest points in Scotland, where the snow would be falling when the sun was shining in Motherwell. The ground, used by Shotts Bon Accord, was the biggest in Scotland, boasting the maximum length and width allowed. It took us twenty minutes to travel there by bus. Another of our training grounds was even further away, and all these considerations had to be weighed before a decision was made. We were the Happy Wanderers with four or five regular training 'grounds'. Shotts was undoubtedly the best when the weather was good, and if you got there early, but from November to February it was bleak, cold, wet and windy. Actually, it was even cold in August.

We had a good pre-season, beating Birmingham City and Cardiff City and winning all of our friendlies. I had only recently returned from the World Cup. There was no family holiday, but Rita had taken the boys away to Tenerife earlier in the summer to give them a break. Bill Dickie moved up to be the chairman at the start of 2002/03; John Boyle became a director. It was fortunate for me I got on with both of them. My only remaining concern was Boyle selling out his share, which could have effectively put me out of work. With the constraints imposed by the administrator we were down to three teams, with me taking the first team, Chris McCart the U-19s, and both of us the reserves. Originally the reserve team was called the U-21s and we were permitted to use only three over-age players other than the goalkeeper. Then it went up to five, and now it's a normal reserve league, though still often called the U-21 League. It was a bizarre situation: the SPL were trying to promote the youngsters but the youngsters were playing on Saturday for the U-18s or U-19s and then most of them would be playing again on Monday for the reserves.

Chris McCart was a joy to work with and has organised a fantastic system throughout the whole youth development structure. He is such a terrific professional and, like Maurice, can be trusted implicitly. Chris and I kept it together so the club didn't have to make a further appointment, even though my wage, despite becoming manager, had been frozen for a year. It was hard times for everyone, and yet another steep learning curve because Chris and I virtually had to do everything. But I did insist on having my days off, and on continuing my radio work. I needed a break from the players every now and then, and they needed a break from me.

Our opening fixture of the new season was on 3 August away to Livingston. I feared the worst when we went 3–0 down, but we came back with two goals which not only made the scoreline look better but was a great encouragement to all of us. However, I was sent to the stand for kicking the ground. The two dugouts were twenty yards or so either side of the halfway line, with the fourth official centrally placed between us. We had a decision go against us and I kicked the ground the way coaches do in baseball to show their ire. The fourth official came over and announced he was reporting me to the referee, who promptly sent me to the stand for the final two minutes of the game. I had to appear before the SFA on 10 September, and the report stated I was sent to the stand for kicking the ground in a violent and aggressive manner. I went armed with a long statement which, though I say so myself, was rather well written. In it I stated I did not swear, did not shout and did not kick dirt towards the referee but away from him. I made my gesture not because of a decision but out of frustration when my centre-forward gave the ball away and then committed a foul. That, I explained, was why I was angry. I pointed out I had no history of bad behaviour on the line (I carefully didn't mention dressing-room doors) and they decided I had no case to answer. I was very pleased with myself. The Rangers secretary Campbell Ogilvie was on the committee and as I left I said it was the first result I had ever had at Hampden with the disciplinary committee. Campbell winked and whispered, 'I hope you do as well later on tonight.' We were playing Celtic at Fir Park and won 2–1. It was rather a good day.

After that Livingston loss we went on to draw at home to Partick Thistle, beat Kilmarnock 3–0, and draw 1–1 at Dundee United. It was a satisfying start for a new team. We were brought down to earth by a two-goal defeat at Hibs, but then of course came coupons-busting victory over Celtic at Fir Park, a game shown live on television. Henrik Larsson should have had a hat-trick in the first half, but we did well to hold out and won it with a penalty from young McFadden. Seventeen-year-old Sean Fagan had scored the first. The first person to congratulate me on the touchline was John Boyle, but it turned out to be a bad public-relations exercise. We had of course been in the public eye, and despite our administration we had been able to bring in players. Although I never paid a transfer fee, a lot of people resented that, and they were turned off by the sight of Boyle hugging me. But we had to survive, and we had to sign players to carry on. Celtic made things better by behaving graciously in defeat. It remains one of my best days as a manager.

We were on television again for the next match, against Hearts, and were two goals up and playing really well. We had signed a big German centre-half, Daniel Sengewald, who I had watched playing for Royal Antwerp in my days with Inside Soccer. He was a giant, comfortable on the ball, and just what I needed. We were a minute away from a 2–0 half-time lead and looking pretty confident when Sengewald fouled the Dutchman De Vries when the striker was going nowhere. The free-kick came in, Sengewald lost his man, and De Vries scored. That gave Hearts a big lift, and in the second half they ran in three goals without reply. Had we kept it at 2–0 going into the break, who knows what might have happened?

There was another boost for us, however, nine days later when we beat East Fife in the League Cup. We followed that by drawing at home with Dundee, and I thought we were back on track. But football has a habit of creeping up behind you when you least expect it, and we were suddenly once again on the slippery slope at home against Aberdeen when Eric Deloumeaux, who I had sold to the Dons after he'd refused to take a wage cut, scored the winner in a 2–1 defeat, the start of a run of nine successive losses.

Nothing went right during that period. My centre-half David Partridge was sent off against Rangers, Livingston hammered us 5–1 at home with a remarkable display of finishing, and we even lost to our great relegation rivals Partick Thistle in a match that saw another sending-off – my skipper Scott Leitch. We were also knocked out of the Scottish League Cup by Aberdeen, Deloumeaux scoring yet again, and even conceded a last-minute goal to lose at home to Kilmarnock. I thought things were on the turn on 23 November when we went to Hibs, where we hadn't won for 70 years, and were one up through Steven Ferguson, a player I had on loan from Spurs. Then Sengewald received two yellow cards and was sent off. He was a funny man. After receiving a head knock in the first half he went down for treatment, but when physio John Porteous came back he was shaking his head. He told me my tough giant central defender had bitten his tongue. Talk about a softie. In the second half he came screaming over to the bench after taking a smack in the mouth from the big Finnish striker Mixu Paatelainen. He wanted an ice cube to suck. I had never heard anything like it. To cap it all, he got that second yellow for losing his temper and lunging in. No sooner was he off than the man he should have been marking, Paatelainen, scored to pull it back to 1–1. After the equaliser, Hibs were rampant. To help them along, Stephen Pearson, a fiery redhead now at Celtic, received a straight red card for a foul, then Partridge got involved in a row about nothing and became my third player to be sent off, leaving us with eight men. Another red card and the game would have had to be abandoned. James McFadden, who was coming back from a long-term injury, tried his hardest. He came on as a substitute and almost immediately fouled our former player Derek Townsley; then, as he walked past the prone player, he stamped on him. Everyone in the ground saw the incident apart from the referee, and he got away with it. I still fined him a week's wages because had the game been abandoned we would have suffered a monster fine and maybe even a points deduction.

We'd had five players sent off in the course of the season so far, and we were not popular with the League authorities. We had a sixth player sent off in our next game at Celtic when Sean Fagan handled the ball in front of goal. We had played well but couldn't cope with a man short and lost 3–1. For most managers a run like that, not to mention the lack of discipline, would have meant only one thing – the sack. But the board kept faith and the run finally came to an end on 4 December in a most unusual manner when we played Hearts at Fir Park and beat them 6–1. We clearly had a Jekyll and Hyde team as well as a Jekyll and Hyde manager, as we went on to prove by beating Rangers on Boxing Day. What's more, we deserved it. Then we went off to Livingston and produced one of our worst displays of the season.

Despite our up-and-down form in the League, we put together a decent Cup run. In the quarter-finals on 22 March we beat Stranraer 4–0 for the right to play Rangers in the last four at Hampden Park. But there was a problem with this run in that Pat Nevin had agreed Scottish Cup bonuses with the players before he left: £1,000 for winning in the third round, £2,000 for the fourth round, and £3,000 for the quarter-finals. We'd only just managed to break even with the bonuses after the third round, then we lost money after the next two games. Fortunately, the four semi-finalists pool their money and share it out, so at least we stood to make up our losses. On the positive side, the Cup run showed how much our fans wanted us to do well. When we came back from the tricky journey to Stranraer they were lining the roads to welcome us home. The owner of the local Poppinjay Hotel, Brian Spence, a Motherwell fanatic, gave us free rooms for the night before the game, where we took 7,000 fans for the lunchtime kick-off.

We were bottom of the table going into the Hampden semi-final and were written off. We feared the worst when we went a goal down after a couple of minutes, but with the pressure off we started to play really well and scored a good equaliser through Stevie Craig, son of Jim Craig of Celtic. Then McFadden scored a superb goal, chipping it in from the right wing, to put us 2–1 up. Seconds before the interval David Clarkson, my seventeen-year-old striker, missed a great chance in front of goal. Rangers brought on Stevie Thompson at half-time and were level within minutes. They then won a dubious free-kick wide on the left. Tony Vaughan, a left-footed centre-half I knew from Ipswich who I had signed on loan from Nottingham Forest, was marking Amoruso but slipped and presented him with a free header. We were still competing well, until David Partridge unluckily scored an own goal to make it 4–2 to Rangers. Even then we pulled back another in the dying minutes and I believe we had Rangers hanging on until the final whistle went. We had lost, but it was a great day and we put up a magnificent fight against overwhelming odds. It's rare that you can bask in defeat, but that is exactly what I did as I sat on my decking at home with Maurice and the family and drank a few beers. Happily, we had also cleared the bonuses.

But the setbacks in the League continued. We played abysmally in a crucial relegation match at Partick Thistle on 26 April. We deservedly lost 3–0, and I think we had yet another player sent off. I have a good memory normally but we had so many players shown red cards that season – eleven in all – I lost track of some of them. The crunch match came on 17 May at home to Aberdeen – a game we had to win to stay up. We lost 3–2, with Deloumeaux scoring against us for the third time that season.

We were guaranteed to finish bottom of the League with one game still to play, but there had been talk all season that First Division champions Falkirk's ground didn't fulfil the criteria set down by the SPL. They said they would ground-share with Airdrie at the new Broomfield, which was SPL compliable, but all the necessary documentation was not in place when they made their application and on the day before our final game of the season against Livingston at Fir Park the news arrived from SPL headquarters that they had been turned down and we were safe. There was total euphoria at the club because we had been saved from another financial nightmare. We had deserved to go down, but here was an eleventh-hour reprieve. We promptly went out and thrashed an injury-hit Livingston 6–2, James McFadden scoring a wonderful hat-trick. The crowd flooded on to the pitch at the end of the game and there were huge celebrations, mainly of relief.

But then Falkirk lodged an appeal with the High Court. It went back to the SPL, the Scottish FA intervened, and it wasn't until 23 June that the decision not to promote them was finally ratified. I was away on a cruise in the Caribbean when the news came through. I had been busy signing players, or at least trying to sign players, including Alex Burns of Partick Thistle, who had scored five goals against us in four games, Stephen Craigan, his centre-half colleague, and goalkeeper Gordon Marshall from Kilmarnock, so it was an incredibly twitchy month for me. It was such a relief to hear the news I went and had a little drink. It was truly a great escape, and more than we deserved considering our form on the field and our poor disciplinary record, for which we were fined £5,000 and another £5,000 suspended until halfway through the 2003/04 season.

I have to say despite our appalling number of red and yellow cards, and despite finishing bottom of the table, I was never threatened with the sack. The board were very supportive, and I had even been given a budget of a little over a million pounds, which I tried hard to exceed but wasn't allowed to. It wasn't until February 2003 that I was permitted to bring in a number two. I was fortunate to land Maurice Malpas, who made a huge difference to both the club and me. He took a lot of weight off my shoulders, helped me with the first team, and took the U-21s. He was also U-21 coach to Rainer Bonhof with the national squad. He didn't want to give the job up, and that was fine with me because it not only helped our image but also kept him in touch with the best of the young players in Scotland. Maurice was an experienced campaigner and I trusted him with my life because I knew what he could do and what he was – a natural winner with a dry sense of humour. It was the first time he had been out of Dundee United for 23 years and he was prepared to drive for an hour and a half to two hours, depending on the weather, to join us every day. He still does now. I had tried to get Alex Smith on board when he was sacked by Dundee United, but he quickly got the job at Ross County. It was only after we had an interview with Maurice over several bottles of good red wine that we realised what a good capture we had. Our relationship has grown since then and we are very comfortable together, despite the hard work. A lot of the credit for our improvement is due to Maurice.

We had no money for a pre-season trip in the summer of 2003 and did all our work at home at Dalziel, for which we were now paying less than 50 per cent of the original fee – a crucial piece of negotiation that gave us a great platform, from the first team down to our U-19s. We recorded a 2–2 draw with Fulham, beat Carlisle 2–0, and generally looked quite good with our new batch of players.

I felt our biggest problem was a mental weakness. Sometimes when things went against us we couldn't handle it and were too brittle. Our expectation levels weren't high, the belief and optimism of the squad was wrong, and I felt we needed someone to help on this front. I persuaded sports psychologist Tom Lucas to come in. He had been working with clubs including Partick Thistle, and with individual players. One of the first things he did was to have a secret ballot where he asked the players to write down where they thought we would finish in the SPL in the coming season. There were one or two who thought we would finish in the top two, including the eternal optimist James McFadden, and another couple who thought tenth and eleventh, but the majority thought we would finish mid-table. I felt it was a positive start, and so did they. It was a clever piece of psychology.

Tom now comes in on a Friday and has lunch. He is as good for me as he is for the players. He started to explain to the players about reaching the top of Everest by the end of the season, and as with every long walk it begins with the first step. Some players switch on and some switch off and don't listen, but as long as it helps at least one player I think it's worth the effort. We also have awards every Friday at one p.m. It's an idea I picked up at Rangers when I wrote a weekly column for the club paper and would nominate the best player, the worst player, the miss of the week, the goal of the week and the moaner of the week. At Motherwell we would have the awards and then the players would see Tom before going home to bed to rest for the game on Saturday. A lot of the votes were, of course, rigged, and I was a regular for moaner of the week with my outbursts. The votes were totted up during the season and the major awards were distributed at the end.

Mind you, I did wonder about the ploy's effectiveness when we lost 3–0 at home to Dundee in the opening match of the season and my new signing Alex Burns missed a penalty. This was followed by a 1–0 defeat at Livingston, who later in the season were to have their own financial problems. We only got our season under way on 23 August when we beat Kilmarnock 2–1, although we should have scored a good deal more.

During this time there was a great deal of speculation about the fate of our top players. During pre-season we'd received a letter from Stephen Pearson telling us he had changed his agent from a local guy in Glasgow to Willie McKay. I didn't really understand why because Willie is rarely in Scotland these days as he is based in Monaco. Stephen put in a transfer request but withdrew it after talking to me a couple of weeks later. His contract was, in any case, due to expire at the end of the season. He was a good player and I knew mentally he would be all right to play. There were a number of clubs showing an interest, but the 'best' offer was from Leicester – a derisory £100,000. James McFadden was also a focus of much speculation. Ironically, we started off the season minus McFadden because of injury, while Pearson was sent off against Partick Thistle in a 2–2 draw on 30 August. We appealed and it was overturned by the SFA. The English transfer window closed later than ours, and suddenly, on the last day, Everton made a bid for McFadden. Davie Moyes was willing to loan me a couple of players to help out, but because our transfer window had closed a day earlier I was unable to take them, so I lost my best young prospect for £1.25 million and was without a replacement.

The next game after McFadden's move was away to Hibs, and as we had done a lot of work pre-season without him he wasn't really missed. We played really well, with David Clarkson and Alex Burns in excellent form, Clarkson scoring twice to win the game for us. We crashed out of the League Cup ten days later on penalties at Forfar, but our form was on the up and up and we didn't lose a game in the next seven. The defeat against Forfar inspired us because not only did it mean a loss of revenue for the club, we also hadn't played well, and a few harsh words had flown about the dressing room afterwards. We must have touched some of the right buttons because it really got us going. Then, at the end of November, we ran out of steam once more and lost four in a row, failing to score in any of them. A point at Hearts in a dreadful goalless match on 27 December at least broke an anxious sequence.

We were rapidly approaching the January transfer window when we knew we would be losing Pearson to Celtic. They wanted him, and he didn't want to go anywhere else. He eventually went for £350,000. He went straight into their team and did well for them for the rest of the campaign.

Clarkson made sure we didn't miss him with a hat-trick against Dundee United and a couple against St Johnstone in the third round of the Scottish Cup. Our Australian youngster Scott McDonald came on as a substitute in that game and also scored. We beat Queen of the South in the snow in the next round, then won a remarkable game against Dundee by five goals to three after going a goal down. Those sort of games are always great when you win them. But once again we suffered a strange reaction: in mid-February we went away to Livingston and were awful in a 3–1 defeat. We bounced straight back with League wins over Kilmarnock, Aberdeen and Partick Thistle, and went into the Cup quarter-final against Inverness in good heart. They were in the First Division at the time under John Robertson and it was a shock when they went ahead through Barry Wilson after ten minutes, a super goal from some 40 yards. It was enough to put us out.

On the heels of a creditable draw at Celtic, there was a strange game at Easter Road. We were playing a very young Hibs side who went two up before the break, but as they came off I could hear them talking to one another wondering what they should now do and how should they play it. They provided me with my half-time team talk. I told our players if they scored Hibs would wobble. I brought on Scott McDonald and made seven positional changes, and suddenly Hibs found themselves facing a totally different team. Because we had such a small squad we had to employ versatile players, so it was no problem for them to switch places, but it was for Hibs, especially when Keith Lasley pulled a goal back. After that it was all us: Derek Adams scored the equaliser, and although they briefly regained the lead, Aussie McDonald won us a deserved point in the last minute.

It was a great fighting point, but consistency continued to elude us. It wasn't until mid-April when we beat Dunfermline at home that we clinched our place in the top six. That was a cause for celebration after finishing bottom the previous season. Needless to say, half a vineyard was consumed through to the early hours. In our last five fixtures we took only a single point, but nothing could take the gloss off a much-improved season.

The day after the season finished with a tremendous game against Hearts, which we lost by the odd goal in five after being 2–1 up, Rita and I left for Massachusetts where our son Edward had taken up an English Speaking Union scholarship. It was a wonderful ten days without pressure, but soon I had to start thinking about football again. I was due in Portugal for the European Championship, but before I went I had to sort out our players. We had offered new contracts but several had chosen not to take them up and went to other clubs. I couldn't blame them, but in the course of a few months we had lost McFadden and Pearson, then vice-captain Derek Adams, striker Stevie Craig, right-side midfield player Keith Lasley and Jason Dair. It was half the team and a third of our squad. In addition, I had to address the state of our pitch. The grass had become diseased and by the end of the season we were playing in thick mud. It didn't suit our style of play because we had developed into a passing side. We eventually had it relaid with undersoil heating. It was much better but still not completely right.

Maurice Malpas and Chris McCart began our 2004/05 pre-season while I was away following England in Portugal, where I stayed on to cover the final as Greece unexpectedly beat Portugal 1–0 – a feather in my cap as I'd never commentated beyond the quarter-final stage before. On my return it was the usual work at Dalziel Park, though in future I'm going to introduce more ball work and a less physical approach. For the first time we had no Premiership or Championship team to play. It had worked like a dream the previous two seasons, but this time we lost to Cowdenbeath, Stranraer and Ross County, and drew with St Mirren. Some of the players complained about not playing a glamour club; others said the bad form was because we couldn't use Fir Park, where the new turf needed time to bed down. But it was simply that we were trying to blend together a new team. We had a number of new players in the squad, including striker Richie Foran from Carlisle, Jim Paterson, a left-sided player from Dundee United who was well known to both me and Maurice, and Brian Kerr from Newcastle United, a big coup for the club as he was a full Scottish international and had turned down Borussia Dortmund. Unfortunately for Brian he missed a big chunk of the season when he damaged his cruciate ligaments in pre-season. We hadn't replaced Keith Lasley on the right side of midfield, but all my funds were gone so it was a case of juggling what we had.

We were given the hardest possible fixture to start with, away to Celtic on a day when the champions unfurled the flag. All very intimidating to a reshaped team. We lost 2–0, and it was far more comfortable for Celtic than the scoreline might suggest. Then came Hibs at home. I had taken on a Celtic player on loan, Kevin McBride, a 23-year-old who had hardly played at the Glasgow club. The board had been very helpful in bringing him in and we signed him full time when we persuaded Celtic to release him from his contract in January. We played well against Hibs but lost 2–1.

But with Kevin's help we embarked on a good run of results, including a 3–0 win over Morton in the CIS (League) Cup – a portent of things to come in the competition. We also beat Hearts 2–0 at home in one of our best performances of the season, and followed it up with a point on the despised plastic pitch at Dunfermline, Scott McDonald scoring a spectacular goal minutes from the end. We warmed up for the next round of the CIS Cup with a 4–2 win against Dundee United, and for once held on to our form in the cup, beating Inverness 3–1 away and thus gaining revenge for our quarter-final cup defeat seven months earlier. And the victory carried more merit as they were now an SPL side.

We were beginning to show a great deal more consistency. The good form continued on 25 September with a 3–2 win at Livingston. After leading 1–0 we'd had a dreadful spell to go in 2–1 down at half-time, leading to a major rant from me which seemed to work. But there were always the likes of Rangers, Aberdeen and Celtic looming somewhere on the horizon, and in October we lost to all three of them. The results affected morale, and it was hardly good preparation for our CIS Cup quarter-final against Livingston away on 9 November. I went there thinking we desperately needed a boost after five straight losses. The tie was to be played on a Tuesday and I spent a week wondering what I could do to change things around. I settled on a 4–3–3 formation, even though we had done no work on it during training. Thankfully we got away to a good start, albeit an own goal, and after that we played really well to win 5–0. It was a real lift for the players and supporters, and good news for the board with the extra revenue.

The confidence came flooding back and we registered six victories on the trot, including a comfortable win against Dundee and two away 1–0 wins: at Hearts to make it four wins in four games against the Edinburgh club, and, much to the joy of Maurice Malpas, at Dundee United. We were delighted with our form. And then the roof fell in once more. Whether it was complacency or just a sudden loss of form I don't know. It began this time a week before Christmas against Inverness at home. That 2–1 defeat was followed by a 4–1 thrashing at Ibrox, a poor performance in a home draw with Aberdeen, and two successive 2–0 defeats at the hands of Kilmarnock, one in the Scottish Cup and one in the League. I couldn't believe the latter as we'd fluffed four one-on-ones with their goalkeeper. We were so much on top but couldn't score. David Clarkson even rounded the goalkeeper once, only to put the ball in the side netting.

We were sliding down the table, and to make matters worse a home game against Hibs was called off because our undersoil heating failed as a result of a broken coupling in the pump. It was our first chance to test the new system, and it let us down. We could have done with the game too as we were due to play Hearts in the semi-final of the CIS Cup on the Tuesday. Once again I changed the system after the awful run of results, reverting to the 4–3–3 formation that had brought us success before. We went a goal up through Stephen Craigan, which settled us, weathered the storm in the second half, and scored again from the penalty spot with five minutes to go. Hearts pulled one back with four minutes of injury time to play, but Scott McDonald immediately cut in from the right to lay on a sitter for David Clarkson – who put the ball over the bar from six yards out. To make it worse, Hearts went straight down the other end to equalise. I screamed and shouted at the players during the short interval before extra time to get them refocused, using the old Alf Ramsey line of 'you've won it once, now go out and win it again'. Goalkeeper Gordon Marshall also had some heated words of advice to pass on. It worked, for we regained our composure and played well. We had a goal disallowed and missed a few other chances, but in the last minute of extra time Marc Fitzpatrick scored the winner. I thought Hearts would launch the ball straight back into our box from the restart, but the referee had already told the players he would blow the whistle immediately. We were through to a final. It was one of the best feelings I have ever had in football. The date 1 February 2005 will live on, not solely for me but for all Motherwell fans. It was their first League Cup Final for a staggering 50 years.

The crowds responded tremendously: we had a couple of 7,000

.dances at home and sold 15,000 tickets for the final against Rangers on 20 March. I had always been jealous of managers and coaches going to Cup finals, and now I was going to one myself with a great bunch of honest professionals, young and old, among the latter 41-year-old Gordon Marshall, 35-year-old skipper Scott Leitch and Phil O'Donnell, who is two years younger and a veteran of Motherwell's 1991 Scottish Cup win. We wanted the day of the final to be an event for the entire family, with the U-17 and U-19 sides plus the Youth Initiative coaches. The club offered packages which included hospitality at Fir Park and transport. We also had to sort out aspects like the distribution of tickets, team suits, corsages, and other post-match things you dare not think about, like an open-topped bus in the event of victory. It resembles a military exercise. People call it a chore, but as far as I was concerned it was wonderful to have these problems, and having done it once we now know what to do next time. We would probably change a few things, like taking the players away the night before the game rather than allowing them to stay at home.

But everything went smoothly in the run-up to the final. The closer we got to 20 March the more I could sense the players didn't want to get injured, especially in the last League game against Livingston on 12 March: as a consequence we gave away a late goal to draw 1–1. It was a game I was happy to get out of the way, and it kept us on course for our top-six place. More to the point, there were no injuries. The training in that last week was the best I can remember, very high tempo, and I was able to pick the team I wanted.

We had a good press day and made all our players available to everyone. But in the match itself we got off to the worst possible start by conceding not one but two goals. It was the sort of opening I'd dreaded. There was hope, though, when David Partridge pulled one back after thirteen minutes. We began to play with a bit more confidence and looked as though we were beginning to enjoy it. Had we been able to hold it to 2–1 at half-time the result might have been different, but a Rangers goal just before the break and one straight after it killed the match stone dead. We couldn't complain about the eventual 5–1 defeat. Rangers were really up for it, and we'd been punished severely early on by indecision. Two moments of hesitation with a ball over the top and a free-kick and we were 2–0 down. The fourth goal had made it a long second half, a nightmare really. After the game I looked at our 15,000 fans, all of whom stayed to the end to applaud the players off the pitch, and I was almost in tears having brought them so far.

Goalkeeper Gordon Marshall didn't even go up for his medal. He felt so bad about the game and how he personally had performed that he booted the door of his locker at Hampden Park, whose beautiful new dressing rooms are so big that they swallow up the Scottish Claymores American football team, with 40 players stripping. The museum, too, is fantastic. Among the displays is my England shirt from the 1989 game against Sweden when I split my head open. I understand they even have one of my England caps – not bad for a Scottish museum. What's more, they didn't send us a bill for the damaged door, which I thought was very noble of them. And Gordon did a good job on that door. I would have been proud of it myself.

I then had to speak to the press in a beautiful amphitheatre. I passed Archie Macpherson on the way, a lovely man – seen it all, done it all. He shook hands with me and said, 'Unlucky today.' I responded, 'Unlucky? What game were you watching?' I felt bad about it afterwards because I didn't mean to have a go at a guy I like a lot, and later I apologised. He had, anyway, taken it the right way. In front of the press all I could do was tell the truth. I said how good Rangers were and admitted we had been given a gubbing – a Scottish word meaning a thrashing. It made them laugh and set the tone. They told me I was pragmatic, but what else could I have said? You have to be realistic. Sometimes you have to hold your hands up.

The easy part was the press conference; the ugly part was the dressing room, where everyone was down. It was not a pretty sight, but I tried my hardest to lift the players, especially because our very next game was against Rangers at home in the League, a fortnight later after an international weekend. I had to find something we could take from the that final and carry forward to the next match, and it wasn't an easy task.

After leaving Hampden we drove back through Motherwell, fans waving at us all the way back. Then I took a call telling me that there were a thousand or more waiting for us at Fir Park. I thought they might be waiting to lynch me after the money they had spent on their day out only for it to end in disaster. It was the last thing I wanted as I felt so distraught for them, but when we got off the bus they raised a huge cheer, which made the hairs on the back of my neck stand on end.

By the time I got into the ground and saw my wife Rita and son

Alistair in the stand I was in tears. It didn't help when the club let all the supporters into the ground and we were asked to go out and acknowledge them. I admit I just broke down in the office. It needed Maurice, Scott Leith andGordon Marshall to get me going again. I had to speak to them, so I told them how sorry we were that we couldn't win it for them, how we would love to go back and play the game again, how we couldn't believe the support, and how we would try to clinch that sixth place in the League for them. It was one of the hardest speeches I have ever had to make, especially with a lump in my throat the size of a football. I had loads of letters and cards over the following weeks telling me we had nothing to apologise for, and how much they had all enjoyed their day out. The whole town and community had made it such a special occasion. They'd decorated shops and given prizes for the best. They'd also arranged street parties and made a massive day of it, which continued regardless of the result. They told us we had given them one of the best days of their lives. That is real support.

We lost again to Rangers in that League fixture, but followed that up with a good run that did indeed clinch that sixth place. It said a lot for the character of the squad. All in all it was a successful season. Had I been offered a Cup Final and sixth place in August 2004, I would have bitten their hands off. That day at Hampden is the high point of my managerial career so far, and for Motherwell and their fans. One thing is for sure: we all want to get there again.

CHAPTER TWENTY-TWO

SCOTTISH FOOTBALL
IS BANKRUPT

Scottish football is bankrupt, even though right at the top the leading clubs, Rangers and Celtic, talk about bringing in £40 or £50 million a year. The most Motherwell could hope for is £2.5 million, with one or two of the others, like Hibs, Hearts and Aberdeen, a touch higher. At most clubs, up to 50 per cent of this income goes out on wages. The gap is so big at the top it's frightening. Rangers and Celtic have far outgrown the rest; they are miles ahead in terms of stadiums, squad, turnover, fan base, and even their own television stations. What's more, they do a first-class job with their corporate hospitality and commercial products. The entire game in Scotland revolves around those two clubs; all the talk in newspapers, on radio and on television is about them.

How would Scottish football survive if they went into the English Premier League or a European League? Personally, I don't see a problem. Everyone would follow them when they were competing, but the remaining teams in Scottish football would then have their own identity and you would have teams who could fight for the championship even if Rangers and Celtic left a presence in the League with their reserves. I am still convinced sponsors and television people would welcome an honest, refreshing and more equal challenge in the League. The biggest problem is lower down. I don't know how the smaller clubs would survive. If they pull in a four-figure gate they have done well. I can only think they must have magnificent commercial departments or wonderful sponsors and supporters to pay all the wages and other expenses. I believe the only way forward for Scottish football is for the smaller clubs to amalgamate, because I just can't see how clubs that attract 150 people to a League game can survive in the professional game.

At the other end there will always be the intense rivalry between the two Glasgow clubs. They will, of course, suffer their ups and downs, as they have done in recent seasons, and we in turn have to change our approach for the games against the Old Firm. Do you take the risk and go with three or four forwards to attack them, be bold and take the risk of them breaking at pace and putting five or six past you? Ian McCall did just that with Dundee United in the February 2005 League Cup semi-final when they were 3–1 down. They went on to lose 7–1, a result that embarrassed their fans and eventually led to his sacking.

It's worrying to think about where Scottish football is heading. I cannot see Rangers and Celtic joining the Premiership, certainly not this year, next year or in the foreseeable future. And I can't see a European League starting in the near future. If they go anywhere I would like to see them go to England – but why would the English take them to the detriment of two of their own clubs? It would be a hard vote to win and would be based totally on financial constraints. Does that mean they'll just slug away against each other year after year hoping to do well in Europe, with us smaller clubs trying to exist with scraps off the table? I'll take that if it means playing the odd Cup Final, as Motherwell did in 2005, but all we can realistically do is manage the maths, balance the books, keep our heads above water and try to survive by any means possible. Throwing money at the problem won't work. That has been proved conclusively by several clubs, including my own. Anyway, the gulf in class between the top two and the rest is just too immense. Hearts have had a complete change since Craig Levein left for Leicester, with new owners from Lithuania. Their new uncertainty has allowed Hibs to close the gap. And with Dunfermline also falling by the wayside as they chased the impossible European dream, the gap is even bigger than before. Hibs, with their young side, are the next challengers to the big two, but we all know what will happen. Such is their dominance that Rangers and Celtic will continue to buy the best of their Scottish youngsters – and then not play them. Rangers don't have a youth academy; what they have is far better facilities, plus their name, which helps them attract the best young players.

Is joining the Old Firm the way forward for the top young players? Maybe not, but if I was a youngster and someone offered to multiply my wages twentyfold and give me the chance of playing Champions League football, what am I going to say? There is only one answer. You back your own ability to climb out of the reserves and put the money in the bank. It's a bleak outlook, and I can't see it getting brighter, apart from the fact there are a lot more opportunities for young Scottish players who are getting more of a chance of playing on a regular basis in the top flight, especially against Rangers and Celtic. In that respect Scottish football is better off.

The other question to ask is how would Scottish football survive without the finance brought in by Rangers and Celtic? It is hard to fill the grounds when either of the Old Firm comes because the games are always on television. Some of the home fans are fed up with Rangers and Celtic and the hype that follows them around, especially when it's eight times a season plus cups. There would still be television money if they left the SPL, but clearly not nearly as much. STV at present covers First Division football regularly on a Monday and can give us some indication of what the future may hold. We would get a better share of the pot without Rangers and Celtic dominating, but how much would the contract be worth without them? If there's a contract at all.

English football, too, has to be careful not to go the same way. I recently watched Crystal Palace play Arsenal and it was like watching one of our lower clubs playing against one of the Old Firm. As well as Palace played, Arsenal turned it on when they had to and won pretty much as they wanted. Chelsea and Manchester United are the same. The gap to fourth place in the Premier League is growing larger by the season. Soon, those top three teams may also begin to feel that they are growing out of the Premiership.

But what if television pulled the plug? It is not so long ago the hooligan problem was decimating the game, with half-empty grounds and no families attending. The game was dying, and it was probably saved by the combination of the formation of the Premiership and the advent of CCTV cameras and better policing. Because of the Premier League and the Champions League the game now has a much bigger impact, although I still believe international football is more important. I cannot believe how international matches have been downgraded so rapidly, with managers like Sven Goran Eriksson littering friendly games with as many substitutes as he can. I find it obscene the way international football has suffered because of selfish club managers and chairmen. It's not so long ago that managers such as Sir Bobby Robson and Graham Taylor were threatened with the sack for losing a friendly international; now we can lose to Australia at home and no one blinks an eyelid. I have to say I enjoy the Champions League – a great format. I even love hearing the music introducing the programme because it tells me quality football is on its way. But the danger with football and its popularity is, if it can go one way so quickly it can go the other just as rapidly. If the television giants found a new plaything, it would have a dramatic effect.

The game on both sides of the border needs to keep pace with society and its changing patterns. Personally, one of the changes I would like to see in Scotland is the introduction of professional referees. I am on the SPL working group, and it's something we've discussed in some depth. I am convinced it would be better for the game, but there is always the problem of cost: many clubs would simply rather spend their money elsewhere. I'm not an advocate of video technology because you will take away a lot of spontaneity from the sport, as has happened in rugby league and cricket. Rugby union is more stop-start, but league is fast-flowing and too many stoppages spoil the spectacle. It also persuades the referees to go to video whenever there is any doubt whatsoever, passing on the responsibility to someone else. It can only be introduced at the top level, as with cricket, for the lower you go down the scale the ability to afford it diminishes. It would further separate the top from the bottom levels of the game.

Let us also be honest: a lot of the game is about controversy and opinions, and always has been. It has always been in my nature to have 'discussions' with officials. We have some right laughs on the touchline and some very heated debates, and now we have the added interest of a fourth official, a job I cannot understand. Why would anyone want to do such a job? Some fourth officials agree with the referee every time because they are all part of the same 'union'; when the man in the middle says something is so, he must be right. To me, that only makes things worse. I will have a go and tell them they are only agreeing because they are mates, and I plead with the fourth official to have a mind of his own. I have discovered the best way for a fourth official on the line to defuse any situation and take the wind out of a manager's sails is simply to answer, 'You're right.' There is simply nowhere to take the argument once those words have been spoken.

I wouldn't be a fourth official for all the money in the world, particularly the way some of us managers and coaches behave. I'm certain we could help by behaving and acting a lot better. But I honestly believe professional referees would help too, especially if the game wants to step up another level with technology. It is evidently working in England, particularly now Keith Hackett has taken over from Philip Don. I see the games live and on television, and I think English officials are far more sensible. For a start they speak to players and keep the game flowing. They even talk to television now and again. I am sure if we followed suit our referees would not only become more efficient, they would earn more respect. They would become a body to answer to, and we would get more from them. Their current image is very different to what it should be.

As for the Scotland national team, there are glimmers of hope. There are, as I said, a lot more young Scottish players coming through now in the SPL, plus a small core of Scottish players in the south after a terrible dearth, almost certainly because of the influx of foreign players. I was disappointed when Barry Ferguson moved back to Rangers from Blackburn. I applaud him for making a brave decision, but it would have been interesting to see the progress he would have made in the Premiership. But whether those Scottish players are of a standard to carry Scotland forward internationally remains to be seen. Still, so low are Scotland in the international rankings it wouldn't take a lot to move them on.

At least in Walter Smith they have appointed a first-rate manager who will get the most out of the players he has available to him. He is an honest grafter who doesn't suffer fools gladly. He demands high standards and appreciates players' commitment and hard work. He is a manager who earns the respect of the players and they both like and want to play for him. They will be happy with him because he will tell them exactly how it is. He is very knowledgeable about tactics and coaching, having learnt at the top both north and south of the border. He also has a softer side helped by a great sense of humour and the support of a lovely family. As a result he has a good public image, and he's excellent with the press, though not a man to mess about. If you muck around with him he will remember and he will eventually sort you out.

We had some great times at Rangers between 1986 and 1990, wonderful times. My quote when he was appointed Scotland manager was that he was a great manager because he likes heavy metal music and red wine – a couple of assets any decent manager should have. It was more Souness I locked horns with than Smith. Walter was the one who organised things like set-pieces and would walk and talk things through with you, like who you were up against and what their qualities were. He was a different character to Graeme, more methodical, more technical, and a perfect foil for the manager. He has a terrific manner about him, an aura that inspires confidence.

He will promote a feel-good factor, and the players will be moulded into a tight, hard-working team. Scotland might not have the flair players they used to have, but they do have players who can get results and hurt the opposition. The fact that there are more Scots playing top-level football now than for some years will help, for in recent years a heavy burden has been placed on young players like Darren Fletcher, James McFadden, Stephen Pearson and David Marshall, who have had to carry an unfair responsibility so early in their international careers. Now the top teams are having to bring on young, homegrown talent, even Rangers, who are producing at last, and Celtic, who have been bringing Scottish lads through for somewhat longer. Even at Motherwell, our U-17s are full time with the U-19s, and below that we have sides ranging from U-15s down to U-11s who all play on Sundays. They have their own excellent coaches and we have a little astroturf pitch behind one of the stands at Fir Park where they train twice a week and sometimes play. We don't have a youth academy because we can't afford one, but we too know we must bring on our own players to survive. Having said that, although there is a nucleus of good young players, I don't see too many outstanding candidates at U-21 level and below who are going to take the senior side by storm. I still believe, though, that under Walter Smith Scotland will improve dramatically.

CHAPTER TWENTY-THREE

ENGLAND, MY ENGLAND

When I first started covering England for Five Live in 1996 it was Glenn Hoddle's debut as manager and David Beckham's first full international game. It was a thrilling experience to be back on the international scene, albeit in a different role. I am still an international freak with a passionate love for football at this level. I covered the European Championship in 2000 with Kevin Keegan in charge and then the World Cup in 2002. I have seen it all change since Sven Goran Eriksson's arrival.

I was a big Sven fan when he was first appointed. Everyone thought I would go the other way, but I felt at the time England needed something different, a manager without the baggage of an English career. In any case, I didn't think there was an Englishman ready to take on the job at the time. When he came he unified the country, unified the team and took us to the World Cup finals in Japan and South Korea by the skin of our teeth when a lot of damage had been done under Keegan. We had taken only one point out of two games, and then against Finland at Anfield in March 2001 we were one down before Michael Owen equalised and David Beckham scored the winner. It was pure drama seven months later against underrated Greece at Old Trafford when Beckham scored the late equaliser in a 2–2 draw. Beckham was even applauded by the press when he came up after the game, something I had never seen before.

It has been sweet and sour for me, the sour bit being those 2002 finals when we went out at the quarter-final stage when I felt we were good enough to win the competition. The saddest thing for me in Japan was the performance of the captain David Beckham. How fit was he? My estimate was only 30 per cent. It was a massive gamble to play him and I thought he did neither himself nor his country any favours. Beckham plus the injury to Michael Owen for the Brazil game played a huge part in our failure to progress that summer. Michael scored, but he wasn't on fire, and I fail to see how any team in the world can take on Brazil with nine fit men and two passengers from the start. Even though Brazil had a man sent off, I felt they ran rings round us and were the better team in the second half. It was like a matador picking off a bull. We looked tired and lethargic. All the talk afterwards was we had trained too hard and could not cope with the heat – a strange excuse when detailed preparations had been the order of the day.

When I played for England we wanted to win every game, whether it was Brazil or Saudi Arabia, but now internationals are seen to be in the way, a hindrance, a necessity you have to fulfil, practice matches and nothing more. No one cares whether you win or lose. There seems to be more animation on a PlayStation. Does it happen because modern superstars play in the top flight of a league shown all over the world, and in the much-publicised Champions League? Are they so good now that everyday football at club or international level is too easy for these top players, and only the very top games turn them on? It infuriates the hell out of me to see a player go through the motions at international level and not put in what we used to put in. If you don't show your passion and give everything when you are playing for your country, there must be something amiss in your character. I don't believe you can turn it on and off like a tap; you should be playing at that sort of tempo all the time. The top players don't play flat out now because in the leading teams there is always someone who will produce the goods. It's only when the top teams play each other that there seems to be 100 per cent commitment.

I feel the only solution at international level is to take out of the equation the very top players for the so-called friendly games. Players with lots of caps, players whose games you know well, can sit out the games and in their place the manager should put in the fringe players, the newcomers, the hungry players, those who want to play. Robert Green, Glen Johnson, Andy Johnson . . . we all know the sort of player who would give everything for a chance to play 90 minutes for England. Why did Beckham have to play in the friendly against Holland in February 2005? What more did we learn about Steven Gerrard or Frank Lampard in that game? Did Lampard really want to play with so many important occasions ahead of him with his club? Even Owen could have gained little from it, although I could see the reasoning in playing him as he was rarely getting a full 90 minutes with Real Madrid at the time. If you don't learn from friendly matches, what is the point of playing them? Why not just have a get-together, something Premiership managers would jump at rather than risk their top players in a game – though of course that would deny the FA their revenue. It amazes me that England can still fill grounds at £50 a ticket when the punters know half the team will change at the break. But for a FIFA ruling the entire eleven could have been replaced. As a manager I am delighted when my players are picked for internationals as it gives them a lift and increases their market value, but I certainly would not want them to play just 45 minutes. Football lasts for 90 minutes, unless someone has changed the laws of the game and not told me. I cannot believe a player would want to come off halfway through an international. And anyway, players need to play for 90 minutes together to build up relationships and understandings. Unfortunately we are in the realm of commercialism. The punters expect to see the top players, but all they are seeing are cardboard cut-outs.

I don't enjoy many England friendlies as much as I used to because they give you nothing new and the public suffer as a result of Premiership deals and agreements. This makes it even more imperative the team delivers in a big championship, especially in 2006 with the World Cup being in Germany with no long-haul travelling or acclimatisation necessary. I personally don't think we can do without international football, despite the competition from the Champions League. There is a groundswell towards moving away from friendlies and restructuring for international weeks, but it's difficult when leagues around the world start and finish at different times of the year. I would vote for continuing with internationals, even, as I said, if it means leaving out the players involved in Champions League games and discovering others for the friendly matches. For me, the World Cup is still the ultimate, not the Champions League. Until you have been in a World Cup finals and experienced it you cannot explain the difference between international and club football. Certainly the supporters want international football, judging by the numbers who continue to turn up for England games, and professional football has to be about the supporters, whether they pay at the turnstiles or watch the game on television. Without them there is no money, no audience, no debate.

And where debate about the England football team is concerned,

David Beckham is always the big talking point. I have found myself in trouble with the current players through doubting their captain and his place in the team. It all blew up in the summer of 2004 during the European Championship in Portugal. For me, he had a wretched tournament. He has now played in two World Cups and two European Championships and has not fulfilled his potential in any of them. Perhaps his best showing was in France in 1998, before he was sent off against Argentina. I was really annoyed with him in the September 2004 game in Austria – a match England should have won comfortably. In fact we were two up at one stage, and then they scored from a free-kick and poor David James made a mistake. But I was more annoyed at the captain because to me he didn't help Gary Neville for the second goal, and in fact rarely tracked back to help his mate. I cannot believe it was under instructions from his manager. He didn't do enough for me. I felt had anyone else played like he did that night he would have been pilloried by the press and would have been out of the side, especially after the poor European Championship he had just suffered.

I happened to express my opinions on the BBC website and told the nation the time had come to say what I thought. There were certain players who it seemed were guaranteed their places irrespective of what they did for their clubs or their country, and I felt it was wrong. Players like Billy Wright and Bobby Moore would turn in their graves because to them the ultimate prize was to play for your country, and to be captain was a huge added bonus. It was meant as a gee-up for Beckham, to get him to pull his finger out. The entire England scenario, I thought, had become Camp Beckham; he appeared to rule the roost. I even wondered whether he had a say in team selection and other international matters. I don't know, of course, but I suspected it to be the case. I also wondered about the commercial interest: was there an unofficial contract stating he must play when he was fit, some sort of agreement similar to the one Brazil had with their kit manufacturers during the World Cup in France?

I posed this question on air: when was David Beckham's last great game for England? In my opinion it was in October 2001, when he scored in that World Cup qualifier against Greece and was England's best player by a huge margin. To some extent he carried them through to Japan. I looked through the books, looked through the programmes, did my homework, and reached the conclusion he had had some good games but no great games for three years. Now, everyone keeps talking about

David Beckham being world class. I thought Sven and everyone else were blinded to the fact he hadn't done a great deal since that pivotal game in 2001. Of course he has the ability, but in 2004 in particular he should not have been in the team. If I had played as poorly as he did I would have been out; more to the point, if someone of the quality of Frank Lampard had been as poor as him he would have been out too.

My observations obviously touched a raw nerve because the reaction was hysterical, and not just among the fans: it made the back-page lead on many of the next morning's newspapers. I accept that that was because the comments came from me, a former England captain; it would not have got the same reaction had it come from a journalist, commentator or punter. But it was said from the heart, not for self-publicity. The reaction from some of the England players was to my mind pathetic, and there were the usual comments about ex-players saying too much. I had stayed with the players in 2004 in the same hotel for the BBC. Not that I had any special access to them, of course, other than seeing them around the hotel. The FA treated me well, as did players like John Terry and Sol Campbell, but we weren't really allowed to mix with the squad. It was a far cry from my days with England when the players and the press travelled together, often stayed in the same hotel, and we made some firm, lifelong friendships with those supposedly on the other side of the fence. Now you need to go through the United Nations to request an interview. Even press conferences have changed. We used to be free to mix with the journalists we wanted to associate with and to talk to whoever we wanted to. Now it's regimented, with players wheeled out accompanied by a minder.

Perhaps, though, some of the criticism has struck home because Beckham's form towards the end of the 2004/05 season seemed to me to show a remarkable turn for the better. His performance against Azerbaijan in March 2005 delighted me. I drove back from St James's Park with a smile on my face, and it was down to one man – David Beckham. People say it's only a minnow country, but I thought because of the pressure he was under he responded really well. He has also been a lot better for his club. His work rate has increased, his form has improved, and he even performed well as an emergency right-back. Of course I wouldn't want to take any credit at all for the transformation, but I wonder if he has had a real good look at himself, or if someone in the England camp has had a quiet word. I know Steve McClaren took him to one side before the game against Azerbaijan; maybe he told him it was time to produce. Beckham was comfortably England's best player on the night. He scored a goal, was very aggressive but controlled, and his tempo was better than it has been for a good few years. That is what we expect from him; it's what we want to see all the time. If he is honest, I'm sure he would admit that we haven't been seeing the real David Beckham for some time. It's amazing how one game can spark off a good run of form, and if he continues to play like that I wouldn't want anyone else in the team, not Shaun Wright-Phillips, not Kieron Dyer, nor anyone else. If Beckham produces the same sort of form and energy in 2006, England will have a very good chance of lifting the World Cup.

My criticism of Beckham has been based on frustration. We all know the quality within him and we're desperate for it not to be stifled and subdued, for whatever reason. But I still feel it is Beckham's England, that the camp has lost the freedom it had in my day when we were all cogs in the machine and a genuine squad. If anyone didn't put the effort in the rest would be quick to tell him. I worry these days that too many play for themselves. If you are to be a successful team, that has to change. In fact, I don't really know where we are with England at the moment. We certainly have some very good players who perform in one of the top leagues in the world, and in the Champions League, yet collectively as a team we consistently fail to deliver when it matters. We have to ask the question of whether we are any further forward than we were four or five years ago. The answer is a tempered yes, because five years ago we were coming off the back of the debacle that was the 2000 European Championship and the defeat by Germany in the last game at Wembley before Kevin Keegan threw in the towel. Of course we have come on since then, but I think we have failed to push on, and now I'm uncertain as to where we are going to go and how we're going to do it.

We should be better than 'not bad' with the quality of players we have available at this moment. We have excellent strikers, for example. I still like Michael Owen and think he has a lot more to offer England. I have been impressed with his attitude at Real Madrid: instead of sulking because he isn't starting enough games it has inspired him to strive even harder. His goals in his first season, coming off the bench and playing when not surrounded by all the Galacticos, were impressive. He seems to have his hunger back, and the complacency, which was creeping into his game, has disappeared. The fear of failing, of not being selected, has spurred him on. He doesn't want to be classed as a failure. In Madrid, for the first time he has found himself under pressure from top players, and he might find the same with England if Jermain Defoe continues to impress and progress. He is a natural goalscorer, eager to learn and seemingly desperate to play for his country. He has pace, is a pest to defenders and finishes well. I also liked the look of Carlton Cole when he played for the U-21, though Shola Ameobi seems to have put the brakes on since Sir Bobby left Newcastle. Another who catches the eye is Jermaine Pennant, now at Birmingham City under Steve Bruce. There is no doubting his rich talent. With the U-21s he has shown phenomenal pace and great skill but not much consistency, which may be because he didn't play enough games for Arsenal. We can only wait and see what happens at St Andrews. Maybe his 30 days in prison will have woken him up to what he can achieve. I think he has as much of a chance as Shaun Wright-Phillips. I didn't particularly rate Lampard when he first emerged, but he has proved me and everyone else wrong, and so could Wright-Phillips.

Then, of course, we have the remarkable Wayne Rooney. Now there's a special lad. He is unpredictable, powerful, aggressive, young, quick, and lives on the edge. He is rash and brash, a player like Cantona who can be brilliant but who can also be a potentially dangerous psychopath – another Mr Hyde (and probably why I like him!). It's a toss of the coin whether he'll just be very good or outstanding. One thing's for sure: he's with the right manager in Sir Alex Ferguson. If you had the choice of who should control him it would have to be the Manchester United boss. He's tailor-made for him. Wayne is an incredibly entertaining player who gives you what you want in terms of unpredictability, excitement, surges of adrenalin, bookings, sendings-off, controversy and, most important of all, goals, which are the lifeblood of the sport. He is a walking blockbuster, absolutely brilliant. Think about his sensational hat-trick in his first ever Champions League game for United, and the two totally different strikes against Middlesbrough. The variety of his goals marks him out as something out of the ordinary. He can hit screamers from outside the box or be incredibly delicate. He is so influential that when he went off in the 2004 European Championship our chances went with him. That was how important he was to England, even as a seventeen-year-old. Steven Gerrard is another who is exciting to watch, a genuine world-class player who can defend and attack.

But my first pick on current form would be Frank Lampard because he not only scores goals but always keeps the ball moving and keeps the team playing. He can play anywhere in midfield and he will do a fantastic job for you. He has to be the most improved player of all time. I saw him against Belgium in the Stadium of Light in October 1999 and I thought he was distinctly average, but at Chelsea he has stepped up several levels. It was a great move for him. If Gerrard is second on my list, third would be John Terry. I prefer my central defenders to be like Terry – uncompromising, clean-shaven with a straightforward haircut, a man who gets on with the job with the minimum amount of fuss. The way he has played over the past two years has been immense, though he still has a lot to learn, particularly at international level. That knowledge will come with experience. I can see Terry and Rio Ferdinand developing into a top international pairing. There is no doubting his quality, but for me Ferdinand takes too many chances. I am not looking for my centre-halves to come out of the back and build up. I want to see a solid defender, someone as rugged as Jaap Stam, someone who can hurt people. Rio can do it, but not always at the right time. Whatever he does, first of all he must be a good defender. Clean sheets mean no defeats. Nothing was ever truer than that little catchphrase used by so many managers. Outside them and Sol Campbell, a class act, there is Ledley King who has done well for Spurs. And it's a great sadness that Jonathan Woodgate can't get fit for Real Madrid. As for my numbers four and five, they would be Rooney and Gary Neville, England's most consistent player and our only right-back. He is a real winner.

For me, then, the England team more or less picks itself: Paul Robinson in goal, probably for some time to come; Neville, Terry, Ferdinand and Ashley Cole; Lampard and Gerrard in the central engine room; and the front two must be Rooney and Owen. The only problem areas are right-side and left-side midfield. If Beckham continues the form he showed against Azerbaijan, the right-side midfield spot is his. If not, maybe Owen Hargreaves could do a job there. He is an honest player but does not get enough opportunities to show us if he can sustain it at this level. He suffers from being a utility player. Maybe it would be a good idea to move from Bayern Munich to a club where he could be seen as a star and played as such. Kieron Dyer, too, might push for Beckham's right-side position as his pace is blistering and he seems to have settled back into Newcastle's team.

The most controversial aspect of the current England team, however, is who should play on the left side of midfield. The best players for England over the last nine years in this role have been Nick Barmby and Emile Heskey, and neither is a natural left-sided player. Remember Heskey against Greece for Eriksson in June 2001? Two great runs down the left-hand side, two crosses, and two goals. Albania away in March that year was another excellent game for the Birmingham City striker. He was always a player who gave of his best wherever he played. Middlesbrough's Stewart Downing should be played out wide to see whether he is good enough, but when he came on against Holland in February 2005 he only played for 35 minutes, and even then he thought he was playing in a 4–4–2 formation, which was nonsense. That night we even had Rooney back in defence clearing the ball and poor Andy Johnson playing right-side midfield on his debut when he is an out-and-out striker who performs on his own up front for Palace. Joe Cole has certainly thrown his hat in the ring with some excellent displays in the qualifiers. He seems to be the most obvious candidate now.

As for candidates to take over from Sven when he goes, there still aren't that many out there. The most obvious is Steve McClaren as he is the number two; he knows the players, knows the system and has done well with Middlesbrough, particularly in Europe in his first season when his injury-ravaged team almost reached the quarter-finals. He would be, without doubt, the number one candidate. Outside him we have the Charlton manager Alan Curbishley. I think he is terrific, but it's a case of whether the current England players would have the ultimate respect for him. Sven has done it in terms of European and international football, while Alan is more of a Graham Taylor type. He has done brilliantly for Charlton but he has not been an international superstar, and he has yet to take a team into Europe. In his favour is the fact he has been consistent for a long time with Charlton and is a genuine football man. He is not a shooting star who will fade quickly. I would like to see him have a go because he is refreshingly honest. He is also studious, he has a great image, and he wants to win. There is an honesty there which I am sure would come out with the players and in press conferences.

And honesty is important. At the moment there seems to be no real spontaneity and honesty in press conferences with Eriksson. He tries to be diplomatic and to reveal nothing, but the public feel distanced from the manager as a result. They deserve more emotion. All I ask for is a bit of honesty. If we play badly, say so – it makes it so much better when we play well. But there is so much spin now, starting with the manager and the captain. They would have a head start in a new career in politics.

Sam Allardyce is another who comes to mind. He has done a remarkable job at Bolton Wanderers and has dealt with some top-class players. Steve Bruce has said he would jump at the job, but he perhaps needs to make some real progress with Birmingham City first to capture the attention of both the FA and the public. Joe Royle is sadly retiring, and I suppose that only leaves young Sir Bobby Robson, who would walk down the A1 to London to take the job again. There have been international managers older than him and it's not as taxing a job as the day-to-day grind of being a club manager, constantly under the cosh. But then Sven has said he wants to go on until 2008, and whatever Sven wants he seems to get.

I believe that with the quality of footballers we have we should be going to Germany in 2006 with real confidence. The players will probably have it, but will the public, having seen them go to the last two tournaments with a great chance only to fail? Certainly no one can blame the FA if England fails, not judging by what they spend on preparations. In the last couple of tournaments the players have had everything they wanted, and perhaps a little more. I suppose when they earn as much as they do they can make almost any demand.

The game has changed hugely since I played, in terms of the pace and rule changes, to mention just two factors, but mainly in terms of money and its effect on play. The players have to protect what they have in some respects, which alters the individuals' perspective of injuries. In our simpler day you wouldn't think about the risk; if a tackle had to be made you would go in and do it whatever the likely consequences. Does Rooney think about the risks? I don't think so because he is so young and fresh, but then Michael Owen was a similar talent at the same age, before he picked up a couple of hamstring injuries which knocked him back and made him a little more careful.

Another way in which the game has changed enormously in recent years is in the number of overseas players in English football. There are currently almost as many players from overseas as there are players born and bred in England. It's one of the consequences of all the money pouring into the game from Sky Television – and one of the disadvantages where England are concerned. When Arsène Wenger picked a non-English squad for Arsenal he was only replicating what had already happened in Scotland, when Dick Advocaat picked a completely overseas squad for Rangers. It cannot be a good thing if a manager can't find a single young English or Scottish player for a top British club. I realise that Wenger was only trying to win by using the best players available, and that his squad make-up has a lot to do with fees and wages, but I also have no doubt he was making a point, and I fear he was wrong to do so. He was certainly doing nothing for the future of the English game.

I believe homegrown players add something to an English team, not weaken it. A lot has happened in Scotland which English players and clubs can learn from. At least Manchester United and Chelsea have a number of top English players, and there is a real need for that, but why should a foreign manager worry about how many English players he plays? Gone are the days of Celtic winning the European Cup with every player from Glasgow, or Liverpool winning it with a British squad; now managers want to win in any way they possibly can. Newcastle had the stated ambition of wanting an all-Geordie team, but football has moved on so much that that sort of opportunity is gone for ever, even though the club announced their intentions not much more than five years ago. Barcelona tried to do the same with Catalan players, and even in Basque country the grip is weakening. It's similar to the religious restrictions at the top Scottish clubs, restrictions that almost certainly cost the clubs major honours. Even more galling for Rangers is there were Protestant players in the Celtic team that won the European Cup. England are lucky to have seen young goalkeepers like Paul Robinson, Chris Kirkland, Robert Green and, to a certain degree, David James come through because a lot of clubs have turned to foreign goalkeepers and stuck by them, and Sven does like to have players in his squad who regularly play Champions League or UEFA Cup games. But the overall lack of Englishmen playing top-flight football must be worrying for all those who care about the England team.

And the problem is, I can't see things changing. The authorities are talking a good game about limiting the number of foreigners in a squad, but as the law stands at the moment it would be illegal, and finding a consensus among all the managers would be next to impossible. It only needs one manager to shake his head. We have travelled a long way from the days when clubs were allowed only three foreign players on the field at any one time; now they are talking about forcing clubs to play three nationals at a time. A complete reversal. It presents a problem for the national manager too: how can Eriksson continue to pick Michael Owen, for example, if he is not playing regular first-team football at Madrid?

Without any doubt the rich will continue to get richer, whether it's through a sugar daddy like Roman Abramovic at Chelsea, a new bigger-capacity ground, or commercial development on a global scale. Just as in Scotland, English players are gradually sinking to the smaller clubs and lower divisions, and the gap between the big and small clubs and the top and lower divisions grows season by season, making it ever more difficult for the players to make that step up.

CHAPTER TWENTY-FOUR

FIVE ALIVE!

One of my great joys over the past few years has been working as a summariser on BBC Radio Five Live, covering mainly England internationals but also League, cup and international tournaments. I had done bits and pieces for them before, but my big breakthrough was when they invited Peter Beardsley and me to attend the Euro 96 quarter-final between England and Spain at Wembley on 22 June. It was a fantastic occasion, and what made it even better was that the BBC then offered me a one-year contract as the next England summariser to replace Ray Clemence and Steve Coppell – hard acts to follow. I was delighted. I knew a few of the commentators but didn't particularly know the two main men, Alan Green and Mike Ingham. When I think about Five Live I think about England games, but also about the way they have been going about their work, developing their sports coverage and becoming more popular. They were reaching a big audience and had access to all the big games. It was a great opportunity for me, not least because at the time I was more or less out of work, taking no wages from my hotel and earning only a small amount with Radio Clyde. This was different. To me, this was the big time.

My first day at the mike was Glenn Hoddle's first game in charge, the World Cup qualifier against Moldova on 1 September 1996. It was also David Beckham's first appearance for his country, so there were new faces all over the place. For me it was a case of going over to the new football nation a couple of days before the game to go through the plans, logistics and requests from the BBC office in London. I had never been to Chisinau before, and on the morning of the game we played the Moldovan press team. On our side were people like FA chief executive

307

Graham Kelly and his successor Adam Crozier, plus, of course, lots of press men overcoming the hangovers of the night before. It was something of a tradition to play these games; many a famous England player and manager had appeared and many a top foreign player had performed against the English press. I remember Trevor Brooking, who was working for television at the time, getting punched by an opponent in Georgia, in 1996. He was cut above the eye, and the wound needed stitches. Now Trevor was rather like Gary Lineker, never in trouble with the officials. Not only did Trevor never kick anyone, nor did he swear; after the incident he simply told his assailant to go away. In those Eastern European countries we would do commentary behind glass panelling that made it a little like a greenhouse. They were not only hot but also quite far away from the pitch. Inside this box was a very old-fashioned Bakelite telephone which suddenly rang. Green picked up the telephone and to his surprise it was Mrs Brooking who had somehow got through to the BBC because a journalist had put the punching story out over the wires and she wanted to find out how her husband was. We were able to tell her it was nothing more than two or three stitches. No wonder she was concerned because her husband is the last person in the world you would expect to be involved in a fight, especially in a press match.

We won that press match in Moldova, as far as I can remember, but afterwards I had to nip off very quickly because we were expected at the ground early to set up our commentary positions and make sure everything was ready for kick-off. We were positioned in a little glass box and you could actually see the terraces through the cracks of the floor below us. It didn't feel particularly safe and we constantly feared we would go through to the ground below. It was so small there was only room for two at the front and we had to perform a hasty change-around when necessary midway through the two halves. It was a hot day, and having played in the morning I was dehydrating in this sauna of a commentary box. I was so flat and tired when it came to the commentary I didn't enjoy it much, even though England won comfortably. Beckham came through his debut better than I did, but then he hadn't been drinking with the press boys the night before. I didn't check out my work on audiotape afterwards because I detest listening to myself on the radio. I just hoped it was going to get better.

It did. I have missed only two England games in nine years: South Africa in Durban in May 2003, and the 1–1 draw with Sweden at Old

Trafford in November 2001, work with Motherwell keeping me away on both occasions. I really enjoy the job, especially because it gives me the chance to work with other pundits like the former England manager Graham Taylor. I've been able to talk to him about Motherwell because it relates directly to how he used to operate with Watford, a club of similar stature. I feel immensely proud to be working for Five Live. The friendlies are not brilliant these days, of course, but it's still good to be there. World Cups and European Championships are something else, and having played in three World Cups I have now been able to see top competitions from both sides of the fence. It really is a treat to go and watch England play and get paid for it. It's my Utopia. The people I travel with are such a good crew and a good bunch of mates. I always look forward to joining up with them, especially as it doesn't happen all that often because I'm based in Scotland. I do north-east games occasionally, but generally England matches dominate my broadcasting. The job has also kept me in touch with the London-based press; it's interesting to mix socially with the old faces and see new faces come in. These days it's as hard to keep up with the movement of journalists as it is with the players. Gone are the days when the number one football reporter had to retire to let the next one through.

Alan Green is a terrific character and has been a great pal to me. There are some people he doesn't get on with all that well because he's a perfectionist, but still he's very relaxed about it. Everyone knows exactly where they are with him. My impression before meeting him was that he was someone who might be difficult to deal with, but I can honestly say I have never had a problem with him. I know his family and we have great heart-to-heart talks about all sorts of matters when we are on the road waiting for the action. There have been one or two slight differences of opinion on air, but they have been nothing compared to the good times we have had together. He is a bubbly character and we are close because while covering major championships we've shared cars, planes and hotels (but never the same bed!).

One difference of opinion occurred during the 2002 World Cup. In their final group game, England drew 0–0 with Nigeria and had they won they would have progressed on a different route. As it was they had to play Denmark and then Brazil, but to Alan's way of thinking if they had gone for the win against the Nigerians and played Senegal in the next round they would have had a much better chance of getting to the final. I was quite happy to see England play the game out and make sure of qualification while Alan felt they should have gone harder for the victory. We discussed it on the radio, me with the experience of being a former player and a manager, Alan from the supporter's and experienced reporter's point of view. Both opinions were valid and sincere. The debate was then thrown on to 6-0-6, the Radio Five phone-in show, and a lot of callers came down on my side. When we phoned home they thought our discussion on air was a 'row', but it really was no more than a professional discussion. I have immense respect for Alan, and for the way he goes about his work. His opinions are strong and forthright, and he will stick with them. He is a purist who wants perfect football all the time, and there is nothing wrong with that, but as someone involved in the game I know as much as we want perfection we won't get it.

We have also had differences of opinion on who has played well and who hasn't, but to me that's good radio, far more interesting than everyone agreeing with every word the other says. I feel we have a terrific rapport and will stick to our respective guns as we slaughter each other, but despite what listeners may think, it is never carried on into the bar afterwards. If we are talking about the finer points of a game he will bow to my knowledge, but he has been to an awful lot of games around the world and has the right to his own views. I respect that experience. He may be from Northern Ireland, but you should see him after an England game when they have played badly or lost. He is desperate for them to do well. It is much easier to cover a winning team than a losing team, but it is our job when the team have done badly to dissect the performance. Some listeners seem to be under the impression we prefer a poor performance because it gives us more to talk about, but that couldn't be further from the truth. It is so much more enjoyable talking about an England win. When England do well, as they did in September 2001 when they beat Germany 5–1, it is a lovely feeling for everyone and a great buzz.

But covering football abroad is about more than the game, and Alan and I have had some great meals together and some very good nights out. Marseille during the World Cup in France stands out. Alan joined us late because he was covering the opening game between Brazil and Scotland. We were in dreadful accommodation – OK as a base for exploring Marseille and Provence, but not when you had to stay in the rooms. There was a small kitchen with a fridge, a bedroom with a bed, a bathroom with a bath, and that was it. No bar, no pool, no restaurant. We were genuinely jealous of the BBC Television crowd who were in top-class hotels and able to relax accordingly. There was a supermarket nearby where I would go to stock up with food and, of course, wine. With two games every evening there wasn't always the time or the inclination to go out to a restaurant, so a meal in front of the television and crashing out afterwards was often the order of the day.

The beach was only five minutes away across a dual carriageway, and on the day before the South Korea–Holland group game we decided to have a day of rest and relaxation and spend a couple of hours sunbathing before heading off for lunch. We met a colleague, Alex, from the BBC who was staying at a nearby hotel and took her over for drinks at a bar and a couple of slices of pizza. We then bumped into commentator Ron Jones who was covering the game the next day, and he joined us for a few more pints. Before long it was nearly five p.m., and we decided to meet up for a meal later in the evening. Alex and Alan went back to their respective hotels while Ron and I wandered back across the dual carriageway to the beach where a game of football was taking place. We asked if we could play, but they said no. Ron then asked them if they knew who I was and gave them a potted history of my career. They still said no.

I was not best pleased and marched off to the supermarket to buy a French stick. Why? I don't know, but I do remember it took me the best part of an hour to find the entrance to the shop while Ron stayed on the beach until the local Moroccans had finished their game, immediately followed by another. This time they agreed Ron could join in with them. Ron was a pretty good player in his younger days, but the ball was a blur to him from the start. Eventually he saw it coming his way, leapt gracefully into the air and headed the ball, immediately collapsing to the ground thinking it had smashed his skull. He knelt on the floor holding his head before deciding he should lie down, which he did, still holding his supposedly shattered cranium. He promptly fell asleep.

The game continued around him in the blazing sun. When he woke up the game had finished and dusk was falling. He felt his head, which was fine, felt for his wallet, which was still there, and decided he had to go back to the hotel, which meant crossing the road. It was now much busier as people were going home from work and the beach. He was still befuddled and couldn't work out the traffic: the cars seemed to be on the wrong side of the road. He dithered for almost half an hour before asking a little old lady to help him across. She took his hand and steered him to the other side where he was able to reach the sanctuary of his hotel bed.

In the meantime I had made it back to my room, clutching my bread, and also promptly crashed out on my bed. Greenie was asleep in his room. When Alex arrived at Alan's room he was still fast asleep, and she couldn't raise either Ron or me on the telephone. The poor girl had to leave on her own, having been promised a night out. I was vaguely aware there were two games I wanted to watch on television, and I awoke to the tone of my mobile telephone and a call from my wife Rita who asked what sort of day I had had. I was still hazy and said I would call her back when the first of the evening's games reached half-time. She promptly told me this was the second game on television and I had slept through the first game completely. She was not impressed and told me to ring in the morning when I was sober.

The next day I went out to buy *L'Equipe* for the team names of the game we were to cover that evening when I bumped into Ron Jones on a similar mission. We were both nursing hangovers and shared our stories. Then Greenie arrived on the scene and told us about letting down Alex. We were three very chastened BBC men, thinking how easy it would have been for any one of the three of us to have been mugged, especially Ron, asleep on the beach in an area notorious for its crime and the scene of a great deal of fighting between English and Tunisian fans before their group game.

Because our digs were so poor we went straight to Paris. Scotland were playing Morocco in the final game of their group, the Scots needing a result to go through, but we passed on the game and decided to go to that superb restaurant La Coupole in Montparnasse for a good meal after the poor fare we had suffered in Marseille. But the waiter was a Moroccan and every time there was a goal or an incident he would come along and tell us, and every time he reported a Moroccan goal we ordered another bottle of Sancerre. By the end of the match we were completely wrecked again as Morocco had scored three times in St Etienne without reply.

We went back to our hotel on the outskirts of Paris near the International Broadcasting Centre. It was my fourth World Cup but the first from the other side of the fence, and it was fascinating to see the outstanding media centres and organisation in France. Anyway, I decided we needed a nightcap. We went to a nice little bar I had used on a couple of occasions to watch matches, ordered some chips and mayonnaise and a couple of pints, and watched a replay of the Scotland game. Two hours later we staggered out, yet I still felt another drink would be appropriate. We decided to go to a Scottish bar called the Auld Alliance where I planned to do a little posturing and mickey-taking. Greenie, playing Jiminy Cricket to my Pinocchio, was trying to haul me back to the hotel telling me I had drunk enough and it was time for bed, but Mr Hyde was ready to go out and play. I eventually piled into a taxi and tried to explain where I wanted to go, but the mixture of my poor French and the alcohol meant the driver hadn't a clue what I was on about. I eventually gave up, which was probably a good thing for my health because I had planned to give it plenty to any remaining Jocks in the bar. We always cheered when the Scots went out, just as they did when the English lost. Mr Green saved my bacon that night. I can't imagine what might have happened to me in the Auld Alliance.

Another night out I remember happened during the trip to Warsaw in September 1999 for an England match in a qualifier. We were set to meet our producer Caj Sohal and went from bar to bar trying to find him. He eventually made contact by mobile and we discovered him in this little bar full of rather attractive, scantily clad women who kept disappearing into little cubicles with the men. There were a few England supporters around so naturally we were careful what we did and said until all of a sudden a huge, imposing guy came over and introduced himself as Gordon Sherry, the Scottish golfer, who was playing on the junior tour in the local open. The bar was full of golfers and punters creating a superb atmosphere. We stood there and talked about golf, something close to the heart of Alan Green, who covers the Open and the Ryder Cup on a regular basis. Fear not, ladies: there were too many people about with cameras for us to do anything other than talk at the bar.

During Euro 2000 we ended up in a restaurant in Amsterdam to celebrate Caj's promotion to BBC Television, and as a thank you to the commentators he took us all out for lunch. There were half a dozen of us enjoying his hospitality when he took a call telling him ITV had just won all the rights to the Premiership while the BBC were left with virtually nothing. What was a celebration lunch became a wake, and we finished up helping him drown his sorrows, eventually moving from the restaurant to the bar where we switched drinks to Sambucca. We caught the tram back to the city centre after that. Needless to say, we were quite boisterous. One of the commentators fell on the floor and because the carriage was moving around a bit he found himself on the rubber piece connecting the two trams and couldn't get up. He squirmed on the floor all the way back to the hotel. It looked as though he was break-dancing! It's nice all the commentators get on so well with one another. It's always fun to be out with them.

One of the great things about travelling around the world is discovering wines. Countries like Moldova, Georgia, Bulgaria, Russia and Hungary are particularly interesting adventures in terms of wine tasting. Many of the reds are totally unknown to us because they are not marketed (at least not widely) in the West. And we found some beauties which slipped down very nicely. I remember one trip with Rangers to Vladikazkaz in Russia. It was fairly bleak over there, and the night before the game we went out with a group of ten or so press men to a restaurant. The food was reasonable, but the wines were glorious. We had been given a police escort to the restaurant and there were only a couple of other tables taken by locals, plus a table for our security guards. They were sitting closest to us and had a meal with our bus driver. They sent over a round of vodkas, wanting to propose a toast to Rangers. We gladly accepted, and we reciprocated before carrying on with our meal. After the course we suddenly found another tray of vodkas in front of us, and the process was repeated, with the vodka downed in one, of course.

This went on all night for four or five hours, with a dozen or more rounds of vodka plus the wine we had ordered with the meal. We were all drunk, not just the journalists but our security and, worse, our driver! We paid the ridiculously cheap bill, obtained the necessary receipt and boarded the coach with a police car in front and one at the back. The streets weren't pitch black but they were dark enough, with what could have been no more than ten-watt bulbs in the few streetlights still working. It was like a scene from Wacky Races, with the police car overtaking the bus and then the bus driver chasing after them to overtake, all the way back to the hotel. The bus was going round corners on two wheels, and by the time we got back to the hotel every one of us was completely sober. We thought we were going to die. They played chicken with us all the way back. The security men and the driver were ready to carry on boozing in the hotel bar but we all went to bed. Frightened? You bet!

But back to the wines. My memories of Le Tournoi in 1997, twelve months prior to the World Cup in France, are among the best, especially as England won the trophy despite losing to Brazil in the last game. We played Italy in a lovely little stadium in Nantes, winning 2–0 and playing really well. It was great to see England beating the Italians at last. It was fairly meaningless, but a good pointer to the big qualifier to come in Rome later that year. We were in very good seats on the halfway line and behind us were the hospitality boxes. The one directly behind our commentary position had the window open to soak up some atmosphere, and through it I could see the guests had departed, leaving lots of unfinished bottles of wine, both red and white. The restaurant staff were cleaning away the food and I asked one of the girls if we could have what was left. I picked up about half a dozen bottles and shared them with the commentators from Capital, IRN and the rest who were sitting near us. We all just sat back with this good wine and enjoyed the feeling of having beaten the Italians.

I remember finding another outstanding wine during the 2002 World Cup in Japan and South Korea. At Osaka airport Mike Ingham had discovered the delicious New Zealand Cloudy Bay Sauvignon Blanc on sale at just £8 a bottle – much cheaper than at home. Every time Greenie and I went through the airport we bought more bottles. Greenie travelled about a lot during that tournament, but I was based in Yokohama. There wasn't a lot to do over there, and the longer the tournament went on the fewer matches there were to watch. Good company was essential, and as a result I have some good memories of that trip. After England's group-stage win over Argentina in Sapporo, we went back to the media hotel nearby where the top floor boasted a lovely bar with a delightful lady singing with a band. The bar was crammed with England supporters and media, though a much more refined and mature bunch compared with usual trips. We could scarcely believe we had won, and when the singer suddenly broke into 'Don't Cry for Me, Argentina' it brought the house down. It must have been the longest, most passionate rendition ever. A great memory.

England played their second-round match against Denmark in Niigata, and after the game we went back to Mike Ingham's hotel where he had a couple of bottles of our favourite Cloudy Bay. That same night BBC presenter Mark Pougatch, Greenie and I went to the local Milan bar, which we had used for a couple of broadcasts and where 6-0-6 were doing their phone-in programme. They finished at about two a.m., and the bar then launched into a karaoke session. It was a surreal evening for the England fans were, for some reason unknown to us, wearing fishnet tights, England shirts and lipstick. Greenie dragged me up on the stage to sing 'You'll Never Walk Alone'. What he didn't realise was as a former Rangers captain it was a minor problem because it was a Celtic song. Thank God no one had a movie camera or tape recorder with them. We stayed on the day after the game to get the fans' reaction and were very impressed with their attitude. The timing also gave us an opportunity to see a show or do some shopping – but no tights, honest!

In Kobe they had a special all-you-can-drink Budweiser night: we paid about a tenner and were served some food and as much beer as we could drink. There was me, Greenie and sound engineer Mike Burgess, and we drank for about two or three hours before a waitress came up and told us we would have to leave. The Japanese limit was fairly low, but we felt after ten or more we were only just getting going. We were disappointed with their attitude, but they insisted we left. There is nothing like a British journalist on his high horse away from home, and we were grateful one or two of our other colleagues weren't with us.

In the Niigata story I mentioned Mike Ingham, but you'll have noticed he doesn't appear in too many of these anecdotes. He is a studious and experienced broadcaster, a thinker, far more intelligent than me. He is a good man and a joy to be with but completely opposite to Alan, who is outgoing, bubbly and emotional. Mike is the ultimate professional. He loves his music and frequently sneaks a musical reference into his commentary. While Greenie and I are looking for a bar, he will be searching out a music shop to buy long-play records or CDs. He loves a quiz, with the top 50 of this, that or the other. It helps pass the time for some, but not for me. Mike also enjoys fine wines, but he is not a boozer. I am more of a quantity than a quality man, but he is the opposite.

In Malta in June 2000 we were all staying in a beautiful Hilton with a restaurant in the central atrium. We were having a gorgeous meal two nights before a game during which both sides switched virtually every player, when we discovered they had our favourite Cloudy Bay. Mike, Alan, BBC producer Charlotte Nichol and I drank six or seven bottles, clearing them out. Having drunk them dry we left for another bar. The next day we discovered that they had ordered in extra supplies of

Cloudy Bay – I don't know how because it's hard to obtain in large quantities. But their delight soon turned to anguish as we had drunk so much the night before no one fancied Cloudy Bay for a second evening. We had just the one bottle, which stood on the table for the entire meal before it was finished.

That's much more Mike's scene: he loves fine wine and good food, but not a lot of it at once, which is why he is so slender. I have never seen him totally inebriated. He's always been a perfect gentleman who thinks the world of his two boys, Marshall and George. He is very knowledgeable where matches, players and stats are concerned, and it's not always the most obvious stat he comes out with. He is quite highly strung before a game, and gets extremely nervous. It is as though he is about to take the field himself. He prepares himself professionally and makes sure his notes are always up to date. It is the mark of a truly professional broadcaster. But you can prepare everything down to the last full stop and still there can be a technical hitch which can throw everything out. This sort of thing used to happen particularly in the former communist countries: the line goes down and there is much shrugging of shoulders until someone brings out his wallet and miraculously everything is suddenly up and running again. Sometimes you feel you are at the mercy of fortune.

Perhaps one day I'll mature into a Mike Ingham type. I've certainly said some unprofessional things on air in my time. When England were knocked out by Romania during France 98 we were all gutted. We had been 2–1 up and lost 3–2. The next game was Spain against Yugoslavia, Spain winning by the odd goal in seven to go through to the quarter-finals. It was a wonderful match and it lifted everyone's spirits. When the Yugoslavs scored they let off scores of flares, and Greenie said in all innocence, 'I wonder how they got those through security.' I replied, on air remember, 'They must have stuffed them down their trousers.' And then I added, to Greenie's mortification, 'The security guards must have asked them if it was a flare down their trousers or were they just pleased to see them.' Greenie almost swallowed the microphone. He quickly glossed over it and went straight back into the commentary, waiting until we were off air before he asked if I had really said what he had heard. It was a stupid thing to say, but I thought it was funny at the time. Fortunately nobody picked it up, though I thought for a while my BBC days were numbered.

But it's an emotional game and it's sometimes hard to keep a check on what you say. I remember once reporting for STV when Rangers were playing Steaua Bucharest and the Romanians were shooting from everywhere. I innocently asked my co-commentator if they were given a bag of salt every time they went for goal – a throwaway line because they were so poor and salt was a luxury even in the best restaurants. It wasn't appreciated, and neither was my comment when striker Adrian Ilie took a knock near the end and I remarked that from Rangers' point of view I hoped it was nothing trivial because he had been such a thorn in their side. I was slaughtered for both comments. It is how you phrase it and how you get it over which is the art, and sometimes you have to engage the brain before you speak. It comes with experience.

The difference between radio and television is knowing when to be silent. On television, silence is golden because pictures can speak for themselves, whereas radio work requires you to illustrate with words, something I really enjoy because I can draw on what I have seen and done. I have done some television work for Channel Five, and there you can just say it was a wonderful save, but with radio you have to describe it. There is not enough time as a summariser on radio to come in if it's a high-tempo match with end-to-end football. You have to know when to speak and, more importantly, when to stop. I don't like to force the commentator to cut in because it means I haven't done my job properly. I try to be as professional as I can be, and I'm sometimes very hard on England and other teams, particularly over the entertainment factor. I can only call it as I see it. I wouldn't be true to myself or the BBC if I sugar-coated my opinions – the result would be bland commentary.

In the summer of 2004 in Lisbon I was in the England team hotel but one or two of the players were ignoring me after some remarks about their own lacklustre performances. But when you play for England the eyes of the world are on you, and I believe you have to play well every time, as I discovered to my own cost. Sometimes I felt remarks about my performances were over the top because I knew I had tried as hard as I could, but now I look at England players and when they play at their very best it is often not for England but for their clubs. It may be said that it is just the clubs and the FA looking after their assets, their prize possessions, but what we want as punters and pundits is value for money in terms of attitude, performance and effort. I feel that sometimes those qualities have been absent, whereas they are almost always present for the

Champions League. I try to bend with the times, to admit it is a different era, but I just can't accept it. Surely to play for your country is the ultimate honour, and anyone who lessens or cheapens playing for England is utterly wrong. As I said, all I can do in the commentary box is be honest with myself and call it as I see it. What people think of me doesn't bother me, to be brutally frank. It would be lovely if they said what a good commentator I was or I speak a lot of sense, but I believe I am an honest person in life so why should I change when I'm in the commentary box? If a player plays well, I will say so. Like all other media men, I love to see England do well because it sells newspapers and attracts audiences to radio and television, but there are times when you have to be critical, and if it's not appreciated then all I can say is, 'Bad luck.' English football is having to fight its corner, and come the big event you have to play with some style if television audiences and the money which goes to pay the high salaries are to be retained. In football, you cannot do just enough. There can be no half measures.

I'm looking forward to going back to Wembley with the England team, and I'm hoping I can keep my contract intact for the opening of the new National Stadium. Wembley holds good memories for me – and the odd bad one. When England beat Poland 3–1 in March 1999 in a rip-roaring game that was Kevin Keegan's first international in charge, my wife Rita and my son Alistair came down to make a weekend of it. I had a BBC pass to go right to the top of the stand to the crow's nest in the old commentary position, where they used to press the button to set off the hare for the greyhound racing. After the game I went to meet Rita and Alistair in the banqueting hall and a young lady asked me if I had a pass. I told her I hadn't but smiled and said I used to play at Wembley now and again, and all I wanted to do was pick up my wife and son who I could see on the far side of the hall. Still she told me I couldn't go through without the correct pass. I then explained I had also just worked for the BBC in their coverage of the game. She remained unimpressed, and after much frustration and anger from me she escorted me to my family and immediately escorted us back out again. Technically she was correct, but I thought as an ex-England captain I would be given a little consideration. Moreover, the FA had promised every ex-player two free tickets for games at Wembley. I hardly ever used this facility, but then Wembley was closed and England moved around the country. I asked for a ticket for Rita for the game against Denmark at Old Trafford in November 2003 but was told to pay £35 by an FA underling. I instructed the jobsworth I was entitled to free tickets, and was then informed even if I wanted a ticket for myself it would still cost me £35! The facility had hastily been withdrawn. I'm hoping the new Wembley will have a different outlook.

Although I adore being behind the microphone, my first priority remains my main profession, which is as a football manager. I always give Motherwell a mention one way or another as I draw on my experience, which is why the BBC employs me in the first place. The radio work is an enjoyable break from the rigours of management – or at least that's what the players say because they are glad to see the back of me when I go. I am eternally grateful to the BBC for giving me these opportunities. At the time of writing I have covered over a hundred games for them – although that's a hundred too many according to Greenie – and I am contracted through to the summer of 2006, which will make it three World Cups as a player and three as a broadcaster. Not a bad record.

POSTSCRIPT

From the very moment the top-six fixtures were published there was always going to be a big climax to the 2004/05 season, especially as we were involved against the two teams challenging for the championship in our final games. Although Celtic had beaten Rangers in a crucial match at Ibrox to go five points clear with four games to go, we still had a feeling we were going to have a significant say in how the title was to be won and lost. Just how dramatic we did not realise – nor did anyone else!

In many ways we hoped everything would be done and dusted by then because you don't want your own fans watching someone else win the championship on your ground and having to play second fiddle to the winners on your last day of the season. That had happened two years earlier when there was a big shoot-out between the Old Firm; Kilmarnock were beaten by Celtic by four goals while Rangers overran Dunfermline 6–1 at Ibrox. We didn't fancy the role of cannon fodder, and personally I felt it could tarnish what had been an outstanding season for us. It would have left a sour taste in the mouth.

We had good results against Hearts (0–0) and Hibs (2–2), but by then Celtic had lost at home 3–1 to Hibs, reducing their advantage to two points. We travelled to Rangers in the penultimate round of matches suffering from a particularly heavy crop of injuries. In fact it had been a crisis for us from the moment we won our place in the top six. To add to the injury problems, suspensions kicked in as well, and we lost David Partridge and Stephen Craigan, our two central defenders who had played together virtually all season, for the game at Ibrox. We fielded a much-depleted team and were seen to be the weakest side in the top six. Rangers hammered us, and Celtic beat Hearts. We were blitzed as they ran riot and we were lucky to concede only four goals, our consolation score coming in the last few minutes when Marvin Andrew deflected the ball through his own net. Rangers were rampant, and their movement was fantastic, with Buffel playing off Prso and Novo on the right and Arveladze on the left. My young defenders were not at the races; we couldn't handle it. But for our goalkeeper Gordon Marshall and some do-or-die defending it would have been eight or more.

Rangers had a superior goal difference, but Celtic's two-point advantage meant that all they had to do to clinch the title was beat us at Fir Park. Nothing Rangers did against Hibs at Easter Road would change that. The situation as to the European places was also to be resolved. Hibs couldn't afford a hammering, which might allow Aberdeen to slip through. Two points looked a good buffer and we were seen as lambs to the slaughter, especially with our injury list. But our build-up through the week was excellent. I worked the players really hard, much to their disgust, and treated the game exactly as we had done our cup final a few weeks earlier. I wanted them to be really focused on the job in hand and to end the season in such a way that we would be really up for the start of 2005/06.

We had Stephen Craigan back from suspension, but David Partridge's injury needed an injection and rest so that he could be ready for a pre-season against top English sides Everton and Southampton. I was also going into the game without my captain Scott Leitch, Kevin McBride, Phil O'Donnell, Paul Quinn and Stephen Hammell – all absent with legitimate injuries; it certainly wasn't a case of resting anyone. We had to cobble a team together who had not played before but who were prepared to go out and do the business.

All week the paranoia was immense, not only with the sectarian problems in Glasgow but also with the east of Scotland, with people talking about Hearts going to Aberdeen on the Sunday and allowing them to score six to put Aberdeen into Europe instead of their Edinburgh rivals Hibs. It was a great week for psychiatrists and tabloid newspapers! They were also saying, of course, that there was no way Motherwell would lie down against Celtic because of their manager Terry Butcher being an ex-Rangers captain. I said all week that I wanted to win for Motherwell and for no one else. We had tried to win the game against Rangers for Motherwell, and this was no different. But few listened. Moreover, we had not won one of our top-six matches in the two seasons we had qualified and we were desperate to finish our season off in style – but for us and no one else. We also needed two points to finish with a higher total than the previous season, and we wanted a win against an Old Firm team too, having lost five games to Rangers and three to Celtic. We had not even come near a point against them and we wanted to give our fans something for the summer.

The other major problem lay in where the championship was to be celebrated, with both contenders playing away from home. Elaborate plans had to be put in place for the award ceremony to take place either at Hibs or Motherwell; there was even a helicopter on stand-by to deliver the trophy. We had talks all week with the SPL, the police, Celtic and television company Santana, discussing everything from where the podium should be set up to controlling the crowd. We knew that Celtic fans had purchased tickets among our supporters. By tradition our supporters always come on to the pitch at the end of the last home game of the season, but we had to appeal to them to stay off. I was concerned it could turn into a real disaster. Should there be any trouble among the fans, or any controversial decisions or sendings-off, we might have a full-blown riot with tensions so high. In the event, the plans for the day were brilliantly drawn up and orchestrated by the SPL and the police.

The media attention was immense; it was more like a cup final than a League decider. We did the media on Thursday with the Sunday papers, dailies, television and radio. I was getting plenty of stick from Rangers fans who were telling me I had to beat Celtic to make sure Rangers won the trophy. I was deluged with emails and text messages from all over Britain. I also received a letter from a Celtic fan telling me that Motherwell was the worst team in the League, that we were rubbish and would lose 6–0. The unsigned letter went up on the noticeboard, as did the message from the Rangers fan that railed on about the Protestants, King William, and making sure we won it for the Queen's XI. All that sort of sectarian garbage. There were also, of course, lots of calls and messages from old Rangers colleagues. The oddity was that my players are predominantly Celtic rather than Rangers. They were all laughing their heads off at the stupidity of the messages from both sides of the divide.

One thing was sure: we would be the centre of attention because Celtic were in the driving seat. I saw it as a big chance for my players to see whether they could handle it and take another step upwards. And they handled the whole day magnificently. What no one, except ourselves, took into account was the fact that we had enjoyed a fantastic season and we did not want to end it on a losing note. We were as up for this game as we could be. Even so, we were aware that we could produce our best performance of the season and still lose to Celtic – a team of great quality. During the build-up I said, somewhat tongue in cheek, that we needed a miracle, having been smashed the previous week and with few changes possible.

After our appearance in the Final and the place in the top six it was a bizarre and weird end to the season. Instead of looking forward to our last five games in a relaxed fashion we found there was something on every game, with Aberdeen, Hearts and Hibs going for Europe while Rangers and Celtic were battling it out for the top prize and the millions of pounds involved in the Champions League. There was no chance of resting players or throwing in youngsters for experience. But I felt it was lovely to be in such a position, playing in games that really mattered. Certainly the six teams below us in the table would have happily swapped places.

The game was very similar to the Cup Final. We didn't want to let anyone down, especially our fans. If I am honest about it the most I hoped for was a draw, but the team went out there and played fantastically well. Admittedly we had plenty of luck – something outsiders always need in Old Firm matches. It was an even first half with Celtic threatening as a result of our mistakes more than their own form, although Craig Bellamy, on loan from Newcastle, was incredibly quick and dangerous. We gave the ball away too often, and eventually our errors resulted in a Celtic goal: Alan Thompson robbed Ritchie Foran, exchanged passes with John Hartson, and when he crossed Gordon Marshall could only push the ball out to Chris Sutton, who put in the rebound.

We went in 1–0 down at half-time and I reminded my players that Celtic had not created a goal through their own play. I added that the next goal, whichever way it went, would be critical. If they scored it would all be over, but if we scored the nerves would begin to eat away at them. I also told my players that the longer it stayed at 1–0 the more nervous Celtic would become. It proved to be prophetic.

We started the second half well, but then they blitzed us with wave after wave of attacks. We couldn't get the ball off them, couldn't get out of our own half. Thankfully Gordon Marshall was at his best in goal, and the back four proved they were real men as they blocked and tackled and threw their bodies in the way for twenty long minutes. I looked at my bench to try and help them out but all I had was two strikers and three youngsters.

And not only did we hold on, we gradually became stronger. Celtic, not having managed a second goal, grew tentative. We began to push long balls forward, our Aussie striker Scott McDonald and Jim Hamilton held the ball up, and suddenly you could sense that our players could achieve something. We began to get crosses into their box and our belief grew as Celtic back-pedalled to defend their single-goal lead.

Time was the only problem. I sent on Clarkson and Britton, but it was McDonald, a Celtic fan, who achieved the breakthrough. He pounced on a loose ball, swivelled and hit it into the top corner. It was an unbelievable feeling as it went in because it was one of those remarkable goals. He had scored a number of fantastic goals during the season, but this one was spectacular, and not just because of the opponents or the magnitude of the game. It was sheer quality. He had been a constant threat to their defenders throughout the game. For a small, pint-sized Australian – albeit strong, quick and tenacious – he was a real handful, despite seeing so little of the ball for long periods.

After his strike Celtic tried to push all their big men forward, lumping the ball through the middle. That suited us and we were able to defend, win the balls in the air and launch counter-attacks. It was from one of these that McDonald again picked up the ball. This time he cut inside Stanislav Varga and from an acute angle some ten yards out hit a shot that clipped Varga's heel and looped over Rab Douglas.

Two goals in two minutes – beyond our wildest dreams! And there was no time for Celtic to hit back as we were already into the three minutes added on, although there was still time for McDonald to try and complete his hat-trick!

It wasn't until the end of our game that I asked the bench what the Hibs–Rangers score was. It was only then that I knew they were champions. If I had been more interested in my old club winning the championship than in my present club beating Celtic, I would have been kept informed of the Easter Road score throughout the match. The only result that mattered to me on the day was ours.

As the helicopter carrying the trophy was suddenly instructed to change course and aim for Edinburgh, the Celtic players disappeared, heads bowed, down the tunnel. We went in, waited for five minutes, and then went back out to salute our fans. Just as we had asked them to, they remained on the terraces and we were able to go round Fir Park and applaud them for their help over the season. It was like winning the Cup as they sang and we did a jig and danced around the touchline. Back in the dressing room there was champagne from the chairman, and afterwards the players carried on their celebrations in the local Mandarin Chinese restaurant while I went home and enjoyed a couple of bottles of beer.

To be honest, I felt devastated for Martin O'Neill, John Robertson and Stevie Walford. I have got on well with them over the years, and in situations like that it's difficult to know what to say. They just suffered, drank a cup of tea and left. Every Celtic player was devastated. It was a real slap in the face for them, especially as the match and the title had been within their grasp and they'd only been three minutes away from lifting the trophy and thumbing their noses at their greatest rivals. Martin O'Neill, whose problems with his sick wife Geraldine had been revealed in the press before the match, was as magnanimous as ever, congratulating us and telling us what a great season we had enjoyed. He must have gone home thinking about all the chances his team had squandered during the 90 minutes, any one of which would have sewn up yet another title.

When I got home I was besieged with messages, including a call from Rangers manager Alex McLeish from the team bus. It was hard to know what to say in the circumstances, so we just congratulated each other. The best call was from a Rangers fan who said the new Celtic jersey for next season was ready. It had 'Carling' on the front and 'Bottled in Motherwell' on the back. I was also told that the Rangers fans at Easter Road had started singing 'There's only one Terry Butcher' after they heard the result from Fir Park. What they did not realise was that if the roles had been reversed and we had been playing Rangers on the last day we would have gone at it just as hard and I would have wanted to win every bit as much. My allegiance is to Motherwell.

I was delighted to be involved in such an incredible end to the season. It gave all of us a taste of what could lie ahead for Motherwell in the future.

TERRY BUTCHER'S CAREER RECORD

Full Name: Terrry Ian Butcher
Born: 28 December 1958 , Singapore

SCHOOLBOY FOOTBALL
Fen Park Primary School, Lowestoft
Lowestoft Grammar School
Lowestoft Schoolboys u/15
Suffolk County u/15
Suffolk County u/19

YOUTH FOOTBALL
Ashlea Boys' Club, Lowestoft

PROFESSIONAL CLUBS

August 1976 – July 1986	Ipswich Town
August 1986 – November 1990	Rangers (£750,000 – Scottish record fee)
November 1990 – January 1992	Coventry City (400,000 – player manager)
July 1992 – November 1993	Sunderland (player manager from Feb 1993)
November 1994	Clydebank

INTERNATIONAL CAREER

England	1980-1990
England under 21	1979-1980
England 'B'	1979
Rest of the World	1986

PLAYING RECORD

Ipswich Town	351 appearances	21 goals
Rangers	176 appearances	12 goals
Coventry City	8 appearances	—
Sunderland	41 (+ 1 sub) appearances	1 goal
Clydebank	3 appearances	—
Total Club Record	**579 (+ 1 sub) appearances**	**34 goals**

England	77 appearances	3 goals
England Under 21	7 appearances	—
England 'B'	1 appearance	—
Rest of the World	1 appearance	1 goal
Total International Record	**86 appearances**	**4 goals**
OVERALL CAREER RECORD	**665 (+ 1 sub) appearances**	**38 goals**

PLAYING HONOURS

Club: UEFA Cup Winners 1980-81 (with Ipswich Town)
League Runners Up 1980-81, 1981-82 (with Ipswich Town)
Scottish Premier Division Champions 1986-87, 1988-89, 1989-90
(with Rangers)
Scottish League Cup Winners 1986-87, 1988-89 (with Rangers)
Scottish Cup Finalists 1988-89 (with Rangers)
Scottish League Cup Finalists 1989-90 (with Rangers)

Country: 1982 World Cup Finals (in Spain), reaching Second Round
1986 World Cup Finals (in Mexico), reaching Quarter Finals
1990 World Cup Finals (in Italy), reaching Semi-Finals
Representative: Rest of the World v. The Americas 1986

MANAGEMENT/COACHING CAREER

November 1990–January 1992   Coventry City, player-manager
February 1993–November 1993 Sunderland, player-manager
August 1997–August 1998   Raith Rovers, reserve team/youth team
coach
August 1998–March 2000   Dundee United, youth team coach
October 2001–April 2002   Motherwell, assistant manager to Eric Black
April 2002 to date   Motherwell, manager

FOOTBALL RELATED WORK

Radio: Football Analyst/Co-commentator, BBC Radio 5 Live, Radio Clyde
Television: Football Analyst, BBC TV Scotland, Scottish TV, Channel 5 TV
Newspapers: Football Columnist, *Scottish Daily Express*
Football Recruitment Consultant 2000-2001

TERRY BUTCHER'S CAREER RECORD IN CLUB FOOTBALL

SEASON	TOTALS		LEAGUE		FA CUP		LEAGUE CUP		EURO/OTHERS		
	A+S	G	A+S	G	A+S	G	A+S	G	T	A+S	G
IPSWICH TOWN											
1977-78	3	—	3	—	—	—	—	—	—	—	—
1978-79	24	2	21	2	1	—	—	—	ECW	2	—
1979-80	46	2	36	2	4	—	2	—	UE	4	—
1980-81	64	6	40	4	7	—	5	—	UE	12	2
1981-82	36	1	27	1	1	—	6	—	UE	2	—
1982-83	49	1	42	1	3	—	2	—	UE	2	1
1983-84	40	1	34	1	2	—	4	—	—	—	—
1984-85	55	2	41	2	5	—	9	—	—	—	—
1985-86	34	6	27	4	5	—	2	2	—	—	—
RANGERS											
1986-87	55	3	43	3	1	—	5	—	UE	6	—
1987-88	18	1	11	1	—	—	3	—	EC	4	—
1988-89	51	4	34	2	8	—	5	—	UE	4	2
1989-90	43	3	34	3	2	—	5	—	EC	2	—
1990-91 (pt)	9	1	5	—	—	—	3	1	EC	1	—
COVENTRY CITY											
1990-91 (pt)	7	—	6	—	—	—	1	—	—	—	—
1991-92	1	—	—	—	—	—	—	—	ZDS	1	—
SUNDERLAND											
1992-93	41+1	1	37+1	—	2	—	2	1	—	—	—

CLYDEBANK

1994-95	3

SUMMARY

Ipswich Town	351	21	271	16	28	—	30	2	22	3
Rangers	176	12	127	9	11	—	21	1	17	2
Coventry City	8	—	6	—	—	—	1	—	0/1	—
Sunderland	41+1	1	37+1	—	2	—	2	1	—	—
Clydebank	3	—	3	—	—	—	—	—	—	—
Grand Totals	**579+1**	**34**	**444+1**	**25**	**41**	**—**	**54**	**4**	**39/1**	**5/0**

TOURNAMENTS

	A+S	G
Football League	314+1	16
Scottish League	130	9
FA Cup	30	
Scottish FA Cup	11	
Football League Cup	33	3
Scottish League Cup	21	1
Zenith Data Systems Cup	1	
European		
- European Cup	7	—
- UEFA Cup	30	5
- Cup Winners' Cup	2	—
TOTALS	**579+1**	**34**

ABBREVIATIONS

A+S Appearances + Substitutes G Goals T Tournament EC European Cup
ECW European Cup Winners' Cup UE UEFA Cup
ZDS Zenith Data Systems Cup (Full Members' Cup)

TERRY BUTCHER'S CLUB MANAGERIAL RECORD

Season	League/Division	P	W	D	L	F	A	Pts	Pos	FA Cup	Lge Cup	ZDS Cup
COVENTRY CITY												
1990-91 (pt)	FL/Division 1	26	8	8	10	31	34	32	16th	R4	R5	—
1991-92 (pt)	FL/Divisions 1	23	8	3	12	25	26	27	(15th)	(R3)	R4	R2
(finished 19th under DON HOWE)												
TOTALS												
Football League		49	16	11	22	56	60	59				
FA Cup		5	1	3	1	4	5	—				
League Cup		6	3	0	3	11	8	—				
ZDS Cup		1	0	0	1	0	2	—				
TOTAL												
COVENTRY CITY	61	20	14	27	71	75		(44.26%)				

Season	League/Division	P	W	D	L	F	A	Pts	Pos	FA Cup	Lge Cup	AI Cup
SUNDERLAND												
1992-93 (pt)	FL/Division 1	21	5	5	11	22	26	20	21st	(R4)	(R1)	—
1993-94 (pt)	FL/Division 1	17	5	2	10	16	27	17	(20th)	(R4)	R3	Prelim
(finished 12th under MICK BUXTON)												
TOTALS												
Football League		38	10	7	21	38	53	37				
League Cup		5	3	1	1	8	7	—				
Anglo Italian Cup		2	1	0	1	2	2	—				
TOTAL												
SUNDERLAND	45	14	8	23	48	62		(40.00%)				

MOTHERWELL		P	W	D	L	F	A	Pts	Pos	SC Cup	SLge Cup
2001-02 (pt)	SPL	2	2	0	0	6	2	6	11th	(R3)	(R2)
2002-03	SPL	38	7	7	24	45	71	28	12th*	SF	R3
2003-04	SPL	38	12	10	16	42	49	46	6th	QF	R2
2004-05	SPL	38	13	9	16	46	49	48	6th	R3	F
TOTALS											
	SPL	116	34	26	56	139	171	128			
	Scottish Cup	8	5	0	3	16	9				
	Scottish Lge Cup	8	5	1+	2	21	14				
TOTAL											
MOTHERWELL		132	44	27	61	176	194	(43.56%)			

(up to end 2004-05)

NOTES

* Although bottom of the SPL, Motherwell avoided relegation through Division 1 champions Falkirk's inability to satisfy the SPL's ground criteria.

+ Drawn match lost on penalty kicks.

ABBREVIATIONS

FL Football League **SPL** Scottish Premier League **AI Cup** Anglo Italian Cup **ZDS Cup** Zenith Data Systems Cup (Full Members' Cup)

TERRY BUTCHER'S INTERNATIONAL CAREER

ENGLAND

Cap	Tournament	Date	Opponents	Venue	Result	Goals	Club
1	F	31 May 80	Australia	Sydney	W 2-1	—	Ipswich Town
2	F	25 Mar 81	Spain	Wembley	L 1-2	—	Ipswich Town
3	BC	27 Apr 82	Wales	Cardiff	W 1-0	—	Ipswich Town
4	BC	29 May 82	Scotland	Hampden Pk	W 1-0	—	Ipswich Town
5	WC	16 Jun 82	France	Bilbao	W 3-1	—	Ipswich Town
6	WC	20 Jun 82	Czechoslovakia	Bilbao	W 2-0	—	Ipswich Town
7	WC	29 Jun 82	West Germany	Madrid	D 0-0	—	Ipswich Town
8	WC	5 Jul 82	Spain	Madrid	D 0-0	—	Ipswich Town
9	ECQ	22 Sep 82	Denmark	Copenhagen	D 2-2	—	Ipswich Town
10	F	13 Oct 82	West Germany	Wembley	L 1-2	—	Ipswich Town
11	ECQ	15 Dec 82	Luxembourg	Wembley	W 9-0	—	Ipswich Town
12	BC	23 Feb 83	Wales	Wembley	W 2-1	1	Ipswich Town
13	ECQ	30 Mar 83	Greece	Wembley	D 0-0	—	Ipswich Town
14	ECQ	27 Apr 83	Hungary	Wembley	W 2-0	—	Ipswich Town
15	BC	28 May 83	Northern Ireland	Belfast	D 0-0	—	Ipswich Town
16	BC	1 Jun 83	Scotland	Wembley	W 2-0	—	Ipswich Town
17	F	11 Jun 83	Australia	Sydney	D 0-0	—	Ipswich Town
18	F	15 Jun 83	Australia	Brisbane	W 1-0	—	Ipswich Town
19	F	18 Jun 83	Australia	Melbourne	D 1-1	—	Ipswich Town
20	ECQ	21 Sep 83	Denmark	Wembley	L 0-1	—	Ipswich Town
21	ECQ	12 Oct 83	Hungary	Budapest	W 3-0	—	Ipswich Town

22	ECQ	16 Nov 83	Luxembourg	Luxembourg	W 4-0	1	Ipswich Town
23	F	29 Feb 84	France	Paris	L 0-2	—	Ipswich Town
24	BC	4 Apr 84	Northern Ireland	Wembley	W 1-0	—	Ipswich Town
25	F	12 Sep 84	East Germany	Wembley	W 1-0	—	Ipswich Town
26	WCQ	17 Oct 84	Finland	Wembley	W 5-0	—	Ipswich Town
27	WCQ	14 Nov 84	Turkey	Istanbul	W 8-0	—	Ipswich Town
28	WCQ	27 Feb 85	Northern Ireland	Belfast	W 1-0	—	Ipswich Town
29	F	26 Mar 85	Republic of Ireland	Wembley	W 2-1	—	Ipswich Town
30	WCQ	1 May 85	Romania	Bucharest	D 0-0	—	Ipswich Town
31	WCQ	22 May 85	Finland	Helsinki	D 1-1	—	Ipswich Town
32	F	25 May 85	Scotland	Hampden Pk	L 0-1	—	Ipswich Town
33	F	6 Jun 85	Italy	Mexico City	L 1-2	—	Ipswich Town
34	F	12 Jun 85	West Germany	Mexico City	W 3-0	—	Ipswich Town
35	F	16 Jun 85	USA	Los Angeles	W 5-0	—	Ipswich Town
36	F	26 Feb 86	Israel	Ramat Gan	W 2-1	—	Ipswich Town
37	F	26 Mar 86	USSR	Tbilisi	W 1-0	—	Ipswich Town
38	F	23 Apr 86	Scotland	Wembley	W 2-1	1	Ipswich Town
39	F	17 May 86	Mexico	Los Angeles	W 3-0	—	Ipswich Town
40	F	24 May 86	Canada	Burnaby	W 1-0	—	Ipswich Town
41	WC	3 Jun 86	Portugal	Monterrey	L 0-1	—	Ipswich Town
42	WC	6 Jun 86	Morocco	Monterrey	D 0-0	—	Ipswich Town
43	WC	11 Jun 86	Poland	Monterrey	W 3-0	—	Ipswich Town
44	WC	18 Jun 86	Paraguay	Mexico City	W 3-0	—	Ipswich Town
45	WC	22 Jun 86	Argentina	Mexico City	L 1-2	—	Ipswich Town

46	F	10 Sep 86	Sweden	Stockholm	L 0-1	—	Rangers
47	ECQ	15 Oct 86	Northern Ireland	Wembley	W 3-0	—	Rangers
48	ECQ	12 Nov 86	Yugoslavia	Wembley	W 2-0	—	Rangers
49	F	18 Feb 87	Spain	Madrid	W 4-2	—	Rangers
50	ECQ	1 Apr 87	Northern Ireland	Belfast	W 2-0	—	Rangers
51	ROUS CUP	19 May 87	Brazil	Wembley	D 1-1	—	Rangers
52	F	23 May 87	Scotland	Hampden Pk	D 0-0	—	Rangers
53	ECQ	14 Oct 87	Turkey	Wembley	W 8-0	—	Rangers
54	ECQ	11 Nov 87	Yugoslavia	Belgrade	W 4-1	—	Rangers
55	F	14 Sep 88	Denmark	Wembley	W 1-0	—	Rangers
56	WCQ	19 Oct 88	Sweden	Wembley	D 0-0	—	Rangers
57	F	8 Feb 89	Greece	Athens	W 2-1	—	Rangers
58	WCQ	8 Mar 89	Albania	Tirana	W 2-0	—	Rangers
59	WCQ	26 Apr 89	Albania	Wembley	W 5-0	—	Rangers
60	ROUS CUP	23 May 89	Chile	Wembley	D 0-0	—	Rangers
61	ROUS CUP	27 May 89	Scotland	Hampden Pk	W 2-0	—	Rangers
62	WCQ	3 Jun 89	Poland	Wembley	W 3-0	—	Rangers
63	F	7 Jun 89	Denmark	Copenhagen	D 1-1	—	Rangers
64	WCQ	6 Sep 89	Sweden	Stockholm	D 0-0	—	Rangers
65	WCQ	11 Oct 89	Poland	Katowice	D 0-0	—	Rangers
66	F	15 Nov 89	Italy	Wembley	D 0-0	—	Rangers
67	F	13 Dec 89	Yugoslavia	Wembley	W 2-1	—	Rangers
68	F	28 Mar 90	Brazil	Wembley	W 1-0	—	Rangers
69	F	25 Apr 90	Czechoslovakia	Wembley	W 4-2	—	Rangers

70	F	15 May 90	Denmark	Wembley	W 1-0	—	Rangers
71	F	22 May 90	Uruguay	Wembley	L 1-2	—	Rangers
72	F	2 Jun 90	Tunisia	Tunis	D 1-1	—	Rangers
73	WC	11 Jun 90	Republic of Ireland	Cagliari	D 1-1	—	Rangers
74	WC	16 Jun 90	Holland	Cagliari	D 0-0	—	Rangers
75	WC	26 Jun 90	Belgium	Bologna	W 1-0	—	Rangers
76	WC	1 Jul 90	Cameroon	Naples	W 3-2	—	Rangers
77	WC	4 Jul 90	West Germany	Turin	D 1-1*	—	Rangers

ENGLAND U-21 INTERNATIONALS

1	F	9 Jun 79	Sweden	Vasteras	W 2-1	—	Ipswich Twn
2	ECQ	11 Sep 79	Denmark	Watford	W 1-0	—	Ipswich Twn
3	ECQ	20 Nov 79	Bulgaria	Leicester	W 5-0	—	Ipswich Town
4	ECQ	12 Feb 80	Scotland	Coventry	W 2-1	—	Ipswich Town
5	ECQ	4 Mar 80	Scotland	Aberdeen	D 0-0	—	Ipswich Town
6	ECQ	16 Apr 80	East Germany	Sheffield	L 1-2	—	Ipswich Town
7	ECQ	23 Apr 80	East Germany	Jena	L 0-1	—	Ipswich Town

ENGLAND 'B' INTERNATIONAL

1	F	12 Jun 79	Austria	Klagenfurt	Abandoned ‡	Ipswich Town

REST OF THE WORLD XI

1	UNICEF	27 July 86	The Americas	Pasadena Rose Bowl	L 2-3	1

ABBREVIATIONS

BC British International Championships **ECQ** European Championship Qualifier **F** Friendly **WC** World Cup (Finals) **WCQ** World Cup Qualifier

NOTES

* Match lost on penalty kicks

‡ Abandoned after 60 mins, England 'B' led 1-0

STATISTICIAN'S ACKNOWLEDGEMENTS

The statistical section was compiled by John Russell, a member of the Association of Football Statisticians (AFS). John would like to thank the following who contributed to the statistics.

Tony Matthews (football author and statistician), Mark Baber (Editor AFS), David Barber (FA Librarian), Bryan Horsnell (Beejay Soccer Enterprises), Pat Goldbold (Ipswich Town Archivist), Emma Koubayssi (Rangers' Press Officer), Peter Rundo (Dundee Utd programme editor), Matthew Elder (*Fife Free Press*), Allan McIntyre (*Motherwell Times*), Jade Quinnell and Emma Biggs. And of course, Terry himself for giving, so freely, his valuable time.

The following publications were used to check the data:

Ipswich Town (The Modern Era), A Complete Record by Rob Hadgraft (Desert Island Books)
Rothman's Football Yearbook (various), edited by Glenda and Jack Rollin (Headline)

INDEX

A-ha 145
Aberdeen, Invery House 187
Aberdeen FC 11, 12, 13, 92
  matches against Motherwell 276, 278, 282, 284, 285
  matches against Rangers 159-160, 161, 173, 179-180, 186-188, 189, 199, 200, 226, 230
  Pittodrie ground 188
  Scottish Cup Final against Celtic 201
  Scottish League Cup matches 176, 189, 197, 201, 224, 276
Abramovic, Roman 306
Adams, Derek 282, 283
Adams, George 269
Adams, Tony 65, 118, 170, 178, 182, 206
Advocaat, Dick 81, 305
Aitken, Roy 59, 158, 164, 166, 185, 190
Aizlewood, Mark 181
al-Sharif (Syrian referee) 146
Albania national team 192, 193, 303
Aldridge, John 132, 211
Alex (BBC colleague) 311, 312
'Alive and Kicking' 144
All Blacks 129
Allardyce, Sam 304
Altobelli (Italian player) 128
Ameobi, Shola 301
Americas, Rest of the World match against 152-153
Amoruso (Rangers player) 278
Amsterdam 85, 313-314
  Sphinx Club 85
Amsterdam Cup 85
Anderson, Viv 84, 93, 125, 129, 130, 136, 138, 140, 169
Andrew, Marvin 321
Andrew, Rob 244
Andrews, Ian 185
Anglia Sport 23
Anglian Combination 24-25
Anthony Nolan Trust 236-237
apprentices' jobs 36-38
Arconada, Luis 101
Ardiles, Ossie 52
Argentina national team 146-150, 151, 218
Aris Salonika football club 77-78
Ark Royal, HMS 16

Armstrong, David 73
Armstrong, Gordon 239, 240-241
Armstrong, Lance 68
Arsenal FC 38, 182, 230, 232, 291, 305
  matches against Ipswich 69, 77, 80, 87, 113, 118
Ashby, Gerald 133
Ashlea Boys' Club 24-25, 27
Aston Villa FC 49, 76, 81-82, 83, 229, 231, 242
Atherton, Peter 229
Atkins, Ian 243, 244
Atkinson, Ron 154, 231, 232, 242
Augenthaler (German player) 129, 199
Australia national team 72-73, 94
Austria national 'B' team 61-62
Austria national team 62, 298
AZ 67 Alkmaar football club 81
Azerbaijan national team 299, 300

Bad Company 29
Baddiel, David 203-204
Bagni (Italian player) 128
Bagshaw, Bob 33
Bailey, Gary 126
Baldry, David 25, 29, 30
Ball, Christopher 21
Barcelona 85-86
Barcelona football club 35, 52, 56-57, 305
Barmby, Nick 303
Barmos (Czech player) 99
Barnard Castle School 244
Barnes, John 109, 110, 114, 125, 128, 129, 177, 178, 192, 193, 264
  World Cup (1986) 143, 147, 149
  World Cup (1990) 212, 214, 216-217, 221
Barnsley FC 238, 239
basketball 21
Basten, Marco van 211-212
Bath University 263
Battiston (French player) 79, 97
Baxter, Billy 20
Bayern Munch football club

156, 199
BBC 28, 181, 200, 208, 258, 311
BBC Radio Five Live 13-14, 31, 190, 260, 267, 272, 294, 306, 307-317, 320
  6-0-6 phone-in show 310, 315
Beardsley, Peter 136, 139, 144, 146, 171, 177, 178, 193, 217, 228, 307
Beasant, Dave 206
Beatles, the 29, 57
Beattie, Kevin 35, 43, 44, 45, 48, 49, 50, 51, 72, 74, 76, 78, 82-83
Beckenbauer, Franz 152, 220
Beckham, David 58, 295-296, 298-300, 302, 307, 308, 318
Belgium national team 214, 217
Bell, Jimmy 199
Bellamy, Craig 324
Bennett, Gary 241
Bento (Portuguese goalkeeper) 142
Berthold (German player) 220
Bertschin, Keith 108
Bessanov (USSR player) 136-137
Best, George 55-56
Betty (Motherwell secretary) 12
Bilbao 95, 96, 98, 100
Birmingham City FC 52, 54, 76, 242, 274
Birmingham University 236
Birtles, Garry 52
Bisham, Black Bull pub 196
Black, Eric 28, 228, 264, 265-266, 267, 268, 269, 270, 271
Blackley, John 260
Blackwell, Kevin 181
'Blaydon Races' 220
Blissett, Luther 61
Blundeston Prison 16, 18, 19, 22
  staff football team 22, 23, 24
Boavista football club 168
Boersma, Phil 170-171, 179-180, 184
Bogart, Humphrey 141
Bologna 214-215, 217
Bolton Wanderers FC 52, 55
Bond, Alan 37-38
Bond, John 82
Bone, Jimmy 20
Bonetti, Peter 25

Bonhof (Cologne player) 79
Boniek (Polish player) 144, 145
Bonner, Packy 158, 164
Bonner, Pat 190, 211
Borussia Mönchengladbach
    football club 168-169
Bouderbala (Moroccan player)
    143
Bowles, Stan 56
Boyle, John 117, 266, 269, 271,
    274, 275
Bracewell, Paul 123
Bradford City FC 87
    fire 121
Brady, Liam 126
Brazil, Alan 37, 38, 39, 53, 70,
    75, 77, 78, 86, 106, 112, 167
Brazil, Jill 112
Brazil national team 114, 171,
    205, 296
Brehme (German player) 129,
    219
Breitner (German player) 101
Bremner, Billy 169
Brentford FC 239, 240
Bridge of Allan 258
    Beaconhurst school 159
    Kenilworth Road 159
    Kipling's restaurant 162
    Old Manor Hotel 17, 245,
        248-249, 250-256, 257
    Rising Sun pub 200
Brighton & Hove Albion FC
    69-70, 77
Bristol City FC 48, 71, 240
Bristol Rovers FC 123, 237-
    238, 240
Britton (Motherwell player)
    325
Brooking, Mrs 308
Brooking, Trevor 95, 96, 98,
    100, 101, 308
Brown, Gordon and Linda 193
Brown, James 129
Brown, John 199, 224
Brown, Nigel 265
Brown, Stewart 265
Brownlie, John 258
Bruce, Steve 122, 304
Bruno, Frank 154
Buckley, Michael 266
Budapest 72
Buffel (Rangers player) 321
Bulgaria national team 62
Bull, Steve 194, 205, 208, 212
Burgess, Mike 316
Burke, Fran 236-237
Burley, George 51, 82, 86, 132
Burnham Beeches Hotel 196

Burns, Alex 279, 281
Burns Club 253
Burruchaga (Argentinian
    player) 146
Butcher, Alistair Ian (son) 13,
    42, 193, 222, 244, 257, 287, 319
Butcher, Christopher Charles
    (son) 13, 42, 86, 91, 100, 101,
    120, 124, 195, 234, 244,
    257
Butcher, David (uncle) 19
Butcher, Edward John (son)
    13, 42, 155, 234, 244, 257, 283
Butcher, Leonard Charles
    (father) 9, 15-16, 17, 18, 19,
    20-21, 22, 23, 24, 30, 34, 35,
    36, 44, 47, 49, 59, 88, 216,
    251-252
Butcher, Rita (wife) 12, 16, 18,
    26, 28-29, 32, 46, 50, 51, 84,
    114, 139, 232, 287
    meets Terry 41-42
    marries Terry 71
    honeymoon 72
    pregancy and birth of first
        child 85, 86
    and Terry's nose injury 88,
        89-90
    at World Cup (1982) 100, 101,
        102
    and Terry's possible move to
        Rangers 141
    in Scotland 154, 162, 165, 166,
        167, 179, 180, 187, 194, 257
    pregnant with Alistair 193
    and Terry's head injury 203
    at World Cup (1990) 207, 216
    and Terry dropped from
        Rangers team 224, 225
    buys Terry a mountain bike
        236
    and Sunderland trial 237
    and hotel business venture
        245, 249, 251, 252, 254, 256,
        257, 260
    and court case 247
    skiing 262
    and company ventures 263,
        265
    on cruise 267
    holiday in Tenerife 274
    USA trip 283
    and Terry at World Cup
        (1998) 312
    at England v Poland match
        319
Butcher, Terry (Terence Ian)
    disciplined life 9, 17, 24
    anger 10-12, 13, 66, 122-123,

133, 187, 200-201
    character 13-14
    birth and early life 15-16
    height 16, 43
    school days 17, 18, 19, 20-22,
        25, 27, 28
    at Denes High School
        (formerly Lowestoft
        Grammar) 17, 20-22, 25
    first interest in football 17, 18
    scalds foot as a boy 18, 19
    and two-footed play 18-19
    watches Norwich as a boy
        19-20
    watches Ipswich matches 20
    plays for Lowestoft and
        Suffolk Schoolboys 20
    enjoys sports at school 21-22,
        25
    discipline at school 22
    schoolboy football 22-23, 27-
        28
    plays for prison staff team
        22, 23, 24
    Sunday-league football 23
    appetite 23, 25-26, 37, 77
    plays for Ashlea Boys' Club
        24-25
    Christmases 26, 29, 77
    after-school jobs 26-27, 33
    'O' and 'A' level exams 28
    and French language 28
    and girls 28, 29
    hairstyles 28-29, 41
    musical tastes 29, 32, 37, 57,
        144, 145, 174
    first visit to pub 29
    summer on the beach 30
    trial for England Schoolboys
        31, 35
    lack of confidence 31-32
    decides to go to Trent
        Polytechnic 32, 33, 34, 35,
        44
    offered trial then youth team
        contract by Ipswich 33, 34,
        35
    pre-training practice 34-35
    jobs at Ipswich 36-37
    in Ipswich youth team 35-41
    injuries 38, 51, 71-72, 76, 87,
        114, 116, 121, 131, 173, 179-
        180, 201-203, 238
    meets and marries Rita 41-
        42, 71
    in Ipswich reserve team 43-
        45
    altercation with Allan Hunter
        44-45

aggressive play 45-46, 64, 65
Ipswich first team debuts 46, 47, 49, 50
and beating Liverpool 51
scores first goal for Ipswich 52, 54
and diving 54
shirts collection 57, 115
and shirt pulling 59
and defending 59-60
selected for England U-21 tour 60
birdwatching 63-64
and hypnotherapy 67-68
honeymoon 72
debut for England 72, 74
and Rita's pregnancy and birth of first child 85-86, 91
aggression 86, 190, 207
broken nose and complications 87, 88-91
World Cup (1982) 94, 95, 96-102
and alcohol 103, 104, 105, 140, 193, 196, 208, 221, 240, 247, 313, 314-315, 316-317
trashes Dutch hotel room 104-105
dog Sadie and puppies 108-109
scores first goal for England 109
captains Ipswich 118
and national anthem 118-119
and captaincy 119-120
captains England 119, 169, 201, 205, 213, 214, 216
rumour of move to Manchester United 132, 134, 141, 152, 154
leaves Ipswich to join Rangers 134, 141, 152, 155
plays for Rest of the World 152-153
Spurs interested in signing 154
moves to Rangers 152, 153-154, 155, 195
first appearance for Rangers 156-157
captains Rangers 119, 158
family moves to Scotland 159
and Rangers winning League title 161-163
awards from Rangers supporters clubs 165-166
and wearing green in

Scotland 166
earns 50th England cap 170
second in Scottish Player of the Year award 172
charged and tried for breach of the peace 176-177, 179, 180, 181, 182, 183
breaks leg and convalescence 179-181, 183
charged with vandalism and breach of the peace 187
head injury in Swedish match 201-203
retires from international football 222
knee problems 222, 225, 226, 228, 229, 237, 262
dropped from team 223-224
offer from Leeds United 224, 225
leaves Rangers 224-225
joins Coventry City as player-manager 12, 168, 185, 225, 226-227
announces retirement from playing 233
sacked as Coventry manager 234
fitness regime 236, 244
works for Sheffield Wednesday 236
bike ride for Anthony Nolan Trust 236-237
coaching in Japan 237
plays for Sunderland 237-238
takes over as player-manager at Sunderland 12, 238
sacked by Sunderland 243-244
hotel business venture 17, 245, 248, 249, 250-256, 257
court case re Coventry contract 245-246, 247
looks for new job 247-248
plays for Clydebank 250
last professional game 250
converts hotel to family home 256-257
as coach at Raith 258-259, 260
as coach at Dundee United 259-262
skiing 262
internet company venture 262-264
player-recruitment company venture 264-267
offered assistant manager's

job at Motherwell 266
researches birthplace 15, 16, 267
joins Motherwell 269
takes over as Motherwell manager 271
called before SFA 275
working as summariser on BBC Radio Five Live 295, 307-317, 320
wine tasting 314-315, 316, 317
broadcasting gaffes 318
Butcher, Valerie May (mother) 15-16, 18, 20-21, 22, 23, 25-26, 27, 30-31, 34, 35, 36, 44, 49, 89, 90, 216, 251, 252
Butcher, Vanda (sister) 17, 20, 49, 70, 245, 248, 249, 250-251
husband Nigel 245, 248, 249, 250-251
Buxton, Mick 243, 244
Byrne, Geoff 181

Cagliari 210, 211-214, 216
Caine, Michael 72
Cambridge, Ronelles nightclub 110
Cambridge United FC 234, 240
Cameroon national team 65-66, 215, 216-217
Campbell, Bob and Marion 108-109
Campbell, Bobby 87
Campbell, Sol 54, 299, 302
Canada national team 139-140
Canete (Paraguayan striker) 145-146
Caniggia (Argentine striker) 219
caps, England 222
captains, inspirational 118
Cardiff City FC 274
Carlisle FC 280
Carlsberg 10
Carter, Tim 240-241
Cascarino, Tony 210, 211
Case, Jimmy 47, 169
Cassidy (Lowestoft striker) 19
Casteneda (St Etienne player) 79
Cathcart, Ian 190
Celtic FC 290
centenary year 175, 184
charity match against Rangers 195
income 289, 291
matches

Falkirk 161
Hibernian 321
Kilmarnock 321
Motherwell 67, 275-276,
    277, 282, 283-284, 322-326
Rangers 11-12, 158, 159,
    160, 161, 175-176, 177, 182,
    185-186, 188, 198, 199-
    200
St Mirren 156
Parkhead ground and
    supporters 160-161
Scottish Cup finals 163, 164,
    190-191, 201
Scottish League Cup finals
    59, 224, 226, 250
supporters clubs 165, 166
win Premier League title 156
Central Auctions 256
Chamberlain, Mark 107, 124
Champions League 292
Chandler, Victor 266
Channel Five 318
Channon, Mick 122
Chapman, Lee 228
Charles, Jeremy 87
Charles, John 22, 56
Charlton, Bobby 56, 154
Charlton, Jack 100, 121, 210
Charlton Athletic FC 242
Chatteris FC 19
Chelsea FC 38, 230, 291
Cherry, Trevor 73
Chester City FC 242
Chievo football club 271, 272
Chivadze (USSR player) 136
Chivers, Martin 267
CIS Cup 284
Clark, Paul 31
Clarkson, David 278, 281, 282,
    285, 325
Clearwater, Holiday Inn 103
Clemence, Ray 47, 62-63, 83,
    307
Clough, Brian 82, 102
Clough, Frank 96
Clough, Nigel 228
Clydebank FC 161, 250
Cobbold, Lady Blanche 117
Cobbold, John and Patrick 39-
    40, 116-117, 118
Coker, Ade 27
Cole, Carlton 301
Cole, Joe 302, 303
Collymore, Stan 238, 239
Cologne football club 79, 80,
    81
Colorado Springs 137, 139
    Broadmoor Hotel 137, 138

Colquhoun, Carol and John
    241
Commonwealth Games 154
Cooper, Alice 29
Cooper, Davie 155-156, 158,
    161, 164, 166, 190, 199, 250
Cooper, Neale 186
Cooper, Paul 49, 55, 63, 106,
    107, 124, 133
Coppell, Steve 95, 97, 101, 307
Corrigan, Joe 62, 73, 99
Cottee, Tony 194
Coventry, Hotel Leofric 232
Coventry City FC 12, 225-234,
    246-247
    1990/91 season 228-231
    1991/92 season 232-234, 235
    court case re Terry's contract
        245-246, 247
    FA Cup Final against Spurs
        226
    Highfield Road ground 228
    matches
        Arsenal 230, 232
        Aston Villa 229, 231
        Cambridge 234
        Chelsea 230
        Derby 230
        Ipswich 70, 71, 88, 113
        Leeds 228
        Liverpool 228, 230
        Luton 232, 233
        Manchester City 230, 232
        Manchester United 228-
            229, 233
        Norwich 229, 230, 233
        Notts Forest 228
        QPR 232
        Sheffield United 232, 233
        Sheffield Wednesday 229
        Southampton 233
        Spurs 228, 230, 233, 234
        West Ham 232
        Wimbledon 234
Cowan (Hibernian player) 157
Cowans, Gordon 61, 110
Cowdenbeath FC 283
Craig, Stevie 278, 283
Craigan, Stephen 279, 285,
    321, 322
Crane, Doc 142, 202-203
Cranson, Ian 'Bull Neck' 122
Crawford, Stevie 250
Croker, Ted 73-74, 99
Crosby, Malcolm 237, 238
Crouch, Nigel 38
Crozier, Adam 307-308
Cruz, Francisco 139
Crystal Palace FC 70, 291

Cullmann (Cologne player) 79
Curbishley, Alan 27, 303-304
Curtis, Alan 87
Czechoslovakia national team
    99, 205

D'Avray, Mich 114
Daily Express 46, 249, 250
Daily Mirror 95, 143, 191
Daines, Barry 77
Dair, Jason 283
Dalglish, Kenny 47, 59, 64, 70,
    194, 226
Darlington 244, 247
Dasaev (USSR player) 136
Davenport, Peter 92, 126, 240-
    241
Davies, Dai 87
De Vries (Hearts player) 276
Deep Purple 29
Defoe, Jermain 301
Deloumeaux, Eric 276, 278
Denes High School (formerly
    Lowestoft Grammar School)
    17, 20-22, 25
Denmark national team 106-
    107, 114-115, 191, 195-196, 205
Derby County FC 121, 230,
    238, 242
Devonshire, Alan 73, 109
Dewhurst butchers 26, 33
Diamantino (Portuguese
    player) 142
Dickens, Alan 132-133
Dickie, Bill 117
Dixon, Kerry 129
Dobson, Colin 227, 234
Dobson, Martin 46
Dobson, Tony 229
Dodds, Davie 159-160
Dollar Academy 245
Dorigo, Tony 204-205
Douglas, Rab 325
Downing, Stewart 303
Dozzell, Jason 113
Drewery, Eileen 67
Drinkell, Kevin 184, 185, 188,
    189, 200, 228
Drogba (Chelsea player) 54
Dundee, Swallow Hotel 200
Dundee FC 10, 13, 161, 163,
    250
    matches against Motherwell
        271, 272, 276, 280-281, 282,
        284
Dundee United FC 259-262,
    290
    Gussie training ground 261
    matches against Motherwell

260, 270, 275, 281, 284
matches against Rangers
157, 163, 188, 189, 200, 223
Tannadice Park ground 200
Dunfermline FC 173, 200, 223,
250, 270, 282, 284, 290, 321
Dunthorne, David 41
Durrant, Ian 42, 158, 161-162,
164, 171, 185, 186, 188
Dyer, Kieron 119, 303
Dynamo Kiev football club
174
Dyson, Paul 71
Dziekanowski (Celtic player)
198

Ear, Nose and Throat Hospital,
Whitechapel 89, 90
East Anglian Cup 20
East Fife FC 163, 276
East Germany national team
124 see also Germany
national team
East Germany U-21 team 71-
72
East Stirling FC 223
Eastick, Brian 228, 233, 235
Edinburgh 157
Norton House Hotel 154,
156, 157
Edwards, Doc 99, 142, 150
Edwards, Jonathan 21
Eggleston, Tommy 72, 88
Egypt national team 135, 213,
214
Eindhoven 103-104
Ekeke (Cameroon player) 217
Ekstrom (Swedish player) 169,
201-202
Elkjaer, Preben 106
Elliott, Paul 198
Elliott, Stuart 272
Ellis, Doug 234-235
Elstrup, Lars 191, 196
Ely FC 19
Enfield FC 231
Engels (Cologne player) 79
England, Mike 179
England 'B' team 94
England national team
acclimatisation training in
Mexico 127-129
Euro 96 matches against
Spain 204, 307
European Championship
match against Austria 298
European Championship
match against Bulgaria 62
friendly matches 296, 297

Canada 139-140
Czechoslovakia 205
Denmark 191, 195-196, 205
East Germany 124
Egypt 135
France 115
Greece 192
Holland 296-297
Italy 204
South Korea 138
Spain 170
Tunisia 207-208
Uruguay 205
USA 129-130
Yugoslavia 204-205
honour in playing for 318-
319
matches
Albania 192, 193, 303
Australia 72-73, 94
Austria 62
Azerbaijan 299, 300
Brazil 114, 171
Cameroon 65-66, 216-217
Denmark 106-107, 114-115
Finland 94, 124, 125-126,
295
France 57
Germany 310
Greece 109, 295, 303
Holland 303
Hungary 92, 109, 115
Ireland 126
Israel 135
Italy 128, 315
Luxembourg 107, 115
Malta 316
Mexico 128-129, 138-139
Moldova 307-308
Northern Ireland 109-110,
116, 125, 135, 169, 170
Poland 195, 204, 319
Romania 125-126, 135
Saudi Arabia 191
Scotland 92-94, 110, 126-
127, 137, 171, 193-194
Spain 83
Sweden 61, 169, 191, 201-
203, 260, 308-309
Tunisia 66
Turkey 124, 125, 135, 177
USSR 114, 136
Wales 92, 109
West Germany 107, 129,
177
Yugoslavia 65, 169, 177-179
matches in Australia 110-111
and new players 296-297
public attitude towards 296

relations with press 210-211,
215, 299
suggested managers 303-304
suggested team 302-303
Varig Cup match against
Brazil 205
World Cup finals matches
Argentina 146-150, 151
Belgium 214, 217
Brazil 296
Czechoslovakia 99
Egypt 213, 214
France 58-59, 97-98, 100
Holland 211-213
Ireland 210, 211
Italy 220
Kuwait 100
Morocco 142-143, 312
Nigeria 309-310
Paraguay 145-146
Poland 143-145
Portugal 142
Romania 317
Spain 101-102
West Germany 100-101,
219-220
World Cup tactics 144, 147,
212, 214, 217, 219
England Schoolboys team 31,
35
England U-21 team 60, 61, 71-
72
English football, future of 291,
292, 306
Eriksson, Sven Goran 19, 119,
143, 291, 295, 299, 300, 303,
304, 306
Escape to Victory 72
Essex Schoolboys team 27-28,
31
Ettori (French goalkeeper) 98
Euro 96: 203, 204
Euro 2000: 313-314
Euro 2004: 298, 299, 301-302
Everton FC 123, 281
matches against Ipswich 46,
47, 70, 76, 87-88, 121, 123-
124, 131-132

Fagan, Sean 275, 277
Fairclough, David 47
Falco, Marc 173, 174
Falkirk FC 161, 157, 173, 278,
279
Falklands conflict 101-102,
146, 151
Fantasy Island 204
Fashanu, John 194
Fashanu, Justin 76

FC Brugge 51
Featherstone, John 243
Fenwick, Terry 140, 142, 145, 146, 148
Ferdinand, Rio 54, 302
Ferguson, Sir Alex 168, 301
Ferguson, Anne 240
Ferguson, Barry 293
Ferguson, Bobby 43, 44, 45, 53, 67, 71, 75, 85, 87, 104, 105, 107, 111, 113, 114, 118, 122-123, 126, 132, 133, 134, 141
as number two at Sunderland 237, 240
Ferguson, Derek 158, 171, 241, 242
Ferguson, Duncan 182, 185
Ferguson, Ian 199
Ferguson, Steven 276
Fernandez (Paraguayan goalkeeper) 146
Fernando (Terry's friend) 170
Ferrere, David 270-271
Ferry, Bryan 37
FIFA 127, 145, 297
Finland national team 94, 124, 125-126, 295
First Wave Management 237
Fitzpatrick, Marc 285
Fleck, Robert 160, 162
Fletcher, Darren 294
Florida 103, 109, 183, 187
Fontainebleau Hilton hotel 183
football, changes in game 304-305
football, physical side of 54-55
football, Surridge Cobbler 39
Football Association 72-73, 126, 139, 145, 204, 206, 208, 218, 215-216, 263, 299, 304, 319-320
international committee 213
Football Writers' Award 75
Foran, Richie 283, 324
Forfar FC 281
Foster, Steve 93
France national team 57, 58-59, 97-98, 100, 115
Francis, Trevor 54, 91, 92, 93, 97, 98, 100, 106, 109, 110, 124, 127, 137, 173, 174
as Sheffield Wednesday manager 236
Fraser, Cammie 250
Fresco, Monte 138
friendly internationals 296, 297
Fuengirola 230

Fulham FC 280
Furlong, Paul 231
Futre, Paulo 142

Gabbiadini, Marco 238
Gallacher, Kevin 157, 189, 228, 229
Ganges, HMS 16
Gardner, Stevie 38
Garland, Chris 71
Gascoigne, Paul 56, 121, 155, 191, 193, 196
Albanian cockerel incident 192
World Cup (1990) 205, 207, 208, 209, 210, 212, 214, 215, 217, 220
Gates, Eric 53, 54, 70, 78, 86, 132
Gateway Builders 159
Geddis, David 34, 46, 48, 49
Gerets, Eric 85, 214
Germany national team 310
see also East/West Germany national teams
Gerrard, Steven 296, 302
Gibson, Terry 91
Giles, Johnny 169
Gillhaus, Hans 212
Gillingham FC 123
Giresse (French player) 97
GKS Katowice football club 190-191
Glanville, Brian 178, 203
Glasgow see also Celtic FC; Rangers FC
Apollo 93
Bellahouston Park 184
Grosvenor Hotel 157
Panama Jacks 164, 165
Ross Hall Hospital 180
Glasgow Green 273
Godbold, Pat 217, 218
Goodman, Don 242, 243
Gornik Zabrze football club 174-175, 177
Gotsmanov (USSR player) 136
Gough, Richard 126, 176
Gould, Bobby 235
Gow, Gerry 71
Gowling, Alan 52
Graham, Tom 263, 267
Grant, Peter 198
Grasshoppers Zurich football club 70
Gray, Andy 123-124
Gray, Phil 241, 242
Gray, Ron 32-33
Greece 77-78

Greece national team 109, 192, 283, 295, 303
Green, Alan 307, 308, 309-310, 311, 312, 313, 315, 316, 317, 320
Green, Robert 296, 305
Greenhoff, Brian 73
Greenwood, Ron 61, 62, 83, 92, 94, 97, 98, 99, 100, 102
Grimsby Town FC 242
Grobelaar, Bruce 171
Gubba, Tony 267
Gullit, Ruud 211-212
Gus (Motherwell groundsman) 273
Gynn, Micky 230

Hackett, Keith 293
Hadziabdic, Dzemal 87
Halliday, Bobby 256
Hamilton, Jim 324
Hamilton Academical FC 158, 163, 185, 188, 189, 273
Hamilton Portfolio 269
Hammell, Stephen 322
Hampden Park 93, 163-164, 285-288
Hansen (Danish player) 106
Harford, Mick 233
Hargreaves, Owen 302-303
Harris, Bob 141
Harrison, Gerry 23
Hart, Paul 133
Hartson, John 324
Hassler (German player) 219
Hateley, Mark 114, 124, 125, 126, 128, 139, 144, 147, 226
Hawaii 39-40, 117
Hayes, Martin 231
Heart of Midlothian FC 156, 161, 188, 223, 290
matches against Motherwell 276, 277, 281, 282-283, 284, 285, 321
Heath, Adrian 123
Heathrow, Post House hotel 71
Henderson, Allan 246
Heskey, Emile 303
Heysel Stadium disaster 121, 123, 127-128, 130, 182
Hibernian FC 10-11, 13, 290, 321, 322
matches against Motherwell 270-271, 275, 276-277, 281, 282, 284, 321
matches against Rangers 156-157, 185, 197-198
High Wycombe, Crest Hotel

110
Hill, Jimmy 81-82, 114
Histon Town FC 19
Hoddle, Glenn 67, 73, 83, 99,
  115, 129, 137, 138
  as England manager 295, 307
  as player-manager at
    Swindon 237
  World Cup (1986) 143, 147,
    148
Hodge, Steve 64-65, 92, 143,
  144, 146, 147, 148, 204
Holland 51
Holland national team 211-
  213, 296-297, 303
Holmes, David 159, 162, 182
Hong Kong 267
Hood, Alistair 176
Houghton, Ray 168
Hover, Graham and Julie 247
Howe, Don 69, 102, 144, 206,
  209, 212, 213, 222, 233, 234,
  235
Hucknall, Mick 207
Huddersfield Town FC 237
Hughes, Emlyn 47, 69, 143
Hughes, Mark 55, 65
Hull City FC 272
Hungary national team 92,
  109, 115
Hunningham 233
Hunter, Allan 43, 44, 45, 49, 51,
  69, 74, 166, 167
Hunter, Norman 169
Hurworth Preparatory School
  244
Huston, John 72
hypnotherapy in football 67-
  68

Ian (Terry's friend) 251, 252
Iceland national team 94
Ilie, Adrian 318
Ilves football club 168
Ingham, Marshall and George
  317
Ingham, Mike 307, 315, 316,
  317
Inside Soccer and website 262-
  264
Inside Soccer Recruitment
  264-267, 276
international football, decline
  in 291-292
Inverness FC 282, 284-285
Inverplan 263
Ipswich, Sporting Farmer pub
  37
Ipswich Town FC 11, 12, 32,

60, 172
1976/77 season 38-40
1977/78 season 43, 46-50
1978/79 season 52, 54, 60
1979/80 season 69-72, 74
1980/81 season 75-83
1981/82 season 86-88, 91-92
1982/83 season 105-108
1983/84 season 112-114
1984/85 season 121-124
1985/86 season 131-134
Bobby Robson team talks 68,
  69
Centre Spot restaurant 37,
  79, 88
Charity Shield match against
  Notts Forest 51
FA Cup matches
  1975: 35
  Bristol City 71
  Bristol Rovers 123
  Everton 123
  Gillingham 123
  Ipswich 123
  Liverpool 52, 53
  Millwall 48
  Notts Forest 82
  semi-final against
    Manchester City 80, 82-83
  semi-final against West
    Bromwich 48-49
  Shrewsbury 82, 112-113
  West Ham 134
friendly against Notts
  County 131
Israel tour 72
laundry 36-37
League Cup matches
  Bradford City 87
  Derby 121
  Everton 87-88, 123-124
  Leeds 87
  Liverpool 89, 107, 134
  Luton 88
  Middlesbrough 76
  Newcastle 121
  Norwich 122-123
  Oxford 122
  QPR 122
  semi-final against Liverpool
    89
  Swindon 132
  Watford 88
matches
  Arsenal 69, 77, 80, 87, 113,
    118
  Aston Villa 49, 76, 81-82, 83
  Barcelona 35, 52, 56, 57
  Birmingham 52, 54, 76

Bolton 52, 55
Brighton 70, 77
Coventry 70, 71, 88, 113
Crystal Palace 70
Everton 46, 47, 70, 76, 121,
  131-132
Leeds 76
Leicester City 75
Liverpool 47-48, 70, 76, 87,
  107
Luton 113-114, 121
Manchester City 70
Manchester United 70, 76,
  83, 86, 114, 121
Middlesbrough 76, 80-81
Norwich 76, 77, 80, 108,
  123, 124
Notts County 107, 108
Notts Forest 52, 54, 64-65,
  69, 92, 114, 124
Oxford 132
QPR 54
Sheffield Wednesday 132,
  133
Southampton 76-77, 118
Spurs 52, 77, 112
Stoke 75, 106
Sunderland 76, 86
Swansea 87
Watford 113
West Bromwich 70, 124,
  131, 132-133
West Ham 11, 92, 121
Widzew Lodz 57
Wolves 49, 50, 69, 70
Norway tour 51
Pioneer Stand 106, 112, 134
Portman Road ground 20
relegated 133-134, 152
reserve team 43-45, 48, 91
School of Excellence 33
tactics 53
training 35-36
UEFA Cup Final against AZ
  67 Alkmaar 81
UEFA Cup matches 35, 70,
  75, 77-80, 92, 106-107
USA tour 103
wins FA Cup against Notts
  Forest 48, 49-50
youth team 35-41
Ireland national team 126, 210,
  211
Irish Troubles 125
Irvine, Brian 161
Irwin, Colin 87
Israel 72, 170-171
Israel national team 135
Istanbul 124-125

Hilton hotel 124-125
Italy, Rangers training in 184-185
Italy national team 102, 128, 145, 204, 218, 220, 315
ITV 214, 313
Ivan, Uncle 17

Jackson, Bryan 271
Jackson, John 95
Jagger, Mick 93
James, David 298, 305
James, Leighton 87, 179
James, Robbie 87
Jankovic, Bosco 81
Janvion (St Etienne player) 79
Japan 237, 272, 315-316
Jardine, Quintin 9
Jefferson, 'Chopper' 20
Jenkins, Ross 55
Jennings, Pat 109-110, 135, 152
Jenny (Coventry secretary) 234
Jersey 222
Joachim, Julian 238
John, Elton 170
John Lawrence Ltd 159
Johnson, Andy 296, 303
Johnson, Glen 296
Johnston, Mo 160, 164, 194, 195, 198-200
Jones, Ron 311-312
Jonker (AZ 67 Alkmaar player) 81
Joshua Tree, The 174
Juventus football club 127-128, 217, 220 see also Heysel Stadium disaster

Kaltz (German player) 101
Katanec (Yugoslav player) 179
Katowice 191
Kaye, Danny 152
Keane, Roy 118
Keegan, Kevin 62, 73, 76-77, 95, 96, 98, 100, 101, 102, 121
as England manager 295, 300, 319
Kelly, Danny 262
Kelly, David 239, 270
Kelly, Graham 74, 206, 213, 220, 307-308
Kelly, 'Rebounds' 213
Kennedy, Nigel 207
Kennedy, Ray 87
Kerr, Brian 283
Kick Racism out of Football campaign 168
Kieft (Dutch player) 212

Kiev 174
Kilcline, Brian 227, 231
Kilmarnock football club 223, 231, 271, 275, 276, 281, 282, 285, 321
King, Ledley 302
Kingston-on-Thames Hospital 38
Kinniburgh, Willie 272
Kirkland, Chris 305
Kirton, Glen 73, 74
Kirton, Trevor 'Wheels' 57-58, 79
Kist (AZ 67 Alkmaar player) 81
Klagenfurt, Austria 61-62
'Knees Up Mother Brown' 220
Koeman (Dutch player) 211-212
Kogl (Bayern Munich player) 199
Konopka (Cologne player) 79
Krankl, Hans 56
Kunde (Cameroon player) 217
Kuwait national team 100

L'Equipe 312
LA Dodgers 139
Lacombe (French player) 98
Lambert, Mick 47, 50
Lampard, Frank (junior) 296, 299, 301, 302
Lampard, Frank (senior) 73
Langley, Mike 106
Larios (St Etienne player) 79
Lasley, Keith 282, 283
Latchford, Bob 46, 47, 70, 87
Latchford, David 46
Latchford, Peter 46
Laudrup (Danish player) 191
Le Tournoi (1997) 314-315
Lea, Cyril 37, 47, 53
Lee, Sammy 110, 115
Leeds United FC 35, 76, 87, 169, 224, 225, 228, 242
Leicester City FC 75, 238, 239
Leitch, Scott 119-120, 276, 286, 287, 322
Lennon, John 57
Lesley (Rita's friend) 41, 42
Levein, Craig 290
Lewis, Doc 67
Leyton Orient FC 20
Lilleshall national rehabilitation centre 180-181, 183
Limpar, Anders 230
Lineker, Gary 56, 118, 126, 129, 136, 139-140, 169, 170, 171,

177, 191, 193, 196, 205
World Cup (1986) 142, 144, 146, 149
World Cup (1990) 211, 212, 214, 217, 219, 220
Littbarski (German player) 79, 101
Liverpool, Holiday Inn 46
Liverpool FC 59
European Cup Final against Juventus 127-128 see also Heysel Stadium disaster
matches against Coventry 228, 230
matches against Ipswich 47-48, 52, 53, 70, 76, 87, 89, 107, 134
Liveston, Graham 260
Livingston FC 10, 275, 276, 277, 278, 279, 281, 282, 284, 286
Livingstone, Steve 229
Lochgilphead, Crinan Hotel 255
London
Fleet Street, Ye Olde Cheshire Cheese 247
Mayfair Hotel 89-90
Park Lane Hilton 83-84
Royal Garden Hotel 50
Strand Hotel 245
Terence MacMillan Stadium 27
London Ballet Company 96-97
London Heathrow Airport, Holiday Inn 153-154
Los Angeles 129-130, 138-139, 152
Hard Rock Café 84
Tramp nightclub 130
Lothingland Hospital football team 24
Lowestoft 16, 17-18
beach 30
Careers Office 31
Carlton Road 18
Denes Oval 30
Fen Park primary school 17, 19, 22, 27
Marquis of Lorne pub 41
South Pier 41
Victoria Hotel 71
Lowestoft and Suffolk Schoolboys 20
Lowestoft Golf Club 71
Lowestoft Grammar School (later Denes High School) 17, 20-22, 25
Lowestoft Schoolboys U-15

football team 27, 41
Lowestoft Town FC 19, 20
Lucas, Tom 67, 68, 280
Luton 221
Luton and Dunstable Hospital
88-89
Luton Town FC 88, 113-114,
121, 232, 233
Luxembourg national team
107, 115
Lyall, John 11, 133

Mabbutt, Gary 107, 169, 170
Mack, Johnny 224, 225, 234,
245
Maddocks, Dan 27
Madness 32
Madrid 73-74, 100
Main, Alan 223
Majorca 51
Malpas, Maurice 10, 12, 13, 68-
69, 261, 269, 278, 279-280, 283,
284, 287
Malta, Hilton hotel 316
Malta national team 316
Manchester airport, Hilton
hotel 225
Manchester City FC 70, 80, 82-
83, 230, 232
Manchester United FC 123,
182, 291
matches against Coventry
228-229, 233
matches against Ipswich 70,
76, 83, 86, 114, 121
rumour of move by Terry to
132, 134, 141, 152, 154
Manning, John 20
Manuel, Carlos 142
Maradona, Diego 55-56, 146,
147, 148-149, 150, 151, 152,
153, 216, 219
Hand of God goal 147-148,
149-150
Mariner, Paul 52, 53, 65, 70, 73,
78, 79, 81, 92, 93, 94, 115, 124,
125, 126
captains Ipswich 118
friendship with Terry 113
trashes Dutch hotel room
104-105
World Cup (1982) 97, 98, 99,
100
Marlborough, Lawrence 159
Marseille 310-312
Marsh, Rodney 56
Marshall, David 294
Marshall, Gordon 163, 279,
285-287, 321, 324

Marshall, Jimmy 159, 187, 189
Martin, Alvin 93, 94, 135, 145
Martlesham, Red Lion pub 48
Marwood, Brian 133
Masons, Scottish 166
Match of the Day 46
Maureen (Dundee United
dinnerlady) 261
Mausser (US player) 129
McAllister, Gary 228
McAvennie, Frank 175, 180,
181, 182, 185
McBride, Kevin 284, 322
McCall, Ian 290
McCall, Steve 82, 86, 124, 133
McCart, Chris 11, 269, 271,
274, 283
McCarthy, Mick 175
McClair, Brian 164, 171
McClaren, Steve 67, 300, 303
McCluskey, George 156
McCoist, Ally 42, 156, 157, 160,
171, 173-174, 175, 176, 185,
188, 199, 200
McCulloch, Ken 248
McDermott, Terry 47, 70, 73
MacDonald, Alan 10
McDonald, Scott 282, 284, 285,
324, 325
McDowall, Kenny 197
McFadden, James 272, 275,
277, 278, 279, 280, 281, 283,
294
McGarry, Bill 20
McGinlay, Brian 200
McGrain, Danny 194
McGrath, Lloyd 231-232
McGurl, Paul 252, 254, 255
McKay, Sheriff Archibald 181
Mackay, Murdo 262, 263, 264,
265, 266-267
McKay, Willie 281
McKechnie, Mr 89, 90
McKnight, Alan 176
McLean, Tommy 259, 260
McLeish, Alex 179, 326
McLintock, Frank 237
McMahon, Steve 208, 211, 214,
216
McMinn, Kevin 'Ted' 155, 167
McNab, Bob 237
McNeill, Billy 194, 200
McNeill, Dixie 227
McPherson, Archie 287
McPherson, Dave 15, 159, 160,
168, 267
McStay, Paul 165
Medhurst, Norman 101, 102,
116, 202, 213

Melville, Andy 241, 242
Mendez, Codesal 217
Metgod (AZ 67 Alkmaar
player) 81
Mexico City
Aztec Stadium 128, 145, 146-
150
Camino Real hotel 127
Reforma Club 127
Mexico City Cricket Club 127
Mexico national team 128-129,
138-139
Middlesbrough FC 76, 80-81,
241, 242, 303
Migueli (Barcelona player) 56
Milla, Roger 215, 217
Miller, Claire 187
Miller, Joe 190
Miller, Willie 187, 201
Millichip, Bert 213
Mills, Mick 77, 80, 91, 94, 97,
104, 106, 108
as Coventry assistant
manager 227-228, 232, 233,
235
Millwall FC 48
Mirandinha (Brazilian player)
171
Miss World 166
Moira (Sunderland secretary)
243
Moldova national team 307-
308
Monterrey 139, 140-141, 142,
145
Moore, Bobby 44, 196, 238-
239, 298
Moran, Kevin 211
Moran, Steve 76
Morgan, John 253, 264
Morocco national team 142-
143, 312
Morton FC 284
Morton's cannery 18
Moses, Remi 114
Motherwell
Dalziel school 272, 273, 280,
283
Popinjay Hotel 277-278
Smithycroft 273
Motherwell FC 10-11, 12, 66-
67, 68, 168, 190, 259, 266, 268
2001/2 season 269-272
2002/3 season 275-279
2003/4 season 280-283
2004/5 season 283-286, 288,
321-326
CIS Cup matches 284, 285-
288

Davie Cooper Stand 271
friendly matches
  Birmingham City 274
  Cardiff City 274
  Carlisle 280
  Cowdenbeath 283
  Fulham 280
  Ross County 283
  St Mirren 283
  Stranraer 283
  income 289
matches
  Aberdeen 12, 276, 278, 282,
    284, 285
  Celtic 67, 275-276, 277, 282,
    283-284
  Hibernian 10
  Livingston 10
  Celtic 322-326
  Chievo 271, 272
  Dundee 271, 272, 276, 280-
    281, 282, 284
  Dundee United 260, 270,
    275, 281, 284
  Dunfermline 282, 284
  Hearts 276, 277, 281, 282-
    283, 284, 321
  Hibernian 270-271, 275,
    276-277, 281, 282, 284, 321
  Inverness 284-285
  Kilmarnock 271, 275, 276,
    281, 282, 285
  Livingston 275, 276, 277,
    278, 279, 281, 282, 284, 286
  Partick 275, 276, 278, 281,
    282
  Rangers 188, 277, 284, 285,
    288, 321, 322
pitch 283, 285
psychology 66-67
Scottish Cup matches
  Dunfermline 270
  Inverness 282
  Queen of the South 282
  St Johnstone 282
  semi-final against Rangers
    277, 278
  Stranraer 277
Scottish League Cup matches
  276, 281
training 272-274
youth teams 294
Motson, John 219
Mott the Hoople 29
Mountfield, Derek 123
Moyes, Davie 281
Moynihan, Colin 220
Muhren, Arnold 52-53, 69, 79,
  82, 83, 106, 107, 212

Müller (Cologne player) 79
Müller (German player) 101
Munro, Stuart 164, 198
Murray, Bob 240, 242, 243,
  244
Murray, David 154
Murray, Len 176

N'kono (Cameroon player)
  217
Naples 215, 216, 218
Naylor, Stuart 132
Ndlovu, Peter 231, 232
Neal, Phil 47, 109, 115
Neville, Gary 298, 302
Nevin, Pat 266, 270, 271, 277
'New York, New York' 136,
  137
Newcastle United FC 121, 236,
  239-240, 305
Newham U-15 football team
  27
News of the World 90
Nichol, Charlotte 316
Nicholas, Charlie 186
Nicholas, Peter 87, 179
Nicholl, Chris 237
Nicholl, Jimmy 125, 250, 258,
  259
Nicol, Steve 113
Nigeria national team 309-310
Niigata, Milan bar 315-316
Nil By Mouth organisation
  168
North American tour (1977)
  28, 39-41
North Berwick, Marine Hotel
  251
Northern Ireland national
  team 109-110, 116, 125, 135,
  169, 170
Norway tour 51
Norwich City FC 19-20, 33,
  123, 133, 229, 230, 233
  matches against Ipswich 76,
    77, 80, 108, 122-123, 124
Nottingham Forest FC 48, 49-
  50, 51, 82, 228
  matches against Ipswich 52,
    54, 64-65, 69, 92, 114, 124
Notts County FC 107, 108, 131

O'Callaghan, Kevin 72
O'Dell, Alan 73
O'Donnell, Phil 286, 322
official, fourth 292-293
officials, English 293
Ogilvie, Campbell 275
Ogrizovic, Steve 227

Ohana (Israeli player) 135
Oliviera (Portuguese player)
  142
Olsen, Jesper 106
onefootball.com 264
O'Neill, Geraldine 326
O'Neill, Martin 52, 108, 326
Ormsby, Brendan 181
O'Rourke, John 20
Osaka airport 315
Osborne, Roger 39, 40, 48, 49-
  50, 53
Osman, Rex 79, 80, 88, 89
Osman, Russell 37, 38, 39, 43,
  44, 45-46, 49, 50, 51, 61, 62, 71,
  72, 73, 76-77, 79, 80, 88, 93,
  94, 106, 110, 114, 122, 124
  and Dutch hotel room
    trashing 104
  captains Ipswich 108, 118
  girlfriend Louise 114
  leaves Ipswich 132
  PFA dinner 83
Oulton Broad, Wherry Hotel
  41
Overton, Paul 49
Owen, Michael 295, 296-297,
  300-301, 302, 304, 306
Owers, Gary 240-241
Oxford United FC 122, 132,
  133

Paraguay national team 145-
  146
Paris 115-116, 312-313
  Auld Alliance bar 313
  La Coupole restaurant 312
Parker, Paul 66, 204, 207, 212,
  219
Partick Thistle FC 275, 276,
  278, 281, 282
Partridge, David 276, 277, 278,
  286, 321, 322
Pasadena, Rose Bowl Stadium
  152
Paterson, Jim 283
Pattelainen, Mixu 276, 277
Payne, Terry 227
Peake, Trevor 227, 231-232
Pearce, Andy 229, 231
Pearce, Stuart 118, 171, 205,
  212, 216, 219, 220
Pearson, Jim 267
Pearson, Stephen 272, 277,
  281-282, 283, 294
Pele 56. 68, 72
Penman family 256
Pennant, Jermaine 182, 301
People, The 106

Peterborough United FC 238, 242

Peters (AZ 67 Alkmaar player) 81

Peters, Martin 54

Petersfield 16

PKF (administrators) 271

Planet Football 262

Platini, Michel 57, 79, 97, 115

Platt, David 205, 212, 214, 216, 217

players, overseas 305-306

players, talented 55-56, 64-65

PlayStation 296

Pleat, David 88, 154

Poland 57-58

Poland national team 143-145, 195, 204, 319

Porteous, John 276

Portland, Oregon 39, 40

Porto football club 48

Portsmouth FC 240

Portugal 150

Portugal national team 142, 283

Pougatch, Mark 315

Powell, Jeff 96

Power, Paul 83

Power Ball 263

Poynton, John 117, 225, 228, 232-233

Prague Bohemians football club 78

Pratt, John 52

Premiership, formation of 291

Presley, Elvis 42

Press Association 265

Prince, Tony 42

Professional Footballers' Association 247
 dinner 83-84
 Player of the Year award 75

PSV Eindhoven football club 206, 210

psychology in football 66-67, 68, 280

Pula Sardinia 208-209

Queen 29

Queen of the South FC 282

Queens Park Rangers FC 54, 122, 232

Quinn, Paul 322

Radio Clyde 249, 307

Radio Luxembourg 42

Radion 203

Rafferty, Bill 50

Raith Rovers FC 23-24, 189, 223, 250, 258-259, 260, 273

Rajkovic, Ante 87

Ramsey, Sir Alf 222, 285

Randall and Hopkirk Deceased 204

Rangers FC 141, 231, 290
 1986/87 season 156-164
 1987/88 season 173-174, 175-180
 1988/89 season 184-190
 1989/90 season 197-201
 1990/91 season 223-226
 charity match against Celtic 195
 CIS Cup Final against Motherwell 285-288
 convention 253-254
 European Cup matches 137, 174-175, 177, 181, 199, 223, 318
 friendly against Bayern Munich 156
 Ibrox ground 156, 158
 income 289, 291
 Israel trip 170-171
 matches
  Aberdeen 159-160, 161, 173, 179-180, 186-188, 189, 199, 200, 226, 230
  Celtic 11-12, 158, 159, 160, 161, 175-176, 177, 182, 185-186, 188, 198, 199-200
  Clydebank 161
  Dundee 157, 161, 163
  Dundee United 163, 188, 189, 200, 223
  Dunfermline 173, 200, 223, 321
  East Fife 163
  Falkirk 157, 173
  Hamilton 158, 185, 188
  Hearts 161, 188, 189, 223
  Hibernian 156-157, 185, 197-198
  Motherwell 188, 277, 284, 285, 288, 321, 322
  Raith 189
  St Johnstone 189
  St Mirren 162, 163, 197
  Stenhousemuir 163
  Stranraer 189
 overseas squad 305
 Scottish Cup matches 163, 164, 190, 191, 200, 277, 278
 Scottish League Cup finals 59, 179, 189, 197, 201, 224, 226
 Scottish League Cup matches 23-24, 223, 224
 supporters clubs 165-166
 testimonial matches 155, 241
 training 184-185
 UEFA Cup matches 168-169, 190-191, 318
 win League titles 161-163, 188-189
 win Scottish FA Cup 164

Ratcliffe, Kevin 123

Rattin (Argentinian player) 146

Ravelli (Swedish goalkeeper) 191

Real Madrid football club 58, 300-301, 306
 Bernebeu Stadium 100, 101

Redford, Ian 157, 262

referees, professional 292, 293

Regis, Cyrille 61, 227, 229, 231

Regis, Mike and Reg 33

Reid, Peter 123, 138, 144, 146, 147, 148, 149

Reilly, George 55

religious sectarianism 167-168, 194-195, 198-199

Rep, Johnny 79

reserve-team football 43

Richard (Dewhurst butchers) 26

Richard, Keith 93

Richards, John 50

Richardson, Mr (Coventry chairman) 246

Rijkaard, Frank 211-212

Rioch, Bruce 17

Rita (Terry's friend) 251, 252

Rix, Graham 61, 97, 101

Robbins, Peter 232, 233, 234

Robert the Bruce 177, 178

Roberts, Dale 43

Roberts, Graham 109, 110, 116, 160, 161, 173, 175, 180, 181, 182, 183, 197

Robertson, John 282, 326

Robinson, Neil 87

Robinson, Paul 302, 305

Robson, Bobby (later Sir Bobby) 304
 as England 'B' team manager 61, 62, 94
 as England Manager 66, 106, 110, 116, 127, 129, 136, 155, 169, 177, 179, 191, 192, 202, 204, 292
 and Dutch hotel room trashing 104-105
 World Cup (1986) 137-138, 142, 143-144, 148, 150

World Cup (1990) 206, 207, 208, 209-210, 212, 213, 215, 216, 217, 218, 219
resigns 206, 210, 221-222
as Ipswich manager 32, 34, 35, 39, 40, 41, 48, 49, 50, 52, 53, 69, 71-72, 75, 77, 80, 82, 85, 86, 103, 104, 116
leaves club 107
team talks 68, 69
and Terry's first team debut 47
and Terry's nose injury 90
and Terry as neighbour 155
Robson, Bryan 54, 61, 73, 106, 110, 116, 118, 119, 124, 125, 126, 127, 129, 135, 136, 152, 166, 170, 177, 178, 191, 192, 193, 196, 204
World Cup (1982) 97-98, 99, 100, 102
World Cup (1986) 140, 141, 143, 144
World Cup (1990) 208, 210, 212, 214, 221
Robson, Stewart 229, 231, 234
Rocastle, David 191, 206
Rodgerson, Ian 241
Rogan, Anton 200, 240-241
Rolling Stones, the 93
Roma football club 106-107
Romania national team 125-126, 135, 317
Rome 106-107
Rooney, Wayne 301-302, 303, 304
Rosario, Robert 229, 232
Rosenthal, Jim 133, 214
Ross County FC 283
Roth, Volker 129
Rotherham United FC 236
Rothmans Yearbook 259, 263
Rough, Alan 156
Rous Cup 137, 170, 193-194
Royle, Joe 71, 304
Rummenigge, Karl-Heinz 101, 107
Rush, Ian 59, 65, 92, 109, 179

St Etienne football club 78, 81
St Johnstone FC 189, 200, 282
St Joseph's school, Woodbridge 21
St Mirren FC 156, 162, 163, 175, 197, 283
Sainty, John 33
Samaras (Greek player) 192
Sampdoria football club 157, 184, 185

San Mames stadium 95
Sansom, Kenny 61, 63, 97, 110, 142, 147, 150, 229, 231-232
Santamaria, José 83
Santana television company 323
Saravakos (Greek player) 192
Sardinia 206-207, 208 209
Is Morus hotel 206-207
Satrustegui (Spanish player) 83
Saudi Arabia national team 191
Sauzee, Frank 271
Schmeichel, Peter 196
Schmidhuber, Aron 211
Schumacher, Toni 79, 86, 101, 129
Scifo, Enzo 214
Scotland national team
future of 293, 294
matches against England 92-94, 110, 126-127, 137, 171, 193-194
Scott, Peter 182
Scottish Claymores American football team 287
Scottish football 155, 159
future of 290-291, 292, 294
income 289-290
Scottish Football Association 156, 157, 187, 275, 279, 281
Scottish Premier League 156, 323
Scottish Television 224, 249, 291, 318
Seggars, Mrs 36
Sellars, Scott 239
Seman (Czech goalkeeper) 99
Sengewald, Daniel 276-277
Sexton, Dave 61, 227
Sharkey, Pat 40-41
Sharp, Graeme 123, 124
Sheedy, Kevin 123, 211
Sheffield United FC 232, 233
Sheffield Wednesday FC 123, 132, 133, 229, 236
Sherry, Gordon 313
Shilton, Peter 62-63, 69, 82, 106, 109, 119, 126, 128, 129, 136, 139, 170, 171, 193, 196, 202, 204, 267
World Cup (1982) 97, 98
World Cup (1986) 142, 143, 144, 146, 148
World Cup (1990) 209, 216, 219, 220
shirts, football 57, 58, 59
Shotts 274

Shrewsbury Town FC 82, 112-113
Shutt, Carl 133
Sierra Nevada mountains 141-142
Sillett, John 226, 227
Simonsen, Allan 55
Simple Minds 144
Simpson, Neil 186
Sinatra, Frank 136
Singapore 15-16
Fullerton Hotel 15
Ripley Crescent 15
Sitton, John 38
Sivell, Laurie 36, 39, 48, 49, 63-64, 72
Skegness Festival 28
Skeid Oslo 70
Skinner, Frank 203-204
Sky Sports 234
Sky Television 235, 246, 305
Slatter (Oxford player) 132
Smith, Alan 206
Smith, Alex 11, 187, 201, 258, 259, 260, 279
Smith, Graham 180, 237
Smith, Tommy 47, 48
Smith, Tony 240-241
Smith, Walter 224, 226, 230, 241, 293-294
Sohal, Caj 313
Soler (French player) 98
Sophie, Great Aunt 17-18, 23, 25
Souness, Graeme 47, 119, 137
as player-manager of Rangers 141, 152, 153-154, 156, 157-158, 160, 164-165, 168-169, 173, 174, 176, 180, 181, 182, 184, 185, 189, 191, 198, 199
drops Terry from team 223, 224
friction with Graham Roberts 197
and Rangers League title win 162
and religious sectarianism 168, 194-195
sendings off 156, 157, 161
and Terry leaving 224-226
leaves Rangers for Liverpool manager's job 226
plays for Sampdoria 157
Soutar, George 191
South, Sir Arthur 80
South East Counties League 36

South Korea national team 138
Southall, Neville 123
Southampton FC 76, 77, 118, 233
Southend United FC 238, 239, 243
Spackman, Nigel 200
Spain national team 83, 101-102, 170, 204, 307, 317
Sparta Rotterdam football club 231
Speedie, David 229
Spelbos (AZ 67 Alkmaar player) 81
Spence, Brian 277-278
Stainrod, Simon 122
Stallone, Sylvester 72
Stam, Jaap 302
Stammers, Steve 101
Stanley, Gary 87
Star 208
Steaua Bucharest football club 175, 181, 318
Stein, Brian 88, 91, 115
Stein, Jock 194
Stenhousemuir FC 163
Stephenson, 'Rocky' 19
Sterland, Mel 189
Steven, Trevor 123, 126, 129, 131-132, 138, 198, 200, 217, 222, 224
   World Cup (1986) 144, 147, 149
Stevens, Gary 123, 146, 147, 150, 190, 203, 213, 222, 262
Stewart, Ray 133
Stielike (German player) 101
Stirk, Johnny 36
Stirling, Hermann's restaurant 269
Stirling, Rainbow Rocks disco 162
Stirling management centre 241
Stirling University 254
Stockholm 61
Stoke City FC 75, 106
Stonehouse, John 16
Stowmarket FC 19
Strachan, Gordon 152, 153
Stranraer FC 189, 277, 283
Streatham Borstal football team 24
Street, Fred 101, 102, 116, 202, 213, 221
Streissleng, Herbert 89-90
Sturrock, Blair 262
Sturrock, Paul 260, 261, 262,

263
Suffolk Schoolboys team 27-28
Suffolk U-19 team 28, 32
Summerbee, Mike 72, 114, 162
Sun 210
'Sun Always Shines on TV, The' 145
Sunday Times, The 177, 178
Sunderland, Alan 73, 114
Sunderland FC 12, 237-244, 247
   1992/93 season 237-240
   1993/94 season 241-244
   League Cup matches 237, 242
   matches
      Barnsley 238, 239
      Birmingham City 242
      Brentford 239
      Bristol Rovers 237-238
      Charlton 242
      Derby 238, 242
      Grimsby 242
      Ipswich 76, 86
      Leicester 238, 239
      Middlesbrough 241, 242
      Newcastle 239-240
      Peterborough 238, 242
      Portsmouth 240
      Southend 238, 239, 243
      Swindon 237, 238
      Tranmere 242-243
      Watford 242
      West Ham 238-239
      Wolves 239
   testimonial match against Rangers 241
Sutton, Chris 324
Sutton, Steve 229
Swansea City FC 87
Sweden national team 61, 169, 191, 201-203, 260, 308-309
Sweden U-21 team 61
Swindon Town FC 132, 237, 238
Switzerland trip 173
Sydney Cricket Ground and Harbour 73

Taggart, Ian 187
Tainton, Trevor 71
Talbot, Brian 52, 53, 73, 113
Taste of Scotland 253
Taylor, Graham 81, 222, 292, 309
Taylor, Paul 237
Tbilisi 136-137
Tel Aviv 135
   Hilton hotel 135

Terry, John 118, 299, 302
Terry Butcher Insurance Consultants Ltd 109
Thatcher, Margaret 182
Thijssen, Frans 52, 53, 70, 75, 81, 82, 83, 85, 106, 212
Thomas, Clive 35, 82, 109
Thomas, Geoff 204
Thompson, Alan 324
Thompson, Max 87
Thompson, Phil 47, 51, 92, 93, 94, 96, 97
Thompson, Stevie 278
Thon (Bayern Munich player) 199
365 (dotcom company) 262
Throw, Louis 187-188
Tigana (French player) 97
Tijuana airport 140
Tiong, Wee 15
Tirana 192
Tol (AZ 67 Alkmaar player) 81
Tooley (Lowestoft striker) 19
Toronto Blizzards football team 39
Toshack, John 87
Tottenham Hotspur FC 91, 154, 155
   matches against Coventry 226, 228, 230, 233, 234
   matches against Ipswich 52, 77, 112
Townsley, Derek 277
Tranmere Rovers FC 242-243
Treasure of the Sierra Madre, The 141
Trent Polytechnic 32, 33, 34, 35, 44
Tresor (French player) 98
Troon, Marine Hotel 193, 231, 232
Troon, Piersland House Hotel 193
Tunisia national team 66, 207-208
Turin 217-218
Turkey national team 124, 125, 135, 177
Turnberry hotel 239
Turner, Robin 72

U2 174
UEFA 123
UNICEF 152
United States, Ipswich tour 103
United States Air Force Academy 138
United States national team

129-130
Uruguay national team 205
USSR national team 114, 136

Val de Lobo, Portugal 150
Val Thorens 262
Valdano (Argentinian player) 146, 149
Valentine, Bob 190
Valletta football club 223
Van der Meer (AZ 67 Alkmaar player) 81
Vancouver 139-140
  World Expo Fair 140
Vancouver Whitecaps 40
Varga, Stanislav 325
Varig Cup 205
Vasteras 61
Vaughan, Tony 278
Venables, Terry 31, 72
video technology and refereeing 292-293
Vieira, Patrick 118
Vienna 62-63
Vierchowod (Italian player) 128
Viljoen, Colin 49
Villa, Ricardo 52
Vladikazkaz 314
volleyball 21
Vujovic, Zlatko 169

Waddell, Willie 225
Waddle, Chris 121, 126, 136, 138, 169, 170, 191, 192, 193, 194
  World Cup (1986) 144, 147, 149
  World Cup (1990) 208, 209, 210, 211, 212, 213, 214, 220, 221
Wales national team 92, 109, 179
Walford, Stevie 326
Walker, Andy 175
Walker, Des 66, 192, 202, 207, 211, 212, 217
Wallace, Danny 228
Wallace, Gordon 'Stubby' 260
Walsh, Ian 87
Walsh, Paul 115
Walsh, Steve 239

Walters, Mark 184, 185, 188, 198, 199, 200
Ward, Mark 73, 133
Wark, John 43, 53, 54, 72, 75, 77, 78, 79, 81, 82, 83, 86, 88, 108, 113
Wark, Tula 78
Warsaw 313
Watford FC 20, 88, 113, 242, 309
Watson, Dave 93, 122, 267
Watts, Charlie 93
Weaver, Paul 90
Webb, Neil 177, 191, 202
Welzl (AZ 67 Alkmaar player) 81
Wembley Stadium 319, 320
Wengel, Jonathan 253
Wenger, Arsène 305
West, Colin 163
West Bromwich Albion FC 48-49, 70, 76, 124, 131, 132
West Germany national team 100-101, 102, 107, 129, 151, 177, 219-220 see also Germany national team
West Ham United FC 11
  matches
    Cambridge 240
    Coventry 232
    Ipswich 35, 92, 121, 132-133, 134
    Sunderland 238-239
West Lodge Park hotel 48
Wharton's butchers 26-27
Who, The 29
Whymark, Trevor 39, 47, 48, 53
Widzew Lodz football club 57, 78
Wilkins, Ray 97, 99, 116, 140, 143, 144, 147, 184, 190, 198
Wilkinson, Howard 66, 215, 224, 225
Williams, Steve 76
Wilson, Barry 282
Wilson, Kevin 'Jocky' 125, 132
Wimbledon FC 234
Wisdom, Norman 193
Wiseman, Jack 213
Withe, Peter 81-82, 95-96, 102, 109

Wizard of Oz, The 152
Wolverhampton Wanderers FC 49, 50, 69, 70, 194, 239
Wood, Ronnie 93
Woodcock, Tony 52, 79, 85-86, 100, 101, 107, 124, 125
Woodgate, Jonathan 302
Woods, Charlie 20, 33, 34, 35, 38
Woods, Chris 23, 61, 122, 128, 139, 141, 156, 162, 163, 169, 170, 175, 176, 179, 180, 181, 182, 183, 185, 186, 188, 190, 192, 193, 194, 196, 198, 200, 203, 222, 223, 262
  at Sheffield Wednesday 236
  World Cup (1990) 208-209, 213, 217
Woods, Clive 48, 53
Woods, Mrs 194
Woods, Ray 229
Woods, Sarah 162, 165
Woodward, Clive 67
World Cup (1982) 58-59, 63, 92-93, 94, 95-102
World Cup (1986) 55, 140-151
World Cup (1990) 119, 206-221
World Cup (1998) 28, 310-313, 317
World Cup (2002) 113, 272, 295-296, 309, 315-316
Worth, Harry 133
Worthington, Frank 52, 55, 56, 65
Wouters (Dutch player) 211-212
Wright, Billy 298
Wright, Brian 250
Wright, Mark 66, 129, 207, 212, 214, 217
Wright-Phillips, Shaun 301
Wyman, Bill 93

Yallop, Frank 140
Yugoslavia national team 65, 169, 177-179, 204-205, 317

Zamora (Spanish player) 83
Zeist sports complex, Holland 12, 70, 85, 103, 104-105
Zenith Data Systems Cup 232
Zimmermann (Cologne player) 79